Narcissism and the Text

PSYCHOANALYTIC CROSSCURRENTS
General Editor: Leo Goldberger

NARCISSISM
AND
THE TEXT

Studies in Literature and the Psychology of Self

LYNNE LAYTON

and

BARBARA ANN SCHAPIRO

Editors

NEW YORK UNIVERSITY PRESS
New York *and* London
1986

Library of Congress Cataloging-in-Publication Data

Narcissism and the text.

(Psychoanalytic crosscurrents)
Includes bibliographies and index.
1. Self in literature.   2. Psychoanalysis and
literature.   3. Literature, Modern—History and
criticism.   I. Layton, Lynne, 1950–   . II. Schapiro,
Barbara A.   III. Series.
PS56.S46N37   1986   809′.93353   86-5112
ISBN 0-8147-5020-6

Contents

Foreword

The *Psychoanalytic Crosscurrents* series presents selected books and monographs that reveal the growing intellectual ferment within and across the boundaries of psychoanalysis.

Freud's theories and grand-scale speculative leaps have been found wanting, if not disturbing, from the very beginning and have led to a succession of derisive attacks, shifts in emphasis, revisions, modifications, and extensions. Despite the chronic and, at times, fierce debate that has characterized psychoanalysis, not only as a movement but also as a science, Freud's genius and transformational impact on the twentieth century have never been seriously questioned. Recently psychoanalytic thought has been subjected to dramatic reassessments under the sway of contemporary currents in the history of ideas, philosophy of science, epistemology, structuralism, critical theory, semantics, and semiology as well as in sociobiology, ethology, and neurocognitive science. Not only is Freud's place in intellectual history being meticulously scrutinized, his texts, too, are being carefully read, explicated, and debated within a variety of conceptual frameworks and sociopolitical contexts.

The legacy of Freud is perhaps most notably evident within the narrow confines of psychoanalysis itself, the "impossible profession" that has served as the central platform for the promulgation of official orthodoxy. But Freud's contributions—his original radical thrust— reach far beyond the parochial concerns of the clinical psychoanalyst as clinician. His writings touch on a wealth of issues, crossing traditional boundaries—be they situated in the biological, social, or humanistic spheres—that have profoundly altered our conception of the individual and society.

A rich and flowering literature, falling under the rubric of "applied psychoanalysis," came into being, reached its zenith many decades ago, and then almost vanished. Early contributors to this literature, in addition to Freud himself, came from a wide range of backgrounds both within and outside the medical/psychiatric field; many later became psychoanalysts themselves. These early efforts were characteristically reductionistic in their attempt to extrapolate from psychoanalytic theory (often the purely clinical theory) to explanations of phenomena lying at some distance from the clinical. Over the years, academic psychologists, educators, anthropologists, sociologists, political scientists, philosophers, jurists, literary critics, art historians, artists, and writers, among others (with or without formal psychoanalytic training) have joined in the proliferation of this literature.

The intent of the *Psychoanalytic Crosscurrents* series is to apply psychoanalytic ideas to topics that may lie beyond the narrowly clinical, but its essential conception and scope are quite different. The present series eschews the reductionistic tendency to be found in much traditional "applied psychoanalysis." It acknowledges not only the complexity of psychological phenomena but also the way in which they are embedded in social and scientific contexts that are constantly changing. It calls for a dialectical relationship to earlier theoretical views and conceptions rather than a mechanical repetition of Freud's dated thoughts. The series affirms the fact that contributions to and about psychoanalysis have come from many directions. It is designed as a forum for the multidisciplinary studies that intersect with psychoanalytic thought but without the requirement that psychoanalysis necessarily be the starting point or, indeed, the center focus. The criteria for inclusion in the series are that the work be significantly informed by psychoanalytic thought or that it be aimed at furthering our understanding of psychoanalysis in its broadest meaning as theory, practice, and sociocultural phenomenon; that it be of current topical interest and that it provide the critical reader with contemporary insights; and, above all, that it be high-quality scholarship, free of obsolete dogma, banalization, and empty jargon. The author's professional identity and particular theoretical orientation matter only to the extent that such facts may serve to frame the work for the reader, alerting him or her to inevitable biases of the author.

The Psychoanalytic Crosscurrents Series presents an array of works from the multidisciplinary domain in an attempt to capture the ferment of scholarly activities at the core as well as at the boundaries of psychoanalysis. The books and monographs are from a variety of sources:

authors will be psychoanalysts—traditional, neo- and post-Freudian, existential, object-relational, Kohutian, Lacanian, etc.—social scientists with quantitative or qualitative orientations to psychoanalytic data, and scholars from the vast diversity of approaches and interests that make up the humanities. The series entertains works on critical comparisons of psychoanalytic theories and concepts as well as philosophical examinations of fundamental assumptions and epistemic claims that furnish the base for psychoanalytic hypotheses. It includes studies of psychoanalysis as literature (discourse and narrative theory) as well as the application of psychoanalytic concepts to literary criticism. It will serve as an outlet for psychoanalytic studies of creativity and the arts. Works in the cognitive and the neurosciences will be included to the extent that they address some fundamental psychoanalytic tenet, such as the role of dreaming and other forms of unconscious mental processes.

It should be obvious that an exhaustive enumeration of the types of works that might fit into the *Psychoanalytic Crosscurrents* series is pointless. The studies comprise a lively and growing literature as a unique domain; books of this sort are frequently difficult to classify or catalog. Suffice it to say that the overriding aim of the editor of this series is to serve as a conduit for the identification of the outstanding yield of that emergent literature and to foster its further unhampered growth.

Leo Goldberger
Professor of Psychology
New York University

Preface and Acknowledgments

While anthologies of psychoanalytic literary criticism are not unusual, what distinguishes this collection is its orientation in post-Freudian theories of object relations and narcissism. In the past few decades, self psychology and theories of pre-Oedipal pathology have gained increasing significance in the clinical world; their impact in the realm of literary criticism is only just beginning to be felt. Our intentions with this book are to provide a readable survey of these theories for nonclinicians and to open up the rich possibilities for their application to literary analysis. We hope the essays in this volume signal the beginning of a promising new direction in psychoanalytic literary criticism.

The editors would like to thank Professor Donald Fritz and Miami University for hosting the 1983 conference "The World as Mirror: Narcissism in the Fine Arts and the Humanities," at which we gathered many of the essays that appear in this volume. We would also like to thank Dr. Bennett Simon and Dr. Ernest Wolf for reading and commenting on the introduction to this volume. Special thanks go also to Dr. Murray Cohen, who helped clarify many of the more difficult concepts that appear in the introduction. Last but not least, thanks to all the friends and study group colleagues who helped us make the ideas presented here comprehensible.

We also wish to thank the following publishers for permission to quote:

"Blake and Women: 'Nature's Cruel Holiness'" by Margaret Storch reprinted by permission from *American Imago,* Summer 1981, Vol. 38, No. 2, pp. 221–46.

"On Narcissism from Baudelaire to Sartre: Ego-psychology and Literary History" by Eugene Holland reprinted by permission from *New Orleans Review*, Summer 1985, Vol. 11, No. 2.

"Sweet Are the Uses of Adversity: Regression and Style in the Life and Works of Henry James" by Joseph D. Lichtenberg reprinted by permission from *Psychoanalytic Inquiry*, 1981, Vol. 1, No. 1.

"'We Perished, Each Alone': A Psychoanalytic Commentary on Virginia Woolf's *To the Lighthouse*" by Ernest S. Wolf and Ina Wolf reprinted by permission from *International Review of Psychoanalysis*, 1979, Vol. 6, No. 37.

We wish to thank Schocken Books, Inc. for permission to quote from FRANZ KAFKA: THE COMPLETE STORIES translated by Edwin and Willa Muir. Copyright © 1971 by Schocken Books, Inc.; from THE DIARIES OF FRANZ KAFKA, 1910–13, translated by Joseph Kresh, ed. Max Brod. Copyright © 1965 by Schocken Books, Inc.; from THE DIARIES OF FRANZ KAFKA, 1914–23, translated by Martin Greenberg, ed. Max Brod. Copyright © 1949 by Schocken Books, Inc.; from LETTERS TO FELICE, translated by James Stern and Elisabeth Duckworth, ed. Erich Heller and Jürgen Born. Copyright © 1973 by Schocken Books, Inc.; from LETTERS TO MILENA, translated by Tania and James Stern, ed. Willi Haas. Copyright © 1953 by Schocken Books, Inc.

List of Abbreviations

AOS   Heinz Kohut, *The Analysis of the Self* (New York: International Universities Press, 1971)

ASP   Arnold Goldberg ed., *Advances in Self Psychology* (New York: International Universities Press, 1980)

DI   Franz Kafka, *The Diaries of Franz Kafka, 1910–13,* trans. Martin Greenberg, ed. Max Brod (New York: Schocken Books, 1949)

DII   Franz Kafka, *The Diaries of Franz Kafka, 1914–23,* trans. Martin Greenberg, ed. Max Brod (New York: Schocken Books, 1949)

FF   Charles Baudelaire, *The Flowers of Evil,* trans. Florence Friedman (Philadelphia: Dufour, 1966)

FZ   William Blake, *Four Zoas,* in *Blake: Complete Writings,* ed. Geoffrey Keynes (London: Oxford University Press, 1966)

I   William Blake, *Infant Sorrow,* in *Blake: Complete Writings,* ed. Keynes

IWER   Otto Kernberg, *Internal World and External Reality: Object Relations Theory Applied* (New York: Jason Aronson, 1980)

J   William Blake, *Jerusalem,* in *Blake: Complete Writings,* ed. Keynes

LF   Franz Kafka, *Letters to Felice,* trans. James Stern and Elizabeth Duckworth, eds. Erich Heller and Jürgen Born (New York: Schocken Books, 1973)

M   William Blake, *Milton,* in *Blake: Complete Writings,* ed. Keynes

MP   D. W. Winnicott, *The Maturational Processes and the Facilitating Environment: Studies in the Theory of Emotional Development* (New York: International Universities Press, 1965)

ORT   Otto Kernberg, *Object Relations Theory and Clinical Psycho-analysis* (New York: Jason Aronson, 1976)

PB   Margaret S. Mahler, Fred Pine, and Anni Bergman, *The Psychological Birth of the Human Infant* (New York: Basic Books, 1975)

PSHI   Harry Guntrip, *Personality Structure and Human Interaction* (New York: International Universities Press, 1961)

RH   Charles Baudelaire, *The Flowers of Evil,* trans. Richard Howard (Boston, David Godine, 1982)

ROS   Heinz Kohut, *The Restoration of the Self* (New York: International Universities Press, 1977)

SFS   Paul H. Ornstein, ed., *The Search for the Self,* vol. 1 (New York: International Universities Press, 1978)

TY   Leon Edel, *Henry James: The Treacherous Years (1895–1901)* (New York: J. B. Lippincott, 1969)

UY   Leon Edel, *Henry James: The Untried Years (1843–1870)* (New York: J. B. Lippincott, 1953)

For works cited repeatedly within a chapter, page numbers in parentheses are incorporated in the text.

Contributors

J. BROOKS BOUSON is Assistant Professor of English at Mundelein College in Chicago. She has published articles on Ted Hughes, Emily Dickinson, and Edwin Muir.

PETER S. DONALDSON is Associate Professor of Literature at M.I.T. He is the editor and translator of *A Machiavellian Treatise by Stephen Gardiner* (Cambridge: Cambridge University Press, 1975), author of monographs and articles on the relation between Machiavellian and sacral conceptions of kingship in the Renaissance, and has recently completed work on his book *Machiavelli and Mystery of State*.

SUSAN GRAYSON is Assistant Professor of French at Occidental College and a psychologist. She is working on a study entitled "Beauty and Narcissism: The Thematics of Alterity" and has recently completed an article (forthcoming) on self and other in Cocteau's *Les Enfants terribles*.

EUGENE HOLLAND is Assistant Professor of French at the University of Iowa. He has published articles on Balzac, Boccaccio and Freud, literary and critical theory, and postmodernism, and is currently completing a book on *The Culture of Masochism*.

PEER HULTBERG is a Danish psychoanalyst currently practicing in Frankfurt, Germany. He also holds a Ph.D. in Polish Literature and has published numerous articles on Jungian psychology, as well as several stories, plays, and translations.

FREDERICK KIRCHHOFF is Professor of English at Indiana University-Purdue University at Fort Wayne. He has published articles on Coleridge, Shelley, Ruskin, D. G. Rossetti, Morris, and Henry James, and he is author of the Twayne studies of Morris and Ruskin.

LYNNE LAYTON has a Ph.D. in Comparative Literature and is currently a Ph.D. candidate in clinical psychology at Boston University. She has published papers on German cinema, Enlightenment drama, Rousseau, and nineteenth-century fiction.

JOSEPH D. LICHTENBERG, M.D., is a practicing psychoanalyst in Washington, D.C. and member of the faculty of the Washington Psychoanalytic Institute and the Program Committee of the American Psychoanalytic Association. He is author of *Psychoanalysis and Infant Research* (Hillside, N.J.: The Analytic Press, 1983) and *The Talking Cure: A Descriptive Guide to Psychoanalysis* (Hillside, N.J.: The Analytic Press, 1984).

BARBARA SCHAPIRO is Lecturer in History and Literature at Harvard University. She has published articles on literature and film, and is author of *The Romantic Mother: Narcissistic Patterns in Romantic Poetry* (Baltimore: Johns Hopkins University Press, 1983).

RODNEY SIMARD is Lecturer in English and Communications at California State College, Bakersfield. He has published essays on various British and American writers and is author of *Postmodern Drama: Contemporary Playwrights in America and Britain* (Washington, D.C.: American Theatre Assn.-UPA, 1984).

MARGARET STORCH is Assistant Professor of English at Bentley College. She has published several papers on Blake and is currently working on a study of Blake and Lawrence.

JOSEPH WESTLUND is Professor of English at Northeastern University. He has published numerous articles and is author of *Shakespeare's Reparative Comedies: A Psychoanalytic View of the Middle Plays* (Chicago: University of Chicago Press, 1984).

ERNEST S. WOLF is currently Faculty, Training and Supervising Analyst at the Chicago Institute for Psychoanalysis, and Assistant Professor of Psychiatry at Northwestern University Medical School. He has collaborated on a number of publications with Heinz Kohut and is author of numerous articles and essays, including chapters in A. Goldberg ed., *The Future of Psychoanalysis* (New York: International Universities Press, Inc., 1983).

INA WOLF has a degree in music and has written on the Bloomsbury group. She has also collaborated with Ernest Wolf in the application of psychoanalytic insights to the study of literature.

Narcissism and the Text

ONE
INTRODUCTION

LYNNE LAYTON AND BARBARA SCHAPIRO

THEORIES OF SELF FORMATION AND SELF PATHOLOGY

In *The Culture of Narcissism* (New York: W. W. Norton, 1978), Christopher Lasch cites several psychoanalysts who report that, in the past few decades, their patients have been complaining of difficulties quite different from those that plagued the hysterical and obsessive-compulsive patients seen by Freud (36–38). While there is no agreement as to whether these symptoms existed before and were simply not "heard" by the analyst or whether they hallmark a new personality and a new disorder, most agree on the description of the problem. Heinz Kohut, theoretician of one branch of recent analytic work on self pathology, captures the difference between Freud's patients and his own in his distinction between Guilty Man and Tragic Man. The guilty human is torn by drive-instinctual Oedipal conflict; the primary anxiety is castration anxiety, and the source of this patient's guilt is incestuous and aggressive wishes. The tragic human, on the other hand, has developmentally more archaic problems. He/she cannot experience him/herself as a center of initiative and suffers from disintegration anxiety. This patient feels despair, shame, boredom, complains of feeling empty, depressed, and, at times, unreal. There is a constant fear of boundary loss, of potential fragmentation; Tragic Man expends his energy in keeping intact and protected what little sense of self he has.

In terms of etiology, where Guilty Man's problems have their source in Oedipal failures, Tragic man's problems have their source in pre-Oedipal failures. Thus, recent psychoanalytic theory of the self shifts its focus from the father-mother-child triangle to the dyad of child and first love-object (usually but not necessarily the mother). Focus is also shifted from the dynamics of ego, id, and superego to those of the archaic forerunners of these structures. Indeed, Kohut and his followers no longer speak of these agencies at all. The failures that may occur in the first few years of life are explained somewhat differently by the various theorists, and it is the differences and similarities in their theories of self formation and self pathology that we will examine in the first section of this introduction. We begin with Kohut, because his theory is markedly different from that of both the British and the American object relations schools examined later in this section.[1]

Heinz Kohut and Self Psychology

Heinz Kohut began writing on problems of narcissism in the fifties and sixties, but the two books that most fully present his self psychology are *The Analysis of the Self* (New York: International Universities Press, 1971, hereafter referred to as AOS) and *The Restoration of the Self* (New York: International Universities Press, 1977, hereafter referred to as ROS). In the earlier work, Kohut takes as his point of departure Hartmann's distinction between the ego, subject of ego psychology, and the self. In his 1950 essay, "Comments on the Psychoanalytic Theory of the Ego," Hartmann had distinguished the ego (a psychic system) from the self, "the whole person of an individual, including his body and body parts as well as his psychic organization and its parts."[2] He further noted that narcissism is not limited to libidinal cathexes of the ego but rather involves any cathexis of self-representations.[3] As had Hartmann, Kohut (AOS) spoke of self representations found within each psychic agency (id, ego, and superego), and he began his text with the following definition (called the narrow definition of the self when compared with his later definition): "The self then, quite analogous to the representations of objects, is a content of the mental apparatus but is not one of its constituents, i.e., not one of the agencies of the mind" (AOS, xv). In his 1978 paper with Wolf, the self was defined in the broad, supraordinate sense in which it had been discussed in ROS:

> the patterns of ambitions, skills, and goals, the tensions between them, the program of action they create, and the activities that strive toward the realization of this program are all experienced as continuous in space and

time . . . they are the self, an independent center of initiative, and independent recipient of impression.[4]

THE BIPOLAR SELF AND THE CONCEPT OF SELFOBJECTS

According to the above definition, the self is bipolar: one pole represents a person's skills and abilities and the other represents a person's goals or ideals. The relative cohesiveness of this self depends upon the relationship between the two poles, which further depends upon the relative integration of two archaic structures that emerge in the early development of the child—the grandiose self and the idealized parent imago. Narcissistic personality disorders arise when there are defects in the psychological structure of the self. We are dealing here not with conflict but with an absence of structure, a deficit in the self; it must be pointed out that other theoreticians of self formation do not agree on this point.

In Kohut's system, the narcissistic patient remains "fixated on archaic grandiose self configurations and/or on archaic, over-estimated, narcissistically cathected objects" (AOS, 3). In ROS, Kohut dropped the notion of narcissistic (as opposed to object) libido, but the point that this term was intended to convey, that one can have a narcissistic relation to an object, remains a major concept in the theory—the concept of the selfobject. For Kohut, narcissism is a subset of object relations. In *The Analysis of the Self,* he states that

> some of the most intense narcissistic experiences relate to objects; objects, that is, which are either used in the service of the self and of the maintenance of its instinctual investment, or objects which are themselves experienced as part of the self. I shall refer to the latter as *self-objects.* (AOS, xiv)

The bipolar self emerges from self-selfobject relations in the following way: According to Kohut,

> The equilibrium of primary narcissism is disturbed by the unavoidable shortcomings of maternal care, but the child replaces the previous perfection (a) by establishing a grandiose and exhibitionistic image of the self: *the grandiose self;* and (b) by giving over the previous perfection to an admired, omnipotent (transitional) self-object: *the idealized parent imago.* (AOS, p. 25)

If the exhibitionism and grandiosity of the archaic grandiose self are gradually tamed by empathic mirroring and approval responses on the part of the mother, who is experienced as part of the self, the archaic structure is integrated into the adult personality "and supplies the instinctual fuel for our ego-syntonic ambitions and purposes, for the enjoyment of our activities and for important aspects of our self-esteem" (AOS, 27–28). If the idealized selfobject is neither unavailable nor traumatically disappointing, the idealized parent imago is integrated as a forerunner of the idealized superego, which provides us with our guiding ideals (AOS, 28). If there is loss or massive disappointment in the idealized selfobject, the person will forever be dependent on others to provide ideals. Because of the structural deficit, however, the narcissistic person will not experience the other as other, but rather as a missing part of the self, that is, as a selfobject. Selfobjects are thus *functions* originally performed by others, which, under optimal conditions, are internalized to form and maintain a structured, cohesive self. As Marian Tolpin has pointed out, the concept of the selfobject can be seen to be the missing link in psychoanalytic developmental theory, the link between early development and the formation of the psychic apparatus.[5]

PATHOLOGICAL   NARCISSISM

Symptomatic results of deficits in the two poles of the self entail the

> fear of loss of the reality self through ecstatic merger with the idealized parent imago, or through the quasi-religious regressions toward a merger with God or with the universe; fear of loss of contact with reality and fear of permanent isolation through the experience of unrealistic grandiosity; frightening experiences of shame and self-consciousness through the intrusion of exhibitionistic libido; and hypochondriacal worries about physical or mental illness due to the hypercathexis of disconnected aspects of the body and the mind. (AOS, 153)

Patients with narcissistic pathology establish specific types of transferences (e.g., mirror and idealizing transferences) different from the classical neurotic transference; a major mark of such transferences is that the analyst is experienced as a selfobject.

Given the important role of the selfobject, it is clear that problems in the nuclear self of the narcissistic person point to problems in the nuclear selves of the earliest selfobjects, the parents. According to

Kohut, the persistence of archaic grandiosity is often due to an unempathic parent (usually the mother), who can neither recognize the child's in-phase needs for merger-mirroring-approval nor gradually discourage out-of-phase demands of the child's grandiose self. The persistence of a need for an idealized selfobject often results from a parent's absence or refusal to allow the child to so idealize and merge with him/her. Yet in Kohut's model, there is apparent a belief in a child's a priori health and in the drive to maintain health.[6] For example, Kohut writes that if the child recognizes that he/she cannot receive what is needed from one parent, the child will turn to the other to try to get it. In fact, the child has two chances, for self-disturbances of a pathological degree occur only when both poles of the self fail to be consolidated (ROS, 185). Unlike Freud's view of a relatively helpless neonate with untamed instincts, Kohut's "baby" is thus "highly complex and preadapted to take an active role in a dialogue with the caretakers in whom it evokes the responses that it needs for successful development" (Personal Correspondence with Ernest Wolf, M.D., 23 Oct. 1983).

In Kohut's analytic method for self pathology, cure entails the slow internalization of missing psychic structure (which he calls "transmuting internalization"). He believes that pathological narcissism arises from a developmental arrest at an early stage of healthy narcissism; in the transference, a self-selfobject relation appropriate to that early stage will spontaneously arise between patient and analyst, and, by means of an empathic mode of observation (reminiscent of Dilthey's concept of *Verstehen*), which carefully guards against inflicting narcissistic injury on the once again very vulnerable patient, the analyst slowly helps the patient to a restoration of self.

It is Kohut's thesis that the chief developmental task of the first few years of life is the development of a cohesive self. Toward the end of many of his analyses, he reports that patients experience a brief Oedipal phase, and, because their self is cohesive, they experience this phase with a "warm glow of joy" (ROS, 229). In affirming that the Oedipal period is more a source of potential strength than weakness, he implies that wherever one sees problems in the Oedipal period, one is probably seeing problems that are a function of earlier difficulties the patient had in attaining a cohesive self. In his 1977 text, Kohut thus absorbs the Oedipus complex into the psychology of self.

Kohut's second major heresy with regard to classical theory is his view that drives are secondary disintegration products rather than primary forces. Destructive rage, for example, results from empathic failure on the part of the earliest selfobjects. Primary is the striving for an enhanced sense of self; this is what motivates us, not drives (ROS, 81–82). On the basis of his psychoanalytic case work, Kohut came to see that the patient's growing empathy with the victim of his rage, the analyst, moves the rage that enslaves the ego toward a more mature aggression—defined as aggression under the control of the ego.[7] What is primary is assertiveness; destructive rage is a regression "motivated by an injury to the self . . . inflicted by the selfobject of childhood" (ROS, 116–117). The same is true, he argues, of libidinal drives (ROS, 121–122). If we remember Freud's description of the human being in *Civilization and its Discontents*, we see how far Kohut has gone in reversing the psychoanalytic theory of human nature:

> The element of truth behind all this, which people are so ready to disavow, is that men are not gentle creatures who want to be loved, and who at the most can defend themselves if they are attacked; they are, on the contrary, creatures among whose instinctual endowments is to be reckoned a powerful share of aggressiveness. As a result, their neighbour is for them not only a potential helper or sexual object, but also someone who tempts them to satisfy their aggressiveness on him, to exploit his capacity for work with compensation, to use him sexually without his consent, to seize his possessions, to humiliate him, to cause him pain, to torture and to kill him.[8]

HEALTHY NARCISSISM

In an early article, "Forms and Transformations of Narcissism" (1966), and in Chapter 12 of *The Analysis of the Self* (296–328), Kohut describes developments in the narcissistic realm that result from a successful analysis. Besides the increased self-esteem and strengthening of ambitions and purposes that result from the integration of the grandiose self, and the strengthening of ideals, self-approval, and admiration for others that result from the integration of the idealized parent imago with the ego and superego, Kohut notes a greater capacity for empathy, creativity, humor, and for that wisdom which involves understanding and accepting human limitations. Healthy narcissim will entail, for example, empathic capacity, for this is a natural outgrowth of a primary psychological experience, that "in our earliest mental organization the feelings, actions, and behavior of the mother had been included in our self."[9]

Kohut also claims that as a result of therapy, the narcissistic patient experiences an increase and expansion of the capacity for object love, but this is considered a "nonspecific and secondary result of the treatment" (AOS, 296). Indeed, Kohut at times calls to mind Nietzsche's transvaluation of values as he rails against the Western value system that disregards development and adaptive usefulness by imposing altruism to such an extent that therapists tend to wish "to replace the patient's narcissistic position with object love" (AOS, 224). As this statement, indicative of Kohut's separation of narcissism from object love, forms one of the major bases for criticism of Kohut's work, we will now turn to Melanie Klein and the British object relations school.

The British Object Relations School

MELANIE KLEIN

The British object relations school includes such theorists as D. W. Winnicott, W. R. D. Fairbairn, and Harry Guntrip. Fairbairn, Guntrip, and the American object relations theorists all acknowledge a great debt to the work of Melanie Klein, although they also distance themselves from some fundamentals of her theory.

Building on Freud's work on the internalization of the ego ideal ("On Narcissism," 1914) and the sadistic superego ("Mourning and Melancholia," 1917), Klein postulated a world of internal object relations that one could intuit from observing children's play and fantasies. In focusing on what she called the first two "positions" of psychological development, the paranoid-schizoid (first half of first year) and the depressive position (second half of first year), Klein was one of the first to shift attention to pre-Oedipal developments, although, as later object relations theorists point out, she seriously underplayed the role of the environment, that is, the real as opposed to the inborn fantasized interaction of mother and child. One reason for this neglect was Klein's strict adherence to a dual instinct theory, which, in her view, regardless of the quality of child care, motored development.

As Kernberg points out in his review of her work, Klein uses self and ego interchangeably.[10] Her theory implies that a primary ego, undifferentiated from the id, exists from birth, and this ego takes as its primary object the mother's breast (called a part-object because the

infant takes the breast for the whole of the mother at this stage). The
first manifestation of the innate death instinct is expressed in oral sadism toward the inevitably frustrating breast. The emotion linked with
this is envy of a breast perceived to be purposely withholding gratification. The breast is thus experienced as persecutory, and this gives rise to
anxiety.

Primitive defense mechanisms, such as splitting, projection and introjection, are also part of the innate ego system. The infant cannot
tolerate the "bad" object as something within and attempts to project
all badness outwards. But the object must be preserved as well, and, to
preserve it, the baby "splits" the object into good and bad. In terms of
libidinal drives, the infant introjects, or mentally internalizes, the
"good" breast, the breast that nourishes, but it also reintrojects the
"bad" breast, which contaminates the self-image.[11] The infant uses the
mechanism of splitting to keep the endangered good object apart from
the endangering bad object; no integration of good and bad self or
object images is possible at this stage of development. A further means
of keeping the good object intact is to project the split-off bad part of
the self and of the object onto an external object, with which the infant
identifies and hopes thus to control; this mechanism is termed projective identification.

If the infant has too much aggression, further splitting may occur,
and the external world takes on a persecutory quality that induces excessive paranoid anxiety. A parallel excessive idealization of good objects
occurs to protect against persecution, but it should be noted that this
idealization arises from the predominance of aggression. Such excesses
in early life mark the schizoid personality described by Fairbairn. But
Fairbairn, who rejects Klein's view of innate sadism, explains that schizoid personalities withdraw from external reality to protect the fragile
good object relations; they are afraid of destroying loved objects by the
sheer strength of their own need for them.

In the next Kleinian phase, the depressive phase, there is an integration of good and bad part-objects, and the developmental task of this
stage is to be able to tolerate ambivalence. Now internal aggression is
"acknowledged rather than split off or projected, and the object is
idealized so it will not be destroyed by this aggression" (IWER, 30).
Characteristic of this phase, and a developmental advance, are guilt
feelings; the infant feels guilty about the wish to destroy the loved
object, and, furthermore, it recognizes its need to preserve this object.

According to Klein, the infant attempts to reduce the guilt by repairing the damage done by its aggression. Klein terms this defensive act reparation, and it involves the expression of love and gratitude to the total object. As Kernberg notes in his review of Klein's work: "The tolerance of ambivalence implies a predominance of love over hate in relation to whole objects" (IWER, 30). This tolerance is necessary to achieve in order to advance to Oedipal relations.

Kernberg summarizes the pathology that results from a failure to resolve the tasks of Klein's depressive position, that is, the failure to establish securely a good internal object in infancy (IWER, 31–34). One possible result is pathological mourning. This is marked by the predominance of a primitive, sadistic superego that demands perfection, shows a hatred of the instincts, and fantasizes the destruction of the world. Another possible result is a group of manic defenses that include (1) idealization—protecting an extremely idealized self "by means of purified exalted states reflecting fantasies of merging of the self with good, unrealistically idealized objects" (IWER, 32–33), (2) manic triumph, and (3) omnipotence, contempt, compulsive introjection, and identification with the sadistic superego (IWER, 33). As Kernberg points out, Klein's narcissistic personality "combines the psychopathology of envy . . . with the personality characteristics reflecting manic defenses" (IWER, p. 34). Kernberg's agreement with this statement alerts us that his view of the narcissist will be less complimentary than that of Kohut.

FAIRBAIRN AND GUNTRIP

Harry Guntrip is a British psychoanalyst who, trained by W.R.D. Fairbairn, has written several *comptes rendus* of the beginnings and development of British object relations theory. In *Personality Structure and Human Interaction* (New York: International Universities Press, 1961, hereafter referred to as PSHI), he took issue with psychobiological and psychosociological schools of analytic theory, proposing Fairbairn's theory of the developing self as a synthesis and corrective. Although he and Fairbairn acknowledge their debt to Melanie Klein, they completely reject her view that human development is motored by innate drives. Like Kohut, they see aggression as a secondary phenomenon, a reaction to injury to the self (PSHI, 74–75). They differ from Freud, Klein, and even Kohut in asserting that human nature is innately neither pleasure-seeking nor self-seeking, but rather object-seeking (PSHI, 79); Guntrip asserts that a

> good personal relationship is not desired merely for the sake of pleasure but is in itself the basic need and aim of men, whose nature cannot be fulfilled without it, while aggression and pleasure-seeking only result from the frustration of this primary aim. (PSHI, 80)

Thus, this theory places relationship, rather than skills and abilities, goals and ideals (Kohut) at the center of the healthy self. As Guntrip puts it: "The two problems of achievement of self-realization and achievement of good personal relationships cannot be separated, for they are two sides of the same process" (PSHI, 169).

Fairbairn had been an orthodox Freudian until 1934, then a Kleinian between 1934 and 1940. As mentioned above, he came to differ from Klein on the issue of instincts as primary. Fairbairn, like Kohut, was more convinced of a primary striving toward health and rejected the innate sadism that instigated the introjections and projections of the Kleinian developmental model. He also criticized her lack of attention to the conditions of external reality.

Fairbairn's Model of the Self
Guntrip writes that Fairbairn's ultimate view of development postulated a unitary and primary ego (= self) from which two repressed structures split off. Each of the three structures is libidinally connected to an object. The primary ego's first engagement with the world is via its object-seeking libido; libido, but not aggression, is innate, and it is reality-, not pleasure-seeking. "The first defence adopted by the original ego to deal with an unsatisfying personal relationship is . . . introjection . . . of the unsatisfying object" (Fairbairn, cited by Guntrip, PSHI, 279). Thus, internal object relations begin with frustration. For Fairbairn, who focused his research on the schizoid personality, "disturbed development results when the mother does not succeed in making the child feel she loves him for his own sake and as a person in his own right" (PSHI, 284).

According to Fairbairn, the two repressed segments of the original ego are (1) the antilibidinal ego, which has a prohibitive antilibidinal object. This would be roughly equivalent to the sadistic forerunner of the superego, and (2) the libidinal ego, seat of desire, which has an exciting, gratifying internal object (PSHI, 328–335; IWER, 65). Problems in the earliest, paranoid-schizoid phase of development (adopted from Klein's theory but elaborated upon by Fairbairn), lead to a terror of any object relations:

> the schizoid person's major internal frustration is an inhibition by acute anxiety of the power to love. The more the need to love is frustrated, the more intense does it become and the unhappy person oscillates between an overpowering need to find good objects and a compulsive flight into detachment from all objects, under pressure mainly of the terror of exploiting them to the point of destruction; for the destruction of the love-object feels then to involve also the loss of the helplessly dependent ego which is in a state of emotional identification with the object. Love-object relationships are the whole of the problem, and the conflicts over them are an intense and devastating drama of need, fear, anger and hopelessness. To attempt to account for this by a hedonistic theory of motivation, namely that the person is seeking the satisfactions of oral, anal and genital pleasure, is so impersonal and inadequate that it takes on the aspect of being itself a product of schizoid thinking. (PSHI, 287)

The main variable of Fairbairn's developmental model is dependence (PSHI, 290–293). The earliest stages of life are marked by infantile dependence, in which both primary identification (merger) and oral incorporative attitudes persist. As in Klein, the first object is the maternal breast and the first libidinal organ is the mouth. In a second, transitional stage, the child struggles to outgrow infantile dependence on the mother and oscillates between the rejection and retention of objects. The final stage is mature dependence, in which the person experiences a full differentiation between self and object. As Kohut's theory makes clear, such full differentiation is a rarely accomplished feat.

Pathology
Fairbairn and Guntrip would seem to agree with Kohut that the neuroses are defenses "against the more serious dangers of the earlier psychotic conditions" (PSHI, 236); they also feel that neurotic resolutions of the Oedipus complex have their ultimate cause in infantile dependence, specifically the schizoid position (PSHI, 311). As noted above, for Fairbairn, internal object relations would not develop were there not a problem with the infant's external object relations. The split between good and bad objects that results from frustration, and the intolerable ambivalence toward one's objects, is the basis of all forms of pathology. Guntrip writes:

> If the mother is a "bad" or unsatisfying object, then separation will threaten to dissolve primary identification all too rapidly and separation-

anxiety will dictate a flight backwards into secondary identification with
an internalized object. (PSHI, 302)

Thus, for Guntrip and Fairbairn, unlike Kohut, pathological narcissism
would not be indicative of a developmental arrest at a normal stage but
of a conflicted pathological self structure that develops and evolves in
response to frustration. Kernberg and the American object relations
theorists agree with the British school on this issue.

Rather than speak of narcissism per se, Guntrip and Fairbairn speak of
a struggle between dependence and independence in characterizing
early pathology. The schizoid person, that is, the person who is extremely
dependent in an infantile manner, experiences all relationships as

> both a mutual swallowing and a mutual merging, and the patient is never
> quite sure at any given moment whether he feels most as if he is being
> swallowed or doing the swallowing. . . . Thus the patient in a state of
> marked infantile dependence is always both inordinately possessive to-
> wards the love-object and yet feels helplessly dependent and loses person-
> ality to the love-object. A great deal of aggressive reaction comes out of a
> struggle not to surrender to infantile dependent relationship with its dan-
> gers to the adult self. (PSHI, 315–316)

According to Guntrip, all immature relationships have a pattern of
hierarchical structuring, that is, one person is superior and the other
inferior. Any reader of contemporary Western literature will recognize
the above-described struggle characteristic of the schizoid position and
those who have not resolved it.

D. W. WINNICOTT AND THE "TRUE" AND "FALSE" SELF

Before leaving British object relations theory, a few words need to be
said regarding D. W. Winnicott's discussion of the true and false self.
Winnicott, who was a pediatrician as well as an analyst, developed the
concept of "good-enough mothering" to refer to normal, non-traumat-
ically frustrating care of the infant by either father or mother.[12] A good-
enough parent "meets the omnipotence of the infant and to some extent
makes sense of it" (MP, 145). The child's emerging self is mirrored and
approved; his/her grandiosity is gradually tamed.

In normal development, a "false," social self protects a "true" self
which alone has the capacity to feel real (MP, 133). The true self precedes object relations; "it means little more than the summation of

sensori-motor aliveness" (MP, 149). If mothering is not good enough, and if the false self alone is treated as real, the true self will feel a sense of futility and despair (MP, 133). As Alice Miller writes in *Prisoners of Childhood* (trans. Ruth Ward, New York: Basic Books, 1982), some infants quickly perceive that it is not acceptable to express their needs, to cry when they need to or be demanding. These infants begin to submerge their needs and comply with the needs of the parent. They may seem precociously independent, but this independence is premature; the infant was not really ready to take over the soothing and mirroring functions of the parent. Such infants have early substituted a false for a true self.

Winnicott writes that a frustrated child endowed with fine intellectual faculties is in danger of making his/her intellect the "seat of the false self" (MP, 134 and 144). This occurs by means of a dissociation between mind and what he calls the "psyche-soma" (MP, 134). An implication of this observation is that over-intellectualization may be a defense used by some people with pathological self structures.

For Winnicott, narcissistic pathology revolves around the relation between the true and false self, the person within the person (MP, 127). The most extreme pathology occurs when the false self sets itself up as real, and the true self remains hidden. The person develops very rigid defenses that prevent growth. Less extreme is when the false self defends the true self, allowing it a secret life. A middle ground is where the false self seeks a way for the true self to come into its own. The healthiest relation is one in which the individual forgoes omnipotence and primary process, forming a compromise between the compliant, false self, and the true self.

Winnicott's work particularly stresses the infant's early environment; in *The Maturational Processes and the Facilitating Environment* he sums up his thesis as follows: "the individual's maturational processes (including all that is inherited) require a facilitating environment, especially in the very early stages" (p. 135).

American Ego Psychology Object Relations Theory: Jacobson, Mahler, Kernberg

In *Internal World and External Reality* (1980), Otto Kernberg presents most cogently a theory of self formation and pathology that is grounded in his own previous work as well as in the work of Margaret Mahler and Edith Jacobson. Through various methods of information-gathering, including psychoanalytic reconstructions and observation of both normal and psychotic infants and their mothers, the three theorists have confirmed and added to each other's work over the years. In Kernberg's view, their work develops an ego psychology object relations theory that expands upon rather than breaks with classical Freudian metapsychology (e.g., see IWER, 18). With such a statement, Kernberg marks himself off clearly from Kohut and his followers. Some of the many differences between the two schools (the latter of which is frequently called "self psychology") are: (1) the Jacobson-Mahler-Kernberg theory incorporates libidinal and aggressive drives, (2) in their view, an ego deficit or deficiency does not preclude conflict, (3) they maintain the tripartite structure of id-ego-superego, while adding to this structural theory a view of the earlier, dyadic relations that contribute to building the structures, (4) as noted above, they do not subscribe to Kohut's view of developmental arrest; the self that the narcissistic patient defends is, in their view, pathologically structured but not structurally deficient, (5) they see object love as inextricably intertwined with narcissistic development whereas Kohut posits object love and narcissism as two separate lines of development that continue to evolve relatively independently throughout life.

In *The Psychological Birth of the Human Infant* (New York: Basic Books, 1975, hereafter referred to as PB), Mahler, Pine, and Bergman present the results of a long-term study of the infant's gradual separation from its primary fusion with the mother; this separation and consequent individuation is what the authors refer to as "psychological birth." In their view, this is a process that is never finished, but its main phase is from the fourth to fifth month of life to the thirtieth or thirty-sixth month (PB, 3). Focusing on these three years, Kernberg, Jacobson, and Mahler have developed a complete theory of the way in which self and object representations are internalized and bind with libidinal and aggressive affective states to build gradually the structures of id, ego, and superego.

SELF FORMATION

For Kernberg, Jacobson, and Mahler, intrapsychic life begins with a self within which ego and id are not yet differentiated and within which aggressive and libidinal drives are undifferentiated as well. The first intra-psychic structure is a fused self-object representation which evolves gradually under the impact of the relationship between mother and infant. (IWER, 95)[13]

In the view of Mahler et al. (1975), primary narcissism precedes the process of separation-individuation. In the first few weeks of life—what they refer to as the autistic phase—the infant is not aware of a mothering agent; in this phase, the internal self-object representation is consolidated and there is a dim awareness by the infant that needs cannot be provided by him/herself. From the second month, the "infant behaves and functions as though he and his mother were an omnipotent system—a dual unity within one common boundary" (PB, 44). The two stages of primary narcissism—autism and symbiosis—occur before *"the emergence of a rudimentary ego as a functional structure . . ."* (PB, 48). A normal autistic and symbiotic phase is a prerequisite for normal separation and individuation.

Separation-individuation begins in the next phase. The main task of this stage, the first task of the early ego, is to differentiate self from object representations. As Jacobson points out, a child's fear of separation and its desire to maintain or regain the original symbiosis are very strong independent of the action of the parent; thus, without help from a mature parent who is able to separate, the child will tend to resist accepting sharply defined boundaries.[14] A defensive refusion of self and object representations protects against pain; pain is kept separate from pleasure by investing some fused self and object representations with aggression. Thus there are now some good and some bad self and object representations in the intrapsychic world. The primitive defense mechanisms elaborated by Klein—splitting, projection, and introjection—are used to keep good representations in and to project bad ones outward. The bad self and object representations become forerunners of the sadistic superego.

In the next phase of the separation-individuation process, the second major task of the early ego must be accomplished: the integration of good with bad self and good with bad object representations (in Klein's terms, the move from part- to whole-object representations characteristic of the depressive phase). A successful resolution of this task leads to object constancy, that is, the ability "to maintain a representation of the good object under the impact of being frustrated by it" (IWER, 3). In this phase, a more mature idealizaton also occurs; ideal self representations are built up which reflect those desired changes in the self that would bring back symbiosis with the mother. Ideal object representations replace the lost ideal mother.

The separation-individuation phase ends with the dual accomplishments of differentiation of self from object representations and integration of libidinally and aggressively determined self and object representations. It should be pointed out that Kernberg stresses in all his books that we never see pure drives but only object relations that incorporate affective drive derivatives (e.g., IWER, 80). The internal world of object representations never reproduces the *actual* world of real people with whom the individual has relationships; "it is at most an approximation, always strongly influenced by the very early object-images of introjections and identifications" (ORT, 33). As the healthy child matures, internal objects are reshaped to resemble more closely external objects (ORT, 34).

In the fourth to fifth years of life, the superego is differentiated from the ego. Ideal self and object representations are integrated into the ego ideal, which is incorporated into the superego. The ideal and the sadistic superegos should tone each other down. Finally, what Kernberg refers to as a third layer internalization occurs: "the realistic, demanding, and prohibitive aspects of the parents that characterize the later stages and completion of the Oedipus complex . . ." (IWER, 99). The superego is thus built up of three layers of object relations.

PRE-OEDIPAL PATHOLOGY

According to Kernberg's model, a failure to differentiate self from object representations in the early phases of development produces psychosis. Symbiotic failures result in "idealized, ecstatic merged states, and terrifying, aggressive merged states" (IWER, 109). If one fails in the developmental task of separation-individuation, that is, integrating good and bad self and object representations, one will show borderline pathology. As described in Kernberg's earlier work, *Borderline Conditions and Pathological Narcissism* (New York: Aronson, 1975, hereafter referred to as BCPN), borderlines are characterized by their use of primitive defense mechanisms—splitting, primitive idealization, projection, denial, omnipotence, and devaluation. The alternating, contradictory states of idealization and devaluation are kept separate (split) in consciousness in order to reduce anxiety; when in one state, the borderline does not recall and cannot relate to the feelings of the other (BCPN, 25–30). Kernberg notes that *identity diffusion* is also characteristic of the borderline. He defines Erikson's term as follows:

> a poorly integrated concept of the self and of significant others. It is manifested typically by a chronic subjective feeling of emptiness, contradictory behavior that the patient cannot integrate in an emotionally meaningful way, and shallow, flat, impoverished perception of others. (IWER, 8)

Unlike the psychotic, however, the borderline is capable of reality testing, that is, distinguishing the self from the non-self.

Somewhere between the time when borderline pathology might develop (around age two to three) and the point of object constancy achievement (around four to five), narcissistic pathology might emerge. In *Borderline Conditions*, Kernberg had said that those with a narcissistic personality structure usually present an underlying borderline organization. Some characteristics of the pathological narcissist are boredom, restlessness, contempt for others, envy, grandiosity that hides feelings of worthlessness, shallow relationships, lack of empathy, and lack of principle. As in the borderline, problems in superego integration make narcissists unable to feel much guilt. Their inability to empathize makes them feel empty rather than lonely. It is their relatively good social functioning, better impulse control, and "pseudosublimatory" potential that distinguishes them from borderlines (BCPN, 229).

Kernberg notes that his narcissistic patients often have "chronically cold parental figures with covert but intense aggression" (BCPN, 234); the narcissist's internal world contains idealized self representations, shadows of others, and dreaded enemies. Their need for others is great, but their fear of dependence, of arousing the dormant hatred and envy caused by early frustration of their needs, makes them unable to acknowledge that they are receiving something from an other. Thus, Kernberg writes, "they always wind up empty" (BCPN, 237). They remain "fearful of a world which seems as hateful and revengeful as the patient himself" (BCPN, 233). In contrast to Kohut, Kernberg stresses "the presence of chronic, intense envy, and defenses against such envy, particularly devaluation, omnipotent control, and narcissistic withdrawal, as major characteristics of their emotional life" (BCPN, 264). Where

Kohut sees idealization of the analyst as a necessary regression to a point of arrested normal development, Kernberg sees it as a resistance, as what the patient usually does to other people in order to control them, devalue them, protect against envy, oral rage, and against receiving something good (BCPN, 279–80). It is Kernberg's conviction that aggression is a key element of the narcissist's pathological self structure, an element that must be analyzed if the patient is to be cured, that perhaps most distinguishes him from Kohut; indeed, Kernberg's belief in the primary nature of this aggression probably accounts for his far more negative view of those with a narcissistic personality.[15]

To summarize, psychosis, borderline pathology, and narcissism are the pre-Oedipal pathologies; they may be complicated by the overlay of later Oedipal difficulties, but their primitive defense mechanisms, such as splitting, mark them off from neurosis, which involves more mature defenses, such as repression.

Conclusion

All of the theorists involved in the study of the self agree that separation from an original state of union with a parent is a key task of the first few years of life, and all agree that this task is very difficult for both infant and parent. The inability to see another person as separate is a function of an early inability to separate from the first love-object;[16] separation is thus crucial both to mature love relations and healthy self-esteem. As Arnold Modell writes, "to love maturely one must accept the *separateness* of the object."[17] And yet, he and others, particularly Kohut, stress that such acceptance is never absolute or final, that the wish to merge is always present.

As part of separation and individuation, the baby who is to develop healthy love relations and healthy self-esteem must learn to integrate good and bad self representations and object representations. The ability to love and hate the same person, to tolerate ambivalence, is stressed by all object relations theorists as a *sine qua non* of healthy development. As Kernberg puts it:

> For practical purposes, object relations in depth involve the capacity both to love well, and to hate well, and particularly to tolerate varying combinations of loving and hateful feelings, and their toned down mingling in the relationship with the same object and with the self. . . . All this is in striking contrast to the frequent blandness and uninvolvement, the lack of

commitment to others as well as to any convictions about himself that one sees in narcissistic patients. Paradoxically, such lack of emotional depth and commitment may permit a better social functioning; for example, in certain political and bureaucratic organizations in which lack of commitments means survival and access to the top. (BCPN, 308)

With his last point, Kernberg opens the way for the subject of his 1980 work—object relations theory applied to the study of large groups, leaders, and institutions. The statement also lends some credence to Christopher Lasch's controversial thesis outlined in *The Culture of Narcissism:*

> Narcissism appears realistically to represent the best way of coping with the tensions and anxieties of modern life, and the prevailing social conditions therefore tend to bring out narcissistic traits that are present, in varying degrees, in everyone. (50)

Thus, it is probably not an accident that, since the nineteenth century, literature seems increasingly to be concerned with the problems of constituting a cohesive self and maintaining a sense of identity. The serious problems in identity formation that we see in many nineteenth and twentieth century works of art are not problems typically found in neurotics; according to Kernberg, neurotics usually have "a solid sense of self" (IWER, 9). Edith Jacobson writes that "serious identity problems appear to be limited to neurotics with specific narcissistic conflicts, and to borderline and psychotic patients."[18] Thus, when confronted with identity problems in texts, knowledge of Oedipal pathology alone will not usually give coherence to the psychological dimension of our literary interpretations. It is our feeling that an understanding of pre-Oedipal development and pathology can lend coherence to interpretations of images, characters, structures, themes—even modes of narration and other stylistic elements—in elusive modern and postmodern texts.[19]

NARCISSISM, ARTISTIC CREATIVITY, AND LITERARY CRITICISM

What are the specific implications of these theories of object relations and narcissism for understanding works of art, particularly literary works? The traditional Freudian view holds a work of art as a kind of substitute for the renunciation of instinctual gratification. The artist, suffering from clamorous instinctual needs, turns away from reality to creation and fantasy, and through the creative act, transforms the repressed wishes of infancy. According to Freud, "the writer is a person with a certain flexibility of repression and the courage to let his unconscious speak."[20] The inadequacy of Freud's theories on creativity, however, prompted his well-known declaration, "before the problem of the creative artist analysis must, alas, lay down its arms."[21] Despite this admission, Freud's theories have spawned a history of debate on the relationship between pathology and artistic creativity.

In his essay "Art and Neurosis" (1945), Lionel Trilling argues that although neurotic people are "likely to see a great deal more of reality and to see it with more intensity" than "normal" people, it is "still wrong to find the root and source of power and genius in neurosis."[22] The artist, he believes, is distinguished less by neuroticism than by health, by the power to control and use his neuroticism. While the artist's neurosis allies him with the common man, "what marks the artist is his power to shape the material of pain we all have" (166). Otto Rank has also argued the distinction between neuroticism and creativity; the neurotic person, he maintains, fears life while the creative artist fears death. The creative act is self-assertive and life-affirmative.[23]

One of the most influential psychoanalytic studies of artistic creativity is Ernst Kris' *Psychoanalytic Explorations in Art* (New York: Schocken Books, 1952). While still relying on Freudian theories of instinctual sublimation and particularly the notion of "flexibility of repression," Kris nevertheless stresses, like Trilling and Rank, the artist's healthiness or, more precisely, his "ego strength." He believes that the artist "borders on pathology and conquers it by his work"; he emphasizes the mastery and conquest of repressed traumatic experience. Although conflict may prompt creative activity, "detachment from conflict," Kris believes, is the key to successful creative work. "It is part of the artist's special gift or endowment which facilitates that detachment."[24]

Kris describes two phases of creative activity: inspiration and elaboration. While the elaborational phase involves "purposeful organization" and problem-solving, the inspirational stage is characterized "by the feeling of being driven, the experience of rapture, and the conviction that an outside agent acts through the creator" (59). This phase has many features in common with regressive processes, with the emergence of repressed impulses and drives and with a passive receptiveness to primary process. In the artist, however, as opposed to the psychotic, the ego is not overwhelmed by these regressive processes. The artist's ego controls primary process and puts it in its service—hence Kris' famous phrase, "regression in the service of the ego." Whereas the psychotic artist seeks no audience and "creates in order to transform the real world," the normal artist creates in order to depict the world "for others he wishes to influence." In all artistic creation, Kris argues, the idea of the public exists; there is thus an implied object relationship and a definite link to reality in the task of production. He then concludes that "art as an aesthetic—and therefore as a social—phenomenon is linked to the intactness of the ego" (169).

Thus while psychoanalysts have generally acknowledged certain connections between pathology and creativity, most seem to feel, like K. R. Eissler, that the psychic activity involved in the creative act is more constructive and organizing than a typical "textbook case" disorder.[25] Phyllis Greenacre, following Freud and Kris, has also conducted some important studies on the creative personality and its distinction from the pathological. "Behavior which, when viewed on phenomenological grounds only, would resemble a state of regression in the more ordinary individual," she claims, "may actually be rather the continued libidinized object relationship to the collective world of the artist."[26] Although Greenacre considers genius a "gift of the Gods" and ultimately unanalyzable, she does distinguish some common characteristics in the childhood of creative or gifted personalities, such as a greater sensitivity to sensory stimulation and an unusual capacity for awareness of relations between various stimuli.

Due to its heightened sensitivity, the gifted infant, she believes, probably has a more intense and demanding relationship to its early personal objects. The primary object which stimulates the intense sensory responses is further invested with a greater field of related experiences. Greenacre terms this field of related experiences "collective alternates," and as the creative personality develops, the collective alternates become libidinally cathected. The artist thus shifts and expands cathexis from primary processes to a "collective love affair" with the world. She concludes that "a love affair with the world is an obligatory condition in the development of great talent or genius" (490). The artistic product is a "love gift," and the creative act partakes of an object relationship (although a collective one) for there always exists the fantasy of a collective audience or recipient.

Two of Greenacre's observations in particular have influenced Kohut and later object relations theorists. The first is that the creative personality is commonly involved in the identification with an idealized image. The gifted child glorifies the parents "in accordance with the peculiar vibrancy and capacity for near ecstasy derived from its own body states" (494). If the real father fails to fulfill this function, a father-figure or father-image will do. The second idea concerns the creative personality's "splits in self representations, going over into even a split in the sense of identity" (p. 498). The artist experiences a schism between its "creative self" and its "social, conventional self."

Although Kohut considers Greenacre's formulation of the artist's love affair with the world as really a narcissistic experience of the world (the self expands to include the world), he agrees that the artist's innate sensitivity to external stimuli is a determining factor. In "Childhood Experience and the Creative Imagination" (1960), he compares the artist's "creative self" to the less developed, more exposed ego of the child. The adult's ego strength, he claims, rests on a "gradually acquired structure built up in consequence of innumerable frustrations of tolerable intensity. This structured ego serves as stimulus barrier and buffer in the interactions with inner and outer environment. It provides for the neutralization of drives and for ever more complex, varied and efficient modes of discharge through action." The artist, like the child, experiences reality with less buffering structures and thus "the near-traumatic impact of new impressions necessitates an inner elaboration of unusual degree."[27] In other words, the creative personality, lacking sufficient neutralizing and buffering structures, employs creative activity in order to safeguard its psychoeconomic balance.

Although Kohut's analysis clearly suggests that the artist's self is more narcissistically vulnerable than that of the ordinary individual, he is careful to distinguish between the creative and the narcissistically disordered personality. He believes that the psychic organization of creative people is characterized primarily by a fluidity of narcissistic cathexis. As he points out in "Creativeness, Charisma, Group Psychology" (1976), the artist may indeed experience periods of enfeeblement and intense disequilibrium, but these are temporary as opposed to the chronic, prolonged state of the pathologically narcissistic patient. Kohut believes the artist's most narcissistically vulnerable period to be in the early stages of creativity, or in what he calls the "precreative" period. At this stage there is a regression, a withdrawal of cathexis from the self and its ideals. The unattached narcissistic cathexis is subsequently put into the service of creative activity. The temporary enfeeblement, exposure and sense of isolation of the precreative period "repeat those overwhelmingly anxious moments of early life when the child felt alone, abandoned, unsupported."[28]

At this point Kohut draws on Greenacre's observations of the artistic personality's identification with an idealized object or image. During the intense precreative period, certain creative persons "require a specific relationship with another person—a transference of creativity," similar to the idealizing transferences of certain narcissistic patients in psychoanalytic treatment. The narcissistic relationship to an alter ego, or idealized selfobject, protects the artist's self from irreversible fragmentation. Kohut points to several examples: Freud and Fliess, Picasso and Braque, Joyce and James Stephens, Nietzsche and Wagner, Hawthorne and Melville.

While Kohut's theories are by no means universally accepted, many recent psychoanalytic theories also assert a strong link between creativity and narcissistic vulnerability or injury. The prevalent view today holds creativity as a variation of a healthy manifestation of narcissism rather than a sublimation of unacceptable drives. Charles Kligerman, for instance, maintains that "the early disappointments of the great artist are not too catastrophically traumatic, usually involving some physical separation or an emotional estrangement due to empathic failures. The ensuing loneliness leads to the rich development of fantasy as a mode of consolation and self-soothing—perhaps a form of play related to the later artistic activity." The artist, Kligerman continues, is concerned with exhibiting a beauty, perfection, and wholeness that "was originally his own (or that of the idealized maternal selfobject)."[29] The concrete work of art is thus a kind of reconstruction of the ideal self or selfobject. Or, as Kohut has explained it, "The broken self is mended via the creation of the cohesive artistic product."[30]

The connection between narcissistic injury and artistic creativity has commanded the attention of several other psychoanalytic theorists as well. From a study of a number of creatively active persons, William Niederland, for instance, discovered "the presence of a permanent and usually severe injury to infantile narcissism." Although he relates this injury specifically to a bodily defect or physical malformation, he admits, "the psychological reverberations which in several cases were archaically tinged . . . outweighed by far the actual physical anomaly."[31]

He thus sees the source of artistic creation in "unconscious restorative strivings" and believes early object loss to be a powerful stimulus for creativity and fantasies of a restitutive character.

Hanna Segal also considers creativity to be of an essentially reparative nature. Her theories are directly related to those of Melanie Klein. According to Segal, creativity arises out of the depressive position, in the desire to reassemble the inner world, felt to have been destroyed by aggressive fantasies, and to make reparation within and without. The creative individual's "realization that the whole loved object has been lost through his own attack gives rise to an intense feeling of loss and guilt, and to the wish to restore and recreate the lost loved object outside and within the ego,"[32] and this wish is the basis of creativity. Segal believes that both the artist and the neurotic share difficulties of unresolved depression and the threat of collapse of the internal world. The artist, however, differs from the neurotic in that the artist has a greater capacity for tolerating anxiety and depression. She concludes that all aesthetic pleasure includes the unconscious reliving of the artist's psychic state and experience of creation.

Winnicott's theories of object relations, and particularly his concept of the "transitional object," have also been central to recent theories about the creative process. As David Schechter explains, Winnicott's transitional objects are "objects that are not part of the infant's body, yet are not fully recognized as belonging to external reality."[33] They may be such things as blankets, toys, or teddy bears, and they reside in an intermediate area of experience between autistic, subjective fantasy, and true object relationship. Winnicott sees this transitional area between subjective and objective realities as containing the root of symbolism. Schechter thus argues that the child's playful engagement in this transitional world is an anlage and precondition for creativity. He maintains further that the creative individual must have achieved, in Winnicott's terms, "the capacity to be alone"; the individual must have access to good internalized object relationships in order not to be overcome by a crippling loneliness or inhibited by a sadistic persecuting superego.[34]

Finally, the contributions of various analysts on the 1971 International Psycho-Analytical Congress Panel on Creativity reflect the heavy influence of object relations and self-theories.[35] Leon Grinberg, for instance, offers the view that in creative activity the self structures undergo a temporary disorganization and then a reintegration on a different basis. The chaotic disorganization phase involves primary process and psychotic mechanisms but, unlike the psychotic, the artistic personality is close to normal in its tolerance of object loss and capacity for abstraction. The artist "can endure the feeling of object loss without overwhelming anxiety " (21). The psychotic mechanisms include splitting, omnipotence, idealization, and projective identification, all of which enable the artist to recreate the lost object. Grinberg believes, furthermore, that during the disintegration stage there is a "fusion with internal objects from which the creative product will emerge. He [the artist] experiences the product as part of himself and himself as part of the work" (22). Another panelist, Bernard Meyer, similarly conceives the created object as a "replacement for part of the self" (p. 24). Grinberg concludes, like Hanna Segal, that every creative act "is based on the working through of depressive fantasies aiming at the reparation of the early lost objects which one feels are damaged" (22).

In a final summary of the panelists' contributions, the reporter, Kligerman, acknowledges that there seemed to be "no unitary formulation to cover the phenomenon of creativity," but he does note the "heavy emphasis on self-object relations . . . compared to earlier formulae of instinctual discharge and sublimation. Many creative persons suffer a structural defect which is temporarily healed by the artistic production. The structural defect often is related to early object loss" (27). These findings have, we believe, important implications for the understanding of a literary work and for the field of literary criticism.

Despite the conceptual differences among the various theorists, they are describing some similar psychic phenomena related to both artistic creativity and general psychological development. These phenomena in turn present exciting territories for critical investigation in literature. Rather than studying the psychology of a literary work in terms of drive-conflict and instinctual sublimation, these theories focus our psychoanalytic attention on identity formation and the vicissitudes of constructing and maintaining a coherent self-structure.[36] Whether it be Kernberg's "integrated self" or Kohut's "cohesive nuclear self," the emphasis and goal are the same. Images and conceptions of the self thus become an important focus of critical inquiry, along with both themes and stylistic manifestations of fragmentation and disintegration.

In view of these theories, the traditional triadic Oedipal configuration would no longer occupy the central spotlight in psychoanalytic literary criticism but would bow to the primacy of earlier mother-child or self-selfobject relations. Merging, mirroring, and idealizing patterns would also become significant areas for critical examination, as would evidence of splitting, grandiose fantasies, and narcissistic rage.

As with all psychoanalytic literary criticism, the charge of reductionism is inevitable. Kohut, in an exchange with the literary critic Erich Heller (*Critical Inquiry*, 1978), offers a cogent defense of the application of modern depth-psychology to literary criticism. Referring to the final line of Yeats's "Among School Children"—"How can we know the dancer from the dance?"—Kohut admits that the line "is beautiful—hauntingly beautiful and evocative—while an analyst's analogous comments about the integration of the self and its actions—even meaningful and important comments, not drive-psychological reductionism—are not. But I admit this fact without shame. It is the very function of art—the essence of its 'being,' as you might say—to be beautiful and evocative; it is the very function of science—its essential objective, as I would say—to be explanatory and clear, to concentrate on the content of its communications and to put formal considerations second to the unambiguous preciseness of its statements."[37]

It is our feeling, furthermore, that object relations theory and self-psychology, when applied to literary criticism, do not reduce the literature but, on the contrary, add to our appreciation of a work's depth and complexity. The purpose of psychoanalytic literary criticism is not to reduce a work to rigid schemata but to illuminate the multiplexities of its emotional and psychological workings and to discern, as does all literary criticism, a work's particular order and coherence.[38] We would certainly not argue psychoanalytic criticism as the only or ultimate theoretical perspective, but along with historical and sociocultural perspectives, among others, it can enhance the intelligent appreciation of a literary work.

In his exchange with Heller, Kohut further defends the importance of psychoanalytic criticism today because he believes that modern man suffers more than ever from the "loss of the secure cohesion, continuity, and harmony of his self" and is in great need of "scientific explanations concerning the significance which the values and meanings that are continuously created by art, religion, philosophy, and by science itself have for him" (449). The comment reflects Kohut's notion, elaborated on in *The Restoration of the Self*, that the twentieth century marks a psychological swing from Guilty Man to Tragic Man. Kohut conceptualizes Guilty Man, we recall, as blocked by anxiety; he experiences conflict over his pleasure-seeking drives and between his ego and superego functions. He may be understood in traditional psychoanalytic terms. Tragic Man, on the other hand, is blocked by despair, by an inability to achieve self-realization. He lacks a cohesive nuclear self and can best be understood in self psychological terms.

In "The Self in History" Kohut speculates that during Freud's time "the involvement between parents and their children was overly intense," children were often "emotionally overtaxed." Conflicts developed as a result of overstimulation; the Oedipus complex was "artificially intensified by overcloseness." The social circumstances and family constellation of the twentieth century, he believes, exhibit just the opposite condition: children are often understimulated due to the absence or emotional distance of significant adults. The familial atmosphere is characterized by "emotional flatness" and "sterility."[39]

The Guilty Man/Tragic Man formulation seems far too simplistic: characteristics of each may, after all, overlap, and we doubt that Kohut would dispute the tragedy of the quintessential Guilty Man, Oedipus. Part of the problem may lie in the semantics of the word "tragic." Kohut gives the term a limited, very particular meaning—his Tragic Man is unable even to experience guilt. The Guilty Man/Tragic Man concept is perhaps primarily meant to be evocative, suggesting that in the history of Western civilization some periods more than others are psychologically characterized by narcissistic enfeeblement, by problems in the cohesion and integrity of the self. This may account for the overrepresentation in this volume of essays dealing with nineteenth and twentieth century literature. As to the reasons, we do not wish to speculate beyond Kohut's tentative remarks. The field is ripe for sociological and psychohistorical inquiry.

APPLICATIONS OF THE THEORIES TO THE TEXTS: A SUMMARY OF THE ESSAYS

The essays in this collection are arranged chronologically and reflect an historical continuity and development. We begin with the Elizabethan period. As Peter Donaldson points out in his essay on Marlowe, the Renaissance was a "decisive period in the emergence of characteristically Western and modern attitudes towards the self, in which outward confidence, assertiveness, and independence are so often attended by fears of inner emptiness, nullity or incoherence." Donaldson argues that although Oedipal conflict informs the external structure of the plays,

Marlowe's tragic vison really occurs at the point at which the conflict structure is perceived as essentially meaningless. The real subject of the plays, he maintains, is the protagonist's sense of incoherence, emptiness, and terror. Donaldson applies Kohut's theories to a careful analysis of characterization and dramatic structure.

Joseph Westlund also uses theories of narcissism, particularly the notion of the grandiose self, in his analysis of Prospero in the epilogue to Shakespeare's *The Tempest*. He argues that Prospero's choice of magic and his use of others as selfobjects reveal his narcissistic omnipotence—one not unlike that of Marlowe's Faustus. Westlund sees this as a fantasy which appeals to all of us, and yet—following Klein and Segal—he demonstrates that the effect is reparative, specifically in the epilogue. Here we, unlike Prospero, can feel guilt for relating to others as selfobjects, and can extend to him the compassion which he seems unable to extend to others. The epilogue, like the play, helps to repair our inner world and make us feel saner and richer.

From the Renaissance, during which an intense interest in the self arose, we turn to the Romantic period and its renewed and more self-conscious interest in identity, in the integrity—and fragility—of the self. Susan Grayson scrutinizes the autobiographical form in her study of Rousseau; she focuses on the problems of the author as revealed in his works. Grayson uses the concept of the selfobject in an intriguing way by asserting that Rousseau's texts themselves function as his selfobjects. Examining the autobiographical *Confessions* and *Reveries*, she shows the many passages where Rousseau's momentary experiences of idealized merger (especially with nature) are followed by severe paranoid episodes. Rousseau's texts are not merely meant to justify his behavior to the world but serve to stabilize his very fragile self.

Ecstatic merger with both nature and idealized female figures is a characteristic Romantic theme, from Goethe's *Sorrows of Young Werther* to Keats's *Endymion*. One of the earliest Romantic expressions of this occurs in the poetry of Blake, which Margaret Storch analyzes in this volume. Storch examines the images of women in Blake's poetry and uncovers patterns that are, she argues, informed by a profound, pre-Oedipal ambivalence towards the mother. Storch uses Melanie Klein's notion of splitting to help understand Blake's alternately idealized and dangerously phallic female figures. Pathological idealization of the selfobject is a core component of narcissism and it goes further than Oedipal explanations in explaining the madonna/whore dichotomy found in so many texts. Storch questions, furthermore, how Blake's subconscious misogyny might affect our analysis of his seemingly progressive political views. Theories of narcissism and pre-Oedipal pathology, as her essay makes clear, have important implications for feminist criticism.

Frederick Kirchhoff further explores the connection between narcissism and Romanticism in his study of Wordsworth's "Intimations Ode." Kirchhoff uses Kohut's notion of "narcissistic adequacy" to explain the poem. He argues that Wordsworth had trouble withdrawing from the idealized, maternal selfobject and introjecting it as an internal structure. Language, Kirchhoff believes, served the poet as "a medium in which the self and its object can interact" and the poetic text "assumes the role of an otherwise missing psychic structure." Kirchhoff studies the diction and stylistic development of the "Ode," arguing, for instance, that the sing-song quality and "conventionalized poetic diction" of the opening lines reflect an "inadequate manifestation of the self." The application of theories of narcissism to stylistic analysis becomes increasingly appropriate as we move into later nineteenth and twentieth century literature and encounter such stylistic phenomena as fragmented prose, disjointed structure or a distanced, ironic narrative stance.

Barbara Schapiro's study of Thomas Hardy reflects many of the same narcissistic patterns found in the Romantics, such as a predominant idealization, a desire for self-annihilating merger, and a split, ambivalent attitude toward women and nature. Schapiro applies theories of pre-Oedipal object relations to an examination of theme, characterization, and imagery in several of Hardy's novels. Two other essays on postromantic writers, Lynne Layton's on Flaubert and Eugene Holland's on Baudelaire to Sartre, both deal with the Second French Empire. Holland takes a sociohistorical approach. He argues that Baudelaire's early poetry is dominated by masochistic imagery appropriate to the early stages of capitalism discussed by Weber, in which the superego is strong, while the post-1850 poetry and prose are marked by ironic distance and narcissistic contempt for all of his earlier sufferings and ideals. Holland draws on Benjamin's study of Baudelaire and Sartre's study of Flaubert to tie the narcissistic character structure of the Second Empire to the beginnings of depersonalized, consumer mass culture. In her study of Flaubert's *Sentimental Education*, Lynne Layton finds the character of the French generation that came of age in 1848 to be marked by narcissistic alternation from exhilarated merger with an idealized person or thing to fragmentation and emptiness. Unlike Holland, she hypothesizes that the generation Flaubert describes in that novel was narcissistic well before the Second Empire, and its narcissism helped bring about the political shift to the right. The alternation described above has referents in the two conflicting ideologies of Flaubert's character and time: Romantic organicism vs. positivism and its mission to demystify the world by breaking down wholes and scoffing at romantic ideals.

By the late nineteenth century, the novel, as has been commonly noted, turns increasingly inward, a move that may be linked to the condition of pathological narcissism. For as the psyche becomes problematic, so does it become a central subject of literature. Brooks Bouson offers a Kohutian reading of Kafka's modern classic of estrangement and disintegration, *The Metamorphosis*. Her approach is similar to a psychoanalytic case study. She examines the character of Gregor Samsa as he exhibits the symptoms of Kohut's Tragic Man. Gregor's transformation, she claims, reveals at once his sense of worthlessness and powerlessness and his repressed grandiosity—his deep-rooted need to control others and be the center of confirming attention.

Joseph Lichtenberg also examines evidence of archaic grandiosity in the life and works of Henry James. His analysis operates within a framework of three separate lines of development, and he sees both progressive and regressive tendencies within these developmental lines. Lichtenberg argues that James's developmental choices are a result of responses to adversity in the author's life, and that the "creative rebounds to adversity" reflected in the work help account for the major stylistic revision of James' later years.

In his examination of E. M. Forster's novels, Peer Hultberg also looks at the author's life history, including the biographical history of Forster's mother, and then traces the course of health/pathology through several of the works. Hultberg discovers some development or working through of the problem in Forster's later novels, particularly in the author's last haunting work, *A Passage to India*. Ernest and Ina Wolf also use biographical information in their psychological study of Virginia Woolf's *To the Lighthouse*. They speculate about Woolf's illness and its roots in her relationship to a mother who was the model for Mrs. Ramsay. The character of Mrs. Ramsay, they argue, "emerges as a narcissistically injured person who needs hyper-activity to keep the people of her environment enmeshed with her own personality in order to protect her defective self from disintegrating. The vicissitudes of human incompleteness pervade the novel and lend it its main theme." The Wolfs examine the novel's imagery and themes in terms of Kohut's psychology of the self. They also point to Virginia Woolf as one of the pioneers of modernism; her works represent the revolutionary modernist shift from the facts of external reality to an introspective, psychic reality. Kohut's psychology of the self, they claim, grounded as it is in "the introspectively graspable data of a psychology of inner experience," lends itself particularly well to the analysis of modernist works.

Critics of twentieth century texts have long focused on the fragmentation of modern form, on the "nothingness" at the center of, for example, a text by Robbe-Grillet or Beckett. Theories of narcissism, we would argue, can help critics to interpret and demystify that nothingness and fragmentation. The nothingness often structures the main character as well as the text. Rodney Simard's essay on Joan Didion's *Play It As It Lays* reveals the emptiness of the central character, indeed of all the novel's characters, and he asserts that this emptiness also results in the short, unsustainable fragment-chapters of the book. Simard further analyzes the protagonist's underlying grandiosity and need for control, as well as the ironic distance both the character and Didion herself maintain.

The issue of irony, from a psychoanalytic point of view, indeed poses something of a critical problem in modern and contemporary texts. A key characteristic of the pathological narcissist is his or her inability really to empathize with another person. This lack of empathy extends to the self, and when a narcissistic writer rains contempt upon characters that are obviously self-projections, the critical problem is raised. Is this irony, be it mere distance or contempt, a further manifestation of narcissistic pathology or is it a criticism and transcendence of the condition? As this type of narrative stance is quite prevalent in the contemporary novel—for example in that of Roth, Handke, Hawkes, Barthelme, to name but a few—this is an important question. In our view, irony is sometimes more of the same and sometimes indicative of transcendence. Gentle irony of the kind found in Fontane entails empathy and is not necessarily narcissistic at all. Contemptuous irony, the coldness characteristic of so many contemporary works, probably, but not unconditionally, reveals narcissism.

We do not mean to suggest that all modern or contemporary texts display pathological narcissism. Bellow's Herzog, for example, although he declares himself a narcissist, suffers only a momentary loss of self due to circumstances. He is rather a guilt-ridden, old-fashioned neurotic; a mark of the narcissist, on the contrary, is the inability to feel guilt (thus the psychopath as main character). Nevertheless, it seems to us that narcissistic pathology has become ever more apparent in the course of twentieth century literature. Thus we would argue that theories of narcissism and pre-Oedipal pathology can open up dimensions in literary texts that have previously resisted analysis from classical psychoanalytic perspectives. The essays in this volume reveal the variety of ways these theories can be applied to literary criticism: Grayson's focus on autobiography, Donaldson's study of characterization and structure, Kirchhoff's stylistic and linguistic analysis, Lichtenberg's and Hultberg's use of personal history—connecting psychological to literary development, Storch's examination of imagery, Westlund's focus on the reader's psychological response, Bouson's case study, or Holland's sociohistorical approach. In their various critical applications, theories of narcissism can, we believe, shed light on the literary texts as well as contribute to our understanding of contemporary experience.[40]

NOTES

1. The essays in this volume draw only on English and American theories of narcissism; Lacan and other French theorists of the self are not included. Many fine works have already appeared which introduce literary critics to the work of Lacan. The same cannot be said for the British and American theories presented here.

2. Edith Jacobson, *The Self and the Object World* (New York: International Universities Press, 1964), p. 6. This definition derives from Heinz Hartmann, "Comments on the Psychoanalytic Theory of the Ego," in *Essays on Ego Psychology* (New York: International Universities Press, 1964).

3. Hartmann, *Essays on Ego Psychology,* p. 127.

4. Heinz Kohut and Ernest S. Wolf, "The Disorders of the Self and Their Treatment: An Outline," *The International Journal of Psycho-Analysis,* 59 (1978), 44.

5. Marian Tolpin, "Discussion of 'Psychoanalytic Developmental Theories of the Self: An Integration,' by Morton Shane and Estelle Shane," in Arnold Goldberg ed., *Advances in Self Psychology* (New York: International Universities Press, 1980, hereafter referred to as ASP) pp. 63–66.

6. See Paul Ornstein, "Self Psychology and the Concept of Health," in ASP, pp. 137–159.

7. Heinz Kohut, "Thoughts on Narcissism and Narcissistic Rage," in Paul Ornstein ed., *The Search for the Self* (New York: International Universities Press, 1978, hereafter referred to as SFS), vol. 2, p. 646.

8. Sigmund Freud, "Civilization and its Discontents," in *Standard Edition,* vol. 21, trans. James Strachey (London: Hogarth Press, 1961).

9. Heinz Kohut, "Forms and Transformations of Narcissism," in *Journal of the American Psychoanalytic Association,* 14 (1966), p. 262.

10. The following resume of Klein's work is taken from Otto Kernberg, M.D., *Internal World and External Reality: Object Relations Theory Applied* (New York, London: Jason Aronson, 1980), pp. 19–38. In the text, we will refer to this work as IWER.

11. For a description of this process, see also Arnold H. Modell, M.D., *Object Love and Reality: An Introduction to a Psychoanalytic Theory of Object Relations* (New York: International Universities Press, 1968), p. 37.

12. D. W. Winnicott, *The Maturational Processes and the Facilitating Environment: Studies in the Theory of Emotional Development* (New York: International Universities Press, 1965), p. 145. We will refer to this book hereafter as MP.

13. This section is largely taken from Kernberg, IWER, pp. 95–117. For Kernberg's model of the connection between object relations and ego formation, see his *Object Relations Theory and Clinical Psychoanalysis* (New York: Jason Aronson, 1976), pp. 25–26, hereafter referred to as ORT.

14. Jacobson, *The Self and the Object World*, p. 58.

15. Stolorow and Lachmann try to integrate the different views of Kernberg and Kohut in *Psychoanalysis of Developmental Arrests: Theory and Treatment* (New York: International Universities Press, 1980). They distinguish narcissistic pathology that results from developmental arrest from that which results from defenses against intrapsychic conflict. Thus they believe that there are two different subtypes of narcissism.

16. In recent years, feminists such as Jessica Benjamin, Nancy Chodorow, and Dorothy Dinnerstein have studied some of the implications of the fact that the first love-object, the first person from whom the baby must separate, is usually the mother.

17. Modell, *Object Love and Reality,* p. 61.

18. Jacobson, *The Self and the Object World,* p. 29.

19. The essays gathered in this volume draw on various aspects of the theory presented in this section of the introduction. In concluding, we should perhaps reiterate that very important differences exist among the various theorists, some of which we have not even mentioned here because they are not relevant to literary study.

20. From Sigmund Freud, "A Special Type of Choice of Objects Made by Men" in *Standard Edition,* vol. 2 (London: Hogarth Press, 1957), p. 165.

21. From Sigmund Freud, "Dostoevsky and Parricide" in *Standard Edition,* vol. 21 (London: Hogarth Press, 1961), p. 177.

22. Reprinted in Lionel Trilling, *The Liberal Imagination* (New York: Harcourt Brace Jovanovich, 1978), p. 160.

23. In Otto Rank, *Art and Artist* (New York: Tudor Press, 1932).

24. Ernst Kris, *Psychoanalytic Explorations in Art,* 2nd. ed. (New York: Schocken Books, 1964), p. 29.

25. Eissler argues this thesis in *Goethe: A Psychoanalytic Study 1777–1786,* 2 vols. (Detroit: Wayne State University Press, 1963).

26. From Phyllis Greenacre, *Emotional Growth: Psychoanalytic Studies of the Gifted and a Great Variety of Other Individuals* (New York: International Universities Press, 1971), p. 542.

27. In Paul Ornstein ed., *The Search for the Self,* vol. 1 (New York: International Universities Press, 1978), p. 272.

28. Also in Ornstein ed., *The Search for the Self,* vol. 2, p. 818.

29. From Charles Kligerman, "Art and the Self of the Artist" in Arnold

Goldberg ed., *Advances in Self Psychology* (New York: International Universities Press, 1980), p. 386.

30. From Heinz Kohut, "The Self in History: Introductory Notes on the Psychology of the Self" in Ornstein ed., *The Search for the Self,* vol. 2, p. 781.

31. From William Niederland, "Clinical Aspects of Creativity," *American Imago,* 24 (1967), 7.

32. From Hanna Segal, "A Psycho-Analytical Approach to Aesthetics" in Melanie Klein et al. eds., *New Directions in Psycho-Analysis* (New York: Basic Books, 1955), p. 386.

33. D. W. Winnicott, "Notes on the Development of Creativity," *Contemporary Psychoanalysis,* 19, 2 (April 1983), 193–199.

34. Arnold Modell in *Psychoanalysis in a New Context* (New York: International Universities Press, 1984) also discusses the importance of the transitional object, and of object relations in general, to an understanding of the creative process (see pp. 187–198). He concludes: "The creation of the transitional object is therefore seen as a derivative of the child's first object relationship. We have suggested that the environment itself may be equated with this, the child's first love-object. The psychology of creativity, which is the psychology of a created environment, can therefore be modeled on the psychology of object relations" (p. 193).

35. As reported by Charles Kligerman in *The International Journal of Psycho-Analysis,* 53, 21 (1972), 21–29.

36. Alan Roland in his essay "Psychoanalytic Literary Criticism" in Roland ed., *Psychoanalysis, Creativity, and Literature: A French-American Inquiry* (New York: Columbia University Press, 1978) makes a similar point: object relations theory, he states, "makes available to the critic a far greater range of unconscious fantasy and emotional stages and experiences from childhood than the psychosexual only—which has figured so ubiquitously in psychoanalytic literary criticism" (p. 252). Roland also provides a fairly comprehensive survey of psychoanalytic theories of creativity and their influence on literary criticism of the past few decades.

37. Heinz Kohut, "Psychoanalysis and the Interpretation of Literature: A Correspondence with Erich Heller," *Critical Inquiry,* 4 (1978), 445.

38. For a comprehensive study of the various uses and value of psychoanalytic literary criticism, see Meredith Skura, *The Literary Use of the Psychoanalytic Process* (New Haven: Yale University Press, 1981).

39. Heinz Kohut, "The Self in History" in Ornstein ed., *The Search for the Self,* p. 781.

40. For further suggestions of literary uses of these theories, see Lynne Layton, "From Oedipus to Narcissus: Literature and the Psychology of Self," *Mosaic,* 18 (1985), 97–105.

TWO

CONFLICT AND COHERENCE: NARCISSISM AND TRAGIC STRUCTURE IN MARLOWE

Peter S. Donaldson

The aspect of the psychoanalytic work of Heinz Kohut that may be most useful for literary work is the shift from a model of the mind based on conflict to one in which the coherence of the self is regarded as prior to any conflicts in which the self engages. From the point of view of the psychology of the self, evidence that would indicate the presence of unresolved Oedipal conflict takes on a different significance. He speaks of a

> shift in the meaning of clinical data—a shift toward a deeper and more encompassing meaning—when we approach them from the point of view of a self struggling to maintain its cohesion—i.e., from the point of view of a self motivated by disintegration anxiety—rather than from the point of view of a psychic apparatus trying to deal with drives and structural conflict.[1]

And later in the discussion of the same case:

> . . . the presence of a firm self is a precondition for the experience of the Oedipus complex. Unless the child sees himself as a delimited, abiding, independent center of initiative, he is unable to experience the object-instinctual desires that lead to the conflicts and secondary adaptations of the oedipal period.[2]

In such a case dream images suggesting castration anxiety, penis envy or other aspects of the Oedipus complex may be merely a mask for deeper fears concerning the cohesion or reality of the self. Kohut held that such fears were in fact more characteristic of our time than the Oedipal conflicts of earlier psychoanalytic practice, that significant shifts in cultural values and the patterns of family life in our century were partly responsible for the increase in cases of self pathology observed in clinical practice. Indeed, Kohut saw such a shift reflected in literary history, and drew a contrast between the nineteenth century novel, which, in its emphasis on conflict and guilt, shares a common ground with classical psychoanalysis, and twentieth century works, such as those of Kafka, which reflect the anxieties of the isolated and unmirrored human self, unable to maintain its cohesion in space and time and fearful of the possibility of complete fragmentation.[3]

But, though the characteristic dislocations of our time provide rich matter for a literature of the self, it would be a mistake to think of the theme of the self's precariousness as a strictly twentieth century phenomenon, for there is a sense in which the Renaissance was an even more decisive period in the emergence of characteristically Western and modern attitudes toward the self, in which outward confidence, assertiveness, and independence are so often attended by fears of inner emptiness, nullity, or incoherence.

Kohut uses the term "Tragic Man" in contrasting the dominant themes of our art and literature with those of the nineteenth century, the products of "Guilty Man" and his Freudian conflicts.[4] But, I would argue, the use of "tragic" in this sense, to contrast a literature of self-cohesion with a literature of intrapsychic and interpersonal conflict, betrays a distinctively post-Renaissance sense of what tragedy is. Ancient tragedy, as Hegel taught, is tragedy of conflict; conflict of persons or principles, conflict in which fully formed selves participate. Agamemnon, Clytaemnestra, Oedipus, Antigone, even Hippolytus, all suffer, enter into conflict, and die as fully formed selves. In Renaissance tragedy, in contrast, the coherence of the self is a more prominent issue, indeed, perhaps the main issue. Interpersonal, even Oedipal conflict provides a frame for the inner drama in plays like *Hamlet, King Lear, Edward II,* and *Dr. Faustus,* but the point here is that such conflict *is* merely a frame, a structure which, like the outwardly Oedipal symptoms of Kohut's narcissistic patients, first masks and then reveals far deeper and more primitive terrors.

This chapter examines the interplay between conflict and coherence in Marlowe's *Tamburlaine* (Parts I and II), *Edward II,* and *Dr. Faustus.*[5] In these plays, which stand at the beginning of the English tragic tradition, the protagonists engage in conflict, but are unable fully to believe either in themselves or in the significance of the conflicts in which they engage, and are left at the end, in one degree of self-recognition or another, with a sense of emptiness and terror. Such self-recognition, such tragic vision as there is in these plays, comes about when conflict— the conflict-based structure of the plays themselves—is abandoned, seen through, or recognized as essentially meaningless. Shakespeare does something more complex, balancing such tragic vision with redemptive reparative gestures, but Marlowe's innovation in tragic form, his tragedy of fragmentation, indelibly altered the Western understanding of what tragedy is, both directly through the example of his own work and indirectly through Shakespeare's reworking of it.

In *Tamburlaine,* the protagonist is a Scythian shepherd who rises to a position of dominance over much of the known world through a series of military conflicts, mostly with older men, that have the character of Oedipal victories, a character underscored by Marlowe's connecting Tamburlaine's conquests to his acquisition of a wife, the daughter of the Sultan of Egypt, who stands last in the series of antagonists overcome by Tamburlaine in Part I. At Tamburlaine's first appearance (I:ii) he has already captured Zenocrate (though she does not yet love him) and the play ends with his victory over her father, her coronation as Tamburlaine's empress, which takes place onstage, and plans for her wedding to Tamburlaine, which is to take place after the play has ended, and to which the last lines of the play refer. Tamburlaine's conquests, then, are framed by the story of his capture, wooing, and wedding of Zenocrate; his fortunes as a lover parallel his successes as a soldier, and both culminate when Tamburlaine achieves a position of unchallengeable dominance over his beloved's father. Yet these victories have at their heart, as many critics have observed, a kind of hollowness. There is little sense of achievement in the military sphere, because Tamburlaine's opponents are knocked down too easily, almost automatically, and there is little sense of intimacy in the gaining of a wife, for, like Tamburlaine's male companions, Zenocrate is to Tamburlaine little more than an extension of himself, or "portion of his glory." Nothing difficult, either in his chosen profession (if we can think of the role world conquerer as a profession) or in his personal relationships is worked through; everything comes too easily. Marlowe's method is to balance external success against inner emptiness: as Tamburlaine moves higher in the world and in Zenocrate's affections, the precariousness of his self-cohesion and his radical dependence upon the mirroring of others becomes more obvious to us, and, I think, eventually also to him.

This precariousness is there from the start—it is our judgment of it that changes. In the beginning, we are closer to sharing the main character's confidence and exuberant self-regard than at the end of Part I, and the process of disillusionment is continued and concluded in Part II. From the beginning, Tamburlaine's miraculous successes are associated with self-display: in his first scene he dramatically casts off his shepherd's costume, revealing the lordly suit of polished armor beneath—"Lie here ye weeds, that I disdain to wear" (I:ii, 40).[6] This exhibition is meant to impress Zenocrate, and, though it fails in its immediate effect, it does impress Tamburlaine's followers (Techelles and Usumcasane immediately become a mirroring chorus, confirming his fantasies and developing further his grandiose self-conception, imagining captive kings already kneeling at his feet). It also initiates the motif of self-display that is quickly seen as Tamburlaine's characteristic mode of action in war as well as love, for Tamburlaine's change of costume has as audience not only Zenocrate, but the Persian general Theridamas whom he is preparing to meet, and his hope is to overcome this enemy through visual display alone. For this parley, Tamburlaine orders an exhibition of conquered treasure ("Lay out our golden wedges to the view, / That their reflections may amaze the Persians, / And look we on them friendly when they come" I:ii,139–41), and tries to awe the opponent with claims that his life is charmed and his victory predestined. Theridamas actually does become entranced by Tamburlaine's self-conception—"won with thy words, and conquered with thy looks" (227)—and gives up without a battle. Tamburlaine always wants to be *looked at:* he calls his estate "mean" because "the nations far removed admire me not" (204), and tends to think of every victory as a forcing of admiration, as a getting of people to look at him:

Our quivering lances shaking in the air
And bullets like Jove's dreadful thunderbolt,
Enrolled in flames and fiery smoldering mists,
Shall threat the gods more than Cyclopean wars;
And with our sun-bright armor, as we march
We'll chase the stars from heaven and dim their eyes
That stand and muse at our admired arms.
(18–24)

As we have seen, exhibitionism contributes to Tamburlaine's success, so that the play, in the early scenes at any rate, seems to endorse its main character's narcissism. Yet the effect of the play's interest in Tamburlaine's impressive appearance and its quasi-magical potency is to point, finally, to his underlying need for assurance of his own worth and coherence, a need that leads him either to avoid conflict or to be unable to be nourished by it in a way that would assuage his hunger for endless repetition of approving, mirroring reactions from other characters.[7] The crown, so often used as a stage property and as a visual image in this play, has a special significance in the pattern of visual narcissism we have been tracing. It is the universal symbol of grandiosity, of course, an attention-getter *par excellence,* and Tamburlaine's quest for it is partly an attempt to gain possession or control over the sources of narcissistic gratification. Yet a crown is something that can not only be admired, but can be touched, handled, handed round, and the play often uses the tactile properties in contrast to the visual, with deflating effect. The crown of Persia is first worn by Mycetes, a comically impotent monarch whose witlessness detracts from the self-proclaimed glory of the man who is destined to conquer him. Mycetes is barely intelligent enough to know when he is being insulted, he needs continual reassurances of his identity as king from his council, and even when asserting his authority he is a farcical and pathetic figure, swearing oaths by his "royal seat" that invite irreverent confusion between the throne and his royal behind ("You may do well to kiss it then" I:i,98). Like the throne, the crown he wears is devalued by an idiotic and infantile gesture, for, when Tamburlaine meets him on the field of battle, he is trying to bury it "in a simple hole" in order to avoid fighting for it. It is thus a symbol of power of doubtful value that Tamburlaine comes upon:

> *Tamburlaine:* Is this your crown?
> *Mycetes:* Ay. Didst thou ever see a fairer?
> (He hands him the crown)
> *Tamburlaine:* Ye will not sell it, will ye?
> *Mycetes:* Such another word and I will have thee
>   executed. Come, give it me.
>
> *Tamburlaine:* No, I took it prisoner.
> *Mycetes:* You lie; I gave it you.
> *Tamburlaine:* Then 'tis mine.
> *Mycetes:* No; I mean I let you keep it.
> *Tamburlaine:* Well, I mean you shall have it again.

Here, take it for a while: I lend it thee
Till I may see thee hemmed with armed men.
Then shalt thou see me pull it from thy head;
Thou art no match for mighty Tamburlaine.
                                        (Exit.)
Mycetes: O gods, is this Tamburlaine the thief?
I marvel much he stole it not away.
                        (II:v,27–42)

Notice that Tamburlaine disdains the tactile transfer of the crown here within his power, preferring to restore it to its place in the highly visual battle ritual he imagines—he must see Mycetes wearing it in more dignified circumstances, and further, it seems important to him that Mycetes see him coming to take it. But the handing back and forth of the crown points to a certain emptiness and circularity underlying the imagined visual pageant. In this theatrical icon of self-mirroring, Tamburlaine will receive back from Mycetes only what he has given him: the crown becomes a gift he bestows upon himself, and the already comically deflated opponent is reduced to facilitating Tamburlaine's self-reflexivity.

We move directly from this scene to one in which Tamburlaine, holding this crown (which we have not see him win) gives it to Cosroe, Mycetes' rebellious brother. Cosroe immediately returns it, appointing Tamburlaine regent of Persia, and repeating the handing-back-of-the-crown motif of II:iv. As with the mother-child games this procedure begins to resemble, there is a relationship between the reassurance provided by the reappearance of the physical object and the need to be attended to, looked at, and admired by the human object.[8] Tamburlaine gives the crown away again, knowing he has the power to get it back, for it was his military victory that won it for Cosroe. But Cosroe has another crown as well, the imperial crown of Asia, and this, too, Tamburlaine allows to slip away only to show how easily he may take it when he wants it. Cosroe leaves for Persepolis, expecting Tamburlaine to follow shortly ("till thou overtake me, Tamburlaine . . . Farewell" 44–46) and dreaming of his triumphant entry into the capital. These dreams, specifically the famous phrase "and ride in triumph through Persepolis" catch Tamburlaine's imagination: by a principle René Girard has called mimetic desire, Cosroe has made the crown valuable to Tamburlaine by wanting it, and he has no sooner left the stage when Tamburlaine sets out after him. Tamburlaine himself recognizes that all this has taken on the character of a game:

> *Tamburlaine:* 'Twill prove a pretty jest, in faith, my friends.
> *Theridamas:* A jest to charge on twenty thousand men?
> *Tamburlaine:* Judge by thyself, Theridamas, not me,
>   For presently Techelles here shall haste
>   To bid him battle ere he pass too far
>   And lose more labor than the game will quite.
>   Then shalt thou see the Scythian Tamburlaine
>   Make but a jest to win the Persian crown.
>   Techelles, take a thousand horse with thee,
>   And bid him turn him back to war with us,
>   That only made him king to make us sport.
>   (II:v, 90–101)

In taking the crown from Cosroe, Tamburlaine is again admiring his own greatness in a mirror of his own construction: yet there is something in the circularity and ease of this exercise ("if I should desire the Persian crown,/ I could attain it with a wondrous ease" 76–77) which, while confirming Tamburlaine's godlike power to make and unmake kings, also betrays a certain emptiness in the process: closely connected to the elation of victory is the growing consciousness that all this is "but a jest," not only easy but worthless.

Tamburlaine's well-known speech to the dying and defeated Cosroe is related to the patterns we have been tracing. It ends with the image of the crown, but only after characterizing the struggle for the crown first as an Oedpial conflict and then as a response to a still deeper incoherence within the human spirit and in the world of nature. The father-son complexities come first:

> *Tamburlaine:* The thirst of reign and sweetness of a crown,
>   That caused the eldest son of heavenly Ops
>   To thrust his doting father from his chair
>   And place himself in the imperial heaven,
>   Moved me to manage arms against thy state.
>   What better precedent than mighty Jove?
>   (II:vii,12–17)

This seems straightforward enough—except that Cosroe does not fit the role of Saturn very well, being himself a rebellious younger brother. Shortly before (II:vi,1–8) he has compared himself to Jove, and Tamburlaine to the Titans, rebels of an older generation against a younger; and Tamburlaine at one point has compared himself in the space of three lines to *both* Jove and the Titanic rebels against him (II:iii,19–21). One of the things that undercuts the Oedipal significance of the battles Tamburlaine fights, here as elsewhere in the Tamburlaine plays, is the

insistent confusion of generations, which tends to blur the sharp op-
positions of Oedipal rivalry, and to suggest an unsettling refusion between the self and the image of the parent. Seeing the role confusion
behind these traditional images of rebellion can help us to understand
the connection between these lines and the apparently inapposite passage on Nature that follows, where the justification for ambition is seen
as a matter of focusing the anarchic restlessness of the unformed self
upon a definite and tangible object:

> Nature, that frames us of four elements
> Warring within our breasts for regiment
> Doth teach us all to have aspiring minds.
> Our souls, whose faculties can comprehend
> The wondrous architecture of the world
> And measure every wandering planet's course
> Still climbing after knowledge infinite,
> And always moving as the restless spheres
> Wills us to wear ourselves and never rest
> Until we reach the ripest fruit of all
> That perfect bliss and sole felicity,
> The sweet fruition of an earthly crown.
>   (18–29)

The anticlimactic quality of the passage has been remarked upon many
times: not only is the weight of centuries of Augustinian Christianity
against our taking an earthly crown as a fit object for the infinitely
aspiring human will, but the stage-business of this particular play has
made the transfer and retransfer of crowns into a kind of nervous sport
or jest. The crown is necessary here not because Tamburlaine has any
real sense of the earthly fruition he claims it represents, but because one
must turn to *something* from the chaotic reflection of man's essence in
nature, from warring elements, wandering planets, reflecting inner
weariness and aimless oscillation. Marlowe mentions the "wondrous
architecture" of the world, but what he presents is not an ordered
universe, but rather one that mirrors the disorder of a fragmented self.
To aim at the crown is really to turn away from the chaos of nature to a
realm of willed coherence. The speech passes from images of fragmenting "natural" energies to the stable but ironic self-icon of the crown.

The marriage subplot presents a related kind of devaluation of the
possible rewards of (Oedipal) conflict, for Zenocrate, too, is turned
into an empty prize by her thorough subordination to Tamburlaine's
need for mirroring.

Tamburlaine has possession of Zenocrate, as he has of the Persian crown, long before he fights for her, and so the build-up to the final military conflict with her father is in one sense pointless. In fact, Tamburlaine's very first lines in the play, addressed to Zenocrate, undo the Oedipal menace his capture of her implies.

> Come lady, let not this appall your thoughts;
> The jewels and treasure we have ta'en
> Shall be reserved, and you in better state
> Than if you were arrived in Syria,
> Even in the circle of your father's arms,
> The mighty Soldan of Egyptia.
> (II:i, 1–6)

When Tamburlaine finally meets her father, the scene is without tension or hostility on either side. Though he is defeated in battle and deprived of his kingdom, with his comrades slain about him, the Sultan doesn't seem to mind; he accepts Tamburlaine's assurances that being Zenocrate's father is a higher title than those he has lost, and is satisfied with Tamburlaine's promise to "render all unto your hands"[9] (V:ii, 384). Though Tamburlaine characterizes himself as a Titanic rebel against Jove in this passage, his relations with the Sultan are cordial, and the scene takes on a fairy tale tone as tensions are unrealistically transcended.

This harmonious mood is the more difficult to credit because Tamburlaine's exhibitionism has taken a savage direction by this point in the play. Earlier, Zenocrate, Theridamas, and Cosroe had been won over by Tamburlaine's shows and displays—his revelations of his armor, his laying out his treasure to their view, his handsome and majestic physical demeanor, etc. But now what he "shows" people becomes identified more and more with Death. The virgins of Damascus know that his sword is made of "fatal steel," but when he asks them to admire it, he is not satisfied with their answer—he wants them to see the personified figure of Death on his sword point (V:ii). And here, too, at the end of the play, what he asks the Sultan to admire, the mirrors in which his self-image is reflected, are the lifeless corpses of Bajazeth, his wife, and the hapless King of Arabia, Zenocrate's former betrothed. The bodies are pointed out to the Sultan: "And see, my lord, a sight of strange import," (V:ii,405) These are "sights of power," (411),

> . . . objects fit for Tamburlaine
> Wherein, as in a mirror, may be seen
> His honor, that consists in shedding blood.
> (412–13)

This is not a threat, in the ordinary sense. What Tamburlaine wants
from the Sultan is not so much his daughter, but that he, too, become a
mirror to Tamburlaine's greatness. And he does:

> Mighty hath God and Mahomet made thy hand
> Renowned Tamburlaine, to whom all kings
> Of force must yield their crowns and empires
> And I am pleased with this my overthrow
> If, as becomes a person of thy state,
> Thou hast with honor used Zenocrate.
>
> (416–21).

The ease of this solution, like the "wondrous ease" with which Tamburlaine wins the Persian crown, call in question the value of the prize:
the Sultan does not display, and is not recognized by Tamburlaine as
having, an authentic, autonomous self, apart from his role as mirror to
his son-in-law.

The unintended irony of the Sultan's use of the word "honor" is
important here—he expects that Tamburlaine has used his daughter
with "honor," but this assertion of paternal right by insistence on sexual
morality is undercut by Tamburlaine's boasting, seven lines earlier, that
honor for him means "shedding blood." The repetition of the word
makes it plain that Tamburlaine's chastity, his sparing of Zenocrate's
hymeneal blood, is related to his savagery, not an alternative to it—both
are attempts to increase his own honor, conceived in self-reflexive terms.

As resentment is absent from Zenocrate's father, so challenge is missing from Tamburlaine's side, for the relationship is desexualized, and
Tamburlaine so merges with the father he has just overthrown that he
can say, intending no sexual pun, that "fair Zenocrate/ will soon consent
to satisfy us both" (435–36). The emphasis falls not on the marriage,
which is to take place after the end of the play, but on her coronation,
and the imagery that attends the act of placing the crown on her head
repeats the relation between conflict and self-coherence we have been
tracing, for she is compared to Juno—but, in the thorough confusion
of Oedipal roles characteristic of Marlowe, not Juno the wife of Jupiter
and the rebel against Saturn, but Juno the *sister* of Jupiter, admiring her
brother's suppression of the Titans; and then to the chaste Diana, as the
image modulates from conflict muted by the reversal of roles to Marlowe's characteristic resort to self-reflection:

> And here we crown thee Queen of Persia,
> And all the kingdom and dominions
> That late the power of Tamburlaine subdued.
> As Juno, when the giants were suppressed,

that darted mountains at her brother Jove,
So looks my love, shadowing in her brows
Triumphs and trophies for my victories
Or as Latona's daughter, bent to arms,
Adding more courage to my conquering mind.
(444–52)

Tamburlaine's marriage is not the outward celebration of any inward growth; Zenocrate is not the prize of a conflict in which fully formed selves have engaged with the risk of injury, nor is it clear that her husband to be has any firm conviction that she possesses a self of her own: she is, like her father and the corpses which are still littering the stage even as he places the crown on her head, just another mirror of a self that must desperately find its reflection everywhere rather than face its own emptiness.

In *Tamburlaine,* Part II, most of the patterns of imagery—crowns, reflections, rebellion, and counterrebellion among the Gods and Titans—are present, and, again, these convey the complexities of the theme of self-mirroring and the devaluation of conflict. A principal difference is that, in Part II, Tamburlaine is a father himself, and his relations with his sons, rather than with father-figures, come to the fore. With this shift in emphasis (which is really no radical change in perspective since, as we shall see, Tamburlaine has trouble distinguishing himself from his sons, just as he had trouble untangling his self-conception in Part I from the kings he overcame) comes a different kind of attention to the special role of women—and especially dying mothers—as mirrors of the self.

To begin with Tamburlaine's relationship to his sons: they are introduced as accompaniments to their mother in one of Tamburlaine's typically visual displays.

Now rest thee here . . . between thy sons
(I:IV,5–7)
. . .

Sit up, and rest thee like a lovely queen.
So, now she sits in pomp and majesty,
When these, my sons, more precious in mine eyes
Than all the wealthy kingdoms I subdued,
Placed by her side, look on their mother's face.
(16–20)

The next line, however, evokes a potential father-son conflict in erotic terms: ". . . look on their mother's face./ But yet methinks their looks are amorous." But what follows shows that Tamburlaine's Oedipal jealousy is less at issue than his anxiety concerning their failure to reflect *his* image: ". . . are amorous./ Not Martial, as the sons of Tamburlaine," and next comes a mocking and reproachful description of their youthful and effeminate beauty. Tamburlaine is not jealous of his sons, but rather needs to identify with them in order to enjoy, through them, the all-important gaze of the mother. Zenocrate defends his sons, describing the warlike spirit of the youngest as he practices in the tiltyard with his "slender rod" (40). Tamburlaine is so pleased with this mirroring that he prefers this youngest son to his brothers: "Thou shalt be king before them and their seed/ Shall issue crowned from their mother's womb" (52–53). The "crowning" of the seed transfers the image of birth to the sphere of masculine achievements, and reduces the female contribution to that of replicating male ambitions. In addition, the ambiguity of pronoun reference, ". . . before *them*/ Shall issue crowned from *their* mother's womb," confuses sons and grandsons, wives and daughters-in-law, so that the "seed" seems to issue from Zenocrate's womb, and neither she nor her sons have a clearly defined existence apart from the exigencies of Tamburlaine's needs.

In this play, Zenocrate and Tamburlaine's sons largely assume the role played in Part I by the conquered kings, that of reflecting back Tamburlaine's grandiose self-image. The death and apotheosis of Zenocrate are of special interest here. Zenocrate, unlike Tamburlaine's victims in Part I, dies a natural death, and, of course, he believes he loves rather than hates her; but what links the two plays is that the mirror in which he seeks to behold his own reflection shows him death. Both his glorious deeds and his idealizing love lead to the same conclusion. And the fact that he has made of Zenocrate a figure of cosmic grandeur merely adds to the potential for inner annihilation when she dies: she has become the unique and all-encompassing object for him, so that her death obliterates not only him but the rest of the world as well.

The totality of the destruction of Tamburlaine's self-image is made possible in part by his own god-challenging, self-deifying, solar rhetoric. He has closely identified with the gods and with the sun:

I hold the Fates bound fast in iron chains,
And with my hand turn Fortune's wheel about,
And sooner shall the sun fall from his sphere
Than Tamburlaine be slain or overcome
(I. I:ii, 73–76)

Smile stars that reigned at my nativity,
And dim the brightness of their neighbor lamps;
Disdain to borrow light of Cynthia,
For I, the chiefest lamp of all the earth

                                        . . . .

Will send up fire to your turning spheres
And cause the sun to borrow light of you.
                        (Part I. IV:ii, 32–40)

But in Part II, it is Zenocrate who gives "light and life" (II:iv,8) to the sun; she is the "world's fair eye,/ Whose beams illuminate the lamps of heaven" (I:iv, 1–2). The beloved's eye, in the tradition of love poetry Tamburlaine adopts here, does not receive but sends forth illumination. Without her gaze, the sun and the world are dark; not merely temporarily eclipsed, but destroyed, as the heavens upon which Tamburlaine has projected his own self-image are reengulfed by the cosmic serpent.[10]

Related to these images of the dissolution of the heavens is the motif of religious skepticism: both that expressed by Tamburlaine when he challenges Mohammed to punish him for burning the Koran if he really is a god, and professes allegiance to a god higher than Mohammed, in whose existence, however, he is not sure he believes; and that expressed by the various god-testing speeches of Turks and Christians. It is the death of Tamburlaine's selfobject, Zenocrate, that brings this skepticism to the surface of Part II. Tamburlaine's own death is logically implicit, ironically present in Part I insofar as he sees himself mirrored in dead bodies, but it is not until Zenocrate falls ill that the consciousness of having "reposed" or invested his self-image in a mortal and transitory object becomes unavoidable. The melting or dissolving of the heavens signifies one aspect of this consciousness and the hints of atheism another.

Zenocrate herself sees the danger in Tamburlaine's inflating of her death to cosmic proportions and of his claim that her death will result in his: it is not just that she unselfishly wants him to live on when she's gone she also recognizes that his merging of his self with her and with the heavens is a greater danger to her selfhood than physical death. She wants to accept death—"But let me die, my love, yet let me die/ With love and patience let your true love die" (II:iv,66–67), and her perception that Tamburlaine's projections threaten the comfort of her hope to meet him in heaven is not so much a matter of respecting the moral prohibitions against suicide as it is a determination to think of herself and of the heaven as existing apart from Tamburlaine's needs and as

resistant to his projections. Her deathbed speech is a strong one, registering a deeper power than Tamburlaine's "high astounding terms," and
the more so because, whatever we may think of him, she continues to
love him while effecting the necessary distinction between selves. She
is even able, in her last lines, to propose her own death as a model for
her children—". . . in death resemble me,/ And in your lives your father's excellency" (75–76). It is *only* in death, of course, but this is
perhaps the one time in either part of *Tamburlaine* where a human self
other than Tamburlaine's has been proposed as a model for imitation.

The wonderful Olympia episode also presents female death as a triumph, and for related reasons. Olympia is a captive, kept alive by
Theridamas who comes upon her on the battlefield and is impressed by
her courage—she has just killed her son and buried her husband's body
to avoid their being dismembered by the Scythians. His falling in love
with her closely parallels Tamburlaine's love-rhetoric—she gives light to
the sun, he needs to watch out for jealous gods trying to steal her, etc.
And his preservation of her life and prevention of her suicide, coming
so soon after Zenocrate's death, suggest that female beauty is something
forcibly kept alive for men to admire and be mirrored by. The kind of
need her beauty serves is suggested when, in stopping her casting herself into the fire, Theridamas says that he would rather fire consume
them both

> Than scorch a face so beautiful as this,
> In frame of which nature hath showed more skill
> Than when she gave eternal chaos form.
> (III:v, 74–76)

Not only the need to stabilize a chaotic self, but the anxiety that it never
can be made cohesive, are present here. The phrase is "eternal chaos"—
chaos persists despite the appearance of form, as Olympia continues to
live (temporarily) despite her commitment to death.

The kind of "love" Theridamas feels for Olympia, kindled on the
instant and based on the belief that her beauty is somehow a stay
against chaos, is no more than a need for narcissistic sustenance, and is
closely related to disintegration fears. That Olympia, like Zenocrate,
has at least partial insight into the source of idealizing male attachment
of this kind is suggested by her brilliant stratagem for achieving her
own death: restrained from suicide by Theridamas, she offers him an
ointment that is supposed to render his skin impervious to all harm,
and then gets him to test it on her throat. That he would want such an

ointment is perhaps no more than the wish of any soldier—but that he believes in the wish enough to run his newly found beloved through the neck suggests that anxiety about the integrity of his own body surface is stronger than, in fact is actually the source of, his feelings of love, as is also the case with Tamburlaine (who also believes he has a "charmed skin").

After the death of his selfobject, Tamburlaine's violence becomes more desperate and gratuitous, and ever less focused on even minimally realistic goals. He burns the town where she died (II:iv;III:i), kills his own son Calyphas, forces the kings of Trebizon and Soria to pull his chariot with bits in their mouths, burns the Koran (V:i)—and, of course, the slaughter of the conquered continues through Part II. His violence goes beyond any measured response to offense or practical pursuit of advantage: what really motivates Tamburlaine after Zenocrate's death is rage at a world that has failed to mirror his self conception. This is quite clear in the murder of Calyphas—this was the son whose looks, more than the others, were "amorous, not martial like the sons of Tamburlaine," and when he hangs back from the battle, playing cards and joking about sex with his servant, Tamburlaine puts him to death, enraged that his son is not more identical to himself, and, more insanely, furious at the gods for having allowed a flawed replication of his grandiose self:

> Here Jove, receive his fainting soul again,
> A form not meet to give that subject essence
> Whose matter is the flesh of Tamburlaine,
> Wherein an incorporeal spirit moves,
> Made of the mould whereof thyself consists,
> Which makes me valiant, proud, ambitious,
> Ready to levy power against thy throne,
> That I might move the turning spheres of heaven,
> For earth and all this airy region
> Cannot contain the state of Tamburlaine.
>   (He stabs Calyphas)
> By Mahomet, thy mighty friend, I swear,
> In sending to my issue such a soul,
> Created of the massy dregs of earth,
> The scum and tartar of the elements,
> Wherein was neither courage, strength, or wit,
> But folly, sloth, and damned idleness,
> Thou hast procured a greater enemy
> Than he that darted mountains at thy head,

Shaking the burden mighty Atlas bears,
Whereat thou trembling hidd'st thee in the air,
Clothed with a pitchy cloud for having seen.
                                   (IV:ii,32–56)

We see here how difficult it is for Marlowe ever to imagine a father-son
conflict that is not seen as a failure of self reflection: Calyphas' sin is not
rebellion against, but difference from, his father; and Tamburlaine's
own rebellion against Jove is made possible by the dwelling of Jove's
own ambitious spirit within him, and motivated by Jove's insult in
sending him a dissimilar son, a son, that is, who, unlike Jove and
Tamburlaine, does not rebel against his father or the gods. What Tamburlaine wants is merger or fusion with his son and with his gods: his
rage against them proceeds from the failure of that fusion. Kohut's
analysis of narcissistic rage is relevant here, and is in fact helpful for
understanding much of Tamburlaine's behavior from this point in the
play onward:

> Aggressions employed in the pursuit of maturely experienced causes are
> not limitless. However vigorously mobilized, their goal is definite: the
> defeat of the enemy who blocks the way to a cherished goal. . . . The
> opponent who is the target of our mature aggression is experienced as
> separate from ourselves, whether we attack him because he blocks us in
> reaching our object-libidinal goals or hate him because he interferes with
> the fulfillment of our reality-integrated narcissistic wishes. The enemy,
> however, who calls forth the archaic rage of the narcissistically vulnerable
> is seen by him not as an autonomous source of impulsions, but as a *flaw in
> a narcissistically perceived reality.* He is a recalcitrant part of an expanded
> self over which he expects to exercise full control and whose mere indepen-
> dence or other-ness is an offense. . . . It is this archaic mode of experience
> which explains the fact that those who are in the grip of narcissistic rage
> show total lack of empathy toward the offender. It explains the un-
> modifiable wish to blot out the offense which was perpetrated against the
> grandiose self and the unforgiving fury which arises when the control over
> the mirroring self-object is lost or when the omnipotent self-object is
> unavailable.[11]

At the end of the play, Tamburlaine suddenly falls ill—whether as
punishment for blasphemy or not remains a matter of debate—and his
reaction to his own impending end painfully illustrates the failure of his
inner world, makes clear what inner emptiness his god-challenging rage
has masked. Zenocrate's picture and her gold-covered coffin are with
him, and he imagines, in his last visual fantasy, that as he dies he will

pierce the coffin with his sight and "glut" his "longings with a heaven of joy" (V:iii,227). Part I ended with a mirror in which Tamburlaine's honor was reflected, and the content of that image was the lifeless bodies of his victims; here the image is of merger, not mirroring, and we are meant to know that the heaven of joy Tamburlaine proposes to himself amounts to fusion with a corpse. In fact, it is because Tamburlaine cannot imagine a relation to others that is not either a perfect mirroring or merging of selves that his only connection to Zenocrate must take this horribly literalizing form. One is reminded of the descriptions by both Kohut and Otto Kernberg of the despair and emptiness faced by patients suffering from acute disorders of the self as death approaches. Death *is* the dissolution of the self, and if the fact of the inevitable disintegration of body and mind has been feared, guarded against, and kept from consciousness by a lifelong reliance upon external mirrors of perfection, the unavoidable confrontation with approaching mortality can be devastating. It is precisely the kind of failure that leads Tamburlaine to imagine a final blissful merging with Zenocrate in her coffin, while being unable to draw on memory of any of her actual qualities for comfort that makes imminent death so terrible for narcissistic personalities:

> the internal resources that an individual has in the face of conflict and failure are intimately related to the maturity and depth of his internal world of object relations. Perhaps the most dramatic example of this situation is incurable illness and the prospect of imminent death; persons who have been able to love other human beings in a mature way retain images of them which provide love and comfort at points of danger, loss, and failure.[12]

Tamburlaine has no such image of Zenocrate, and his possession of her portrait and her coffin cannot substitute for it. Tamburlaine's failure is seen also in his inability to pass on anything of value to his children. He wishes to believe that his dreams of immortality, which have failed with his wife's death and are threatened by his own impending end, may be rescued by his children. But the sons who survive have been reduced to mirror images of their father to such a degree that he cannot really believe that his own death does not somehow entail theirs, just as Zenocrate's death implied his. Again, to use Kohut's language, Tamburlaine has been one of those parents whose fragmented or fragmentation-prone selves are closed to that empathetic merger with their children that would allow them to delight in their children's growth and assertiveness. Optimal parents . . . are people who, despite their stimulation by and competition with the rising generation, are also sufficiently in touch with the pulse of life, accept themselves sufficiently as transient participants in the ongoing stream of life, to be able to experience the growth of the next generation with unforced, non-defensive joy.[13]

And Kohut offers, as symbolic images of parents who, because of a defect in their own self-cohesion, are unable to do this, those literary figures who, like the Flying Dutchman or the Wandering Jew, are unable to die.

On his deathbed, Tamburlaine passes on his dominion to his son, but he does so joylessly, warning him that the chariot he must guide is like that of Phaeton, who was destroyed when he tried to manage the horses of the sun, usurping his father Apollo's prerogative, or like that of Hippolytus, who was dismembered, torn apart by his horses as a punishment for dishonoring his father Theseus' second wife. On their surface, these images speak to Tamburlaine's competition with his sons, his unwillingness to relinquish his power because he regards them with jealousy. But the Phaeton image is one that Tamburlaine has used of *himself* (see Part I. II:iv, 49) and its use here shows that he has taken no joy in his apparent victories—what Tamburlaine bequeaths to his sons is not a threat, but the legacy of a self that has triumphed in the external world of conflict only to be haunted at the end by confusion of self with others, of one generation with its predecessor, of conquest with rebellion, of aspiring men and divine power. He is unable to die and, at his death, passes on to his son a wearily useless warning against dismemberment because he has never sufficiently accepted himself as a transient being, never distinguished his own being from the other selves and from the heavens he looked to to mirror it, never enjoyed the fruits of the conflicts he has engaged in because he never really believed in the cohesiveness of the self that entered into those conflicts.

Our treatment of the other tragedies must necessarily be brief and our effort will be to suggest how they build upon the basic Marlovian conception of tragedy as we find it in *Tamburlaine,* a structure in which the action is carried by a conflict or a series of conflicts which are apparently Oedipal in character, involving rebellion against figures of authority or defense against rebellion from youth, but in which the conflict gradually comes to seem empty or transparent, as it opens upon questions concerning the cohesion of the self.

Edward II is built around a series of conflicts between the king and his rebellious nobility. One of the barons, Edmund Mortimer, eventually succeeds in having Richard murdered and consummating an affair with the queen. He, in turn, is defeated and beheaded by the young king, Edward III, who also sends his own mother to prison on suspicion of her connivance with Mortimer in the death of Edward II. But the play is not so much about these conflicts as it is about Edward's inability to participate in them in any meaningful way. The king is a homosexual, and his homosexuality is portrayed as a turning away from the world of political reality to lovers who are worthless themselves, and who are valued only because the king is mirrored in their affection. The turning away from participation in the conflicts by which sons replace fathers in the world of male responsibilities is made clear in the opening line, where Gaveston is reading a letter from the new king, who has just ascended the throne: "My father is deceased, come Gaveston/ And share the Kingdom with thy dearest friend." But Edward's choice of Gaveston is based on no intrinsic qualities—when the barons ask him why he loves a man whom the rest of the world hates, his only reason is "because he loves me more than all the world" (I:iv,77). When the barons force his exile, Edward speaks of being banished from himself, and, in a theatrical image of their mutual mirroring, they exchange pictures at their parting. This gesture, like Tamburlaine's keeping of Zenocrate's picture, is related to the failure to maintain the constancy of inner objects. The arbitrary, empty character of Edward's choice of love-object is emphasized in his almost immediate turning to another lover, equally base in character, as soon as he has news of Gaveston's murder. More, Edward's love is seen as proceeding from a self so enfeebled that, although he is king, he cannot take steps to protect his lover from banishment and death. When the lords first insist on Gaveston's exile, Edward's first reaction is that he would rather set the island of Britain adrift to wander through the sea. When he is threatened with deposition by the archbishop, he takes up a posture of resistance, "Yet I will not yield./ Curse me, depose me, do the worst you can" (I:iv,56–7). But this quickly gives way to an offer to let the lords divide the kingdom up, so long as "some nook or corner" is left the king to "frolic" in with his lover. Yet he neither resists nor resigns the kingdom—instead, as the barons insist, he signs the order banishing the man he "loves more than all the world," and these waverings all take place in less than forty lines, and reflect no real change in the external situation; the barons merely continue to insist and Edward undoes himself before them. It is not really that he has chosen love over politics, for he is not true to the implications of his choice: rather his kind of love is a piece with his inability to fight for it—both reflect a central defect in his sense of himself.

Though Kohut avoids defining the self strictly, his various attempts to delineate his usage emphasize the individual's sense of cohesion in body and mind, the continuity in time and space of this feeling of unity, and "the sense of being an independent center of initiative and perception." It is this latter aspect of self that Edward lacks, and it is one that Kohut mentions as requisite to the ability to grow through conflicts:

> Unless the child sees himself as a delimited, abiding, independent center of initiative, he is unable to experience the object-instinctual desires that lead to the conflicts and secondary adaptations of the oedipal period.[14]

The play begins with this lack of initiative, closely related to a need for love that is narcissistic and self-reflective, and, as the conflicts develop, the other aspects of the self—cohesiveness, continuity in space and time—come into prominence as the barons begin to use their perception of Edward's defective self-organization against him in more and more sophisticated and sadistic ways.

The first phase of this involves the translation of Edward's indecisiveness into spatial terms. As the nobles send Gaveston away, Edward recalls him, he is exiled again, sneaks back, and is captured and moved from one place to another, so that a giddy rhythm of spatial dislocation is generated. When regarded in the context of this pattern, Edward's image of England cast adrift to wander in the ocean expresses not the defiance he intends, but the disorientations of a self without a strong sense of its own spatial location. That the barons understand how to use this feeling of shuttling back and forth for their own ends is evident in the discussion of whether to recall Gaveston. They have just sent him away, when Mortimer suggests recalling him—his argument being that it will be easier to have him murdered at home than abroad, but also that it will humiliate Gaveston to recognize that he can be sent out and called back at the lords' command. Once he returns, he is captured by the lords and the sense of spatial disorientation is developed by his

transfer from their custody to that of Pembroke, who promises to take
him to the king for a final visit before his execution; then to that of
James, Pembroke's man, when Pembroke, in a sexually ironic turn, ab-
sents himself for the night to go home to his pretty wife; and finally he
is turned over to Warwick's men, who actually execute him. The discussion of whether to behead or hang him, and the debate over what part
of his divided body to send the king, continue the development, in
dramatic imagery, of the consequences of Edward's indecisiveness—from
symbols of spatial disorientation to images of actual fragmentation.

What happens to Gaveston prefigures the humiliation of Edward in
the last act, as he is transferred from the custody of the monks to that of
Leicester, then to Berkeley, then to Gurney, and finally handed over to
the murderer Lightborn. In Mortimer's instructions to Gurney, it is
plain that the moving of the king is not motivated by merely tactical
reasons but by a desire to assault his personality.

> Seek all the means thou canst to make him droop,
> And neither give him kind word nor good look . . .
> And this above the rest: because we hear
> that Edward casts to work his liberty,
> Remove him still from place to place by night,
> Till at the last he come to Killingworth,
> And then from thence to Bartly back again,
> And by the way, to make him fret the more
> Speak curtly to him; and in any case
> Let no man comfort him if he chance to weep,
> But amplify his guilt with bitter words.
>
> (V:ii,54–65)

The actual murder, which takes place after Edward has been kept in the
lowest vault of the castle, up to his knees in sewer water, is among the
most violent onstage deaths in all dramatic literature, for, as in Marlowe's historical sources, the murderer, in a sadistic parody of Edward's
sexual delinquency, presses him down upon a featherbed brought for
the purpose, and dispatches him with a red hot spit. Marlowe balances
this sadistically punitive death, for which he had historical warrant,
with an even more horrible scene of his own invention enacted just
prior to the murder, between tormentor and victim. This involves Edward's self rather than his body. Lightborn, in a brutal analogy to the
king's need for affection to stabilize the chaos of an unformed self,
becomes Edward's comforter, and with almost maternal ministrations
puts the king to bed and extracts professions of trust and need from him

before killing him. Edward, at this point, describes his torments, which have left him without a clear sense of his physical coherence: his captors have kept him sleepless for ten days by beating a drum, his

> mind's distempered and my body's numbed,
> and whether I have limbs or no I know not,
> O, would my blood dropped out from every vein,
> As doth this water from my tattered robe.
>   (V:v,64–66)

Lightborn's comforts are meant to effect a parallel breakdown of Edward's emotional self: it is not that Lightborn tricks Edward into trusting him, but that Edward has no psychological alternative but to turn to him, despite his clear perception of his mission. Edward recognizes, fully, though fitfully, that Lightborn has come to murder him, but he needs to rest, and at this point can only sleep in the presence of a comforting, soothing person. At the end he actually asks Lightborn to stay with him, on the theory that, if he really is a murderer he will come back anyway. Like much else in Marlowe, what is enacted here has roots in the psychological hazards of very early life, in the infant's fear of annihilation, and in the inability to integrate contrary perceptions of the mother, who is the source of the infant's nourishment and the mirror of the infant's self-cohesion on the one hand, and the cause of frustration on the other.[15]

Lightborn's sadism is gratuitous: that is, like Mortimer, his need to destroy the king's mind goes beyond the necessities of his duties as a professional murderer. But, as with Mortimer too, the sadism is made possible by and is in some sense a response to the defects in Edward's psychological makeup. As the death by spitting is a punishment by analogy for Edward's sexual behavior, Lightborn's eliciting of infantile dependence from the king is an analogy and an extension of the defect in the self Edward's homosexuality is seen to proceed from—his radical dependence on the mirroring of others to remedy an incoherent sense of self. At the end he is forced to bring this need to full consciousness when he can no longer make any use of such self-knowledge, forced to recognize that he'll turn to anyone, even his murderer, for comfort, just as he has throughout the play turned to anyone for erotic excitement and mirroring response.

The invention of this scene, like so much else in Marlovian tragedy, has the effect of shifting attention from the external conflict—here over the crown—to the fragmented condition of the self. Mortimer is the actual antagonist, yet Marlowe handles the historical material in such a way that we tend to forget the political struggle almost entirely. As the king is transfered from one keeper to another, the evil that befalls him becomes less a matter of a conflict of will, purposes, and personalities, and more a confrontation with an underlying horror inherent in the character of human emotional need. What Mortimer inflicts on the king is done through several intermediaries: Lightborn himself has been hired not by Mortimer, but by Matrevis and Gurney, with instructions merely to kill the king in a way that will not be readily detectible: his assault on Edward's self is his own idea, and its gratuitousness has a universalizing effect: Edward is facing the dissolution of the human physical and emotional self which, in Marlowe's tragic vision, is essentially empty and cruelly mocked by a world in which its need to find a mirroring object is answered by death.

The final scene of the play concerns Edward III's assumption of power, and represents Marlowe's final statement on the hollowness of the political world and the father-son relationship that lies behind the conflicts in the political arena, for Edward achieves in a moment, yet without any sense of triumph or achievement, the suppression of the antagonist who had tortured his father.

Like the accession of the good son Fortinbras to the Danish throne at the end of Hamlet, the assertive triumph of Edward III resolves none of the questions the play has raised about the human self, and which Edward's sufferings have exemplified. Rather, the final scene is a turn toward superficiality and a closing off of tragic vision—the world of firmer selves, of sons ready to succeed their fathers, punish rivals, and discipline mothers, the world of Oedipal conflict and success, is inimical to depth. The deepest concern of the play is not centered upon either the conflicts that destroy Edward II or those that establish his son as the great king he would go on to be, but rather with Edward's tendency to fragmentation, and his growth to tragic stature as he becomes conscious of both the urgency of the need for cohesion and the impossibility of achieving it.

A few observations about *Faustus* will conclude this argument. The subject of Faustus' sense of emptiness, worthlessness, and incoherence of himself, and the way in which he reaches for goals and objects which are themselves empty in order to stabilize his fragmentation has already been treated brilliantly by Edward A. Snow in ways that anticipate Kohut's later views on disintegration anxiety.[16] As the concern of this play with issues of self-coherence is well recognized, it will be sufficient to remind ourselves that here too we find the tragedy of the self sustained by a structure based on conflict, rebellion, transgression, and punishment, and that this structure, as in the other plays we have examined, gradually becomes transparent to the issues concerning the self that lie below the surface. Think, for example, of how Faustus' conflict with the Pope himself is trivialized by its farcical treatment, or how much more important to him is his encounter with Benvolio, whose great sin has been to fall asleep while Faustus was performing his magic. But it is not merely the Pope whom Faustus cannot regard as a serious antagonist: he also, until the very end, turns away from, will not recognize, and trivializes his conflict with God, which is, in a sense, the central action of the play.

The prologue contains an image that may stand as an emblem of the complex interplay of conflict and coherence in the work, as indeed, in Marlovian tragedy generally. The prologue speaks of Faustus' fall in terms drawn from the myth of Icarus:

> Till, swoll'n with cunning of a selfe conceit
> His waxen wings did mount above his reach,
> And melting, heavens conspired his overthrow.
> (20–23)

On the surface this passage offers an image of conflict between the overreaching Icarus, who has usurped the secrets of his father's craft, and the gods, who punish him by melting his wings and casting him to earth. But the vision of the gods as hostile, as 'conspiring his overthrow' is punitive in a way that reveals, and is meant to reveal, its own excess: Icarus' wings melt because it is the nature of wax to melt near the sun—there is something in his own project that is *self*-defeating, *self*-undoing. This recognition that Icarus has actually destroyed himself is already present in the myth Marlowe uses—but he goes further: Icarus destroys himself by coming too close not to the sun but to "melting heavens"—the adjective hovers between Icarus' wings and the heavens themselves—and they are 'melting' not only because they can soften wax, but because they are themselves, as in Tamburlaine's so often repeated image, capable of melting or dissolution, of refusing to cohere in ways that reliably mirror human aspirations and human selfhood. As does the play as a whole, the image of revolt against the Gods and the inevitable punishment that follows, is made to contain a deeper significance, to suggest the more profound anxieties of a self in danger of fragmentation and unable to find, or to believe in, the external mirror of cohesion it so desperately needs.

The final soliloquy works in the same way: Faustus' vision of God's impending punishment seems powerful, but is relatively mild when compared with the vision of the dissolution of the self with which Faustus afflicts himself, imagining his fragmentation into drops of water, to be drawn into the clouds and spewed forth never to be found.

Christ's blood streaming in the firmament—a vision he sees but cannot reach or make use of—is also an image of a self dissolved, and of a way of regarding the dissolution of the self that could be redeeming, not ruinous. Its removal from Faustus' grasp at this final moment recalls Kohut's description of the sense of guiltless despair of patients suffering from narcissistic personality disorders, who realize in late middle age that they can no longer reassemble a fragmented self in the time at their disposal, and that they face a failure of overwhelming magnitude. Kohut believed that it was the achievement of self-cohesion, more than any other factor, that enabled some to accept death as "an integral part of a meaningful life," while others regard "death as a proof that life is utterly meaningless—the only redeeming feature being man's pride in his capacity to face life's meaninglessness without embellishing it."[17] Where there is severe self pathology the inevitable dissolution of the self cannot be accepted because its full cohesion has never been achieved.

Again, Marlowe has used the language of Oedipal revolt and punishment to speak of a deeper tragedy, that of the unmirrored and fragmented human self. Marlowe's tragic protagonists are not able to reconstruct or repair the self, as perhaps Shakespeare's tragic heroes do: rather they move from an uneasy belief in their own grandiose self-conceptions toward a recognition of the emptiness and fragmentation they have tried to deny. Marlowe's tragic effects depend upon the interplay of conflict and coherence, upon the juxtaposition of Oedipal and pre-Oedipal interpretations of the same events, and in creating them he not only revived a *genre,* but gave it a new direction, for after Marlowe the term tragedy itself is altered in meaning, and tends to suggest, to us as it did to Shakespeare, recognition of the precariousness of the cohesion of the human self.

NOTES

1. Heinz Kohut, ROS, p. 222.
2. Kohut, ROS, p. 227.
3. Kohut, ROS, p. 286.
4. Kohut, ROS, pp. 132–3,206–7,238–43,285–90.
5. Of other psychological approaches to Marlowe, perhaps the most impressive is Edward A. Snow's dense and brilliant essay "Marlowe's *Doctor Faustus* and the Ends of Desire" in Alvin Kernan ed., *Two Renaissance Mythmakers: Christopher Marlowe and Ben Jonson* (Baltimore: Johns Hopkins University Press, 1977), pp. 70–110. Snow's approach to the "oral-narcissistic dilemma" in *Doctor Faustus* is indebted, at least indirectly, to object relations theory, especially as taught by Fairbairn and Guntrip, and is very much in harmony with my own views. Constance B. Kuriyama's *Hammer or Anvil* (New Brunswick: Rutgers University Press, 1980) is a full-scale psychoanalytic study of Marlowe from a classically Freudian point of view, and a most valuable contribution to Marlowe studies, though the author tends to emphasize neurotic elements in Marlowe's life and art at the expense of the pre-Oedipal material. The psychological side of C. L. Barber's work on Marlowe in "'The Form of Faustus' Fortunes Good or Bad,'" *Tulane Drama Review*, 8, (1964), 92–119 and "The Death of Zenocrate: 'Conceiving and Subduing Both' in Marlowe's *Tamburlaine*," *Literature and Psychology*, 16 (1966), 15–26, is still valuable, though in some respects superseded by Snow and Kuriyama. Stephen Greenblatt's chapter on Marlowe in *Renaissance Self-Fashioning* (Chicago: University of Chicago Press, 1980) is a lively study of the theatricality of Marlowe's heroes and their attempt to assure themselves of their own existence by self-reference, and is relevant at a number of points to the issues discussed here.
6. References are to *The Complete Plays of Christopher Marlowe*, ed. Irving Ribner (Indianapolis: Bobbs-Merrill, 1963).
7. In this connection it is interesting that the occasion of Tamburlaine's first demand for visual attention is his failure to establish other kinds of contact with

Zenocrate. Compare Kohut's discussion of the hypercathexis of vision or gaze in narcissistic patients:

> The visual area is often clearly overburdened by cathexes channeled into it after the failure of other modes of interaction . . . . By looking at the mother and by being looked at by her, the child attempts not only to obtain the narcissistic gratifications that are in tune with the visual modality, but also strives to substitute for the failure that had occurred in the realm of physical (oral and tactile) contact or closeness. Heinz Kohut, *Analysis of the Self* (New York: International University Press, 1971), p. 117.

8. Compare D. W. Winnicott's remarks in MP, pp. 180ff: "The infant experiencing omnipotence under the aegis of the facilitating environment *creates and recreates the object.*" See also the description of the "practicing subphase" of the separation-individuation process in Margaret S. Mahler, Fred Pine, Anni Bergman, *The Psychological Birth of the Human Infant* (New York: Basic Books, 1975), pp. 70–74, especially their observation that at this time the "infant's peek-a-boo games seem to turn from passive to active the losing and regaining of the need-gratifying object and then the love-object" p. 71. For a contrasting interpretation of these passages in Marlowe, see Kuriyama, *Hammer or Anvil*, p. 26.

9. This is a verbal gesture of reparation similar in function to the return of the crown to Mycetes in Act II—its real purpose is to enable the Sultan to give everything back in the next speech.

10. Zenocrate's absence
   makes the sun and moon as dark
   As when, opposed in one diameter,
   Their spheres are mounted on the serpent's head,
   Or else descended to his winding train.
                         (II:iv, 52–54)
The reference here is not, as Ribner thought, to the constellation Scorpio, but to the "nodal dragon," who according to widespread ancient belief, consumed the sun in eclipses.

11. Heinz Kohut, "Thoughts on Narcissism and Narcissistic Rage," in Ruth S. Eissler, Anna Freud, et al. eds., *The Psychoanalytic Study of the Child,* Vol. XXVII (1972), (New York: International University Press, 1973), pp. 385–86.

12. Otto Kernberg, ORT, p. 73. See also Kohut, ROS, pp. 238–42. Both practitioners agree that late middle age is often a period of intense suffering for narcissists, even when there has been surface adaptation in earlier life. Kernberg writes eloquently of the reasons for this in a passage that sheds light on the relation between the pathological character of narcissism and the universals of human experience: "If we consider that throughout an ordinary lifespan most narcissistic gratifications occur in adolescence and early adulthood, the individual must eventually face the basic conflicts around aging, chronic illness, physical and mental limitations, and above all, separations, loss, and loneliness—then we

must conclude that the eventual confrontation of the grandiose self with the frail, limited and transitory nature of human life is unavoidable" (BCPN, pp. 310–11).

13. Kohut, ROS, p. 237.
14. Kohut, ROS p. 227.
15. See Melanie Klein, *Envy and Gratitude* (New York: Basic Books, 1957).
16. Snow, "Ends of Desire."
17. Kohut, ROS, pp. 241–42.

THREE

OMNIPOTENCE AND REPARATION IN PROSPERO'S EPILOGUE

Joseph Westlund

Most people find the epilogue to *The Tempest* strangely moving, yet critics fail to explain why this should be so. They all too often address abstract intellectual issues at the expense of emotional ones and do not attend to the tone of the speech. Instead of dealing with the character as a character they tend to regard Prospero as simply a spokesman for the playwright.[1] Let us assume that the speaker is Prospero and that we hear his voice.

In order to do so we need to sharpen our sense of Prospero's character, for interpreters tend to make him appear too enigmatic by treating him as a magician without examining the implications of this role. From his behavior before he was deposed, and from his reluctance to give up magic at the end, we can assume that his choice of magic arises from his characterization, from the "personality" Shakespeare creates for this extraordinary figure. Even while Prospero is actively engaged as a magician he reveals by his assumption of magical powers a grandiose sense of himself, and he embraces grandiose ideals as well. His perception of himself and the goals he creates suggest that he seeks to confirm his feeling of worth. Prospero attempts to bolster his sense of vigor, greatness and perfection; in a way he behaves as though he were god-like. When critics blandly agree that he *is* godlike, they confuse the issue and mislead us about our response to the play.[2]

Prospero aspires to perfection. He seeks it by idealization of himself and of those who mirror his greatness: Ariel, Miranda, Gonzalo. Conversely, he degrades those who call it into question: Caliban, obviously, but also Antonio, whose usurpation is in some ways Prospero's responsibility. Prospero repeats painful experiences from his past, apparently in hope of gaining the perfection he feels he lost. In Milan, he abandoned worldly duty in pursuit of an idealized goal: Art "which, but by being so retir'd, / O'er-priz'd all popular rate" (I:ii, 91–92). On the island, he pursues another idealized goal: to be once again "the prime duke, being so reputed / In dignity" through all the signories (I:ii, 72–73)—not so much because he wants to rule, for he will again be retired and think of his grave, as simply to regain the perfection of being "the prime duke." His repetition fails to achieve exactly what he wishes: both wicked brothers fail to repent; Caliban's repentance strikes him as inadequate. Prospero's melancholy at the end of the play—a tone which Anne Barton among others finds there—stems from his unwillingness to give up magic and be an ordinary prince. Some deep, continuing need remains unfulfilled. At least, the pattern suggests this: he sought to perfect his Art at the expense of the state; on the island, he controls everyone in quest of some ideal solution; at the end he feels entitled to something significant, but deprived of it. Throughout *The Tempest,* Prospero's attitude, which many find austere and hieratic, also has unpleasant overtones; he is, as Stephen Orgel puts it, "arbitrary, illtempered, vindictive."[3]

Prospero becomes less enigmatic if we place him in the context of other of Shakespeare's more obviously problematic characters. Helena in *All's Well That Ends Well* manipulates everyone so that she can get Bertram—whom she idealizes beyond our comprehension—regardless of what he wants, or of the inappropriateness of the match. To Helena, Bertram is a perfect mate; the irrational nature of her fantasy indicates that she, like Prospero, seeks an archaic state of bliss which would confirm her heroic yet grandiose sense of self. In her case, she seeks to be a perfect combination of "a mother, and a mistress, and a friend"— and a countess. Prospero also has much in common with Vincentio in *Measure for Measure,* who tries to manipulate everyone so as to establish himself as a perfect ruler, and who makes an issue of his self-esteem by taking the real or imaginary waywardness of his subjects so personally. Both dukes want to attain impossibly high goals—the reform of sinners by means of ideal statecraft—and not simply because this would be desirable, but in order to prove their perfection to themselves and to others. We should cast a skeptical eye on the grandly conceived goals which they pursue so intensely, and whose apparent attainment leaves them, and the endings of their plays, touched with sadness.[4]

The psychological explanation of this quest for perfection is that such an achievement would create a state of bliss: either remembered somehow from the womb when needs are fulfilled before they are even felt, or briefly attained during infancy and pursued, with great futility, forever after. Whatever the cause, a disordered sense of self-esteem has at its root self-contempt for being imperfect. Paradoxically, this can make someone concentrate psychological interest upon the self in a manner which gives the impression of excessive self-love. Self-love, clearly, is something everyone needs. When people lack a firm sense of their own worth, when they feel it severely undermined and fragile, they compensate by so inflating their self-esteem and their goals that they lose touch with everyday reality and with their own instincts—neither of which can ever be perfect. If this state persists untempered by frustration, people lose touch with themselves and with those around them. I summarize this theory with the intention of showing that narcissistic disorders are an extreme version of a common human problem. Helena, Vincentio, and Prospero are not pathological extremes in the sense of belonging in some case history. Still, we can better understand them by attending to their inflated, and consequently fragile, sense of self.[5]

From this perspective, let us turn to Prospero's enigmatic, poignant epilogue. As the play itself ends, he asks the others: "Please you, draw near" (V:i, 318). He begins to draw toward others in a gesture which we have never before seen. However, as soon as the characters depart he assumes another self-inflated role: the magician who gave up all. The speaker sounds too much like Prospero for us to be very much aware of the actor playing his part. Indeed, Prospero's characterization takes on new depths during the epilogue, ones implicit all along.

Throughout the play Prospero makes us believe that he means one thing, while actually meaning another. He often professes to give up "this rough magic," but continually values it and misses his former omnipotence. His tone hardly changes, even during the epilogue. Now, however, he claims to need us:

> Now my charms are all o'erthrown,
> And what strength I have's mine own,
> Which is most faint: now, 'tis true,
> I must be here confin'd by you,
> Or sent to Naples.

>   (Epil.:1–5)

He protests that he is merely mortal, but persists in controlling others to achieve not merely applause but something far more grand—as his extraordinary phrasing indicates. He perceives his request as the result of weakness, or unconsciously disguises it as such. Because his strength is "most faint," we in the audience must help him get what he wants. As is usual with such maneuvers, he employs his weakness to control us: we must confirm his greatness because it is his due. His faint strength seems a bit suspect; although no longer omnipotent, he has become Duke of Milan before our eyes: an august, powerful ruler. What he really wants is not power in the form of applause and cheers to drive his ships back to Milan, but appreciation itself. And he wants it not for the play called *The Tempest,* but for himself. He seeks to confirm what is always in question: his self-esteem. And unique among Shakespeare's epilogists, Prospero concentrates exclusively upon himself during the epilogue. The other epilogists draw attention to their play and to the whole company. For example, Puck promises that "If you pardon, we will mend," and Feste says that "we'll strive to please you every day." The king after the end of *All's Well* asks "that you express content; which we will pay, / With strife to please you." Rosalind, more modestly, asks that you "like as much of this play as please you." Prospero, however, makes mention neither of the play itself, nor of the company as an on-going group devoted to its audience's pleasure. Instead, he refers only to himself—and uses the personal pronoun fifteen times in twenty lines.

Prospero reverses the role which he had during the play while sole arbiter of everyone's destiny; now he becomes the subject—the Ariel, Caliban, Miranda—and we the audience have strength to determine his fate. We may do with him as we wish; and yet, he himself sets up the terms: we can either confirm his self-esteem, or undermine it. Prospero's motivation becomes clearer than ever before: he asks us to demonstrate our appreciation of his achievement—of his "project" which is not simply, as he states here, to please, but to gain his dukedom and, perhaps, revenge; as he remarks in the first line of the final act: "Now does my project gather to a head." Ultimately, as I have suggested, this appreciation amounts to the love which he feels can be won by perfection—an insight which W.H. Auden's poetic commentary on the play supports.[6] Prospero's appeal for applause has an especially ingratiating effect, for he provides us with the power to be benevolent—to work our own spell:

> Let me not,
> Since I have my dukedom got,
> And pardon'd the deceiver, dwell
> In this bare island by your spell;
> But release me from my bands
> With the help of your good hands;
> Gentle breath of yours my sails
> Must fill, or else my project fails,
> Which was to please.
>   (Epil: 5–13)

This indicates a need to manage the response of others which goes far beyond that of an actor's relationship to an audience. The startling conceits draw attention to the speaker; the exhibitionistic, grandly formulated phrasing is exactly what we have grown to expect of the duke:

> Now I want
> Spirits to enforce, Art to enchant;
> And my ending is despair,
> Unless I be reliev'd by prayer,
> Which pierces so, that it assaults
> Mercy itself, and frees all faults.
>   (Epil: 13-18)

This is an extraordinary sort of request. Not only is it difficult to imagine it coming simply from an actor asking for applause, but also it seems strange that so many people have thought they could detect Shakespeare's own voice here. The voice is Prospero's, right down to the unexpected, hyperbolic word "despair." It suggests his sense of emptiness, as in his notion that his every third thought will be of the grave. The grandiose attitude derives from Prospero's feeling that life and the world are insubstantial, baseless. In the passage just quoted—as in the revels speech—he relentlessly demands all, or finds nothing: perfection, or an acute sense of emptiness. Rather than perceiving life as essentially sad and finite—and thus getting on with it by finding gratification in the everyday world—Prospero seeks something quintessential and unattainable. This accounts for his extraordinary terms: the prayer of applause must pierce and assault mercy itself and free all faults. This beautifully phrased, yet grandiose plea sums up what he seeks throughout the play.

What makes his request so effective is that he now works on us, rather than on the characters. He makes a striking invitation for audience response:

As you from crimes would pardon'd be,
Let your indulgence set me free.
                    (Epil: 19–20)

Prospero "shifts the role from that of fellow sinner to that of homilist, the voice of conscience."[7] I think that Prospero assumes this attitude from the start of *The Tempest*; now it comes right into the open. All along, he sees himself as Destiny, as Fate, as someone entitled to behave in a godlike manner. In a way, the nature of his role as benign magician and duke thrusts this attitude upon him. Still, as in the case of Marlowe's Faustus, we can believe that he chose to be a magician, and that his choice arose from a richly detailed and coherent character.[8] Prospero longs to be superior, and remains so to the final couplet of his epilogue. Many critics accept the last lines at face value: "As you from crimes would pardon'd be, / Let your indulgence set me free" (Epil: 19–20). He reminds us of our misdeeds, and asks that we not judge him harshly; we should—although he merely alludes to the idea—do unto others as we would have them do unto us. However, he still has a tin ear. Why bring up the provocative issue of "crimes"? The word is grand, yet troublesome, for he raises an idea better left unstated. He was remiss when "the government I cast upon my brother, / And to my state grew stranger" (I:ii, 75–76). Now he apparently intends to retire there rather than, so far as we can tell, take an active role. Nor has his attitude toward characters who intend or commit crimes been remarkably charitable. Prospero assumes our guilt, and skips over his—yet again—to ask for our indulgence. Although he plays upon our sympathy and compassion, his tone remains rather superior and deprecating.

The epilogue's effectiveness stems from other, better strategies. The epilogue marks the culmination of a process which operates throughout *The Tempest* and may account for the inexplicable pleasure which the play gives. Although it is difficult to account for the sense of well-being which the play creates, one reason must be our satisfaction at the happy winding up of events. Still, the reconciliations are more limited than we expect at the end of one of Shakespeare's comedies or romances: Alonso repents and becomes reconciled with Prospero, who regains his dukedom and marries his daughter to Alonso's son. Three important characters are not admitted to this scheme: Antonio, Sebastian, and—by Prospero's frown—Caliban. Gonzalo remains just as he always has been. Ariel simply disappears into the spirit world.

That Prospero is a magician is the most potent factor in bringing pleasure to the audience, for his omnipotence allows us to partake vicariously in his ability to master the external world. If it can be his oyster, then perhaps it can be ours. However, this fantasy can also create ambivalence in the viewer, for the play lets us identify with the characters whom he controls and whose individuality he devalues by his magic and by his attitude toward them. Insofar as we identify with Prospero's subjects—look at them through *our* eyes, rather than his— we can sense the unpleasant reality of living under his great power. We can spot the frightening implications of being so over-controlled, and we can perhaps see how frightening it might be to have such power over others, to subject them to our will.

Prospero makes it difficult for us to be sure what other characters feel, for he controls our response to them. But if we approach the duke as a motivated, lifelike figure, we can appreciate what it might feel like to live under such domination, benign though it usually is. Critics infrequently respond in this way. One exception is the fact that they often seem to like Caliban despite Prospero's view—and despite their own distaste for this would-be rapist and assassin. Although Caliban is listed in the dramatis personae as "a salvage and deformed slave," and born of the devil upon a witch, Caliban behaves in a way every bit as "human" as that of the wicked Italians. Modern viewers side with him when he complains that Prospero has usurped his island and enslaved him; we see Caliban as a victim of colonialism, a response exacerbated by the duke's superior learning, power, and attitude. Most of Shakespeare's audience would not have sided with Caliban on this subject; this may be why Caliban, like Shylock in similar circumstances, is made vividly human so that he transcends the age's prejudice. On the other hand, Shakespeare's audience was far more sensitive than many modern audiences to the disadvantages of living under an absolutist ruler. Modern critics sentimentalize the ruler's godlike manner in a way which, for example, members of the Parliamentary sessions of 1609 and 1610 most certainly did not.[9]

Audiences react to different aspects of a play, but we can generalize about three distinct responses to *The Tempest:* the elation of identifying with Prospero's omnipotence, and also a sobering awareness of how his attitude and power devalue those who must submit. As a result the play can stir up a third response: feelings of guilt—on some level of consciousness—for we are all like Prospero in his desire to master; we treat others at times with control, triumph, and contempt. Clifford Leech finds Prospero "the dream-figure of ourselves which we all from time to time imagine, elevated by a special dispensation to a position of full authority over our enemies and even our friends, able with a nod to perplex, to chastize, to pardon."[10] I suspect that this dream-figure is also accompanied by some nightmare-figures. We may be quite unaware of our inner conflict on such matters, but it probably is there—as attested by the defensive quality of so much criticism: its abstractness where emotions must be relevant, and critics' tendency to sentimentalize Prospero's relentless control.

The epilogue helps to focus our response so that we feel an elation different from that of omnipotence. The epilogue invites us to assist Prospero—not control him—by ensuring the success of his "project . . . Which was to please." The duke has lost what we, too, can find wonderfully desirable; thus, we can share his feelings, and yet extend him sympathy and our modest aid. We are better off than Prospero, for we never had magical power; our sense of loss is less plangent. For this first time, we are clearly in a superior position: released from awe at his power, and relieved of whatever resentment we may feel about his control. Now that the rest of the characters have left the stage, the power relationship central to its action exists solely between him and us—and with us, or so he says, in control of his fate.

At this point, our guilt—actual or potential—for vicariously acting out fantasies of omnipotence can be channeled in a "reparative way." To encourage this, the epilogue employs a strategy similar to the one which allows Beatrice and Benedick to fall in love in *Much Ado about Nothing*. The lovers are given a chance to admit what they feel; indeed, they are led to believe that they must do so for altruistic reasons, since the other party pines for affection. Rather than remain self-centered and defensive because they fear being manipulated, Beatrice and Benedick come to the aid of someone who needs them—and, simultaneously, to Hero's aid.[11]

The epilogue to *The Tempest* encourages us, members of the audience, to come to a character's aid: to transcend, say, the defenses which we may raise because of Prospero's manipulation of others during the play, and to admit our admiration—and even sympathy—for a duke who clearly needs it, but would never admit to such a weakness. Prospero's attitude and quest during the entire play suggest that he seeks to repair an injury to his self-esteem, to achieve success and the affection which it might entail. His name itself intimately links him to the notion of success, the need for which defines his nature. "Prospero" stems from *prosperare*: "to cause (a thing) to succeed, to render fortunate"—an etymology made even clearer when he is referred to as "Prosper". He must prosper, must achieve his goals, for they establish, or so he apparently hopes, his sense of greatness and worth. Success takes on such inordinate importance because it seems a way—even *the* way—to attain love.

The epilogue offers viewers the chance to be needed, for only we can validate the success of his projects: to get his enemies at his mercy, to gain his dukedom, and finally "to please." That the chance comes from a character who has proven so studiously self-sufficient adds to its luster. We can bestow on Prospero the compassion which he so parsimoniously offered to others. He gives the impression of needing no one's repentance, or even love—with the exception of Miranda's (which he compulsively controls) and Ariel's (which, because Ariel is a spirit, he cannot get). As father, ruler, and magician Prospero remains unneedy, distant, and superior.

We cannot help but be surprised when Prospero makes so extravagant a bid for our approbation. Since he rarely gives others a chance to exist in their own right—conceives them as part of himself which he can thoroughly control—they cannot give him much in return. Even Miranda cannot love him as a whole "person" with a wide range of feelings—say, her wry, ironic, hard-headed attitudes which we, but not Prospero, spot. He casts her in the role of a supportive daughter, and she dutifully carries it out. Prospero's avowed neediness in the epilogue can stir up our compassion: he wants to implicate us in his situation, to establish some fellow feeling; this may be one reason for his overly strenuous terms: prayer, guilt, mercy, conscience.

"Compassion" proves an especially useful concept here, for it indicates an acknowledgement of the individuality of others as outside ourselves rather than subject to our absolute control. We perceive them as our equals, and "suffer with" them; *com-pati* is the root. One of the definitions of compassion is "suffering together with another, participation in suffering; fellow feeling" (OED). Like Prospero, we may indulge in fantasies of control and needlessness, and we experience the elation of such states. However, because he behaves so grandly most of the time, Prospero dulls our sense of fellow feeling. Only occasionally does he engage us in the way he attempts during the epilogue. The most effective moment comes just after the revels speech; Prospero addresses Ferdinand, with Miranda present:

> . . . and our little life
> Is rounded with a sleep. Sir, I am vex'd;
> Bear with my weakness; my old brain is troubled:
> Be not disturb'd with my infirmity:
> If you be pleas'd, retire into my cell,
> And there repose: a turn or two I'll walk,
>   To still my beating mind. (IV: i.157–63)

This request is unusually considerate and touching in its broken rhythms and shifts of thought, especially after so grandly conceived a view of life. However, audiences probably grow confused and even dismiss this plea for sympathy, for as soon as Prospero gets the lovers off stage, he roundly curses Caliban and proceeds to deal with the conspiracy. Prospero seems disingenuous: he asks for compassion and seems to suffer, and yet as soon as Ferdinand and Miranda leave he changes his tune. Prospero seems to cover up his neediness, seems unwilling to reveal any trace of vulnerability. Nonetheless, the lovers behave in laudably compassionate fashion, as we expect of them, for it is their best trait; they say, comfortingly and in unison: "We wish you peace" (IV: i, 163).

In doing so, they prove compassionate in the other major sense of the word: they "take pity" toward a person in distress as "one who is free from it, who is, in this respect, his superior" (OED). Viewers are in one vital sense superior to Prospero. We may suffer with him in his longing for omnipotence and for the love which it seems to bring within reach; yet we are largely free of his distress, for we were never actually omnipotent. When he admits, at the very last moment, to some pale semblance of the human need for affection, he provides us with an excellent occasion for giving it to him. We can show our gratitude for *The Tempest*. Although *The Tempest* is part of the ordinary world insofar as it is a play performed in a theater, it approaches the perfection for which we yearn. Here is a chance for elation. On the other hand, the epilogue gives us a chance to repair the damage implicit in our indulgence of fantasies of omnipotence. We can extend compassion to someone who at last begins to seem like us at our best and sanest—someone who finally begins to admit what we ourselves try to avoid admitting: our neediness in an imperfect world.

NOTES

1. Frank Kermode summarizes the principal interpretations in his Arden Edition (London: Methuen, 1954), pp. 133–34. I use this as my text.

If the speaker is Shakespeare, another problem arises: he had a hand in two more plays. Still, critics may ultimately be right in sensing a kinship between Prospero and Shakespeare, but for reasons other than those which they advance. One reason why this play is so moving in the context of Shakespeare's career is that an enduring bias remains: he idealizes in order to preserve the possibility for something extremely good. Shakespeare's weakness may be the source of his creativity and strength. It helps him to create tragic heroes who convey with terrible accuracy the destructiveness inherent in idealizing and degrading: the eternal struggle between fusion on the one hand, and isolation on the other. And it allows him to create comic heroines, and occasional heroes, who convey with wonderful effect the possibility that someone ideal exists who can create or preside over a benign and trustworthy world. Such idealization is dangerous. One pays for it, as Shakespeare's characters demonstrate in a multitude of ways in his works. And yet his own propensity gives his reparative strategies a conviction which a more tempered view could never give. For further speculation on this, see Joseph Westlund, "Conclusion," in *Shakespeare's Reparative Comedies: A Psychoanalytic View of the Middle Plays* (Chicago: University of Chicago Press, 1984).

2. Many critics assume Prospero to be more admirable than he is. Stephen Orgel, one of the best of these critics, says that Prospero's suffering is "essentially behind him," and that he leads the play "through suffering to reconciliation and a new life"; and yet Orgel also appreciates the incomplete, even tragic quality of the ending in "New Uses of Adversity: Tragic Experience in *The Tempest*," in R. A. Brower and R. Poirier eds., *In Defense of Reading* (New York: E. P. Dutton, 1963), pp. 114, 125. Also see Orgel's *The Illusion of Power* (Berkeley: University of California Press, 1975). Harry Berger, Jr., terms Orgel's the best of the "sentimental" readings, and offers his own more "hard-nosed" account in

"Miraculous Harp: A Reading of Shakespeare's Tempest," *Shakespeare Studies,* 5 (1969), 253–83. Berger finds the play more self-reflexive than I do; the control which we both find so crucial an issue is to him "exerted nowhere but in the never-never land of magic and romance" (p. 270). I argue that Prospero's manipulative nature is an exaggerated version of the everyday compulsion to master others.

Most critics devote themselves to more abstract issues. Frank Kermode discusses "ideals-in-poetry" in the Introduction to the Arden Edition. A. D. Nuttal declares the play "metaphysical in tendency," although we cannot pin it down in *Two Concepts of Allegory* (New York: Barnes and Noble, 1957), p. 81. Colin Still, in a similarly perplexing way, declares that *"The Tempest* (if it have any underlying significance at all) is the expression of a definite and coherent moral philosophy" in *Shakespeare's Mystery Play* (London: Cecil Palmer, 1921), pp. 237–38). Derek Traversi, whom Berger puts in the sentimental school, also emphasizes the "symbolic" spirit of the play, rather than considering it from a "purely realistic point of view"; otherwise, he argues, the suffering of the lovers may seem "abstract and even perfunctory," in *Shakespeare: The Last Phase* (London: Hollis and Carter, 1954), p. 255. Traversi, like most critics, thinks the play presents a vision of a "redeemed, ennobled humanity" (p. 255).

3. Orgel, *The Illusion of Power,* p. 48. I emphasize Prospero's character and motivations in greater detail than most interpreters. This seems an obvious approach, but critics usually delve no further than to find him wise, august, harsh—and perhaps vindictive. Anne Righter [Barton] in her Introduction to the New Penguin Edition of *The Tempest* (London, 1968) nicely sums up the feeling: *"The Tempest* is not a play that can be reasoned with in terms of character [unlike, say, *Hamlet*]. Even Prospero, its most dominant and fully displayed figure, is curiously opaque"; "the theatre audience . . . is never really allowed to penetrate his consciousness" (p. 11). Barton continues: his "words reflect a variety of emotions . . . transmitted powerfully by the verse. . . . Their causes, however, at a number of important moments, remain hidden and unexplained. From this distancing of the central character spring many of the problems of the play" (p. 11).

4. For this interpretation of *All's Well* and *Measure for Measure,* see Joseph Westlund, *Shakespeare's Reparative Comedies.*

5. One aspect of "narcissism" is made clear by the myth from which it gets its name: Narcissus himself "is only in love with his owne perfections" (as Sandys puts it in *Ovid's Metamorphoses Englished*). This nicely captures a central aspect: the love of and quest for "perfection."

I largely rely upon Kohut; for a fine summary, see Heinz Kohut and Ernest S. Wolf, "The Disorders of the Self and Their Treatment: An Outline," *International Journal of Psycho-Analysis,* 59 (1978), 413–25. A decade or so before Kernberg and Kohut, Béla Grunberger published several excellent essays in French and gathered them into a book which has only recently been translated (*Narcissism: Psychoanalytic Essays,* trans. Joyce S. Diamanti [New York: International Universities Press, 1979], originally published in French [Paris: Payot, 1971]). He strikes me as clearer and more orthodox. Following Freud, Grunberger sees the origin of narcissism in prenatal existence—a state in which the fetus was literally in its own perfect world which provided everything needed, and, crucially, before the need was even felt. We can spot such wishes in infants, but their world is far more frustrating, and thus not—except for moments of fusion with mother in a blissful state where all needs are met—exactly what other theorists find as the optimal existence for which, on some deep level, everyone longs. Grunberger resolves some of the issues which Kohut and Kernberg raise. Marion Oliner summarizes Grunberger's views in her Foreword to the book: The aim of narcissism is an attempt to gain lost omnipotence by overcoming the narcissistic injury of dependency on objects, differences between sexes and generations, and man's finite existence. The strivings for lost omnipotence take the form of an attempt to achieve uniqueness through merger with idealized objects (roughly Kohut's selfobjects). Unlike the narcissistic personality, the mature one accepts gratifications obtained from the real world as adequate, rewarding, valuable—and this gratification by objects helps to support the renunciation of claims to omnipotence, needlessness, and grandiosity. Again, Grunberger and Kohut insist that a sense of narcissistic wholeness, greatness, and the ineffable subsists within each of us throughout life, and is of immense value—so long as we can also find gratifications in the real, imperfect, finite world.

6. W. H. Auden, "The Sea and the Mirror," in the suggestively titled section "The Supporting Cast: Sotto Voce" (the other characters know their place) *For the Time Being* (New York: Random House, 1944). Auden also has Prospero describe himself ("Prospero to Ariel") in a way which directly captures the narcissistic injury of infancy and the quest for omnipotence which results (Prospero tries to be "godlike" as we see in "I am that I am"):

> When I woke into my life, a sobbing dwarf
> Whom giants served only as they pleased, I was not what I seemed;
> Beyond their busy backs I made a magic
> To ride away from a father's imperfect justice,
> Take vengeance on the Romans for their grammar,
> Usurp the popular earth and blot for ever
> The gross insult of being a mere one among many:
> Now, Ariel, I am that I am, your late and lonely master,
> Who knows now what magic is;—the power to enchant
> That comes from disillusion.

7. Berger, "Miraculous Harp," 279.

8. Joseph Westlund, "The Orthodox Christian Framework of Marlowe's *Faustus,*" *Studies in English Literature,* 3 (1963), 191–205.

9. Parliament was dissolved by James in January of 1611 after prolonged and contentious discussion of a number of problems: the new impositions by the king on imports; the clash with Coke on whether the king is absolute and above common law; Cowell's *Interpreter* (1607)—a law dictionary which exalted the royal prerogative beyond all measure. These problems raised the basic question of how omnipotent the ruler was in fact to be.

10. Clifford Leech, "The Structure of the Last Plays," *Shakespeare Survey,* 11 (1958), 25–26.

11. For this interpretation of *Much Ado,* and for further discussion of Klein's theory of reparation in relation to comedy, see Westlund, *Shakespeare's Reparative Comedies.* I find Klein's theory of "reparation" persuasive, and especially useful for discussing literature. She sees reparation as a means of resolving conflict and dealing with the real or imaginary destructiveness bound up with living. By accepting guilt for such destructiveness, we can—and indeed must, at the same time—find ways of repairing its real or imagined consequences (say, by raising children more lovingly so that we need not continue to suffer guilt for hating siblings). Klein's clearest discussion is in "Love, Guilt and Reparation" (1937), rpt. in R. E. Money-Kyrle ed., *Love, Guilt and Reparation and Other Works, 1921–1945* (London: Hogarth Press, 1975), pp. 306–43. Hanna Segal summarizes Klein's view of manipulative, unsuccessful attempts to repair without admitting one's guilt; such "manic reparation" helps to define Prospero's attitude (*Introduction to the Work of Melanie Klein,* revised [1964; London: Hogarth Press, 1973], pp. 83–84).

Alice Miller clarifies the reason for such manic, controlling behavior: "one's use and abuse of power over others usually have the function of holding one's own feelings of helplessness in check"; this means that the "exercise of power is often unconsciously motivated," and hence "rational arguments can do nothing to impede this process," in *For Your Own Good,* trans. H. and H. Hannum (New York: Farrar, Straus Giroux, 1983), p. 278; originally published as *Am Anfang war Erziehung* [Frankfurt: Suhrkamp, 1980]). This helps to account for the difficulty we all have in comprehending characters such as Prospero.

FOUR

ROUSSEAU AND THE TEXT AS SELF

SUSAN GRAYSON

"'So intimately . . . were Rousseau's writings associated with his life that it is impossible to comprehend them without a detailed knowledge of his curious and remarkable career.'"[1] The puzzling overlap of Rousseau's life and career continues to intrigue biographers, critics, and psychologists alike. Rousseau himself does not always separate the personal from the artistic in his works; for him, writing and passion spring from the same well. Creativity represents an affective moment, not a vocation,[2] when the celestial fires of inspiration fan an ardent pen; and it is Rousseau's own life which informs this urgent inspiration.

> The ideas that Rousseau began to formulate and express around 1750 concern his life, and the individual lives of his readers, in a unique and revolutionary way . . . in the preface to *Narcisse* in 1753 he wrote, 'Il faut, malgré ma répugnance, que je parle de moi' . . . From that date on, the writer's self has never ceased to be the topic of central interest. . . . Ultimately, then, in spite of his repugnance, he was forced to write not just about, but *exclusively* about himself. Few people have ever so fully transformed their lives into a literary text.[3]

While Rousseauists generally acknowledge this blend of self and subject matter, they are divided in their reaction to it. Some critics, notably Crocker, analyze Rousseau's personality as part of his literary production. They respect Rousseau's own choice of self-disclosure and account for his behavior as revealed in his autobiographical works. These critics necessarily dwell on certain well-known aspects of Rousseau's character: the paranoia; the obsessive ideation; the compulsive health rituals; and the curiously self-defeating conduct, including his troubled interpersonal relationships.

At the same time, the whole of Rousseau is greater than the sum of these unhappy parts. Other critics maintain that exclusively psychological explanations tend to obscure Rousseau's contribution to the intellectual life of the Enlightenment. Gay finds that the "genetic explanation" can reveal "why an author writes a certain book, and why he holds certain beliefs—but the objective validity of his doctrines is unaffected by the personal history of their creator."[4] De Man agrees that this interpretation "reduces Rousseau from the status of philosopher to that of an interesting psychological case. . ."[5]

We must presume the "real" Rousseau to lie somewhere between the distorted and the indispensable psychological foundations. But is it irrelevant to consider Rousseau the person when we read him for his contribution to literature and philosophy? Even his contemporary Saint-Lambert writes, exasperated, in a farewell, "'I promise you, sir, for my part, to forget your person and remember only your talents.'"[6] It is my position that we cannot ignore the personal component, however unflattering; for if critics have been lured by Rousseau the man, he has demanded as much, preoccupied as he is with himself. Palpably present in his works, Rousseau begs to be understood as fully as the thoughts he presents.

Rousseau is not the only Enlightenment author to inject some form of himself into his writings. We are comfortable, however, with the narrative personae of Voltaire and Diderot, unaware of them as people. We rarely catch them adjusting their masks. Their works are intentionally polemical in a political sense, where Rousseau's are written from "virtuous indignation"[7] at more personal offenses. In Rousseau, the self pierces the identity of philosopher, and we see him in various stages of psychological undress.

The reader cannot assume full blame for voyeurism. Rather, Rousseau, in a psychological sleight-of-hand, piques our interest by opening and shutting the window to his soul. This device disconcerts the reader as much as it confused the author's friends.

Rousseau haunts us because he haunts himself and poses himself as the object of inquiry. For him the autobiographical enterprise is an ontological act.[8] It is for this reason that we consider him narcissistic. He sets up a double mirror, seeking reflection in both his works and the reader's reaction to them. "The veritable project of the *Confessions* is the quest for *transparency* at the interior of the self and with regard to the reader."[9] He offers himself, not as the Classical Age offered the "honnête homme" or the Enlightenment the philosopher, but as the Romantics will offer the misunderstood hero. For Rousseau, the "I" of autobiography is author, narrator, and hero,[10] a self worthy of our attention.

Paradoxically, it is in this capacity that Rousseau echoes his century, for the philosophers advocated reason because they knew the self to be forever at odds with the social order. Voltaire and Diderot, for example, realized that passion, political and sexual, respectively, will dominate unless checked. They coincide with Rousseau in condemning the reigning morality which corrupts well-meaning individuals.

Rousseau further belongs to his era in his praise of freedom—personal, artistic, and financial. Those who like himself must forge their own way can find solace in Rousseau's rejection of the glittering society he was unable to penetrate without anguish and sacrifice. Indeed, the Revolutionaries, admirers of Rousseau, destroyed that very society for similar reasons. Rousseau thus sets the tone of the late Enlightenment and announces the Romantic Age, as he proclaims the primacy of special individuals over a social order that refuses them.

Is the French Enlightenment, then, a narcissistic culture? Certainly not compared to the glorification of the individual found in French Romanticism, where to live in a world without seeing reflections of oneself was at once alienating and gratifying, confirming one's uniqueness. Nor can one speak of narcissism when eighteenth century ears ring with the cries of liberty, equality, and fraternity issued from the early days of the Revolution. Throughout the Enlightenment, individual questions were subordinated to public, political ones. Yet in the pre-Romantic stirrings of Rousseau, narcissism—both personal and artistic—finds its voice.

Rousseau, ever the exception, presents himself as a narcissist in a century of concern for human institutions and social issues. The ideals which inspire Enlightenment philosophers undergo a very personal metamorphosis in Rousseau's hands. Rousseau as writer and man exemplifies narcissism in both the popular and Kohutian senses; popular because he is self-involved and self-referential, using his ego as a starting point for philosophy; Kohutian or clinically narcissistic in his need for constant mirroring and adulation, his rage at not having them, his easily fragmented self, his avowed split (into "Jean-Jacques" and "Rousseau"), and his use of artistic endeavor as a means of self-cohesion.

Rousseau the writer sees his texts as the mirrors he never had, as the only unfailing selfobjects in his delusional system. His texts reflect him as could no person in his life. Nowhere are Rousseau's narcissistic struggles more apparent than in his *Confessions* and *Reveries*. Painfully revelatory, these works represent that most narcissistic of genres, the autobiography, but abound in narcissistic preoccupations not inherent in the genre. In them and in his *Dialogues,* Rousseau acknowledges his split self and names two identities: Rousseau the writer, the fallen self of civilization; and Jean-Jacques the man, the idealized self of Nature. He organizes himself around this split.

He writes of his exile and alienation from a society in which his paranoid eyes see only negative images of himself. He cannot tolerate this rejected, compromised self of Culture. Thus, removed from the pernicious influence of others (that is, their inadequate mirroring of him), Rousseau lives his grandiose delusion as the self-proclaimed authentic voice of Nature. His grandiosity, however, has a decidedly paranoid flavor; indeed, his feelings of persecution, real or imagined, keep him from a soothing merger with appropriate individuals in real life, and he turns to his texts for solace.

Comfort him they do, but at the price of new conflicts which displace but never completely mask the old. Rousseau's personal struggles predate and clarify his literary ones. The events of his early life explain the unhappiness he never overcame. Rousseau entered the world plagued by misfortunes. His mother died shortly after his birth, leaving a sickly infant who would cling all his life to his identity as a fragile physical specimen. "I was born infirm and ill; I cost my mother her life. . ."[11] he writes. His widowed father, Isaac, received his "sad fruit" without consolation, and seemed to see his wife again in the child. Rousseau felt in his father's embraces "a bitter grief mixed with his caresses."[12]

Always traumatic, the death of a parent is especially so for a young child. In Kohutian terms, the event fueled Rousseau's grandiosity, albeit negatively, for he felt responsible for his mother's death. Normal magical thinking and the wish to be powerful became fearful realities for Rousseau. The event also led to his idealization of the mother he never knew and, by extension, of other women; for there was no reality testing in the form of contact with her. Thus began his lifelong search for substitutes, culminating in his relationships with Mme. de Warens and, later, Thérèse Levasseur, his eventual wife and mother of his five abandoned children.[13]

Rousseau suffered an unstable youth as an "undisciplined boy" and wandering "supertramp".[14] He sought refuge from an erratic father who abused his elder son, François, as much as he praised Rousseau. The latter witnessed and intervened in many a scene.[15] These early incidents stimulated his sadomasochistic fantasies; later he would expose himself to women on the street[16] and describe genuine excitement at beatings he received from older women.[17]

Isaac Rousseau's brush with the law and flight from Geneva left Jean-Jacques to fend for himself. He endured some unsatisfactory and abusive apprenticeships where, intelligent and sensitive, he felt ill-suited to this station in life. He emerged narcissistically wounded and convinced that he merited a greater destiny. Eventually (1728) he was sent to Mme. de Warens, a Catholic convert, at the advice of a curate who wished the wayward Rousseau to follow her example.

Rousseau found in her household a haven, and his idealized descriptions of her fill the pages of the *Confessions*. But his naïveté keeps the reader naïve; we must wait for Rousseau's biographers to reveal Mme. de Warens as scheming and pleasure-loving. Nonetheless she was generous and patient with the inexperienced boy. Eventually she tired of the responsibility for his sentimental, social, and religious education. Later, Rousseau was crushed to find himself replaced in her heart, bed, and household by a more ardent young man.

Rousseau's pet name for her, "Maman," speaks for itself. For Rousseau, Maman and her house represented happiness, idyllic innocence, "childhood reconquered under the maternal protection of Mme. de Warens . . . the symbol of spiritual renaissance in a found Eden."[18] He needed her, and she him. She stabilized him as no one else had. He was able to preserve a positive memory of her among all his acquaintances. Unaware of how dissatisfied she was with him, he left her to find his fortune in a series of undistinguished positions in the world.

Rousseau would find a substitute for Maman in the semi-literate Thérèse Levasseur, his inferior in all respects, but a devoted servant and therefore suitable caretaker. She functioned as both nurse and scribe. They married in 1768, after 23 years and 5 children, all rejected as Rousseau's own father had rejected him.[19] Rousseau's attraction to her puzzles his chroniclers, but we may speculate that she had few interests in anything that would distract her from his bidding.

While Thérèse was his lifelong companion, Maman emerges as the more significant figure, occupying a prominent place in his works. His relationship to her set the tone for later encounters with higher stakes: women in the Holbach literary clique.

Rousseau was a stranger to the literary salons until he won first prize for his *Discourse on the Sciences and Arts,* submitted to a contest sponsored by the Academy of Dijon. His fame was immediate:

> Thus, after an unusually variegated career as apprentice to an engraver, lackey, seminarist, music-master, gigolo (of a kind), clerk, tutor, diplomat, secretary, composer and writer, Jean-Jacques, in the year 1750, had at last arrived. And he had arrived, not with a whimper, but with a bang that blew open the doors of all the best houses.[20]

Rousseau soon found the companions and infatuations of his adult life: Grimm and Diderot, Mme. d'Epinay and Mme. d'Houdetot, respectively. But these idealized relationships ended in disaster. Suspicions and jealousies inflamed Rousseau's paranoia and caused him to break definitively with his circle of friends. Ultimately, in 1765 he withdrew to the island of Saint-Pierre to escape personal and professional retaliation.

Writing allowed Rousseau to compensate in part for these failures. He reworked many painful experiences into literature of great merit, ponder though he did the paradox of expressing himself through the written word which he denounced and contested.[21] His days as a lackey and tutor, for example, are transformed in *La Nouvelle Héloïse* and *Emile.* The perceived breaches of friendship and conspiracies are central to the conception and execution of the *Confessions* and *Reveries.*

Yet literary triumphs do not remove psychological scars. The *Confessions* and *Reveries* lay bare the deepest, most distorted levels of Rousseau's being and attest to the interpenetration—indeed, the identity—of self and subject matter. These works arose from Rousseau's need to expose and defend his character, anticipate and denounce his detractors, and petition future generations of readers to judge him kindly as the victim of cruel schemes. No mere memoirs, the *Confessions,* begun in 1765 and read to the public in 1771, recount Rousseau's life in astonishing detail and exhort the reader to believe and forgive him.

Rousseau abandons the need to justify himself in the *Reveries,*[22] begun in the period 1772–1776, and finished shortly before the author's death in 1778. The work is a collection of ten promenades, thematically varied and punctuated by bursts of paranoia. Ironically, the Rousseau who condemns sentient beings as depraved animals now reflects as he walks. The *Reveries* are an incomplete confession, where Nature attends without judging or absolving, acting rather as a mirror for Rousseau.

The form is original, free and lyrical, and the tone serene if melancholy. An "intimate journal"[23] like the *Confessions,* the *Reveries* turn to the self and Nature as agents of coherence,[24] causing the interior to take precedence over the exterior.

Both the *Confessions* and the *Reveries* represent a narcissistic mode of self-observation unusual even for autobiography. Rousseau's injured self permeates these works and shows him out of step with both himself and the prenarcissistic culture which torments him. There is a threefold narcissism, then, to this author. First, relative to his century, the pre-Romantic Rousseau monitors the nuances of his inner states, having assumed our interest in the minutiae of his life. Second, he displays an eccentric, self-absorbed, personal basis to such works as his two *Discourses* and *Essay on the Origin of Languages.* Underneath the concern for public welfare, the works grapple with some of his own needs and justifications. As in *Héloïse* and *Emile,* these works present a distanced version of Rousseau's frustration and inability to maintain self-cohesion in his daily life. When "transplanted into the turmoil of the world of men—the social world," Rousseau discovers his sensibilities "impotent against that world, which threatened to shatter them. Thus Rousseau, the sentimental enthusiast, became the radical political thinker."[25]

But Rousseau is narcissistic principally in the Kohutian sense. His narrative stance as the innocent, sensitive victim, his tragic sense of specialness, and his estrangement bespeak narcissistic personality organization. While these traits are also a function of his genius and vision, their psychological component suggests a Rousseau split into two self poles and unable to mediate them with his personal resources.

In the *Confessions* and *Reveries* we see the injured core of Rousseau, who has learned to organize himself around paranoia. His fragile observing ego retrenches when the pain of remembered wounds forces a retreat into defensiveness. This mechanism explains the oscillation between lyrical and self-righteous passages in the works. Bruised, Rousseau remains torn between the two Kohutian poles, the idealized and the grandiose, and cannot glue himself together consistently through artistic production.

The *Reveries* represent the intended but unwritten third volume of the *Confessions.* Though chronologically later, the work is affectively closer to the author's early personality organization and most intense longings. Let us consider now the idealized self, the Jean-Jacques identity which utters the *Reveries.* Kohut states that the idealized self seeks a soothing merger with a selfobject who lends a sense of perfection. The serious disruptions in Jean-Jacques' early life—his mother's death and father's rejection of him—made soothing or healthy mirroring from caretakers rare if not impossible. He thus turns to writing, Nature, and his inner life for consolation.

In self-imposed exile on the island of Saint-Pierre, undisturbed by the overstimulating presence of others, he abandons himself to a rhapsodic appreciation of Nature. "It is on this island that I sought refuge. . . . I found my stay here so charming. . . ."[26] he writes. "Nothing is more singular than the raptures, the ecstasies that I felt at each observation that I made on vegetable structure and organization."[27] He sees Nature as he sees himself: perfect but vulnerable to encroachment and despoliation.

In effect Jean-Jacques renounces Culture and attempts merger with the forces of Nature as idealized selfobjects. At times he finds soothing mirroring, seeming to fuse himself with the waters around the island. "I let myself go and drift at the water's will, sometimes for several hours, plunged in a thousand reveries confused but delicious."[28] These natural mirrors, unlike the brittle and unforgiving glass of civilization, flatter him. If inaccurate, these mirrors are no more so than those of Culture, which claim reflection but are distorted.

In solitude, able to integrate the few stimuli available, Jean-Jacques suspends his persecutory fantasies and reveals his vulnerability safely to the unknown reading public. He speaks of his favorite pastime, his herbarium, the symbol of time preserved. Arranging the herbarium, he composes the primordial book without words, the eighteenth century Book of Nature, a book not part of the mediated world of Culture. His other occupation is music copying, the aural equivalent of the visual, tactile, and olfactory herbarium. These pursuits recall the way an infant apprehends and processes stimuli: the world of the infant, like that of Nature, is one of sensation unmediated by intellect.

Music and botany represent a regressive mode but a bridge from Culture to Nature. Released from the struggles of civilization, Jean-Jacques experiences life primitively through his eyes and ears, and he is calm. He communes with himself preverbally, authentically. Ironically he rejects the resources and skills which could successfully repair his split self. He is a better writer than musician or botanist, yet disdains his identity as a writer in the real world, preferring elemental forms of expression to the artistic imperative.

Removed from the salons, Saint-Pierre offers few failures, disappointments, or rebuffs to the author's self-esteem and allows him to escape fragmentation. Jean-Jacques feels more consistency of self in time and space in ecstatic states during which he experiences wholeness. The continual noise of the waters "sufficed to make me feel with pleasure my existence, without troubling to think."[29] Released from the urgent "brooding" (Kohut's term) and lifelong hypochondriachal preoccupations aggravated by his mental states, his overburdened self is at repose. Suspended is his mirror-hungry thirst for confirming, admiring human selfobjects, as the island offers none. He may miss the potential for mirroring, but not the torment of empathic failure, the usual result of his quest.

The island also serves the contact-shunning side of his personality. Kohut uses this term to indicate those who avoid social contact and become isolated not through disinterest but through too intense a need for others, hypersensitivity to rejection, and fear of self-annihilation or loss of self-integrity in union with others. Jean-Jacques, the eighteenth century apologist of Nature against Culture, avoids risk in choosing a union with the forces of Nature. Rousing himself from a "long and sweet reverie," he glances at the surrounding verdure: "I assimilated to my fictions all these amiable objects. . . . I couldn't mark the point of separation of fictions from realities."[30]

We see equally the author's grandiosity, for he wishes to merge with the entire world—global merger, literally and figuratively. This world for him is omnipotent, infallible. He can share in its power and perfection enough to compensate for defects in his self, and " . . . he finds a new source of happiness that can never dry up."[31] Nature, an empathic and wise mirror, lends him a nonpunitive superego. He is happy to proclaim himself her child, abandoned as he was by his parents. The pre-Romantic interest in Nature assumes new significance when understood for its psychological meaning in this author.

The merger with Nature is also a function of Jean-Jacques' ideal-hungry personality, perpetually searching for others to admire. Perfect others allow the admirer to experience himself as worthwhile. Kohut comments that the inner void is filled unsatisfactorily by these means. Yet Jean-Jacques notices no lack in Nature as opposed to people, who remain untrustworthy selfobjects.

We turn now to the promenades themselves. The first shows that attempts to regulate tension are not always successful. Jean-Jacques admits to feelings of "incomprehensible chaos" in solitude: the more he contemplates the less he understands. He evinces narcissistic fragmentation as, without human mirrors, he is engulfed by panic. He pays the price of alienation for the comfort of isolation. The earth seems a "strange planet" to him, now that he has left his persecutors. In his emptiness he worries about "defamation, depression, derision, opprobrium."[32]

This fragmentation produces time dysfunctions or elasticity, prolonged in agony, contracted in pleasure—the theme of the second promenade. In rapturous moments of suspension, Jean-Jacques experiences a fusion of emotional and physical states and believes he has returned to the equilibrium of the noble savage. He is convinced he no longer needs human contact. The ecstatic fusion in Nature represents narcissistic gratification on an infantile level. The author has returned to the synchronic time of primary process and therapy, from the diachronic time of civilization. Time does not impinge upon the senses when needs are met.

The third promenade reveals how Jean-Jacques turns to paranoid processes to close off his narcissistically wounded core. The vocabulary—persecutors, traps, plots against him—belies the claim that he is comforted. Developmentally, primitive-level frustrations like these are later justified with the adult's intellectualized defense of paranoia. Repeated earlier rejections, such as the disheartening attempts to make a place for himself in various households, can explain Jean-Jacques' hesitation to trust and accept others.

The childhood incidents, detailed in the *Confessions,* were so painful that Jean-Jacques "lies" about them, idealizing his youth. His frightening adult relationships contrast with his early experiences where, "tranquil in [his] innocence [he] imagined only esteem and good will for [himself] among men."[33] He is surprised when expectations are not met. In fact he never develops empathy, the adult ability to change perspective.

The fourth promenade continues the discussion of white lies, embellishments, and prolonged moments of pleasure. We see in Jean-Jacques' praise of abstract truth a clinical resistance to uncovering old wounds. One does not always owe the truth to others, he writes; the questions must be to whom and at what price.[34] Truth and pain define each other yet are intolerable together. Jean-Jacques remains puzzled and embarrassed at his inability to separate them.

Mirroring would alleviate the dilemmas of pain. The fifth promenade, the highlight of the *Reveries,* illuminates mirroring in terms of
the Nature–Culture conflict. Searching for tranquility in solitude,
Jean-Jacques suspends his writing and fills his room with the objects of
Nature (flora), not Culture (books). Impulses, even sexual, are safe in
the plant world. Jean-Jacques finds himself "enchanted" by the repro-
ductive parts of flowers and vegetables. The truths of life which fragment him in society delight him in Nature. The pleasures of Culture
dim beside those of a Nature which lull Jean-Jacques into states of
ecstasy. The rhythmic music of the waters, like the cooing voices of the
caretakers he never had, cradles him ("bercer"), and like a contented
infant he transcends the limits of time and space: " . . . night surprised
me without my having perceived it."[35]

Jean-Jacques describes this happiness as full and perfect, but, faced
with memories which continue to agitate him, he admits that these
moments are rare and "too rapid to constitute a state, and the happiness
that my heart regrets is hardly composed of fugitive instants but of a
simple and permanent state. . . . "[36] Jean-Jacques avoids disappointment only in depressive or lethargic states of withdrawal, if not paranoia; preferring internal safety to external stimulation, he confuses
internal and external cues. Clearly, he prefers to live his desires and
fantasies than to test or re-experience reality.

Physical and psychological withdrawal is a cure as drastic as the
complaint. The sixth promenade reveals the author's regrets at having
become a public figure through his writings. The creative impulse,
with its potential to restore, has brought only "chains of engagements";
living in society corrupts Jean-Jacques' artistic "penchants."[37] Isolation
on Saint-Pierre allows him to preserve some positive sense of himself,
his primeval virtue, and his life experiences. Born "good," he says, we
later face a conflict between duty and desire, and cannot reconcile them
in civilization. Here Jean-Jacques veils but thinly the child's conflict
between gratification and frustration. Socialization and reality testing
temper this conflict; withdrawal maintains it.

The seventh promenade returns a strained Jean-Jacques to his herbarium. An effort of cataloging, not creativity, the herbarium distracts
him from angry feelings with tasks that bind and absorb his energies.
His paranoid ideation reappears in an old form, the Nature–Culture
conflict. Even the herbarium is not immune and can turn against him.
Jean-Jacques speaks of medicinal uses of herbs by apothecaries, and

contrasts this with the Garden of Eden, that paradisal coincidence of
the infant's needs felt and fulfilled. Herbs belong to both Nature and
Culture, for they cure the illnesses which people bring on themselves.
Jean-Jacques' hypochondriacal fixations lead him to see Nature as the
perfect mirror, repairing the diseases of civilization. He asks Nature to
heal him as a hurt child requests comfort from a caretaker.

The eighth promenade embroiders these themes, while the ninth
reveals still more examples of disruptions in the author's specular self.
Jean-Jacques discusses how he abused, then abandoned his illegitimate
children, replaying his own traumatic abandonment; rejected, he rejects.

He writes about children, whom he says he doesn't like. In a sort of
repetition-compulsion familiar to paranoids trying to curb their anxiety,
he returns to the orphanage and acts out his wish for the heartfelt, "pure
caresses" from a child. He wants to see in its eyes "the joy and content-
ment of being with me."[38] The eyes of children represent mirrors in
which many narcissistically wounded adults hope to find reflections
they never received; Jean-Jacques here is no exception. Such positive
mirroring would obviate the need "to seek among animals the benevolent regard which has been henceforth refused me among humans."[39]

The ninth promenade reiterates the Nature–Culture conflict, again
favoring natural pleasures over the opulent ones of civilization. Symbolically, Jean-Jacques suggests that no distractions in social life can
compensate for the emptiness of improper mirroring. The return to
Nature, from a Kohutian viewpoint, is the search for what Jean-Jacques
never knew but sensed that he lacked and needed. On another level,
these wishes are pre-Romantic as well, in the desire to abjure worldly
pleasures, indulge in melancholy, and commune with Nature. Pre-
Romantic, too, is the adolescent, narcissistic lack of a solid self core.
Jean-Jacques is easily tossed about, confirmed or broken by others.

The brief but poignant final promenade renews Jean-Jacques' tribute
to Mme. de Warens, the most fully available idealized object in his life.
Intense in its simplicity, this promenade reveals how profoundly merged
the maternal figures of Nature and Maman remain for the author.

From the obvious deficits in self-regulating mechanisms in Jean-
Jacques' idealized realm, we turn to his grandiose realm of ambition and
achievement, evaluation, judgment, and separation rather than merger.
This is the Rousseau identity, the self of Culture who writes in the
established genre of confessions to make public a private act. Rousseau
invites narcissistic wounding by comparing his enterprise to other con-

fessions and defying the reader to find his lacking. Yet his self-defeating grandiosity uses reality-testing to humiliate rather than temper; if truthful, he will have to reveal secret shames.

The *Confessions* pose important conflicts: truth, fiction, and error; the spoken and written words; the plenitude of Nature and emptiness of Culture—all conflicts which remain unresolved throughout the twelve books of *Confessions*. But Rousseau seems content to expose and justify, for there is no resolution to his pain. The *Confessions* represent narcissistic grandiosity in their exhibitionism. Ironically, Rousseau, like a child, reveals all, expecting positive mirroring and appreciation; yet consciously he reminds the reader that confessions are to be judged. Rousseau the penitent asks for forgiveness but must first display the sins which even Rousseau the judge despises.

Rousseau's grandiosity in the *Confessions* is evident conceptually, thematically, and textually. Denigrating his predecessor, Montaigne, for admitting only to likeable faults, Rousseau is "emboldened" to gain "by showing myself as I was" and "other people as they were," so that "I should never have to blush before anyone."[40] He writes the *Confessions* absolutely convinced that they will clear his name and incriminate his foes; yet he is uneasy enough to remind us of this on several occasions.

Examples of merger, fragmentation, and idealization are sprinkled through the *Confessions* as well as the *Reveries,* but the former additionally contain many thematic examples of Rousseau's grandiosity. His portraits of significant figures are exaggeratedly good or evil: for example Maman, as contrasted with his father, or Grimm. His fears of bodily disintegration alarm him: every illness places him at death's door. His picture of himself, too, is painted in extremes of purity and decadence. Rousseau's humiliation is masochistically pleasurable in its grandiosity. Various youthful incidents of petty theft or adult incidents of social awkwardness are unbearably, almost unnecessarily painful. Finally, Rousseau is grandiose in his misery and melancholy, as are the Romantics. Book twelve begins with a chilling, sombre description of the depressive state to which he has sunk. He wallows in this abyss, having found, it seems, his rightful place.

Textually, the grandiosity of the *Confessions* is best seen in three moments: the motto or "devise," the epigraph, and the beginning and closing paragraphs. These boundaries of the work act as a skin which Rousseau must open to drain the abcess of his narcissistic wounds. The first book begins with the slogan "inside and in the skin" ("Intus et in cute"). Skin is an important metaphor for Rousseau. His own delusional system shows a permeable skin which cannot separate internal from external cues. The screen between Rousseau's conscious and unconscious processes, to use a more Freudian conceptualization, is of too wide a mesh and leads to confusion and pain.

Popular narcissism sees skin as the packaging of a product. Rousseau himself refers to the body as a "deciduous envelope," an unreliable package. Then, too, he was acutely aware of the skin's function as an excretory organ. Due to his chronic urinary tract condition he was at times unable to void and made himself sweat by exercising to rid his body of toxins. In the *Confessions,* the same is true of his soul.

The second boundary, the epigraph, is grandiose and hyperbolic in tone and vocabulary: "Here is the only portrait . . . in all its truth . . . which probably ever will exist . . . unique work . . . only monument to my character. . . ."[41] The conclusion echoes these exaggerated claims. Not convinced, Rousseau anticipates and condemns in advance negative reactions to the work. He begs his readers' indulgence while accusing them of vengeance. He thus validates the reader's presence—ironically, for he claims to write for himself, to reveal the truth without regard to repercussions, and to condemn writing as the inauthentic arm of Culture. Rousseau violates this most sacred code. He is caught between the roles of judge and penitent, subject and object, participant and observing ego.

The opening paragraphs of the *Confessions* indicate just how much he violates his code. Having established the uniqueness of his enterprise "without example" or imitation, he invokes the trumpet of the Last Judgment—neither spoken nor written word, but a clarion, thus less vitiated. The trumpet recalls Rousseau's music copying, a more palatable form of writing; when he must communicate in civilization, music is a more acceptable medium. Yet he will appear on Judgment Day, book in hand, and present his writing rather than himself, in a gesture reminiscent of Derridian supplementarity. The book is more authentic than Rousseau himself, a complete reversal of his lifelong stance. Rousseau's grandiosity knows no bounds; he can tell the God of judgment how to evaluate, forgetting that such a God should need no book.

The book as self, not just selfobject, raises the key question of the relation between narcissism and art. Rousseau confesses that his book is an extension of himself, a selfobject which, unlike people, remains under his complete control. It mirrors him in "all the truth of Nature." In fact it is distorted to reflect a more merciful portrait of Rousseau. He wishes to substitute art for life. Yet by admitting a faulty memory, embellishments, and fibs in the text, Rousseau perjures himself.

In contrast to the merger-seeking *far niente*[42] of the *Reveries,* the *homo faber* or creative self dictates the *Confessions.* "I have resolved on an enterprise which has no precedent, and which, once complete, will have no imitator."[43] The grandiose creative self allows Rousseau to maintain an objective distance between subject and object, the heart of auto-biography. Admitting his split fosters Rousseau's sense of uniqueness. Again he compares himself with God, but this time with the God of creation rather than judgment.

Rousseau's grandiosity and split are textually evident in his opening words: "Je veux montrer à mes semblables un homme dans toute la vérité de la nature; et cet homme ce sera moi. Moi, seul. Je sens mon coeur et je connais les hommes." ("I wish to show to my kind a man in all the truth of nature; and this man will be myself. I alone. I feel my heart and I know mankind.")[44] In this passage the cohesive nominative pronoun "je" contrasts with the disjunctive pronoun "moi," set apart and fragmented. "Je forme" opens the first paragraph with a complete sentence; "Moi, seul" opens the second with a fragment. The "je" of creation invents the "moi" of the *Confessions.*

Splitting is a later defense than primitive merger and requires con-scious recognition in order to be bridged. For Rousseau this awareness comes during the creative act. Self-cohesion is available to him, then, but attenuated and at the price of using the tools of Culture to attain it. Rousseau thus maintains the "je-moi" split by choosing to codify him-self through the deceitful vehicle he always has condemned, writing. He presents himself in what should be a most humble, penitent, truth-ful form, but is grandiose and untruthful.

He concludes the *Confessions* with a solemn warning to the reader. "I have told the truth," he declares.[45] Any disbeliever who does not verify the facts is unjust and dishonest. Here then is confession without abso-lution on two accounts. First, Rousseau supplies the only acceptable judgment: he disculpates himself with a grandiose condemnation of dissenters. Second, absolution is not possible in someone whose exis-tence depends on separated split-self realms to insure a fragile psycho-logical equilibrium.

Can artistic production mediate this split? Is writing the self-glue, are books the mirrors which offer reflection and cohesion? Rousseau asserts that the trumpet of confession and the authentic voice of Nature are pure, while language and writing are not; they are unsuitable means to an end. A Kohutian explanation of these assertions suggests that self needs were better met in infancy, when the author's cry elicited attention, without his needing the cognitive structures to know he was doing so. Needs were met without coercion, pleading, or seduction; they were anticipated.

Adults and older children, however, must ask for help. So it is for Rousseau, who in his chosen career must compromise himself by writing to receive praise, approval, and mirroring from others. Rousseau waxes poetic about the superiority of Nature, or symbolically of having his needs foreseen and soothed. He deplores the conditional fate of life in society where narcissistic supplies are earned. Nevertheless this is what he must do and does.

Rousseau's prognosis, as it were, for bridging his split is guarded, for his narcissistic need to be mirrored makes him unable to tolerate the pain of facing his wounds in order to allow healing. To take in positive mirroring from both the internal and external worlds he would have to accept, not just acknowledge, an image of himself as imperfect or merely human. As he cannot, will not renounce the wish to be perfect, he re-experiences the wound each time he is mirrored in the real world. Thus he reinforces the split so that the two poles, the idealized and the grandiose, preserve his fantasy of perfection not available through merger.

This split in turn fuels his delusional system. The fond wish for perfection which most of us share becomes an imperative for Rousseau, no longer a wish. It underlies his paranoia, which now clearly emerges as the mechanism by which he functions with the split. Mirroring feeds the paranoia, as it offers an image which Rousseau neither wants nor believes. This is the image he projects onto his persecutors.

There is an all-or-nothing, desperate quality to Rousseau's thought processes. It is adolescent and typically narcissistic. Ironically, he sequesters himself to achieve the longed-for global merger. Seemingly counterproductive, this solitude is necessary because Rousseau accepts mirroring only from Nature, which is a fantasy; or from his own books, works about himself and as carefully edited and screened as is the paranoid's therapy hour. The creative impetus can provide self-glue, but of a qualified type: only when Rousseau can create or invoke tolerable mirrors. Rousseau's self-glue is water soluble. Improper mirroring dissolves it and loosens its binding properties.

Like Narcissus, Rousseau is obsessed not with his "self" but with a reflection of that self, an orchestrated version of his own creation. The Jean-Jacques Rousseau of the *Confessions* and *Reveries* is a self washed clean of exactitude, a self of psychological rather than historical truth.[46] Rousseau takes us beyond the mimetic. Art *becomes* life, and life art.

The tragedy of Rousseau is his ambivalence toward the only possibility of cohesion: writing, the healing coincidence of ambitions and ideals. He divorces his literary talents from his merit as a person.[47] Success, far from wiping out his afflicted past, brings him new entanglements without the unequivocal confirmation of his genius.

Vitam impendere vero—to risk one's life for the truth—was no intellectual exercise for Rousseau but a mortal struggle during which he experienced the death of the self through fragmentation. The *Confessions* and *Reveries* became his legacy, selfobjects over which he had complete control. In them he could preserve an idealized version of himself not subject to correction. This mythic self restored for him an illusion of continuity and coherence.[48]

In the *Confessions* and *Reveries* Rousseau confers on his readers a sacred trust which we must take care not to violate. He offers himself in the spirit if not the practice of truth. How then can we do justice to Rousseau the visionary, worshipped by the Revolution as a moral hero, when facing the pathology of a clearly troubled individual? Rousseau supplies the answer. We must refuse the role of the "hypocritical reader," as Baudelaire puts it, by accepting without judging, without declaring ourselves "better than that man."[49] To recognize the positive side of his Edenic longings is to allow his work to "come into being before our eyes in accord with its own inner law."[50] Rousseau demands the same justice and empathy for humanity that he requires for himself. "He will always be searching for the ideal and unattainable. His writings will look back nostalgically to a mythical past, the innocent childhood of mankind, or look forward to a golden future in which men will be redeemed."[51]

NOTES

(All translations are mine unless otherwise stated.)

1. "Rousseau," in F. J. C. Hearnshaw, ed., *The Social and Political Ideas of Some Great French Thinkers of the Age of Reason* (London: Harrap, 1930), p. 172. Cited by Peter Gay in his introduction to Ernst Cassirer, *The Question of Jean-Jacques Rousseau,* trans. Peter Gay (Bloomington: Indiana University Press, 1975), p. 15.

2. Marc Eigeldinger, *Jean-Jacques Rousseau, Univers mythique et cohérence* (Neuchâtel: Editions de la Baconnière, 1978), p. 30.

3. English Showalter, Jr., "Madame de Graffigny and Rousseau; between the two *Discours,*" in *Studies on Voltaire and the Eighteenth Century,* 175 (1978), 89.

4. Peter Gay, in Cassirer, *The Question.*

5. Paul de Man, *Blindness and Insight, Essays in the Rhetoric of Contemporary Criticism* (New York: Oxford University Press, 1971), p. 113.

6. Jean-Jacques Rousseau, *The Confessions of Jean-Jacques Rousseau,* trans. J. M. Cohen (Baltimore, Md.: Penguin Books, 1954), p. 462.

7. Ibid., p. 459.

8. Marc Eigeldinger, "*Les Rêveries,* solitude et poésie," in *Jean-Jacques Rousseau, Quatre études* (Neuchâtel: Editions de la Baconnière, 1978), p. 115.

9. Eigeldinger, *Rousseau, Univers mythique,* p. 73.

10. Ibid., p. 217.

11. Jean-Jacques Rousseau, *Les Confessions, tome I* (Paris: Livre de Poche, 1963), p. 24.

12. Ibid.

13. How many children, and whether or not they were all Rousseau's, are still subjects of some controversy.

14. "Rousseau," in Hearnshaw, ed., *The Social and Political Ideas.*

15. Lester G. Crocker, *Jean-Jacques Rousseau, The Quest (1712–1758),* vol I (New York: Macmillan, 1968), p. 18.

16. Rousseau, *Les Confessions,* pp. 145–46.

17. Crocker, *Rousseau, The Quest,* p. 24.

18. Eigeldinger, *Jean-Jacques Rousseau*, p. 80.

19. Crocker, *Rousseau, The Quest*, p. 19.

20. J. H. Huizinga, *Rousseau, The Self-Made Saint* (New York: Grossman, 1976), p. 2.

21. Jean-Jacques Rousseau, *Les Confessions, tome II* (Paris: Livre de Poche, 1972), pp. 164–65.

22. Eigeldinger, "*Les Rêveries*", p. 100.

23. Ibid.

24. Ibid., p. 103.

25. Cassirer, *The Question*, pp. 106–7.

26. Jean-Jacques Rousseau: *Les Rêveries du promeneur solitaire* (Paris: Garnier-Flammarion, 1964), p. 96.

27. Ibid., p. 98.

28. Ibid., p. 99.

29. Ibid., p. 100.

30. Ibid., p. 104.

31. Cassirer, *The Question*, p. 86.

32. Rousseau, *Rêveries*, p. 37.

33. Ibid., p. 66.

34. Ibid., p. 77.

35. Ibid., p. 100.

36. Ibid., p. 101.

37. Ibid., p. 111.

38. Ibid., p. 159.

39. Ibid.

40. Rousseau, *The Confessions*, trans. Cohen, p. 479.

41. Rousseau, *Les Confessions, tome I*, p. 20.

42. Rousseau, *Les Rêveries*, p. 97. Rousseau's favorite "occupation" is to be what he calls "lazy."

43. Rousseau, *The Confessions*, trans. Cohen, p. 17.

44. Rousseau, *Les Confessions, tome I*, p. 21.

45. Rousseau, *Les Confessions, tome II*, p. 476.

46. Eigeldinger, *Rousseau, Univers mythique*, p. 70.

47. Crocker, *Rousseau, The Quest*, vol. I, p. 203.

48. Eigeldinger, *Rousseau, Univers mythique*, p. 313.

49. Rousseau, *Les Confessions, tome I*, p. 22.

50. Cassirer, *The Question*, p. 39.

51. Crocker, *Rousseau, The Quest*, vol. I, p. 17.

FIVE

BLAKE AND WOMEN: "NATURE'S CRUEL HOLINESS"

MARGARET STORCH

There is an inescapable contradiction between Blake's expressed sympathy for women within his schema of cultural history, and the actual emotional impetus that lies behind his characterizations of women in most of his major poetry. His concern over women's plight in a degrading world is in tension with deep-rooted feelings of animosity towards them.

Blake is rightly regarded as a radical thinker, who had his own thoroughly regenerative vision of society and was in harmony with the most advanced social radicalism of his age. An essential element in his critique of society, first fully elaborated in *Visions of the Daughters of Albion,* is his recognition of the debased and exploited position of women, which is, he realizes, a facet of capitalistic greed, class division, and the repressive force of established religion. Women suffer greatly in the fallen state and will partake fully of the happy rejuvenation of all creation that will come about in the redeemed world.

But we cannot ignore certain other aspects of Blake's treatment of women: the fact that women, as emanations, are subservient to men since they have no true existence except in the state of the division of men's psyche; and the cruel and sinister forces women often represent in Blake's myth of the fall. Furthermore, when we consider what moral and intellectual value Blake attaches to "the definite," we cannot overlook the significance of the fluidity and vagueness with which his women are customarily associated. This is not to impugn the integrity of Blake's ethical posture, but to suggest that he had personal and partly unconscious feelings about women that shaped his conception of the fall of humankind, and determined the destructive function he often gave to women.[1]

The subservient role of the emanations is often overlooked as a mere narrative and expressive device, and we are reminded that in the perfect state of Eden there will be no separation of the sexes, as there will be no class divisions:

> Los answer'd swift as the shuttle of gold: "Sexes must vanish & cease
> "To be when Albion arises from his dread repose, O lovely Enitharmon."
> *(Jerusalem* 92, 13–14:K739)[2]

However, it is in the image of man that human nature is redeemed; the female emanations are restored to the breast of man as actor and agent. The very notion of women having a separate existence is threatening. When women are united with men they live only to give them pleasure: as distinct beings, they exert a castrating influence over them:

> And Many Eternal Men sat at the golden feast to see
> The female form now separate. They shudder'd at the horrible thing
> Not born for the sport and amusement of Man, but born to drink up all
>   his powers.
> *(Four Zoas* IX, 621–23:K373)

Enitharmon says defiantly to Los in Chapter 4 of *Jerusalem* (hereafter J) that she will maintain her identity separate from him as a manifestation of rationalist authoritarianism and hypocritical chastity, a statement which has vast sinister import:

> . . . "This is Woman's World, nor need she any
> "Spectre to defend her from Man. I will Create secret places,
> "And the masculine names of the places, Merlin & Arthur,
> "A Triple Female Tabernacle for Moral Law I weave,
> "That he who loves Jesus may loathe, terrified, Female love,
> "Till God himself become a Male subservient to the Female."
> (J 88, 16–21:K733)

The argument of Los's which she rejects makes clear her ideal relationship of dependence on him:

> "How then can I ever again be united as Man with Man
> "While thou, my Emanation, refusest my Fibres of dominion?"
> (J 88, 12–13:K733)

The triple female power for destruction is enormous and frightening, and yet in her ideal relation to man, she has no capacity to bring about a fruitful change of herself. Jerusalem, lamenting her banished state, complains to Jesus:

"Shall Albion arise? I know he shall arise at the Last Day.
"I know that in my flesh I shall see God; but Emanations
Are weak, they know not whence they are nor whither tend."
(J 62, 15–17:K696)

To this Jesus replies not that Jerusalem, the most richly symbolic of the emanations, has some existential significance of her own, but merely that she should believe and trust in him.

We must consider why Blake was compelled to structure reality in the way he does. It is not sufficient to say that his characterizations of women are simply part of the intellectual system through which he gave shape to his view of history. There is a powerful antagonism behind his depictions of women, a true resentment at man's sensuous ties with women, that arises from the deeper sources of his being. If he gave this significance within his allegory, it was because his view of social reality was colored in a correspondingly hostile way.

The presence of such strong feelings of animosity toward women, as distinct from Blake's stated social and political beliefs, requires explanation. Psychoanalysis can suggest the nature of his prevailing mental state and specifically the nature of his attitude toward women. The roots of such elemental emotions must surely lie in the tensions of his early family life:

A man's worst enemies are those
Of his own house & family;
And he who makes his law a curse,
By his own law shall surely die.
(J 27, 81–84:K652)

We have little direct knowledge of Blake's childhood, his relationship with either of his parents, or their personalities. Blake does not refer to them in any extant material, and the childhood anecdotes of the nineteenth century biographies are unreliable. From these, we gather chiefly that as a young boy he had childhood visions for which on one occasion his mother beat him and on another saved him from a thrashing by his father.[3] If these are actual memories of Blake rather than biographers' readings of the visionary poet, they remain difficult to interpret without further information. Yet, in a sense, Blake never stopped talking about his parents: the cruel, jealous, authoritarian Nobodaddy-Urizen, and the destructive, imprisoning Vala-Tirzah-Enion, together with the often repeated paradigm of the cruel parents, or mother alone, binding up and torturing a baby. As well as expressing insights of social or imaginative truth, art organizes and resolves the scattered images of the unconscious mind, and thus is a rich source of information about the total self of the artist. Blake's method of giving form to his analysis of intellectual and moral decadence was determined by the material of his own psyche.

There is a strong division in Blake's emotions toward women, from feelings of hostility toward the threatening and evil female figures, to total admiration for the benevolent figures of Ololon and Jerusalem, union with whom brings about the spiritual salvation of Milton and Albion respectively. Melanie Klein's notion of "splitting" in early infancy leads to a description of these conflicting extremes. Splitting is a defensive device, employed to counteract anxiety and the child's fears of its own overwhelming feelings of aggression against its mother in a situation of frustrated desire.[4] When these emotions threaten to destroy the ego, for example in the case of withholding of food by the mother, the infant in fantasy splits the mother, or at an earlier phase of object relations, the breast, into a good and bad part. The idealized good part the infant attempts to assimilate or introject, while the hateful and bad part is projected out of the child's mental world so that it may not harm the ideal good object. Thence develops a fantasy image of a good mother and a bad mother, each an aspect of the actual mother: the infant's perception of the nurturing good mother is modified by an accompanying experience of the bad mother, who sometimes withdraws her comfort and nurture, leaving the child in a state of painful loss. The child's internal world thus constructed remains as the foundation of adult patterns of emotion: intense love conflicts with powerful impulses of hatred and destructiveness, as a result of which both love and hate are colored by guilt. Even in the most normal and happy development such tensions will be present, but where there is reason for a greater sense of rejection by the mother, the child will be overwhelmed by anger and aggression that will remain in adult relationships. Threatening women are such a powerful and insistent element in Blake's work that one must suspect a real experience of hostility toward his mother.

There are three short poems which give us pertinent information about Blake's unconscious emotional patterns in relation to his mother: the Cynic's *Song* from *An Island in the Moon,* the earliest recorded version of the cruel parents theme; and two poems from the Pickering

manuscript, *The Mental Traveller* and *The Crystal Cabinet*. What the
three poems have in common is an ever-shifting perspective on the
relationship of child and parent. The most complex of these is *The
Mental Traveller*. As the baby, the "frowning Babe" of Experience,
grows older, the mother-figure, who at the beginning of the poem was a
sadistic old woman, grows younger. The episodes incorporate the essential relationships of men with women and the ways in which these
relationships are bound up together. The anguish of babyhood, when
the child is subject to the cruelties of a threatening mother, is transformed into the pain of adulthood when the man is no less subject to
the torments of woman as mistress, which he can deal with only by
turning his aggression upon her:

> Till he becomes a bleeding youth,
> And she becomes a Virgin bright;
> Then he rends up his Manacles
> And binds her down for his delight.
> (K425)

The man becomes an old man and the cycle is completed as he pursues a
coy maiden through a harsh wilderness: the true relationship is re-
established as he becomes again a baby and she an old woman who nails
him down upon the Rock. The compensatory aggression of the male
toward women as a result of maternal rejection or cruelty is less constant and less effective than his fundamental experience of her malicious
torment of him.

Blake's treatment of the parent-child theme reveals strong feelings of
resentment toward both father and mother. Taking his responses to the
maternal figure, it is evident that there is a great deal of aggression
toward her, and also anger at man's emotional bonds with women,
whether as mothers or lovers; in both of these relationships, an identical pattern of tormentor and victim is revealed. In the Cynic's *Song,* the
central figure is apparently a father, "Old Corruption," but several elements reveal that it is really a hybrid parent who is being referred to and
that important responses to the mother are also a theme. "Old Corruption" feeds the child "with his own milk," meaning perhaps that he is a
phallic mother[5] whose breast to the child has the aspect of a threatening
phallus. The syntax at this point of the poem is obscure but it seems
that there is an identification between "he" the male parent and "he"
the child; thus it is from both of them that the harsh mother withdraws
the nurturing breast:

3

"He call'd him surgery, & fed
  "The babe with his own milk,
"For flesh & he could ne'er agree,
  "She would not let him suck."
(K50)

The mother is referred to impersonally as "flesh," the omnipresent
element of nature. The rejected child feels anger and a sense of revenge
toward the mother, and follows through an appropriate fantasy:

4

"And this he always kept in mind,
  "And form'd a crooked knife,
"And ran about with bloody hands
  "To seek his mother's life."

5

"And as he ran to seek his mother
  "He met with a dead woman,
"He fell in love & married her,
  "A deed which is not common."
(K50)

Since he does not find but "forms" a knife, this weapon seems to be an
expression of Blake's own phallic aggression toward his mother. In fantasy, he does indeed kill her, since she is the dead woman, thus acting
out his anger, and in the same act fulfills his concomitant Oedipal
desire for her by marrying her, or making her a passive victim of his
erotic aggression.[6] The poem concludes with the son, now a father,
tying down his own diseased offspring and experimentally cutting holes
in him in order to reveal the child's guts. Several passages in the later
poetry reveal Blake's morbid fear of his entrails or "veiny pipes" breaking free from the enclosing "definite outline" of his skin, an element
which contributes to the horror of the birth of Enitharmon: the butcher-
surgeon father threatens him with bodily disintegration, cruelty which
is in turn an aspect of the poet's own wish to inflict pain.

The Crystal Cabinet subdues feelings of anger and aggressiveness
toward women and deals rather with the relationship that gives rise to
them. In adult relations with women the free and autonomous male,
dancing in the wild, is imprisoned by a beguiling mistress and locked in
a crystal cabinet which expresses at the same time the encircling prison
of the womb or dependence upon women which is both desired and

resented, and, in its crystalline nature, what Blake feels to be the sexual
frigidity and lack of any change or living response in the dominant
female. Within the cabinet he sees the world only through the split
three-level perspective of fallen nature, since the overbearing female's
withholding erotic gratification is associated with the power of the
female will. The male's attempt to grasp the essence of the "threefold"
reality results in his breaking out of his prison, the hated and desired
womb, to the total isolation of the baby apart from his mother:

> A weeping Babe upon the wild,
> And Weeping Woman pale reclin'd,
> And in the outward air again
> I fill'd with woes the passing Wind.
> (K430)

Although the mother is present here she is physically separate from the
child and also suffering in this emotional wilderness, yet unable to
restore the bond of love. As both children and infants, males are subject
to the power of women, agonized whether trapped within the circle of
their cruelties or cast outside overwhelmed with loss.

A recurrent, almost obsessive, pattern in Blake, partly emergent in
the Cynic's *Song*, is that of the cruel parents binding or torturing a
child. One of the earliest examples is Tiriel's description of his own
childhood, a paradigm of human experience, which has brought him to
his reptilean old age:

> The child springs from the womb; the father stands ready to form
> The infant head, while the mother idle plays with her dog on her couch:
> The young bosom is cold for lack of mother's nourishment, & milk
> Is cut off from the weeping mouth: with difficulty & pain
> The little lids are lifted & the little nostrils open'd:
> The father forms a whip to rouse the sluggish senses to act
> And scourges off all youthful fancies from the new-born man.
> (*Tiriel*, 25–31:K110)

The infant, who leaps like a fiend into the dangerous world and sulks
upon his mother's breast bound in swaddling bands by his father in
Infant Sorrow is met again many times. The cruel parents of the *Songs of
Experience* transmit to the child the repressive force of church and state
but are themselves the most painful embodiment of it. The sad state of
the lost or tormented children of Experience is returned to later as an
image of human despair:

> Humanity is become
> A weeping Infant in ruin'd lovely Jerusalem's folding Cloud.
> (J 81, 13–14:K724)

In the first night of the *Four Zoas,* Enion gives woeful birth to two children who "wept upon the desolate wind" (I 192:K269) and then "sulk upon her breast" (I 211:K270), later to wander away so that she must seek for them in vain.

Each of the parents has a distinct function in the torture of the child. The father usually binds the child, first in the shade of a myrtle tree in the early drafts of *Little Boy Lost* in the Notebook, a theme which develops into the complexities of Urizen's chaining of the serpent Orc beneath the tree of mystery in the later epics. In both *Little Boy Lost* and the binding of Orc in the *Book of Urizen,* the mother, in the latter case Enitharmon, aids the father in binding and tormenting the child. In *The Mental Traveller,* the mother's specific form of cruelty is explored: she pierces the child and cuts him, an activity which in the fully-fledged state of the theme in the epics appears as the cruel and malicious delight of the women who violate with knives Luvah, the eternal form of Orc.

What this repeated pattern of images suggests about Blake's unconscious emotional state is that he had experienced destructive feelings toward his parents. As a result of infantile frustrations, the child builds up feelings of anger and hatred toward the parents which produce an unbearable burden of guilt. Guilt and fear are then dealt with by being projected into an image of parents who are themselves cruel and threatening,[7] such as a castrating mother. Where the pattern of parental cruelty is as insistent as it is in Blake, it probably points to actual and specific harshness on the part of the parents. A way of resolving hostility toward cruel parents can be found in Night the Ninth of the *Four Zoas* (hereafter FZ) when Tharmas and Enion, the "parent powers," are reduced to the state of immature children, ineffectual in the social sphere. They are hence rendered safe and robbed of their threatening presence.

A related set of images is that of the lost children in the *Songs of Innocence and Experience,* and in the earlier Notebook versions of those poems. Melanie Klein states that among children in analysis she frequently found fantasies of being lost or turned out of the home.[8] These she interpreted as manifestations of the children's anxiety about unconscious aggression or about harm they had actually done. The children experienced guilt for angry feelings toward parents and siblings which they converted into fantasies of aggression against themselves in order to contain them. Applied to Blake, this poetic theme could perhaps have its source in violent childhood feelings which were repressed and converted into an image of loss and desolation.

One of the most monstrous embodiments of evil in Blake is the hermaphrodite. The hybrid male-female form is often a dragon and is associated with the violent passions of love and war. There are two types of hermaphrodite, the female hidden within a male and the even more threatening male hidden within a female, who is the dragonlike Rahab or Babylon:

> -these are the Female Males,
> A Male within a Female hid as in an Ark & Curtains.
> Abraham, Moses, Solomon, Paul, Constantine, Charlemaine,
> Luther: these Seven are the Male Females, the Dragon Forms,
> The Female hid within a Male; thus Rahab is reveal'd,
> Mystery, Babylon the Great, the Abomination of Desolation,
> Religion hid in War, a Dragon red & hidden Harlot.
>
> (J 75, 14–20:K716)

Earlier the shadow of Milton is said to be hermaphroditic, usually interpreted as a version of the Selfhood, or the self-centered fusion of subject and object.[9] The hermaphrodite is far from being a combination of male and female qualities in a positive sense, which one might have imagined is what Blake meant in saying that in Eden "sexes must vanish & cease to be." The composite form is an image of the union of the parents, the fantasy of which reduces the child to impotence and envy.[10] An earlier version of a hermaphrodite shows the actual copulation of Enion and the Spectre of Tharmas:

> a bright wonder, [that] Nature [shudder'd at]
> Half Woman & Half Spectre; all his lovely changing colours mix
> With her fair crystal clearness; in her lips & cheeks his poisons rose
> In blushes like the morning, and his scaly armour softening,
> A monster lovely in the heavens or wandering on the earth.
>
> (FZ I, 183–87:K269)

The most frightening aspects of the female males and of the male females are ultimately associated with female power. The male hidden in a female, or in the female will, is concealed in the forbidden holy ark of sexuality. The male females are male-lawgivers, related to Urizen, and at the same time are dragons, possessing all the aspects of the phallic mother who in turn has incorporated the father's power. The child's sense of powerlessness is felt in the unyielding authoritarian figure that emerges, the father's power redoubled by association with the mother's, and the mother's deep roots in nature and sexuality producing an aura of impregnable mystery. The composite monster is associated by extension with the sense of society's aggression toward the individual, which has feelings of parental mystery and authority at the heart of it, "Religion hid in War." The child's own feelings of aggression toward the parents are transformed into the hybrid monster and then in turn directed against the threat that monster poses to the social order.

In the second book of *Milton* (hereafter M), Blake makes a statement of the theme of his poem that might be taken as the essential theme of all his later poetry:

> that . . . I might write all these Visions
> To display Nature's cruel holiness, the deceits of Natural Religion.
> (M 36, 24–25:K527)

Each of the elements he selects for censure here—the realm of nature; its cruelty and forbidden mysteries; and the rationalisation or "female will" associated with the philosophers of Natural Religion—has a specifically feminine context. Fear and awe of women is the dominant emotion behind Blake's critique of society. Even the cold mechanistic power of Urizen is ultimately subsumed into the Female Will, and no male figure in the poetry is capable of the range and subtlety of cruelty that often characterises the women. Apart from Urizen, the male figures suffer while female figures in the fallen state are often active principles of evil. The mother against whom Blake feels such rage for the frustration of love and desire exerts her influence in every aspect of his experience: in her withholding of maternal comfort; in her withholding of sexual gratification which for the adult male is the counterpart of maternal consolation; and in her associated suppression of sensuous response to the natural world, which is an extension of herself.

Some of the sketches and illustrations Blake made in the manuscript of the *Four Zoas,* partly erased and never intended for public view, make clear the quality of his feelings toward women.[11] Some of the most striking of these illustrations are grouped together on page 26. The text which accompanies them describes Luvah sealed up in the furnaces of Affliction, whose flames Vala "fed in cruel delight." The relationship of Luvah and Vala embraces the ambivalence of the male's relationship with females: she is wife, mistress, mother, and child. Luvah recalls how he walked with her "in bliss in times of innocence and joy," and then how she began life as an earthworm whom he nurtured until she became a serpent and then a dragon:

>   she grew
> "A scaled Serpent, yet I fed her tho' she hated me;
> "Day after day she fed upon the mountains in Luvah's sight,
> "I brought her through the Wilderness, a dry & thirsty land,

"And I commanded springs to rise for her in the black desart,
"Till she became a Dragon, winged, bright & poisonous."
(FZ II, 84–89:K282)

The process is repeated at the human level as Vala becomes a child in relation to Luvah, a child whom he nurtures until she is able to bear his children. The one relationship that is not mentioned is the mother-son relationship, and yet the overall feeling of the situation is that Vala is a cruel mother, an impression built up by her general role in the *Four Zoas,* the paradigm of the cruel mother in the Notebook versions of the *Songs of Innocence and Experience* and in *The Mental Traveller,* and Vala's role of a repressive parent echoing that of Urizen binding down Orc beneath the Tree of Mystery. The fundamental relationship, that of the mother and son, is here suppressed because Blake had so many tensions about it which he displaced instead into symbolic expression.

The illustrations on the page bear this out.[12] The most striking is an ornate dragon form with serpentine undulations. With her three breasts she can be associated with the Great Mother of mythology, but her malevolent characteristics and phallic lower breast align her more exactly with the threatening mother of Freudian and neo-Freudian theory who, in the eyes of the child, has such power over the potent and nurturing breast. The figure above this is a bird of prey with a hooked beak and an enlarged vagina. The legs are ambivalent, being scaly like those of a dragon but, in that there are two, being birdlike and suggesting the devouring chicken mother of folklore.[13] The other two sketches depict the female in two stages of growing into the threatening dragon: the upper one is a girl child with butterfly wings, malicious in her prettiness, and the lower one a woman with dragon wings. In all is implicit the recurrent theme of the phallic worm becoming a dragon, or Blake's own phallic forces turning against him as a menacing and overwhelming monster. These drawings are not amusingly scurrilous as they are sometimes regarded, but expressions of a deep obsession with an overpowering mother-figure, made plain by the perverted features of the enlarged vagina and phallic breast. In these private sketches Blake depicts in unaccustomed detail the images which disturbed him, images which nevertheless have some counterparts in his finished engravings.[14]

The essence of Blake's expressed criticism of women is their capacity to withhold erotic satisfaction from men. The women in *Visions of the Daughters of Albion* have been deprived of the possibility of sensual fulfillment, a painful state necessarily shared also by men. In the later

poetry women more often withdraw from sexuality, thus being associated with forbidding social forces instead of sharing the role of victim
with men. In the prophecy section of Europe, Enitharmon speaks in
her role of Virgin Goddess who is to be worshipped throughout the
Christian era:

> "Go! tell the Human race that Women's love is Sin;
> "That an Eternal life awaits the worms of sixty winters
> "In an allegorical abode where existence hath never come.
> "Forbid all Joy, & from her childhood shall the little female
> "Spread nets in every secret path."
>
> (*Europe*, 5, 5–9:K240)

She establishes a reign of repressive chastity, in which the male is
reduced to helpless impotence. The image of a man in the totality of his
life experience as a "worm of sixty winters" is found frequently, for
instance at the end of *Tiriel*. It expresses the notion of man as a phallic
form deprived of all strength or power to act, and when associated with
the recurrent idea of the worm as a child in the womb—

> Yet helpless it lay like a Worm
> In the trembling womb
> To be moulded into existence.
> (*Urizen*, 19, 21–23: K232)

—it includes each phase of a man's life in relation to women, from his
subjection to his mother as an infant to the adult version of the same
experience where he is bound sensually to a chaste virginal woman.
This state of deprivation is intimately connected with the other evils
that accrue to man: he lives in an "allegorical abode," namely the state
of memory and the closed-up senses where all contact with higher
forms of living is impossible. Thus a man's fear and frustration under
woman's domination are the cause of his intellectual stultification and
sense of separation from his living surroundings, referred to as the
Female Will.

Furthermore, in this cruel chastity, or maternal rejection on the part
of women, lies the essential "mystery" which is universally hated in
Blake. The little females who "spread nets in every secret path" are one
version of a prevalent notion, that of women's power associated with
what is shadowy and secret. The essential, hated secret is the genital
nature of women—

> "Why a little curtain of flesh on the bed of our desire?"
> (*Thel* 6, 20:K130)

which is endowed with an aura of worship by the frustrated male:

> "—the youth shut up from
> "The lustful joy shall forget to generate & create an amorous
>   image
> "In the shadows of his curtains and in the folds of his silent
>   pillow."
>   (*Visions of the Daughters of Albion* 7, 5–7:K194)

The feeling of mystery and secrecy arises from the taboo which sur-
rounds the female genitalia and the place of parturition. The word
"holy" extends to an object of fascination which is both desired and
feared, wrapped in delightful secrecy.[15] Therefore the "mystery" which
Blake abhors in all of its forms is what is loved and wished for but, since
possession of the mother and, in her image, of other women, is forbidden by a powerful taboo, the consequent rage and sense of deprivation
can be dealt with only as a hatred which encompasses all of nature. The
fearful holiness which is a frustrated object of desire is alluded to also in
the image of the female tabernacle ("A triple Female Tabernacle for
Moral law I weave" [K733]); the longed for and forbidden possession
of the mother is converted into a hated and menacing womb which
stifles and sets up moralistic barriers.

One method of dealing with the fear of the enclosing womb is the
process by which Los's emanation, Enitharmon, is born, an anguished
parody of normal parturition from the mother:

> "My loins begin to break forth into veiny pipes & I saw writhe
> "Before me in the wind englobing, trembling with strong vibrations
> "The bloody mass began to animate. I, bending over,
> "Wept bitter tears incessant. Still beholding how the piteous form
> "Dividing & dividing from my loins, a weak & piteous
> "Soft cloud of snow, a female pale & weak, I soft embrac'd
> "My counter part & call'd it Love."
>   (FZ IV, 94–100:K300)

The process begins with a partial disintegration of Los's circumference
of identity. The womblike globe of blood is associated with the circle
and other limited and imprisoning forms, such as the crystal cabinet
and the sun of generation, which pose a threat to man unless he can
control them, here by giving hideous birth to a weak and vulnerable
woman. Similarly, in *Milton* Los maintains tight control over his own
imaginative life by re-creating every day "The red Globule of the un-
wearied Sun. . . " (M I, 29, 23:K517).

Blake's fundamental state is one of anxiety about the disintegration of his physical being. What he describes as the predicament of contemporary man, with his atrophied senses and distorted three-fold vision, is first of all an urgent portrayal of his own mental condition, as the exaltation at the renewal of the unity of the senses expressed at the end of *Milton* and *Jerusalem* is Blake's own. The source of this intense anxiety is a conflict in the child-mother relationship. Blake's most unequivocal address to a threatening maternal figure, or the bad mother, is *To Tirzah,* an addition to the *Songs of Experience.* The cruel mother is responsible not only for the oppressive domination of the male child, but for the very stultification of the senses which Blake focuses upon as the essential evil of his culture:

> Thou, Mother of my Mortal part,
> With cruelty didst mould my Heart,
> And with false self-decieving tears
> Didst bind my Nostrils, Eyes, & Ears:
>
> Didst close my Tongue in senseless clay,
> And me to Mortal Life betray.
> The Death of Jesus set me free:
> Then what have I to do with thee?
>   (K220)

This she does by cutting the child off from spontaneous joy in nature, which is a repetition of the blissful state she herself had provided and withdrawn during the child's infancy. The senses become deadened when the child is unable to make sensuous contact with the mother, who by extension is all the material of nature. As a defence against the loss of what is most desired, hatred is directed against the loved substance of nature and the senses atrophy. This produces an experience of separation from the physical world which leads Blake to deny the world of nature. He expresses scorn for the "natural vision" of Wordsworth's poetry, since, he contends, the only true insight is within the imagination:

> I see in Wordsworth the Natural Man rising up
> against the Spiritual Man Continually, & then he is
> No Poet but a Heathen Philosopher at Enmity
> against all true Poetry or Inspiration.
>   (K782)

The realm of nature, or generation, is split off from the true vision of the imagination.

Blake's resistance to nature was an unusual one among his contempo-

raries. We might view the absorption of the Romantic poets in the
sensuous apprehension of nature, or the later eighteenth-century interest in landscape painting, which Blake despised, as a manifestation of
the need to heal the breach between human beings and the rest of
creation. In terms which Blake would heartily support, the self in the
early industrial era feels a sense of loss and pain as a result of the
deadening effect of mechanistic thinking applied to many aspects of
life. What Blake would not agree with is that the essence of the loss lies
in separation from the enduring natural order. He believes that what
must come about is a renewal of all human capacities, both sensory and
mental, within the existing psyche, whereas the tendency of some of his
contemporaries is to reestablish a union with nature, by being absorbed
in, and also taking into the self, fundamental natural impulses.[16] For
some, this is a necessary stage in developing personal strength: Blake
will not acknowledge his need of an outside agency which represents
the withdrawn, and therefore hated, maternal love.

At the beginning of the second book of *Milton* Blake gives an unusual
portrayal of the infant's blissful narcissistic union with its mother as an
image of the joyful state of Beulah:

> But Beulah to its Inhabitants appears within each district
> As the beloved infant in its mother's bosom round incircled
> With arms of love & pity & sweet compassion.
> $\qquad$ (M 30, 10–12:K518)

This is an integrated picture of the relationship with the good mother,
which appears as an evanescent ideal at several points in Blake's art as a
contrast to the much more powerful and overwhelming image of the
threatening and destructive mother. This reference to the happy infant
in its mother's bosom is followed by a passage which creates a tangible
experience of natural beauty exceptional in Blake after the early period
of the *Poetical Sketches*. It begins with a description of the song of the
lark, who draws together the disparate realms of the poem and is to lead
Blake back to London with the new wisdom and strength of Felpham:

> Mounting upon the wings of light into the Great Expanse,
> Reechoing against the lovely blue & shining heavenly Shell
> His little throat labours with inspiration; every feather
> On throat & breast & wings vibrates with the effluence Divine.
> $\qquad$ (M 31, 32–35:K520)

This release from hostility toward maternal protection is continued in
an evocation of flowers which recreates their presence:

. . . . first the Wild Thyme
And Meadow-sweet, downy & soft waving among the reeds,
Light springing on the air, lead the sweet Dance: they wake
The Honeysuckle sleeping on the Oak; the flaunting beauty
Revels along upon the wind; the White-thorn, lovely May,
Opens her many lovely eyes listening; the Rose still sleeps,
None dare to wake her; soon she bursts her crimson curtain'd bed
And comes forth in the majesty of beauty.

                                    (M 31, 51–58:K520)

The flowers are instinct with a sense of feminine sexuality, seen from the
male point of view, especially the rose which, in bursting her "crimson
curtain'd beauty" displays her erotic openness to men. The image of
sexually provocative women, usually regarded as threatening to male
integrity, is here indulged by Blake in his state of harmonious acceptance of the fundamental relationship.

Another version of the association of nature and maternal power is
found in Night the First of the *Four Zoas,* when Enion, after her copulation with the spectre of Tharmas, gives painful birth to two children,
Los and Enitharmon. Enion, who is to become the aged mother wandering in search of her lost children, is shown to have mysterious com-
plicity with nature on account of her power of parturition:

Enion brooded o'er the rocks; the rough rocks groaning vegetate.
Such power was given to the Solitary wanderer.

                                    (FZ I, 202–3:K269)

The effect of Enion's brooding is to make the bark of trees break open,
whereupon small birds emerge and other aspects of nature surround the
human children to give them strength and protection:

. . . twittering peep forth little beaks & wings,
The Nightingale, the Goldfinch, Robin, Lark, Linnet & Thrush.
The Goat leap'd from the craggy cliff, the Sheep awoke from the mould,
Upon its green stalk rose the Corn, waving innumerable,
Infolding the bright Infants from the desolating winds.

                                    (FZ I, 206–10:K270)

Later, however, Blake chose to delete this entire reference to Enion's
power within nature. It was not, like the image of mother and infant in
the state of Beulah, an acknowledgement of the good and loving mother;
the link between mother and nature is seen to be distorted and to carry
an incipient threat. Yet the healing effect of nature was still maintained.
In the version which Blake later settled on this view of nature is suppressed: Enion is the lonely and deserted mother condemned to seek
her scornful children in despair;

They sulk upon her breast, her hair became like snow on mountains:
Weaker & weaker, weeping woful, wearier & wearier,
Faded, & her bright Eyes decay'd, melted with pity & love.
And then they wander'd far away, she sought for them in vain:
In weeping blindness, stumbling, she follow'd them o'er rocks &
    mountains . . .

(FZ I, 211–15:K270)

The children of Experience had created the state of being lost as an image of the haunting fear that their parents would desert them because of their own aggression toward them: now they turn deeper hatred and vengeance against the parents. The mother-figure's possessive power is controlled as she is condemned to total suffering, bereft of all hope or consolation.

Although the overwhelming weight of emphasis in Blake's poetry is upon women who are destructive, threatening, and representative of social ills, there are of course several female figures who stand for what is good, positive and creative, embodiments of the good mother and her nurturing love. Enitharmon in some of her manifestations has this function, but is also subject to conflicting emotions about the role of wife and mother. The purest versions of the good mother are Ololon and Jerusalem, the emanations respectively of Milton and Albion, two male figures with whom Blake identifies but from whom he is more distanced than from Los, Enitharmon's consort. The poems *Milton* and *Jerusalem* each end with the mystical union of Milton and Albion with their emanations, whereupon a tremendous outburst of energy and release is experienced. Blake assimilates the qualities of the good mother and is restored, at the end of *Milton,* to a joyful union with nature, and at the end of *Jerusalem* to vividly awakened sense experience. The sense of salvation comes from the dissipation of the inability to make contact with his natural surroundings, an incapacity which the threatening mother produces in him. More fundamentally there is a release from his own destructive feelings of aggression toward her. The ultimate emotional necessity is not to destroy the source of nurture but to be reunited with it. The forms of the male figures united with their emanations have nothing of the monstrous union of the hermaphrodites. The normal perspective of men and women is restored. But the implication is that the females have now returned to the male bosom and have ceased to be threatening because they no longer have independent existence. Women are benevolent only if they are under male domination.

NOTES

1. It is often acknowledged that there are problems in reconciling Blake's negative images of women with his view of them as social beings: see David Erdman, *Prophet Against Empire,* revised edition (New York: Doubleday, 1969), pp. 253–54. Irene Taylor ("The Woman Scale," *Bulletin of the Mid West Modern Language Association,* 6 [1973], 74–87) argues that the temporal divisions between men and women vanish in the eternal form of the unified human being. Susan Fox ("The Female as Metaphor in William Blake's Poetry," *Critical Inquiry,* 3 [1977], 507–19) states that we must recognize and accept both Blake's metaphoric use of women, with its tendencies to abstractness, and his concrete social observations. D. Aers ("William Blake and the Dialectics of Sex," *ELH,* 44 [1977], 500–14), in a Marxist analysis, finds that, while Blake presents an ideal response to oppressive society in the person of Oothoon in *VDA,* he later portrays women more realistically when they adopt the Female Will as a strategy for survival. Diana Hume George ("Is She also the Divine Image? Feminine Form in the Art of William Blake," *Centennial Review,* 23 [Spring 1979], 129–40 and *Blake and Freud* [Ithaca, N.Y. & London: Cornell University Press, 1980] considers that Blake sees the feminine as part of the perfection of human nature, although in the fallen state women are the vehicles and victims of repression. George acknowledges that the notion of the Female Will is paradoxically close to abstraction. I will argue that the dichotomy has its roots in Blake's personality and probably is not completely resolved artistically.

2. Quotations from Blake are taken from *Blake: Complete Writings,* ed. Geoffrey Keynes (London: Oxford University Press, 1966), hereafter referred to in the text as K.

3. G. E. Bentley, Jr., *Blake Records* (Oxford: Clarendon Press, 1969), pp. 519 and 7.

4. Hanna Segal, *Introduction to the Work of Melanie Klein* (London: The Hogarth Press and the Institute of Psycho-Analysis, 1973), pp. 3–5 and 27–30. (Although not written by Melanie Klein, this study by a colleague is the standard exposition of her theories, otherwise scattered through her work.)

5. Jean Hagstrum, in "Babylon Revisited, or the Story of Luvah and Vala," in Stuart Curran and Joseph Anthony Wittreich eds., *Blake's Sublime Allegory* (Madison, Wis.: University of Wisconsin Press, 1973), discusses versions of the phallic woman theme in Blake's more mature work (pp. 108–10), but does not see this motif as having its source in Blake's own personality.

6. Melanie Klein's view of the Oedipus complex is essentially the same as Freud's with the important difference that in her theory it begins to develop at a much earlier stage of childhood, Segal, *Melanie Klein*, pp. 103–16.

7. Segal, *Melanie Klein*, pp. 5–6, and p. 56; Melanie Klein and Joan Riviere, *Love, Hate and Reparation* (New York: W. W. Norton, 1964), pp. 109–10.

8. Klein and Riviere, *Love, Hate*, p. 109.

9. Northrop Frye, *Fearful Symmetry* (1947: rpt. Boston: Beacon Press, 1962), pp. 135, 172.

10. Segal, *Melanie Klein*, pp. 107–8.

11. The drawings are reproduced in G. E. Bentley's *Vala; or, The Four Zoas* (Oxford: Clarendon Press, 1963). John E. Grant discusses them in detail in "Visions in Vala: A Consideration of Some Pictures in the Manuscript," in Curran and Wittreich ed., *Sublime Allegory*, pp. 141–202, basing his comments upon infra-red photographs of the manuscript.

12. These drawings are discussed by Grant, "Visions in Vala," pp. 153–160, and by Christine Gallant, *Blake's Assimilation of Chaos* (Princeton: Princeton University Press, 1978), p. 61.

13. The Russian cannibalistic ogress Baba Yaga, one of the transformations of the devouring witch who lives in a little house in the forest (Vladimir Propp, *Morphologie du Conte*, trans. Marguerite Derrida [Paris: Editions du Seuil, 1965], pp. 106–7) is characterized by the chicken legs on which her house stands. The house itself is one of the forms of the imprisoning mother.

14. Grant, "Visions in Vala," pp. 159–60, gives parallels in the engraved works.

15. Compare Hagstrum, "Babylon Revisited," pp. 113–14.

16. See, for instance, Stuart A. Ende, *Keats and the Sublime* (New Haven, Conn. & London: Yale University Press, 1976), pp. xv–xvi.

SIX

RECONSTRUCTION OF THE SELF IN WORDSWORTH'S "ODE: INTIMATIONS OF IMMORTALITY FROM RECOLLECTIONS OF EARLY CHILDHOOD"

FREDERICK KIRCHHOFF

The gap of "two years at least"[1] between the composition of the first four stanzas and the remainder of Wordsworth's "Ode: Intimations of Immortality" argues that the poem should be read as a problem and its solution. The problem is that of completing the poem—of Words-worth's finding a way to write himself out of the corner in which he places himself at line fifty-seven; its solution, the myth of pre-existence, loss, and recovery that organizes stanzas five through eleven. To this much, I think, most readers of the poem would agree. But readers are less inclined to agree on just how the myth in fact solves the problem of closure—just how the poem's glorification of "Early Childhood" en-ables Wordsworth to substantiate the "philosophic mind" (line 187) in which both the logical and emotional dynamics of the poem ultimately come to rest.

In a recent essay, Michael Friedman argued that "the question of how to establish a stable identity was Wordsworth's dilemma of self."[2] Work-ing with the postulates of ego psychology, he outlined a conflict in Wordsworth's personality between what he termed "the princely sense of self"—an experience of mastery over and, at times, merger with the outside world—and the "contracted" self—an experience of separation from nature in which "the outside world . . . began to seem unreal." Friedman attributed these opposing states to a single source: Wordsworth's failure to develop a stable identity, secure "in relation to what is not the self."[3] I maintain that it is in terms of this failure—hence, need—to develop a stable identity that the "Ode: Intimations of Immortality" should be read, and that the formal difficulty of bringing the poem to closure and the psychological difficulty of evolving a coherent adult self are two aspects of the same problem.

It can be argued that the poem resists completion because Wordsworth was unable to face the Oedipal conflict underlying his own rejection of the "Immortality" that "Broods" over the child as "a Master o'er a slave" (lines 119–20); and that lines 58–204 constitute an elaborate strategy through which Wordsworth, by reversing the roles of child and father and becoming, ultimately, a parent rejected by the child figures of his own poem, transforms Oedipal guilt into tragic vision. I do not wish to reject this reading of the ode. However, I would like to suggest, as an alternative to its reliance on the model of Oedipal conflict, a reading based on Heinz Kohut's psychology of the self. For the notion of narcissistic adequacy central to Kohut's theory not only explains the poem, but, insofar as its text is a fragment of the poet's evolving self, does so within the logic of the poem itself.

The breakdown Wordsworth faces in the opening stanzas resembles a crucial stage in the process to which Kohut attributes the development of the self—the recognition that external selfobjects can no longer perform their selfobject function.[4] Parents are the child's ordinary selfobjects. As the child begins to experience disappointment with aspects of these idealized figures, their positive aspects are—under favorable circumstances—introjected in the form of internal structures able to perform the functions formerly performed by the selfobjects (e.g., providing a sense of self-esteem). This process, which Kohut calls "transmuting internalization," is not limited to childhood development. It is, he maintains, characteristic of the latter stages of the psychoanalytic treatment of narcissistic personality disorders, when elements of primal narcissism, reactivated in the course of analysis, are withdrawn from the analyst. Extending this concept, transmuting internalization offers a general model for human behavior: the pattern of merging with objects or persons and subsequently internalizing aspects of those objects or persons as structures of the self accounts, at least in part, for the continuous, lifelong transformation of the self. Thus, the notion accounts, on the one hand, for the epochal events of childhood and psychoanalytic recovery and, on the other, for an area of human experience less dramatic than these extremes: the adult's attempts to deal with less than pathological narcissistic inadequacies—like the insecure, incompletely developed "sense of identity" Friedman attributes to Wordsworth.

This is not the place for a detailed examination of Wordsworth's psychological development. The relevant events appear to be the death of his mother just a month before the boy's eighth birthday and, four years later, the death of his father. In the years following his mother's death, Wordsworth lived with his grandparents—whom he disliked—and saw his father only on holidays. It was a period of unhappiness for the boy, who at one point seems to have contemplated suicide and at another attacked a family portrait with a whip.[5] In his extended analysis of Wordsworth's autobiography, Richard Onorato argues that Wordsworth, because of the need to deny the loss of his mother, persisted in "the fantasy of unimpaired possession of the mother 'within' him, and, in her projected form, around him as the Presence in Nature"; and that "his special sense of the power of a Poet derives from the enormous power of fantasy originally associated with his mother's permissiveness, now felt by projection as Nature's permissiveness."[6] Onorato perceives this fantasy as an Oedipal regression. However, his link between the power of the poet (that is, the adult self Wordsworth sought to affirm) and the power with which he invests the natural world suggests a simpler explanation: that, at least in the text of *The Prelude,* Nature assumes the narcissistic role of the missing parent; and that its power derives not from the experience of the mother's permissiveness but from the selfobject idealization that the traumatic loss of or separation from his parents precluded him from internalizing in transmuted form. The archaic wish to merge with an omnipotent selfobject thus remains a force in Wordsworth's adult behavior, attached in this instance to Nature—just as, in what Kohut termed the "idealizing transference," the archaic wish for selfobject merger can become attached to the analyst of a narcissistically enfeebled patient.[7]

Wordsworth continued to experience states of archaic grandiosity both as a child and, less frequently, as an adult. The childhood symptoms, as he reported them to Isabella Fenwick near the end of his life, included "a sense of the indomitableness of the spirit within me," accompanied by "a feeling congenial to this" that is clearly akin to primal narcissism: "I was often unable to think of external things as having external existence, and I communed with all that I saw as something not apart from, but inherent in, my own immaterial nature."[8] The point is not that Wordsworth was trapped in this state, but that he experienced it within the period of conscious memory and thus lived with the conscious recollection of acute loss. He sought to repair this loss by cultivating a form of meditation on landscape that (temporarily) restored the archaic experience of power. (His ability to accomplish this is the subject of "Lines Composed a Few Miles above Tintern Abbey.") He appears, in other words, to have had difficulty withdrawing from and internalizing the omnipotence with which he had invested the natural world, and was only able to experience a powerful self by regression to an archaic selfobject relationship.

This predicament would seem to be inherent in the selfobject identification with nature. For the natural world is not, under normal circumstances, a discrete entity with which the developing self is able to engage in a manner comparable to its engagement with (and disengagement from) fellow human beings. Its radical otherness blocks the identification of the self with its idealized projections that would, in turn, ground the recognition of less than radical differences. And it is precisely the recognition of less than radical differences that enables transmuting internalization to occur.

But there is a context in which the natural world functions as a discrete entity and in which the identity of self and its natural object are possible—the context of the written word: of the poem itself. For language is a medium in which the role of nature, both as the expression of the boy's omnipotence and—less satisfactorily—as a mirror of his exhibitionist grandiosity, assumes objective status. Moreover, written language is also a medium in which the self and its object can interact. It is here, then, that Wordsworth is able to undertake a controlled regression to his earlier experience, with the hope—or intuition—that he will be able to internalize elements of his own primal narcissism and thus strengthen his adult self.

The opening stanzas of the "Ode: Intimations of Immortality" dramatize the dilemma of recovering narcissistic energy from a natural world the otherness of which seems to deny the human origin of its potency. The poem begins at the point at which the role of nature as selfobject has begun to break down. The poet, in a state of narcissistic inadequacy, attempts to compensate for it by selfobject participation in the natural world conceived as a literary subject, but nature refuses to cooperate. Instead, through the experience of writing a text that denies this participation, the poet is forced to recognize that nature is something other than and therefore unresponsive to the self. This recognition is a necessary stage in his advance to psychic and intellectual maturity. However, because the poet fails to internalize the potency with which he has invested the world when he experienced it as a selfobject—because he fails to recognize that the authority and significance he saw in nature was in fact his own authority and significance— his recognition of discontinuity is as yet only a confrontation with loss. He lacks confidence in himself and in his own power as a human being—specifically, he lacks confidence in his own power as a poet and therefore his ability to bring the poem to closure.

For this reason, the formal inadequacy of the opening stanzas is not their reflection of a natural world that has become repetitious, but their reflection of a repetitious circularity in the poet's expressive mode. The only way he is able to write verse, it would seem, is an inadequate manifestation of the self. One senses this inadequacy in the sing-song quality of stanza two:

> The Rainbow comes and goes,
> And lovely is the Rose,
> The Moon doth with delight
> Look round her when the heavens are bare;
> Waters on a starry night
> Are beautiful and fair . . .

> (10–15)

Instead of offering him the coherence of landscape, as it has in his earlier poetry, Nature has fragmented into unrelated parts—the rainbow, the rose, the moon, the waters on a starry night.[9] These images are the counters of lyric poetry, but not its organizing vision, and as items in a list are unable to mirror the complex totality of the poet's self. Mired in this conventionalized poetic diction, Wordsworth would seem to lack the self-assurance needed to mold language to his own purposes.

Underlying this inadequacy, however, is a counter-effort to reaffirm the self by recapitulating an even earlier stage of infant development. The poem begins with attempts to differentiate the self from its prior experience of the natural world; that is, it begins by postulating time as a means of differentiating the self from a past self or selves. In stanza three this pattern is replaced by an analogous spatial differentiation of self from other within the present. These gestures suggest Wordsworth's effort to ground the poem in the fundamental material of being. However, the perspective of these lines is not the child's but the adult's. Their repetitive structure is at odds with the needs of the mature poet working in a sophisticated literary form. Consequently, the poet is trapped in a pattern of simple alternation between past and present, external and internal moods. He is able only to differentiate. The self is determined through its denials rather than its assimilations.

The one break in this seesaw pattern is telling:

> A timely utterance gave that thought relief,
> And I again am strong; . . .
>
> (23–24)

Strength, not understanding ("thought") is the object of Wordsworth's desire. And strength lies in the gesture of utterance. The self is "strong" insofar as it verbalizes its thoughts, but the relationship of thought to language is not necessarily mimetic. Language gives "relief" to thought. Wordsworth might have written "release," suggesting that his problem is simply the pent-up nature of uncommunicated mental activity. He does not. However the significance of what he does instead is not itself entirely clear. Utterance may simply be an aspirin for the headache of introspection. On the other hand, it may come to the aid of introspection, an auxiliary power that enables thought to come into being (not through release, but by augmentation). In either case, writing need not imitate thinking. It is, imitative or not, something of another order—an affirmation of the "strong" self capable of action (i.e., writing) in the world. The poet who writes manifests a self; the thinker who thinks only imitates its possibility. Moreover, the poet's artifact offers a way out of the circularity of the opening stanzas of the ode. Backing away from what he has written, the poet is able to distance himself from and thus establish a new relationship with the states of mind in which he has been enmeshed. Perversely, however, Wordsworth attempts to sustain this affirmation of the self through yet another identification with the otherness of nature:

> My heart is at your festival,
> My head hath its coronal,
> The fulness of your bliss, I feel—I feel it all.
>
> (39–40)

The desperation of the attempt is clear from the hyperbolic tone of the verses, as well as from their attempt to achieve unified vision by juxtaposition rather than meaningful connection. Yet the result is not just another breakdown, but a clarification of the reasons why the natural world cannot embody the omnipotence of the poet:

> —But there's a Tree, of many, one,
> A single Field which I have looked upon, . . .
> (51–52)

The nature Wordsworth had experienced as a selfobject was a unity—Nature with a capital "N." What the poet now confronts is the fact that nature is not an indivisible whole; that it, too, can break up into individual parts. The fragmentation of the idealized selfobject is now explicit. And the recognition of its divisibility gives the final blow to the illusion of omnipotence.

This fragmentation is appropriate to the recathexis of the poet's self;[10] however, it is also a blow—although not a final one—to the ode itself. Since nature could no longer function as a selfobject, Wordsworth could no longer express himself adequately in the kind of nature poetry he had written (or attempted unsuccessfully to write) in stanzas one through four. To continue the poem, a new literary mode was necessary—a mode able to replace the authority of nature without denying the individual being of the poet; able to invest the individual experience of the poet with significance without at the same time alienating him from the source of its power. Myth, in which universal and individual experience merge, was just such a mode.

The myth of pre-existence that renews the poem's effort of self structure performs two seemingly dissimilar functions: it justifies the grandiosity of primal narcissism and it accounts for its transience. The second function needs no explanation. The first, however, may be unexpected, since its immediate effect is not to lessen but to intensify the sense of loss established by the opening stanzas. There is, one notes, a shift in the mode of treating childhood. The first four stanzas worked by differentiation rather than by assimilation. What was lost was the other. Stanza five reverses this tactic: what is lost is a temporal component of the self. The tense shift from "There was a time" (line 1) to "Our birth is but a sleep . . . " (line 58) indicates a shift from differentiation to assimilation. Moreover, the movement from individual to general experience suggests a new relationship with the past: the poet is now able to identify himself with his own past self by means of the generalizing power of language. Contrast the concluding couplets of stanzas four and five:

> Whither is fled the visionary gleam?
> Where is it now, the glory and the dream?
> (56–57)
> At length the Man perceives it die away,
> And fade into the light of common day.
> (76–77)

What is absent in the first and present in the second (in addition to the affirmative mood) is the "Man" whose perception of "it" ("the vision splendid") dying away gives substance to the lines. The "Man" is, of course, only the last of a sequence because he is most closely related to the poet. Through this figure Wordsworth is able to place himself within the text of the poem, not merely as a percipient first person, but as a third person of indisputable being. Friedman recognizes the significance of the "small child's psychic sense of his vastness and omnipotence," as well as its confirmation in the "beloved Presence" of his mother.[11] Translating these terms into Kohut's psychology of the self, they become two components of primal narcissism: the infant's grandiose exhibitionism and his identification with an idealized parent imago. Wordsworth's characterization of the child affirms grandiosity with a vengeance:

> Thou, whose exterior semblance doth belie
>   Thy Soul's immensity;
> Thou best Philosopher, who yet dost keep
> Thy heritage, . . .
> . . . .
> Mighty Prophet! Seer blest!
> (109–12, 115)

Similarly, his elevation of the mother imago into "Earth" herself (lines 78f.) represents an extreme of idealization. Nature is no longer the objective order of the natural world. It has been transformed into a mythic figure, the very being of which depends on the subjective imagination of the myth-maker. When the objective order no longer functioned as a selfobject, its radical otherness blocked transmuting internalization. There was no strong basis for an analogy between natural and human potency. On the other hand, treating nature as an anthropomorphic foster-mother establishes a paradigm for the narcissistic recathexis of the nuclear self of the poet. The relationship between poet and nature is now a quasi-human relationship and can therefore be expected to develop by the logic of human development. (Indeed, that the mother imago is now a "homely Nurse" [line 83], not a biological parent, may be a first stage in this process.)

The notable instance of internalization in the ode is Wordsworth's assumption of the role of mirroring parent in stanzas six through eight. Instead of repeating the pattern of loss, he now openly admires the condition of his own childhood. He looks at a version of his former self and so affirms his identity as a being that can be looked at. Moreover, this admiration is a fact of the poem. The text assumes the role of an otherwise missing psychic structure—the experienced sense of narcissistic power Wordsworth has hitherto failed to incorporate in his adult self. Its role is prosthetic; as such it enables Wordsworth to achieve the closure of the poem.

However, the attributes of Wordsworth's primal narcissistic self-image have a specific as well as a general function. They do not merely confirm him as a being capable of admiring himself (in retrospect); they also explain his relationship to the set of external conditions that threatened his self-esteem in the first stanzas of the ode. Again, Friedman's notion of two selves is useful. The state of mind he identifies with the contracted self is familiar to readers of Wordsworth's poetry. It is the state "when the fretful stir/ . . . and the fever of the world, / Have hung upon the beatings of my heart" ("Lines Composed a Few Miles above Tintern Abbey," 52–54); the condition of withdrawal from and therefore oppression by the external world for which the "blank confusion" of London in Book Seven of *The Prelude* is Wordsworth's extended expression. This state reappears in stanza eight of the ode:

> Full soon thy Soul shall have her earthly freight,
> And custom lie upon thee with a weight,
> Heavy as frost, and deep almost as life!
>
> (127–29)

The ruling image here—as elsewhere in Wordsworth's poetry—is one of weight, a perception of the external world as an alien order, constraining growth and upward movement. However, the tone of lines 127–29 is very different from the anxious malaise of the opening stanzas of the ode. Depression has given way to tragic vision. Recognizing his condition as a universal human experience, the poet is no longer merely a victim of his moods. He writes from a new perspective; experience enables him to predict the future, to act as the poetic spokesman for his race.

The route to this new power is the childhood self-image of stanza seven. The child playing with fragments "from his dream of human life" establishes an alternative to passive acceptance of the soul's "earthly freight." The child dominates the external world by treating it as the materials of playful self-expression. It is his "dream"; hence, reality is something conferred by the dreamer, for whom "The glory and the freshness of a dream" is evidence of the potency of the self. Wordsworth has at last been able to identify the source of the power he had alienated from himself in the opening stanzas of the poem.

For the adult poet, the "dream of human life" is language—his reconstruction of the world in the medium of verse. Thus, the power he reclaims is specifically poetic. This power manifests itself in the new relationship between self and other that characterizes the closing lines of the ode. The need to "feel" (line 41) the bliss of the natural world has been replaced by the anticipation of joining it "in thought" (line 172). "Feel" (line 175) becomes an imperative verb directed to nature itself. "Thought," i.e., self-consciousness, is the mode appropriate to mature human experience; feeling, i.e., thoughtless immediacy, is appropriate to nature. If "the meanest flower that blows can give / Thoughts that do often lie too deep for tears" (lines 204–5), it is the difference between the two orders of being, not their similarity, that comforts the poet. The lines that best define this new relationship occur in the last stanza:

> The Clouds that gather round the setting sun
> Do take a sober colouring from an eye
> That hath kept watch o'er man's mortality . . .
>
> (197–99)

Here again it is difference that gives the poet his sense of a coherent, independent self. Yet cloud and eye, nature and human awareness, meet in a perception of the natural world through which the clouds become, without losing their otherness, the means of expressing the poet's complex state of mind. Nature, in other words, is once more the poet's material.

The sing-song of "The Rainbow comes and goes"—the implicit discontinuity between the poet and his literary medium—has been replaced by a mature control of language, by the recognition that participation in language represents not a restraint, but an enlargement of the field of self. And it is in this respect that the ode is not "a poem about growing old," but, as Lionel Trilling suggests, "about growing up."[12] Wordsworth has achieved the attributes of personality Kohut identifies with healthy narcissism—creativity, the ability to be empathic, the capacity to contemplate one's own impermanence, wisdom.[13]

The significance of the conclusion of the ode is not, I admit, merely this manifestation of a secure self. It is also the set of affirmations the secure self is able to voice. Yet the "philosophy" of the conclusion is only possible through the restructuring of the self and the recovery of self-esteem. If it rings true, it is not because we have been convinced by Wordsworth's reasoning. (His "irrational" elevation of the child to "best Philosopher" has disturbed more readers of the poem than Coleridge alone.)[14] The process by which Wordsworth reaches the "philosophic mind" is more psychological than intellectual. And the poem is a satisfactory whole, regardless of whether or not we give credence to Wordsworth's vision of human destiny, because it is not Wordsworth's vision, but Wordsworth himself whose fate is the central issue of the ode.

Yet if the poem is a medium of restoring narcissistic potency, its ultimate purpose is not poetic. Or at least it does not lead to further poems of a similar nature. Wordsworth continued to write until he died, forty-six years after completing "Ode: Intimations of Immortality." But the decline of his poetic power during these last years of his life is a noteworthy phenomenon. In place of the daring of his early poetry, his later work offers settled belief; in place of its earnest self-scrutiny, it offers, in David Perkins' words, "an attitude of disengaged, objective contemplation."[15] But is not this attitude precisely the goal of the ode and the other poetry of his early and middle years that continues to engage the modern reader? Trilling considers the ode Wordsworth's "dedication to the mode of tragedy," but goes on to acknowledge that "the tragic mode could not be Wordsworth's." For Wordsworth, he argues, lacked "the 'negative capability' which Keats believed to be the source of Shakespeare's power, the gift of being able to be 'content with half-knowledge,' to give up the 'irritable reaching after fact and reason,' to remain 'in uncertainties, mysteries, doubts'".[16] One senses this inadequacy in the affirmations of the ode itself—in its promise of a "Strength"

> In the soothing thoughts that spring
> Out of human suffering . . .

                    (184–85)

Tragedy is presented not as the (vicarious) experience of suffering, but as its belated effect on the "philosophic" human observer. Even "the meanest flower that blows" gives "Thoughts" and not feelings. Instead of the "uncertainties, mysteries, doubts" of Shakespeare, we have the "soothing thoughts" of a poet who stands between his reader and tragic experience. Yet it is precisely this mediacy that confirms the self of the poet. Appropriately, Wordsworth made it a practice to place "Ode: Intimations of Immortality" at the very end of his collected poems: it represents, in a real sense, the terminus of his creative life. It is the irony of Wordsworth's career that his most successful poems were successful in restoring a self able to write poetry that no longer interests us.

NOTES

1. Wordsworth began the poem in 1802 and completed it in 1804. His account of its composition was dictated to Isabella Fenwick in 1843. (See *The Poetical Works of William Wordsworth,* ed. E. de Selincourt and H. Darbishire [Oxford: Clarendon Press, 1966], vol. 4, p. 463. Citations to the text of the ode also refer to this edition.)

2. Michael Friedman, "The Princely and the Contracted Wordsworth: A Study of Wordsworth's Personality in Terms of Psychoanalytic Ego Psychology," *The Wordsworth Circle,* 9 (1978), 411.

3. Ibid., pp. 410, 411.

4. See Heinz Kohut, *AOS,* pp. 49–50.

5. Mary Moorman, *William Wordsworth: A Biography: The Early Years, 1700–1803* (Oxford: Oxford University Press, 1957), p. 174.

6. Richard Onorato, *The Character of the Poet: Wordsworth in* **The Prelude** (Princeton: Princeton University Press, 1971), p. 174.

7. See Kohut, *AOS,* p. 53.

8. Wordsworth, *Poetical Works,* vol. 4, p. 463.

9. I disagree with Barbara Schapiro's view that these lines describe a "former existence" (*The Romantic Mother: Narcissistic Patterns in Romantic Poetry* [Baltimore: Johns Hopkins University Press, 1983], p. 115); they describe, in the present tense, a collection of natural events taking place in the generalized present of the poem, but excluded from the poet's visionary consciousness. Although generally sympathetic to her arguments, I also disagree, as will be seen, with her belief that the ode works toward an acceptance of "the mother as a whole reality" (p. 119). The direction of the ode, it seems to me, is not toward acceptance but toward rejection of the mother-imago.

10. Kohut, *AOS,* p. 49.

11. Friedman, "The Princely and the Contracted Wordsworth," pp. 406, 408.

12. Lionel Trilling, "The Immortality Ode," in *The Liberal Imagination* (New York: Viking Press, 1950), p. 131.

13. Heinz Kohut, "Forms and Transformations of Narcissism," in Paul Ornstein ed., *SFS,* vol. 1, p. 446. (Only one of Kohut's categories—humor—is missing in the final lines of the ode; it appears also to have been largely missing in Wordsworth.)

14. See Samuel Taylor Coleridge, *Biographia Literaria,* ed. J. Engell and W. J. Bate (Princeton: Princeton University Press, 1983), vol. 2, p. 138.

15. David Perkins, *Wordsworth and the Poetry of Sincerity* (Cambridge: Harvard University Press, 1964), p. 232.

16. Trilling, "The Immortality Ode," p. 152.

SEVEN

THOMAS HARDY AND THE "WELL-BELOVED" SELF

Barbara Schapiro

Thomas Hardy's last published novel, *The Well-Beloved* (1897), is perhaps his least successful but most personally revealing work. Written between the publication of *Tess* and *Jude the Obscure, The Well-Beloved* reveals patterns in theme, characterization, and structure that are reflected in the two greater novels. As J. Hillis Miller has pointed out in his introduction to The New Wessex Edition, "*The Well-Beloved* has great importance for understanding all Hardy's work in fiction and in poetry."[1]

The novel tells the story of Jocelyn Pierston, a man who believes himself the descendent of a "visionary race," doomed and "cursed" from birth to pursue an elusive idealization, the "Beloved," as it is incarnated in one woman after another. As Pierston bitterly complains, however, each incarnation, "each shape, or embodiment, has been a temporary residence only, which she has entered, lived in awhile, and made her exit from, leaving the substance, as far as I have been concerned, a corpse, worse luck!" (54). In other words, Pierston cannot stick to one incarnation because, he explains, "When I grapple with the reality she's no longer in it" (69). The novel traces Pierston's pursuit of the "Beloved" in three generations of women in a single family, all of whom are named Avice. He courts the first Avice, a childhood sweetheart, until she kisses him and acknowledges her love. At this point, Pierston explains, the Beloved departed her body and "unmistakably moved under his very eyes" into that of another woman, Marcia Bencomb. Pierston has a temporary affair with Marcia while Avice, feeling hurt and betrayed, marries another man, bears the second Avice, and after several years, dies. Upon learning of her death, Pierston is suddenly stricken with remorse and claims that she "is the only one I shall ever regret" because she was the "only woman whom I never rightly valued" (87). Hardy adds, "He loved the woman dead and inaccessible as he had never loved her in life" (88).

Pierston also feels bound to Avice through a shared ancestry: "Like his own, her family had been islanders for centuries. . . . Hence in her nature, as in his, was some mysterious ingredient sucked from the isle; otherwise a racial instinct necessary to the absolute unison of a pair" (89). Pierston then pursues the daughter, the second Avice. She, however, is secretly married to another man who, coincidentally, is a distant cousin of Pierston's and shares his last name. Upon learning of the marriage, Pierston angrily departs, only to return twenty years later to fall in love with the daughter from this marriage, Avice the Third, who now bears his own surname. Ignoring the fact that he is old enough to be her grandfather, Pierston pursues this third Avice. Hardy comments that despite Pierston's sixty-one years, his figure differed "but little from what it had been when he was half his years," and that "he might have been of any age as he appeared to her at this moment" (157). Avice the Third first accepts his advances and his marriage proposal but ultimately elopes with another man (the son of Marcia, the woman with whom Pierston deceived the original Avice). This last betrayal leaves Pierston defeated and resigned. He rejoins Marcia in a quiet, passionless relationship and lives out his last years a hollow, "grey shadow" of a man. After his death he is remembered by the townspeople, Hardy concludes, as "a man not without genius, whose powers were insufficiently recognized in his lifetime" (206).

Even without much knowledge of psychoanalytic theory, one can recognize obvious narcissistic elements in this story. Miller indeed observes in his introduction that Pierston "in his deepest moment of self-understanding, recognises that his evasive well-beloved . . . is really his own self-image, his 'wraith' or double 'in a changed sex'" (p. 11). This view is enforced throughout the novel: the second and third Avice bear Pierston's own name and even come to reside in Pierston's childhood home, with Avice the Third inhabiting his boyhood room. Furthermore, Pierston's statement, as quoted earlier, about his shared ancestry with the original Avice betrays a fantasy of twinship: in their natures "was some mysterious instinct sucked from the isle." The metaphor suggests the oral and maternal roots of their bond. Miller concludes that "such a union would be a kind of incest and so is subject to a powerful taboo. . . . The narcissistic desire to join oneself to a double of the opposite sex is, moreover, a displacement of the deathwish" (p. 21). While traditional Freudian drive-conflict theory is not inappropriate here, neither is it wholly adequate in accounting for all of the novel's various strains: the predominant idealization, the fantasy of Pierston's agelessness and unrecognized genius, the constant devaluation of others and the self, and the general sense of depletion and despair. Contemporary theories of narcissism and object relations can offer a coherent view of the novel as it expresses the interpsychic dynamics of a narcissistic personality.

In Hardy's novel, Pierston's "Beloved" can be understood as an idealized selfobject, or in Kernberg's terms, as the undifferentiated ideal self and ideal object image.[2] Behind such idealization, as both Kohut and Kernberg have shown, is a frustrated, highly ambivalent relationship with the original love-object, the mother. Pierston's Beloved is indeed inextricably bound up with an ambivalent maternal attachment. Hardy highlights the maternal role by making the original Avice first the mother, then the grandmother, of Pierston's Beloved ideal, and all three relationships are marked by ambivalence and betrayal. The unconscious aggressive content in Pierston's relationship with his Beloved is evident in his inexplicable betrayal of the original Avice as well as his violent shifts of feeling toward all his ideal women: in a moment of anger, for instance, he questions whether the second Avice is a woman at all, but rather "a witch, sprite, troll" (p. 121). The destructive rage at the real rejecting mother that lurks behind the ideal also insures that the Beloved remain disembodied and inaccessible; fear of the enraged aggression in both the mother and the self, as well as the forbidden Oedipal striving, precludes any real union with the Beloved.

The title "The Well-Beloved" is indeed ironic as it refers to both the mother and the self: the mother is as much hated and feared as she is loved, and the self does not feel well-beloved at all, but empty, hungry, and enraged. Pierston's continual pattern of devaluating the Beloved after time, as well as the devaluated self images at the end of the novel (the "hollow" and "grey shadow" of a man that he becomes) project the narcissist's deepest sense of a "bad," unloved, unappreciated self. Pierston's denial of his declining years, and Hardy's concluding statement about him as a "genius" whose "powers were insufficiently recognized," reflect the compensating grandiose fantasy.

The original narcissistic wound results in feelings of anger, fear, and revenge that lead, in Pierston's case, to a repeated pattern of hurting and rejecting the loved one and a consequent overwhelming sense of guilt. The novel suggests that Pierston's rejection by the two succeeding Avices is merely just punishment for his original betrayal; his guilt indeed leads him to expect the same treatment he inflicted on the original Avice—rejection and abandonment. The fact that he returns unhappily to Marcia, the representative of his original crime, and that Avice the Third betrays him with Marcia's son, enforces this idea.

In Michael Millgate's recent biography of Hardy, we can see similar narcissistic patterns in the author's life, as well as a possible source for his condition in the story Millgate tells of Hardy's birth and infancy. After experiencing a difficult delivery, Hardy's mother reportedly cast the young Thomas aside as dead before he was finally rescued by the midwife. The story, Millgate admits, may be apocryphal, but there is evidence that Hardy was a sick and weakly child, that his mother may have thought him an "idiot," and that he was reared largely by a woman neighbor. Both parents, Millgate suggests, "perhaps took little interest in, or feared to make any great emotional commitment to, a weakly child whom they had not wanted and who was unlikely to live."[3] Millgate tells of problems in his rearing, of "parental impatience at his unresponsiveness," and of the boy's "extreme emotional dependence on his mother." The "tenacity of that maternal attachment," Millgate believes, accounts for Hardy's "prolonged immaturity" and for the problems he encountered at all stages of his first marriage.[4]

Throughout his life, Hardy, like Pierston, was subject to infatuations with idealized, inaccessible women. The first of these was an obvious idealized mother-figure, a Mrs. Martin, who, according to Millgate, "overwhelmed the child with her cultivation, elegance, and voluptuousness." He notes that Hardy himself described his feeling toward her as "almost that of a lover," but that the relationship "loomed larger in his imagination than elsewhere."[5] Millgate also describes a childhood incident in which the young Hardy pushed a favorite female classmate against the schoolroom stove, causing her to burn her hands. This was the first of those experiences of love, Millgate explains, "the slighting of the loved one and subsequent guilt which were to recur throughout his life." Like Pierston, Hardy suffered emotional swings "between romantic enthusiasm and sullen self-reproach" and was subject to lifelong fits of depression.[6]

Such guilty depression, which Pierston and many of Hardy's other characters also experience, does reveal some integration or resolution of narcissistic splitting and ambivalence. As D. W. Winnicott, as well as Kernberg and others have discussed, the ability to experience depression, to feel regret over one's aggression and to mourn over one's lost good objects, represents an achievement in the personality. Severely narcissistic or borderline patients are often unable to experience guilt, to move beyond feelings of persecution and impotent rage, or what Kohut describes as "empty" depression. Winnicott explains that "a sense of guilt is anxiety linked with the concept of ambivalence, and implies a degree of integration in the individual ego that allows for the retention of the good object imago along with the idea of a destruction of it."[7] He calls this "the capacity for concern," for the anxiety of guilt drives one toward constructive, reparative, actively loving behavior.

The conclusion of *The Well-Beloved* reveals such a reparative gesture. There are, in fact, two endings to the novel, one composed in 1892 and another five years later, the ending which appears in the final 1897 publication. Miller provides both in his edition of the novel. The first version has Pierston resolve to commit suicide by drowning. In the second, Pierston returns, as mentioned, to Marcia, and in the novel's final paragraphs, Hardy describes how Pierston spent his last years devising a "scheme for the closing of the old natural fountains in the Street of Wells, because of their possible contamination, and supplying the townlet with water from pipes, a scheme that was carried out at his expense, as is well known. He was also engaged in acquiring some old moss-grown, mullioned Elizabethan cottages, for the purpose of pulling them down because they were damp; which he afterwards did, and built new ones with hollow walls, and full of ventilators" (205–6).

These are curious details, though understandable in the logic of the intrapsychic world. The fountains and houses have oral and maternal associations; the fact that the old natural fountains were felt to be contaminated and the old cottages cold and damp, suggests a rupture in the past oral/maternal relationship and recalls the original narcissistic wound. The act of destroying the old fountains and homes and building new pipes and new houses with ventilation systems is at once destructive and constructive and reflects the primary ambivalence. Whereas in the first version Pierston wishes to drown, to die in an oceanic merging, in this version he channels and controls the maternal waters through the pipes. The second ending ultimately reveals an attempt to repair a relationship felt to be polluted by rage and aggression. The reparative gesture suggests some integration and control of the narcissistic rage and ambivalence that characterize the novel as a whole.

The earlier ending, in which Pierston deliberately rides a frail craft out to a turbulent sea, represents a more regressive conclusion. Although Pierston is saved from drowning, this version ends with his bitter "hysterical" laughter as he wakes to find Marcia by his side and realizes, "His wife was—not Avice, but that parchment-covered skull moving about his room" (248). This ending reflects less resolution of narcissistic rage and allies the story more closely to its sources in Shelley's poetry. Not only is the novel's epigraph drawn from "The Revolt of Islam," but as Miller points out, "Hardy's work is in fact steeped in echoes of Shelley throughout" (12). Shelley's "Alastor," for instance, tells the story of a poet pursuing an elusive ideal maiden and the poem ends with the poet steering his small craft out toward certain death by drowning. Shelley's poetry repeatedly expresses a desire for regressive refusion with the mother that is also a deathwish, and it rarely resolves an enraged ambivalence that keeps his female figures split and abstract.[8]

Hardy, unlike Shelley, usually achieves some resolution of narcissistic rage and ambivalence in his work, and most of his novels and poems reflect a higher degree of self-integration. This distinction is evident in the fact that Hardy's work, unlike Shelley's, is steeped in guilt. Guilt and the consequent desire for reparation, like Pierston's constructive gesture in the final version of The Well-Beloved, reflect, in Winnicott's terms, a more highly integrated "capacity for concern." Moreover, Hardy's major female characters, excepting the Avices, are generally not abstract and disembodied, but represent some of the finest achievements of his art. The specific nature of these women characters is nevertheless deeply determined by the dynamics of Hardy's narcissism.

Although The Well-Beloved is the most overtly narcissistic of his novels, all of Hardy's major works betray patterns that are determined, on the deepest level, by narcissistic ambivalences and fantasies. His characteristic themes of fatalism, idealism, and frustrated love, his powerful, destructive, and self-destroying women, his passive, shadowy, victimized men, and his ambivalent attitude toward nature are all rooted in the narcissistic condition. His novels ultimately deal more with person-

ality, with the psychic dynamics of self, than with a closely observed
social reality. Even of *Jude the Obscure,* generally considered his most
"social" novel, A. Alvarez has noted that all of the characters are projections of Jude, are only parts of him, "existing only in relation to him."
The entire novel, he claims, "is simply the image of Jude magnified and
subtly lit from different angles until he and his shadows occupy the
whole Wessex landscape. And Jude in turn is an embodiment of loneliness, deprivation and regret."⁹ It is not the social world but the personality, and the universe as colored by that personality, that creates the
real tensions and drama of Hardy's novels.

Jude, as Hardy states in the Preface to the First Edition, is a "tragedy
of unfulfilled aims." Like *The Well-Beloved* it chronicles the central character's self-destructive pursuit of idealized selfobjects. Jude's first idealized figure is Phillotson, the schoolmaster, who leaves the boy to
pursue his academic career in Christminster. The university itself then
becomes invested with the same idealized significance; it stands in the
boy's mind for Phillotson and the idealized image of himself as a great
scholar. Yet such idealized grandiosity only masks a deeper narcissistic
ambivalence and split; at bottom the boy feels worthless and unwanted,
terrified and enraged. He is an orphan who as a boy identified with
nature's most lowly, disregarded creatures; he could not even bear to
step on a worm. Hardy describes how he "carefully picked his way on
tiptoe among the earthworms, without killing a single one" (p. 36).
When sent to chase away rooks from a farmer's field, "his heart grew
sympathetic with the birds' thwarted desires. They seemed, like himself,
to be living in a world that did not want them" (p. 34). The boy
perceives the environment as cold and brutal: "Nature's logic was too
horrid for him to care for. . . . All around you there seemed to be
something glaring, garish, rattling, and the noises and glares hit upon
the little cell called your life, and shook it, and warped it. If he could
only prevent himself growing up! He did not want to be a man"
(37–38).

The images of the self as thwarted and feeble and of the environment
as cruel and rejecting ultimately prevail. Christminster, which the boy
first views from an elevated distance, gleaming in "points of light like
the topaz," becomes, when he actually arrives, only another reflection
of his wounded, broken self:

What at night had been perfect and ideal was by day the more or less defective real. Cruelties, insults, had, he perceived, been inflicted on the aged erections. The condition of several moved him as he would have been moved by maimed sentient beings. They were wounded, broken, sloughing off their outer shape in the deadly struggle against years, weather, and man. (103)

Phillotson, too, ultimately mirrors this same injured self-image: by the end he is enfeebled and ineffectual and, like Jude, thwarted in both ambition and love.

The female characters in the novel are products of this same wounded narcissism. The women are, first of all, split into the animalistic, sexual Arabella and the ethereal, asexual Sue. Both women are cruelly manipulative and are made to seem largely responsible for Jude's tragic end. At first Jude even manages to idealize Arabella, who resides on a pig farm and first attracts his attention by smacking him on the ear with a pig's pizzle. Hardy comments that although Jude realized she "was not worth a great deal as a specimen of womankind," he "kept up a factitious belief in her. His idea of her was the thing of most consequence, not Arabella herself" (78).

It is Sue, however, who is the recipient of Jude's most intense idealization; even as he comes to know her, she remains, Hardy says, an "ideality" to him. She indeed bears many similarities to Pierston's beloved Avices. Like the shared ancestry between Pierston and Avice, Sue and Jude are cousins and, as Jude's aunt informs him, Sue was born in Jude's boyhood home. Alvarez also notes the many references to the similarity between the pair, such as Phillotson's remark that "They seem to be one person split in two," and Jude's exclamation at seeing Sue attired in his clothes, lent to her after she arrives at his flat soaking wet: "What counterparts they were! . . . Sitting in his only arm-chair he saw a slim and fragile being masquerading as himself on a Sunday, so pathetic in her defencelessness that his heart felt big with the sense of it" (164). After observing her a few moments more, however, Hardy adds that Jude "saw in her almost a divinity." Sue is indeed a projection of Jude's own split self—of both his fragile, wounded, defenceless self and his idealized, grandiose, "godlike" self.

The identification between the two is so complete that Hardy invests both characters with the same narcissistic ambivalence, the same self-censure and paralysing guilt. Just as Jude claims, "I have the germs of every human infirmity in me," and that "I never know in what new form a suppressed vice will break out in me," Sue cries, "I cannot humiliate myself too much. I should like to prick myself all over with pins and bleed out the badness that's in me!" (365). While the guilt both feel has a sexual, Oedipal component (Jude feels himself a "wicked worthless fellow" for having given vent "to an animal passion for a woman," and Sue feels they deserve punishment for "loving each other too much—indulging ourselves to utter selfishness with each other!"), the guilt also has a deeper, pre-Oedipal source in rage over narcissistic injury. Both feel they harbor an evil, vicious "bad" self that deserves punishment.

This enraged "bad" self-image is also projected onto the external world in the novel; from the beginning, Nature, Fate and Society are portrayed as if in conspiracy to prevent the characters' self-realization or fulfillment. Both Sue and Jude are warned never to marry because of their family's tragic marital history. Jude's parents had parted in bitter strife, his mother had drowned herself soon after and his father had simply disappeared. Sue's parents had met a similar fate, and thus due to their tainted past, Sue and Jude are warned that their love relationship is doomed from the beginning. This idea that a cursed history of family relationships is responsible for a tragic future in love is a common theme in Hardy's novels. It draws its psychological source from Hardy's frustrated, "cursed" relationship with his first love-object. All future love relations will be invested with and endangered by the unresolved rage and aggression experienced in the original love relationship.

The malevolent forces of Nature and Fate in the novel project this enraged aggression. For the infant, the mother *is* the environment and her power may indeed be felt as overwhelming; so in Hardy's novels, the environment is often one of inscrutable powers that buffet and punish the characters and prevent them from achieving either their ambitions or fulfillment in love. Jude refers to "the scorn of Nature for man's finer emotions, and her lack of interest in his aspirations" (p. 197); Sue speaks of Fate having "given us this stab in the back" while Jude replies, "Nothing can be done, . . . Things are as they are, and will be brought to their destined issue" (358). This fatalistic, passive, and resigned attitude is another common feature of Hardy's characters and reflects, again, an infantile attitude toward an ambivalent and overwhelming maternal environment.

The same passive, fatalistic attitude, as well as the self-destructive pursuit of idealized selfobjects and the underlying ambivalence and rage, also characterize *Tess of the d'Urbervilles*. The character of Tess, perhaps one of Hardy's finest creations, draws vitality from the author's empathic identification with her. On the one hand, Tess is female and associated with the powerful, ambivalent mother; she is capable of murder and maintains throughout a compelling mystery and strength. On the other hand, Hardy identifies with Tess. One characteristic of the narcissistic personality may be the close identification of the self with the mother, and in this case, by identifying with Tess, Hardy endows her with his own deepest terrors and strivings, his own narcissistic vulnerability. Like Pierston, Jude and Sue, Tess pursues idealized self-images and suffers from a split inner condition; her ultimate victimization is as much self-inflicted as it is due to the malevolent forces around her.

The critic Evelyn Hardy has noted the self-destructive element in Tess' character, her "tendency towards martyrdom and self-sacrifice."[10] He points to the passage in which Tess furiously cries to Alec, "Now punish me! . . . Whip me, crush me; . . . I shall not cry out. Once victim, always victim—that's the law!" (379). Evelyn Hardy sees Tess' self-punishment as arising out of guilt over her own strong sensuality. There is also evidence, however, that this guilt has an even deeper source in a wounded narcissism.

Tess' feelings of shame and guilt, first of all, emerge directly out of two incidents in which she inappropriately falls asleep. In the first instance, she drowses off while driving the family's cart into town, as a result of which the family horse is killed. Hardy states, "Nobody blamed Tess as she blamed herself" (62), and her guilt over the loss of the horse leads her to accept the offer from the d'Urbervilles, from which all of the trouble ensues. The second instance occurs in the woods with Alec and results in the pivotal seduction. Evelyn Hardy sees these sleeping incidents as merely evidence of the vulnerability of the flesh; Tess feels guilt over her carnal nature, her vulnerable, fleshly nature that is responsible for the "accident" of falling asleep. Such sleeping episodes, however, which also occur elsewhere in the novel, are not merely "accidents" of the flesh. They suggest a regressive desire to escape reality, a fantasy of refusion, a deathwish.

In the seduction scene, for instance, Hardy describes Tess asleep on the ground as if she has merged or fused with the environment. She blends into the brush and leaves and is figuratively divested of both her form and consciousness: "With the setting of the moon the pale light lessened, and Tess became invisible as she fell into reverie upon the leaves where he had left her." And when Alec returns, "he could see absolutely nothing but a pale nebulousness at his feet, which represented the white muslin figure he had left upon the dead leaves" (106–7).

Tess' love scenes with Angel reflect a similar fantasy of regressive refusion; she yearns for an absolute union that also means death: "Her one desire, so long resisted, to make herself his, to call him her lord, her own—then, if necessary, to die—" (254). Or again, when Angel carries her in his arms in the sleepwalking scene, Tess thinks, "If they could only fall together, and both be dashed to pieces, how fit, how desirable" (291). The final scenes with Angel, after the murder of d'Urberville, are of a similarly regressive and escapist nature. The two hide out together and both, Hardy says, "seemed to implore something to shelter them from reality" (p. 429). During the final night at Stonehenge, Tess is blissfully happy in her union with Angel only because she knows it is doomed. When the soldiers finally arrive to escort her to her execution, she exclaims, "It is as it should be. . . . Angel, I am almost glad—yes, glad! This happiness could not have lasted. It was too much. I have had enough; and now I shall not live for you to despise me!" (447).

The "despised" bad self that Tess has secretly harbored all along is her deepest source of guilt. It is not merely ironic that Tess' liberating moment of self-realization is in the destructive and ultimately self-destroying act of murder. The act is an outward expression of the rage and aggression formerly directed inward. The angry, bad self lies behind her idealized conceptions of both Angel and herself. For Tess, Angel, as his name implies, is a being as ethereal and divine as Avice is to Pierston, as Sue is to Jude. The pattern is perhaps the most characteristic one in Hardy's work. As Miller has observed, if Hardy's fiction has a single theme, it is "fascination—the love of a human being who radiates a divine aura."[11] Tess regards Angel, Hardy states, "as an intelligence rather than a man" (164). Of Angel, he comments, "he was, in truth, more spiritual than animal; . . . he was less Byronic than Shelleyan; could love desperately, but with a love more especially inclined to the imaginative and ethereal; it was a fastidious emotion which could jealously guard the loved one against his very self. This amazed and enraptured Tess . . . " (234). Tess is indeed enraptured by the ideal, grandiose image of herself that Angel reflects. Hardy states that her love for him "sustained her dignity; she seemed to be wearing a crown" (234).

Tess perhaps could have saved herself had she confessed the truth of her past to Angel at the beginning, but she could not bear to part with the ideal of herself as perfect and pure, which Angel believes. He, for instance, considers her "a visionary essence of woman," an "idyllic creature." Thus when she finally confesses, Angel's brutal response terrifies her but is no less than she expects; he expresses her own deepest terrors about herself:

> He looked upon her as an impostor; a guilty woman in the guise of an innocent one. Terror was upon her white face as she saw it; . . . The horrible sense of his view of her so deadened her that she staggered. (272)

Angel suffers from the same internal split as Tess; she is as much an idealized selfobject to him as he is to her. He cannot accept her imperfect reality, which significantly includes her sexuality, because he cannot accept it in himself, cannot bear to part with his own idealized self-image. Sexuality is too bound up with the rage and aggression of the original love relationship with the mother. In Hardy's universe, the impossibility of union with the beloved has both Oedipal and pre-Oedipal roots; it is due both to forbidden libidinal urges toward the mother and to the deeper narcissistic rage, the intense ambivalence that stems from an empathic failure in the original love relationship.

Angel finally does decide to accept Tess, but only after she has married Alec and her inaccessibility is insured. Miller makes the point that "It is the law of life in Hardy's world that if someone by nature seeks complete possession of another person he is doomed to be disappointed over and over, either by his failure to obtain the woman he loves or by his discovery that he does not have what he wants when he possesses her."[12] In psychoanalytic terms, one is bound to be disappointed if the object of one's love is merely an idealized, as well as intensely ambivalent, selfobject. The pattern is not confined, however, to Hardy's men; his most complex female characters are caught in the same narcissistic bind.

Like Tess, Eustacia Vye in *The Return of the Native* pursues an idealized image of herself in the form of the two men in the novel, Wildeve and Clym Yeobright. Both Tess and Eustacia are also loners, cut off from the social world, Tess by the "crime" of her illegitimate pregnancy and her guilt, and Eustacia by her isolated life on the heath. Both are more in love with disembodied abstractions than with real men. Of Eustacia, Hardy comments, "She seemed to long for the abstraction called passionate love more than for any particular lover" (96), and he adds that she spent "the spare hours of her existence by idealizing Wildeve for want of a better object" (98). When Clym arrives from Paris, he replaces Wildeve as the object of her fantasies only because of the "fascination which must attend a man come direct from Paris— laden with its atmosphere, familiar with its charms" (141). Hardy states, "The perfervid woman was . . . half in love with a vision" (143), a vision of herself as part of the glamour, status, and power she associates with Clym and the Parisian world. When Clym fails her by not returning with her as his wife to Paris but becoming instead a lowly furze-cutter, she turns again to Wildeve. Yet before she runs off to Wildeve at the novel's end, she questions, "Can I go, can I go? . . . He's not *great* enough for me to give myself to—he does not suffice for my desire!" (371). He does not suffice, in other words, her grandiose fantasy of herself.

At times there is evidence that Hardy recognizes the danger and destructiveness of such romantic idealizations. He clearly condemns Angel, for instance, portraying him as hard and selfish in his inability to accept Tess in her imperfect reality. More often, however, Hardy's sympathy is with his self-destructive idealists. He says, for instance, of Eustacia, "The fantastic nature of her passion, which lowered her as an intellect, raised her as a soul" (143), and of Wildeve, "To be yearning for the difficult, to be weary of that offered; to care for the remote, to dislike the near; it was Wildeve's nature always. This is the true mark of the man of sentiment" (237). Clym, too, is an idealist who, as his mother observes, is "an enthusiast about ideas, and careless about out- ward things. He often reminds me of the Apostle Paul" (302). Hardy adds that Clym's mind was not "well-proportioned," but that a well- proportioned mind would never cause a man to be "applauded as a prophet, revered as a priest, or exalted as a king" (197).[13]

Hardy's sympathy is clearly with his idealists; he places the responsi- bility for their tragedies less on the destructive nature of their idealism than on the inscrutable forces of a coldly indifferent universe. The power of a cursed ancestry, for instance, plagues Tess as it does Sue and Jude, and Hardy concludes with the bitter remark that "the President of the Immortals . . . had ended his sport with Tess." Similarly, Eustacia feels that she has been punished by "some colossal Prince of the World," and she cries, "How I have tried and tried to be a splendid woman, and how destiny has been against me! . . . I do not deserve my lot! . . . O, the cruelty of putting me into this ill-conceived world! I was capable of much; but I have been injured and blighted and crushed by things beyond my control!" (372). Such a desperate cry of wounded narcissism is at the psychological core of all of Hardy's major characters. It is also a key determining factor in his portrayal of nature, both in the novels and the poetry.

One of the most significant aspects of nature in Hardy's world is the author's ambivalent attitude toward it. Nature is alternately portrayed as a source of benevolent harmony with which the self is organically interconnected and as a cruelly indifferent force that annihilates the self. The depiction of nature reflects the infant self's ambivalent experience of the mother. In *The Return of the Native*, for instance, Hardy vacillates between describing Egdon heath in distanced, objective terms as a presence inscrutable, "other," and indifferent to the human, and in subjective, lyrical terms, as an integral part of and/or reflection of humanity. On the one hand, the heath is a "great inviolate place," "eternal and immutable," a "Titanic form," an "enemy" of civilization: "The sombre stretch of rounds and hollows seemed to rise and meet the evening gloom in pure sympathy, the heath exhaling darkness as rapidly as the heavens precipitated it. And so the obscurity in the air and in the land closed together in a black fraternization. . . " (33–34). Hardy emphasizes here and elsewhere the heath's alien "obscurity"; in this passage the heath and sky are "closed together" in a darkness that is closed-off and exclusive of the human. In the second chapter, in which "Humanity Appears upon the Scene," the human form is described as "a moving spot," a "single atom of life," and throughout the novel the human is commonly figured as a "speck," a "blot," or an insect in relation to the natural environment. As Hardy states, the heath, "having defied the cataclysmal onsets of centuries, reduced to insignificance by its seamed and antique features the wildest turmoil of a single man" (342). In its alien otherness, the heath overpowers and reduces the human.

On the other hand, Hardy's frequent personification of Egdon intimately links it to the human. Indeed the heath, Hardy suggests, expresses the essence of the human soul: "It was at present a place perfectly accordant with man's nature—neither ghastly, hateful, nor ugly: neither commonplace, unmeaning, nor tame; but, like man, slighted and enduring; and withal singularly colossal and mysterious in its swarthy monotony. As with some persons who have long lived apart, solitude seemed to look out of its countenance. It had a lonely face, suggesting tragical possibilities" (35). Hardy is here endowing the heath with the nature of his own wounded psyche: like so many of his characters, it is "slighted and enduring," isolated in a lonely, tragical solitude. Hardy identifies with the heath as he identifies with his powerful female characters; the heath is in fact allied with the central woman in the novel.

Eustacia is introduced as her expression of lonely solitude intertwines with that of the heath: "The bluffs, and the bushes, and the heather bells had broken silence; at last, so did the woman; and her articulation was but as another phrase of the same discourse as theirs. Thrown out on the winds it became twined in with them, and with them it flew away" (82). Or again, Hardy describes her on the heath during a storm: "Never was harmony more perfect than that between the chaos of her mind and the chaos of the world without. . . . Between the drippings of the rain from her umbrella to her mantle, from her mantle to the heather, from the heather to the earth, very similar sounds could be heard coming from her lips; and the tearfulness of the outer scene was repeated upon her face" (371).

Clym, too, is frequently described in harmony with the heath, but his alliance threatens his identity and diminishes him as a man; his mergence with the heath becomes a kind of death:

> He was a brown spot in the midst of an expanse of olive-green gorse, and nothing more. . . . His daily life was of a curious microscopic sort, his whole world being limited to a circuit of a few feet from his person. His familiars were creeping and winged things, and they seemed to enroll him in their band. . . . Huge flies, ignorant of larders and wire-netting, and quite in a savage state, buzzed about him without knowing he was a man. (273–74)

As in *Tess,* merging with nature means death or disaster for it exposes a regressive fantasy of refusion with the mother. Hardy's ambivalent portrayal of nature is even more pronounced in *Tess* than in *Return of the Native.* Lyrical scenes of organic harmony contrast sharply with descriptions of nature as a fiercely antagonistic foe. He describes Tess and her fellow field workers, for instance, as "soaring along in a supporting medium . . . themselves and surrounding nature forming an organism of which all the parts harmoniously and joyously interpenetrated each other" (98). Similarly, he states, "a field-woman is a portion of the field; she has somehow lost her own margin, imbibed the essence of her surrounding, and assimilated herself with it" (123).

On the other hand, the natural environment, like the heath in *Native,* also diminishes and destroys the human: "Not quite sure of her direction Tess stood still upon the hemmed expanse of verdant flatness, like a fly on a billiard table of indefinite length, and of no more consequence to the surroundings than that fly" (142). Or, "They trudged onwards with slanted bodies through the flossy fields, keeping as well as they could in the shelter of hedges, which, however, acted as strainers rather than screens. The air, afflicted to pallor with the hoary multitudes that infested it, twisted and spun them eccentrically, suggesting an achromatic chaos of things" (335).

At times the environment envelopes or swallows the people. Referring to Angel alone in his room, Hardy writes, "The night came in, and took up its place there, unconcerned and indifferent; the night which had already swallowed up his happiness, and was now digesting it listlessly; and was ready to swallow up the happiness of a thousand other people with as little disturbance or change of mien" (278). The metaphor here reveals an oral component to Hardy's ambivalent attitude toward the environment, suggesting roots in the infant's first mode of connection with the mother.

The depiction of nature in Hardy's poetry reflects this same ambivalence. Some of his poems, such as "Transformations," celebrate a joyous harmony between humanity and nature while others, like "Nature's Questioning," rail against nature's brute injustice and destructiveness. Several poems also reveal the ambivalence underlying the fantasy of refusion with nature/mother. The lyric, "A Thought in Two Moods," for instance, explicitly connects mergence with nature with thoughts of death:

I saw it—pink and white—revealed
Upon the white and green;
The white and green was a daisied field,
The pink and white Ethleen.

And as I looked it seemed in kind
That difference they had none;
The two fair bodiments combined
As varied miens of one.

A sense that, in some mouldering year,
As one they both would lie,
Made me move quickly on to her
To pass the pale thought by.

> She laughed and said: "Out there, to me,
> "You looked so weather-browned,
> "And brown in clothes, you seemed to be
> "Made of the dusty ground!"[14]

The poem's split in attitude, the "Two Moods" of the title, displays the author's characteristic ambivalence. Hardy's narcissistic injury is also at the core of many of his love poems; often they are structured on the contrast between a past state of ideal love and union and a present state of loss, isolation, and diminishment.

Hardy's narcissistic wound, finally, plays a profoundly determining role in all his work. As a result of the initial injury to his self, of his feeling thwarted in the realization of his identity, his central male characters often remain hollow, passive, and insubstantial, never emerging from the shadows of the powerful women. Michael Henchard of *The Mayor of Casterbridge* is perhaps his strongest male character, and he achieves his vitality precisely because he is able to vent outwardly his narcissistic rage toward the mother, and by extension, toward women in general. Henchard, Hardy admits, was "by nature something of a woman hater," and he expresses this at the novel's outset by drunkenly abusing his wife and selling her to a stranger at a country fair. Of course, Henchard is ridden with guilt throughout the rest of the novel. Although he complains, as do most of Hardy's characters, of a "sinister intelligence bent on punishing him," he admits that his punishment "was what he had deserved," and by the end, his self-devaluation is complete.

Hardy's major female characters represent the author's greatest achievement, for through them he transcends his narcissistic rage. His women are generally not merely hollow abstractions, and even if the female characters are initially split, often by the end of the novels the good/bad division is no longer clear. In the case of Sue and Arabella, for instance, the evil, sexual Arabella is ultimately more generous and feeling than Sue, and while Sue shrivels in self-torture, Arabella drinks and laughs and merrily survives. Hardy finally makes Arabella far more likeable than Sue, and even allows Arabella the novel's last words, the final pronouncement on Sue: "She's never found peace since she left his arms, and never will again 'till she's as he is now!" (p. 491). Sue and Jude's love is equated with death while Arabella lives.

In the case of *The Return of the Native*, early manuscript notes reveal that Hardy originally intended to make Thomasin the "pure" heroine and Eustacia the sinister "witch."[15] In the creative process of writing the novel, however, Hardy obviously transcended such severe, primitive ambivalence. Although the women still reflect authorial ambivalence—they are destructive to the men and are often punished for their sexuality—the ambivalence is on a more mature, integrated, Oedipal rather than pre-Oedipal level. Hardy's finest women are at least whole and embodied and allowed sensuality. Moreover, they are allowed to suffer; these women are not merely the abstracted objects of the men's pursuit. Through his narcissistic identification with them, Hardy invests the women with his own deepest yearnings and terrors, thereby humanizing them. His greatest female characters perhaps represent Hardy's most profound reparative act toward his loved and hated mother.

NOTES

1. *The Well-Beloved* (London: Macmillan, New Wessex Edition, 1975), p. 14. All quotations and page references from Hardy's novels refer to the New Wessex Editions.

2. See Heinz Kohut, *AOS,* and Otto Kernberg, *BCPN.* For an introductory summary of their theories, see the Introduction to this collection, Part I.

3. Michael Millgate, *Thomas Hardy* (New York: Random House, 1982), p. 16.

4. Ibid., p. 23.

5. Ibid., pp. 46, 47.

6. Ibid., pp. 41, 93.

7. D. W. Winnicott, *MP,* p. 73.

8. For an analysis of the narcissistic patterns in Shelley's poetry, see Barbara Schapiro, *The Romantic Mother* (Baltimore: The Johns Hopkins University Press, 1983).

9. A. Alvarez, "Jude the Obscure," in Albert J. Guerard ed., *Hardy: A Collection of Critical Essays* (Englewood Cliffs, N.J.: Prentice-Hall, 1963), pp. 120–21.

10. In Evelyn Hardy, *Thomas Hardy, A Critical Biography* (London: David Higham, 1954), p. 231.

11. In J. Hillis Miller, *Thomas Hardy: Distance and Desire* (Cambridge, Mass.: Belknap Press of Harvard University Press, 1970), p. 114.

12. Ibid., p. 149.

13. For an analysis of Clym's narcissistic and melancholic character, see Mary Ellen Jordan, "Thomas Hardy's *The Return of the Native*: Clym Yeobright and Melancholia," *American Imago,* 39, 2 (Summer, 1982), 101–18.

14. In *Collected Poems of Thomas Hardy* (New York: Macmillan, 1972), p. 457.

15. As discussed by John Paterson in *The Making of The Return of the Native* (Berkeley: University of California Press, 1960), pp. 17–30.

EIGHT

ON NARCISSISM
FROM BAUDELAIRE TO SARTRE:
EGO-PSYCHOLOGY AND
LITERARY HISTORY

Eugene Holland

Soon after the concept of the narcissistic personality was developed by clinical psychologists, it gained currency in the study of contemporary culture and society.[1] The work of Christopher Lasch in particular incisively demonstrated how narcissism pervades what he calls our "age of diminishing expectations."[2] By comparing contemporary goals and values with the classical image of nineteenth-century values and the Protestant work ethic, Lasch is able cogently to unite a broad range of cultural phenomena—from business managerial styles to professional sports, from theories of education to relations between the sexes—under the rubric of the culture of narcissism. I say the classical *image* of nineteenth-century values and the Protestant work ethic, because Lasch's account of the historical origins of cultural narcissism has inspired a great deal less confidence than his description of the phenomenon itself in post-World War II society. While Lasch's historical derivation of narcissism from the decline of the family has provoked controversy, nonetheless few would deny that his work has shed considerable light on contemporary culture in America.

But there is a curious omission from Lasch's anatomy of our narcissistic age: he never mentions the popularity in this country of Sartre and Camus, indeed never discusses existentialism at all. Yet existential philosophy directly addresses many of the issues Lasch raises in connection with narcissism, and when today we reread *Nausea* or *The Stranger,* what we see is in fact a proto-typical narcissistic hero. If there is any recent fictional character who—to quote from Lasch's portrait—"sees the world as a mirror of himself and has no interest in external events except as they throw back a reflection of his own image,"[3] it is Sartre's Roquentin. And virtually the entire catalogue of narcissistic personality traits apply: who is unable to form lasting commitments to other people and institutions, if not Roquentin? He may get excited about his fits of nausea, but in relations with other people, he is as unemotional as is his counterpart, Meursault, at the funeral of his mother or when he shoots the Arab on the beach. Roquentin may appear more anxious or bored than placid Meursault, but Camus' prose on the other hand conveys strikingly the remarkable emptiness of Meursault's inner life. Except for their indifference to others' opinions of them (a central tenet of existentialist philosophy), both existentialist heroes are practically type-cast narcissists.

Moreover, existentialism achieved extraordinary popularity in this country at just the same time that narcissism was forcing itself on the attention of the therapeutic community: in the 1950s—a good two decades before the so-called "me-generation" brought the idea of narcissism to popular attention. But then again, Sartre wrote *Nausea* in the 1930s, well before many of the social forces to which Lasch attributes narcissism were in full force. Perhaps existentialism would give narcissism a good name; or perhaps it emerges too early for Lasch's account, disrupting the convenient contrast he repeatedly refers to— often only by implication—between postwar narcissism and the culture of solid nineteenth-century values and virtues he pictures preceding it. This anomaly would by itself be far from damning: pervasive cultural narcissism can hardly be expected to have appeared overnight. But if, as I shall argue, Sartre's "narcissistic" philosophy and characters in fact derive from aesthetic developments of the mid-nineteenth century, then Lasch's account of the origins of narcissism in twentieth-century decadence would appear very suspect indeed.

To raise the question of historical origins is to pose the problem of historical causality. Many critics have attacked Lasch's use of the nineteenth-century nuclear family as a model and ideal standard of comparison for the very different families of today, asserting for instance that the decline of the bourgeois-patriarchal family cannot serve as grounds for condemning contemporary narcissism because such a family-type has always been the exception rather than the rule, or because it was not a worthy ideal in the first place.[4] The family is indeed the linch-pin of Lasch's account, and not only because of his earlier study of the family, *Haven in a Heartless World.*[5] For one thing, even in *The Culture of Narcissism,* Lasch maintains an orthodox psychoanalytic emphasis on the family as prime determinant of psychic life:

> The emergence of (narcissistic) character-disorders as the most prominent form of psychiatric pathology . . . derives from quite specific changes in our society and culture . . . and in the last instance from changes in family life. . . . Psychoanalysis best clarifies the connection between society and the individual, culture and personality, precisely when it confines itself to careful examination of individuals.[6]

This position, let us note, is a good deal more orthodox than Freud's own, for Freud insisted that psychoanalysis not be confined to individual analysis and family romance, but applied to culture and society as a whole[7]—a particularly appropriate strategy, one would think, if the family has succumbed to corrosive social influences as Lasch suggests it has. But more important, Lasch mistakes the nineteenth-century nuclear family for the last bastion of precapitalist values and interpersonal relations, when on the contrary the private space of the nuclear family in fact arose as a *product* of capitalist development, not an exception to it.[8] Only by considering the so-called "demise" of the nuclear family in the context of society and culture as a whole, I want to suggest, may we arrive at a thorough understanding of the historical emergence of cultural narcissism.

Here, I would like to consider the relation of Baudelaire's poetry to the emergence of narcissism. Not that he invented it first, of course, or all by himself. Rather I will argue that his elaboration of a modernist poetics is emblematic of a host of social developments affecting not only the internal structure of the family in the mid-nineteenth century, but the status of social authority as well. Now Baudelaire is usually associated with masochism rather than narcissism—and for good reasons. But my claim is that the shift in Baudelaire's poetics from Romanticism to Modernism entails a shift from masochism to narcissism—and furthermore that masochism plays a crucial transitional role in the rise of narcissism to cultural predominance. Taking bourgeois social authority as a baseline of comparison (rather than the nuclear family alone), we can better understand the role that a culture of masochism played in preparing the ground for the culture of narcissism that prevails today.

It may seem tenuous to base the characterization of a broad cultural development from masochism to narcissism on one emblematic figure. Critics from René Laforgue in the 1930s to Leo Bersani more recently have agreed, however, on Baudelaire's masochism.[9] Among these critics, Sartre not only confirms this assessment of Baudelaire, but in his study of Flaubert claims that the novelist, too, and a group of Second Empire writers Sartre calls the "Knights of Nothingness" were masochistic as well, arguing that the "loser-wins" strategy they all employ was part of the "objective neurosis" of late nineteenth-century culture.[10] Furthermore, Sartre's historical analysis is corroborated by the immense popularity and international acclaim during this period of Sacher-Masoch himself and his novels, for the same "loser-wins" strategy forms the core of Masoch's own masochistic stance and appears throughout his best fiction.[11] For economy's sake, then, I take Baudelaire's masochism as an emblem of this entire cultural complex.

Yet, as convincing as Sartre's biographical study may be, in its own way, the association of Baudelaire exclusively with masochism is questionable. Other critics have written with equal conviction of the sadism of Baudelaire.[12] And indeed, in the later works, particularly in the prose poems, the poet seems as likely to take the side of violent aggression as of passive submission. This paradox is best understood, I suggest, in light of a shift in Baudelaire's poetics leading in the direction of borderline-narcissistic pathology. Baudelaire has become a widely acclaimed figure in Western culture; as Walter Benjamin puts it, Baudelaire anticipated a reader who could appreciate a certain structure of experience, and his renown seems to confirm Benjamin's contention that "Baudelaire was eventually to find the reader(s) at whom his work was aimed."[13] Among these readers, I want to include not only Rimbaud, Huysmans, Mallarmé, and Proust, but also Sartre and the countless enthusiasts of existentialism whom Baudelaire reached through works such as *Nausea*. For Sartre's existential novel, as we shall see, can be considered a direct descendent of Baudelairean modernism. But first, let me give one vivid illustration of masochism in Baudelaire's works and then a brief sketch of the masochistic "loser-wins" operation.

Baudelaire once claimed that the best way to end the *Flowers of Evil* would be an "Epilogue" in which he would address himself to an anonymous "Madame" and exhort her thus:

> If you want to please me and rekindle my desires, be cruel, treacherous, licentious, lewd and thievish. . . .[14]

Now the point of actively soliciting such ill treatment, in the masochistic scenario, is not simply to submit to the tyranny of a woman, but to do so in order to invalidate the punishment thereby meted out. Since punishment is willingly sought by the masochist, not merited, the punishment backfires and disqualifies the authority responsible for it. Thus, by soliciting unwarranted punishment, the masochist invalidates punishing authority and emerges triumphant. The dynamic of this "objective neurosis" is particularly clear-cut in Cézanne: he repeatedly sent his most avant-garde paintings to the traditional Salon competitions, sure that as long as he was refused, he was on the right track.[15] The masochist submits to punishment, then, in order to invalidate social authority and idealize the martyred self.

Baudelaire's masochism is a commonplace in the critical literature, so I will not dwell on it here. We can trace his evolution from masochism to narcissism, as I have suggested, through the shift in his poetics from Romanticism to Modernism, a shift that has been the subject of some of the best recent work on his poetry.[16] For our purposes, this complex transformation can be summarized as a combined process of disintegration and "distanciation."

Baudelaire begins the *Flowers of Evil*[17] with a series of poems that reiterate the familiar romantic theme of the misunderstood artist at odds with society. The opening poem, "Benediction" (RH, 11), promises the poet a mystical halo of pure light and understanding in exchange for the suffering he endures:

> Thanks be to God, Who gives us suffering
> . . .
> that best and purest essence which prepares
> the strong in spirit for divine delights!
> I know the Poet has a place apart
> among the holy legions' blessed ranks;
> . . .
> I know that pain is the one nobility
> upon which Hell itself cannot encroach;
> that if I am to weave my mystic crown
> I must braid into it all time, all space
> . . .
> for it will be made of nothing but pure light

Subsequent poems depict on the one hand an ungainly poet cruelly taunted by uncomprehending humanity, as in "The Albatross" (RH, 13):

How weak and awkward, even comical
this traveller but lately so adroit—
one deckhand sticks a pipestem in its beak,
another mocks the cripple that once flew!

The Poet is like this monarch of the clouds
riding the storm above the marksman's range;
exiled on the ground, hooted and jeered,
he cannot walk because of his great wings.

While on the other hand, poems like "Elevation" (RH, 14) depict a poet soaring high above the mortifying world of earthly existence:

Free from the futile strivings and the cares
which dim existence to a realm of mist,
happy is he who wings an upward way
on mighty pinions to the fields of light;
whose thoughts like larks spontaneously rise
into the morning sky; whose flight, unchecked,
outreaches life and readily comprehends
the language of flowers and of all mute things.

Included in this first cycle of poems is the well-known sonnet, "Correspondences," (RH, 15)—often regarded as the quintessential expression of the Baudelairean aesthetic:

The pillars of Nature's temple are alive
and sometimes yield perplexing messages;
forests of symbols between us and the shrine
remark our passage with accustomed eyes.

Like long-held echoes, blending somewhere else
into one deep and shadowy unison
as limitless as darkness and as day,
the sounds, the scents, the colors correspond.

In fact, the aesthetic of correspondences is precisely what the rest of the *Flowers of Evil* will work to undermine and eliminate.

On one level, this revision process involves simply rejecting the romantic myth of the inspired artist communing with nature: the living temple of familiar symbolism in "Correspondences" becomes in a latter poem, "Obsession" (RH, 72), a ghastly cathedral echoing with sounds of death:

Forest, I fear you! in my ruined heart

> your roaring wakens the same agony
> as in cathedrals when the organ moans
> and from the depths I hear that I am damned.

The beacons of past artistic greatness ("Guiding Lights," RH, 16) become the ironic beacon of Baudelaire's conscious evil—"la conscience dans le Mal" ("The Irremediable," RH, 80):

> Distinct the heart's own exchange
> with its own dark mirror,
> for deep in that Well of Truth
> trembles one pale star,
>
> ironic, infernal beacon,
> graceful torch of the Devil,
> our solace and sole glory—
> consciousness in Evil!

And by the end of the prose poems, as we shall see, the mystical halo awarded to poetic inspiration will be disdained and abandoned by the Modernist poet.

But the *Flowers of Evil* do not depict the disintegration of one myth, the Romantic myth, simply to replace it with another one. Rather, on a second level, the process of disintegration undermines the integrity of representation itself—or at least of the kind of essentializing representation expressed in the first cycle of the collection. The poem "Correspondences" celebrated equivalence and synaesthesia through its use of simile and metaphor, promoting a poetic vision able to unite interior and exterior, essence and appearance, in an organic whole. Baudelaire's anti-Romantic, Modernist aesthetic—presented in the opening poem of the next cycle in the *Flowers of Evil,* "Beauty" (FF, 40)—emphasizes exteriority, randomness, mechanical causality, and fragmentation instead. Rather than look into Beauty's eyes to grasp her inner essence, as it were, the poet now remains on the outside and at a distance: her eyes are now mirrors that only reflect beauty onto objects around her:

> For I, to charm each docile devotee,
> Have mirrors that enhance beauty's delights:
> My eyes, my glorious eyes of quenchless light!

Defying metaphoric comparison and totalizing expression, Beauty is now appreciated through her incremental effects on the external world. And in the subsequent poems of the cycle, Beauty appears only in fragments and random images, valued not for or as an essence, but for her contingent impact on the poet. This metonymic aesthetic comes to predominate in the *Flowers of Evil,* as Leo Bersani's study suggests; and its predominance is even clearer in the prose poems, as Barbara Johnson's comparisons between verse and prose versions of several poems have shown.[18]

In the verse poem "Tresses" (FF, 48), for example, a woman's hair inspires a whole set of metaphoric equivalences, becoming a forest, then an ocean, and so forth:

> A whole world, distant, strange and almost lost,
> Lives in these depths, this forest fragrant, sweet;
> (. . .)
> You hide, O ebony sea, a dazzling dream
> Where sails and oarsmen, masts and pennants meet—

In the prose version, by contrast, her hair merely possesses a series of properties that serve to stimulate the poet's imagination:

> Your hair holds a whole dream of masts and sails. . . . In the ocean of your hair I see a harbor teeming with melancholic songs. . . . In the caresses of your hair I know again the languors of long hours lying on a couch in a fair ship's cabin. . . .[19]

Similarly, the metaphoric equivalence between woman and country in the verse "Invitation to the Voyage" (FF, 89), a relation inspired by the poet's desire, gives way in the prose version (XVII, 32) to a series of banal clichés about foreign travel, and the woman becomes more a casual friend than a young lover:

> My sister, my child,
> (. . .)
> Together we travel afar!
> (. . .)
> In lands whose reflection you are!
> The sun that is shrouded
> In skies lightly clouded
> So fair to my spirit appears,
> As rich for surmise
> As your treacherous eyes,
> So brilliantly shining through tears.
> There is a wonderful country, a country of Cocaigne, they say, that I dream of visiting with an old friend.

In the same vein, the poetic inspiration that in the early version of

"Projects" (XXIV, 48) creates a whole set of imaginary landscapes is replaced in the final version by a process of mechanical repetition by which the poet merely reproduces a series of scenes encountered by chance in the course of an evening walk. This loss of "inspiration"—a state of mind connected in Baudelaire with the aesthetic of organic wholeness and metaphoric equivalence—this loss of inspiration is itself allegorized in the prose poem "The Loss of a Halo" (XLVI, 94), where the poet loses his halo in heavy traffic and then decides against trying to recover it. As an ironic reference to the mystical halo of pure light granted the inspired poet at the beginning of the *Flowers of Evil,* this late prose poem reiterates the disintegration of the Romantic myth of the poet; but it can also symbolize the disintegration of poetic experience itself, as the poet's allegedly privileged understanding turns out to be mere fascination with proliferating images which are themselves meaningless.[20]

The second development in Baudelaire's poetics—what I termed "distanciation"—is also particularly evident in the prose poems. Johnson's comparison of the verse and prose "Invitation to the Voyage" shows a shift from first- and second-person interaction in the verse to third-person in prose; we no longer see dreams inspired by and addressed to a lover, but hear third-person accounts of foreign lands. Indeed the presence of a narrator distancing us from events and emotions is characteristic of virtually *all* the prose poems; even where the "I" appears, it is often narrating a scene involving others.

Take for example the transformation of an anecdote in Baudelaire's "Intimate Journals" into the finished prose poem "Loss of a Halo." In the original sketch, the poet manages to retrieve the halo, but gets the feeling its temporary loss was a bad omen and is left with a sense of foreboding the rest of the day:

> As I was crossing the boulevard, hurrying a little to avoid the carriages, my halo was dislodged and fell into the filth of the macadam. Fortunately, I had time to recover it, but a moment later the unhappy thought slipped into my brain that this was an ill omen; and from that instant the idea would not let me alone; it has given me no peace all day.[21]

In the final version, however, the poet decides it was "less unpleasant to lose my insignia than to get my bones broken," and opts instead for a life in which he can "stroll about incognito, do nasty things, and in-

dulge in vulgar behavior just like ordinary mortals." So much for
Romantic delusions of grandeur. What's more, the poet in the prose
poem is recounting the episode to an acquaintance he meets in a brothel;
here, in an effort to save face for having lost the halo, he boasts of how
he will ridicule anyone old-fashioned enough to pick it up and wear it:

> Dignity bores me. And besides, I can just picture some poor poet finding
> it and daring to try it on. What a pleasure, to make someone happy—
> especially someone who will make me laugh! Imagine X, or Z! That sure
> will be funny!

The loss of the halo is now not merely the subject of a story: it is an
event recounted by a narrator to a listener *within* the story; it has
become an occasion for the narrator to exercise an invidious superiority
over his fictitious audience. The poet is now at one remove from his
own experience: Baudelaire has transmuted the original account and
the uneasy feeling it provoked into the snide banter of a world-weary
and slightly sullied roué.

The hostility latent in this prose poem—and blatant in several others—
has led critics such as Charles Mauron and Leo Bersani to equate the
appearance of the narrator in the prose poems with a shift to sadism
and an identification with a persecutory social self against the original
artistic self.[22] But they overlook the numerous prose poems in which
the narrator apparently identifies with the artist-figure instead. On
balance, Baudelaire identifies with neither the persecuting sadist nor
the persecuted artist (as Jean Starobinski has shown): the narrator
intervenes precisely to remain at a *distance* from everything, even from
his own former selves and from his own experience.[23] The poet of the
prose poems has withdrawn from the world, and now only watches it—
just as intently, perhaps, but with an unbreachable reserve and at an
unbridgeable distance.

What this distance reveals is not sadism, but borderline-narcissistic
pathology. Indeed Baudelaire's prose poem collection could very well
serve as a textbook illustration of the features—personality-splitting,
obsessive self-reference, alternating states of hostility and indifference,
and so forth—that constitute the pathology of borderline and severe
narcissistic conditions.[24] The final version of "The Loss of a Halo," for
instance, illustrates its basic defense mechanism: splitting. Splitting of
the self into separate compartments in the prose poem enables the

narrator first to detach himself from his earlier attempt to recover the halo, and then to subject others similarly tempted to scorn. This devaluation of others and even of one's own former sentiments is typical of narcissism, as is the narrator's self-inflation that accompanies it.

The tendency toward self-reference after which narcissism is named is strikingly illustrated in the prose poem entitled "Windows" (XXXV, 77). This account of someone who takes pleasure in inventing stories about people he glimpses through their windows begins with the following curious but very revealing proposition:

> Those who look into an open window never see as much as those who look in through a closed one. . .

Here is someone who, as Lasch puts it, "sees the world as a mirror of himself," preferring to look through a closed window, "and has no interest in external events except as they throw back a reflection of his own image" (47). Indeed, when challenged at the end of the poem as to the truth of the stories he makes up, the narrator answers,

> What difference does it make what external reality may be, if it helps me to live, to feel *that* I am and *what* I am?

That this exclusive self-reference can become callous and even brutal is clear from the poem "The Bad Glazier" (IX, 12). After asking a glazier to carry his wares up six flights of narrow stairs, the narrator berates him for having no colored panes, and shoves him out the door. Then, just as the glazier is leaving the building, the narrator leans out the window and drops a flower-pot on him, knocking him over and of course breaking all the glass. The narrator allows that such pranks are sometimes dangerous and often costly, but concludes that the instant of infinite pleasure is well worth eternal damnation:

> Such erratic pranks are not without danger and one often has to pay dearly for them. But what is the eternity of damnation compared to the infinity of pleasure found in a single second?

Moreover, the narrator describes how he is sometimes compelled to commit such heinous deeds, while ordinarily he feels quite apathetic:

> There are certain natures, purely contemplative and totally unfit for ac-

tion, which nevertheless, moved by a mysterious and unaccountable impulse, act at times with a rapidity of which they would never have dreamed
themselves capable.

The narrator here evidences that quintessential Baudelairean emotion
(if it can be called that), ennui.

Ennui or apathy, and perhaps even more so, this kind of vacillation
between very different and completely discrete personality types, are
basic traits of the borderline-narcissistic personality. Perhaps this propensity for extreme vacillation can help explain why some critics cite
Baudelaire for sadism when many poems nonetheless manifest a touching empathy for suffering. Among Baudelaire's prose works, "A Heroic
Death" (XXVII, p. 54) and "The Old Clown" (XIV, 25) perhaps represent the opposite poles of Baudelaire's vacillations—but they share an
aesthetically and psychologically crucial common denominator: the narrator's distance from emotional involvement in the scene he is narrating.

Now the point of correlating poems with symptoms this way is not to
diagnose Baudelaire a narcissist, of course, but rather to explain the
impact of his poetry on a culture that has itself become increasingly
narcissistic. Since I suggested earlier that Baudelaire achieved such an
impact in part through the widespread popularity of the existential
novel, let me sketch the relation between the evolution of Baudelaire's
aesthetic and the shape of Sartre's *Nausea*.[25]

The distance Roquentin takes from his own experience is plain
throughout the book. With the exception of his experience of nausea
itself, he shows very little interest in the experience of other people or
his own actions: he abandons work on his biography of Rollebon
(97–98), gives up on contact with Annie (152–54), and generally lives
at one remove from life. Even events of some magnitude—such as the
expulsion of the Self-made Man from the library (166–68) or the scene
with the flasher in the park (79)—are gripping without being engag-
ing: Roquentin remains frozen in his role of observer. This distance—
and the borderline personality-splitting it implies—is perhaps most
dramatically illustrated when Roquentin stabs himself in the arm . . .
and then watches dispassionately as his blood trickles across the table
(100). Here, the borderline-narcissistic lack of emotion distances the
character from his own body.

The process of disintegration characteristic of Baudelaire's poetry
characterizes Sartre's novel as well—and operates on both levels we iden-

tified. For one thing, Roquentin engages in a constant demythification of his social environment—starting with the symbolism of the statue in the square (28), continuing with the portraits of local notables in the Bouville museum (92–93), and culminating in his rejection of the basic myth, what he and Annie called "adventure" (147–48), the myth of narrative itself.

But the central development in the novel is not the disintegration of these interpersonal and social myths, but rather the disintegration of experience itself. The feeling Roquentin calls "nausea" results precisely from his inability to process his everyday experience in the usual way: the codes and categories he uses to classify things, to attribute properties to things so as to make sense of them, no longer function effectively. *Nausea*'s ultimate climax in fact occurs when Roquentin confronts the chestnut-tree root in the park, and finally comes face-to-face with bare existence (129–35). The poetic failure Baudelaire invokes, of no longer being able to portrary beauty in terms of metaphor, similarities, essences and the like becomes in Sartre's novel an inability to live everyday life in terms of the standard essentialist categories and codes of reference. Roquentin's experience becomes random, unwholesome, untotalizable. *Nausea*, in other words, re-presents the Baudelairean aesthetic in prosaic terms.

That *Nausea* portrays experience typical of narcissism is clear from psychiatrists' use of Sartre's novel (and his early philosophy) as an illustration of this personality type.[26] They note in Roquentin certain defensive patterns of response to the disintegration of self and experience that recur frequently in cases of narcissism: a kind of hyper-reflective attention paid to the disintegrating self, as evidenced in Roquentin's obsessive journal-keeping; an attraction to music and especially to melody, for the sense of temporal continuity it affords an ego whose own ability to synthesize is weak; and finally, two ways of relating to other people, which correspond to the basic forms of narcissistic transference observed in therapy. Roquentin first attempts a form of "idealizing transference" in relation to the subject of his biography, Rollebon, whose imposing figure confers value on his own existence (98). But when he realizes that Rollebon is flawed (just like everyone else), he rejects both the historical personage and the biographical project in a typically narcissistic reversal. Roquentin then takes up a position of aloof disdain for other people, tinged with a mute and somewhat disparaging pity. Exactly this "projective identification"—where a flaw of one's own is projected onto another, yet still evokes some emotional response—typifies the narrator's stance in Baudelaire's "A Heroic Death" and "The Old Clown," as well.

By presenting borderline-narcissistic pathology in the texts of Baudelaire and Sartre this way, we are already on the verge of translating ego-psychology into a historical semiotics. As valuable as the work of Kernberg et al. proves in shedding light on the overall shape of late nineteenth- and twentieth-century culture, ego-psychology remains notoriously unable to account for historical changes in personality type.[27] When Heinz Kohut, for example, explains that children become narcissistic because . . . they have narcissistic parents, he simply begs the question of how the parents themselves became narcissistic, of how narcissism started in the first place.[28] The borderline-narcissist's relative ego-instability is best understood, I would suggest, as an effect of the historical dislocation and disarticulation of social codes that are responsible for the stability of meaning and self-experience in the first place.[29] The poetics of Baudelaire take on significance in this light as an original reaction to the initial installation of unalloyed bourgeois economic rule in France during the 1850s.

Marx said in the *Communist Manifesto* that capitalist market society would tend, in his words, "to strip the halo" from all previous forms of social intercourse.[30] Walter Benjamin's remarkable study of Baudelaire is invaluable because it provides mediations between the underlying motor of historical change in this period—the rapid spread of market relations, of the "cash nexus"—and the effects registered in Baudelaire's poetry. In the *18th Brumaire of Louis-Napoleon,* Marx had shown on one level why the reign of Louis-Napoleon and the age of capital he inaugurated spelled the eclipse of bourgeois social authority—why, that is to say, under democratic conditions capitalists would have to forfeit direct political rule and cultural expression to maintain their economic rule intact behind the scenes.[31] Benjamin goes on to show how, on a second level, the poet's loss of his halo reflects a general "atrophy of experience" (as Benjamin calls it) brought about by changes in city life, the mass media, and the development of mass consumption. In reaction to the shocks of increasingly rapid traffic, the sudden transformation of the urban landscape, the fragmentary human contacts typical of crowded city streets, the speed of rail transportation, the invention and marketing of matches and photography, and ultimately the fetishization of commodities itself, Baudelaire adopted what Benjamin calls a shock-defense. This defense mechanism works to isolate and encapsulate discrete incidents which, due to their brevity and/or novelty, could not be assimilated into regular patterns of experience. In the same vein, mass-circulation newspaper stories present increasingly discrete bits of information and no longer integrate them into larger and more comprehensive narratives or world-views. The mass media first replace older narration with information this way, and then proceed to replace information with mere sensation, with a culture of images. Finally, the growing fetishism of commodities replaces more or less competent evaluation of goods with superficial fascination by images: exchange-value, in a word, replaces use-value; mindless fashion supplants tradition as the arbiter of taste. Baudelaire's poetry, as both Barbara Johnson and Benjamin suggest, is the poetry of nascent consumerism.[32]

This disintegration of experience, codes, and values produces an unstable self no longer able to integrate the incidents of everyday life into coherent experience. And what I have called "distanciation" supervenes, as Otto Kernberg has explained, when this weakness of the ego is itself used as a defense mechanism to protect it: the borderline mechanism of splitting serves to segregate incompatible facets of the personality in order to forestall complete breakdown. These are the processes, disintegration and distanciation (splitting), that lead Baudelaire from masochism to borderline-narcissism.

We are now in a position to consider the role of masochism in the historical development of today's narcissistic culture. I mentioned at the outset that the isolated nuclear family was not an exception to but a product of capitalist development. In its early stages, the isolation of the family from larger structures of society and social authority (such as the Catholic church) called for increasing reliance on internalized authority and hence magnified the role of the superego. Even if we believe the superego to be a universal psychic structure, its functions are no doubt considerably increased in early bourgeois culture through the internalized conscience of the Protestant ethic and the internalized rationality of the Enlightenment.[33] The family occupies a separate space, but it does so as an agent of social change: at this stage, its values are consonant with the social values of the bourgeois class and actively support the consolidation of bourgeois hegemony. In the culture of narcissism, by contrast, the superego has ceased to function as purveyor of social values. Lasch attributes this to narcissists' unwillingness or inability to internalize social directives, and speaks conversely of modern institutions' "loss of ability to command allegiance."[34] But this loss, historically speaking, is not some secondary consequence of the narcissistic personality; rather, it results from the culture of masochism—for isolating the private individual from public values was a primary goal of masochistic strategy. Baudelaire throws his own example of individual corruption in the face of society to prove its malfeasance: by willingly playing its victim to the hilt, he denies bourgeois society its legitimacy and institutionalizes the split between individual and social authority, thereby paving the way for narcissism. (Baudelaire himself then proceeded to elaborate the narcissistic grandiose self of the dandy as compensation for and repudiation of his own earlier sacrifice.)

Cultural masochism, then, is an essential precondition for the culture of narcissism, and provides the social context for the so-called demise of the nuclear family. Starting in the mid-nineteenth century, what in fact distinguishes family life is the increasing pressure of consumerism it is called upon to bear. Capitalism had earlier separated wage-labor and social production in the public sphere from reproduction and the nuclear family in the private sphere; to this domestic sphere it now adds consumption, spurred by the drive to realize profit on mass-produced consumer goods.[35] The public–private split thus takes on a new dimension: the good realm of domesticity, haven in a heartless world, becomes increasingly distinct from the jungle of capitalist competition, and domestic consumption becomes the compensation and reward in one realm for the oppressive "productivity" of the other. Consumers bent on redeeming their nine-to-five of toil or drudgery take "Living well is the best revenge" as their slogan. Positive though commodified leisure-time and negative, exploited work-time exist side by side, but without any intrinsic relation between them, separated by the gulf of the market which becomes increasingly difficult to bridge. This rift fosters narcissistic disorder: for borderline and narcissistic pathology, as psychologists and psychiatrists explain it, result precisely from an inability to synthesize good and bad experience into a coherent, nuanced apprehension of the world.[36] Furthermore, the pressures of consumerism have this additional effect: paradoxically, under the whip of fashion and the imperative to consume—Baudelaire's slogan is "To the depths of the unknown to find something new!"—paradoxically, the imperative to consume makes true satisfaction impossible. Consumer society promises everything, but can allow no one enough satisfaction . . . to stop consuming. What was supposedly a haven from a heartless world turns out, as the locus of consumption, to have denial and frustration at its very core. This inevitable frustration, too, contributes to narcissistic disorder: for borderline and narcissistic conditions result from a contradictory response to desire, and produce the impotent rage of oral aggression against an entire society (not just mothers!) that continually nourishes desires but never finally satisfies them.[37]

What I mean to suggest, then, is that cultural narcissism is a social affliction prepared by the cultural masochism of the nineteenth century; that it was fostered by consumerism and the split between public and private life, between production and consumption; and that its ultimate source is not just the vicissitudes of modern family life, but the basic structure of capitalist social relations themselves. This is not to say that the nuclear family and other social institutions included in Lasch's account are not important factors, even immediate causes, of the culture of narcissism—for they certainly are. But their effects would be far less pervasive if they did not resonate throughout a society whose very libidinal-economic structure fosters and continually reinforces the borderline-narcissistic personality.

NOTES

1. Among the first social commentary articles were Peter Marin's "The New Narcissism," *Harper's,* (October, 1975) and Tom Wolfe's "The 'Me' Decade and the Third Great Awakening," *New York* (23 August 1976). The central clinical study is Otto Kernberg's BCPN, itself based on (and an advance over) Heinz Kohut's earlier AOS. Kernberg's formulations are generally more acute than his predecessor's (Kernberg himself addresses their differences explicitly in Part II, Chapter 9, "Clinical Problems of the Narcissistic Personality"), primarily because Kernberg considers narcissism in relation to "both libidinal and aggressive drive derivatives" (BCPN, p. 271), whereas Kohut "concentrates almost exclusively on the role of libidinal forces" alone (AOS, p.xv). The resulting divergence is considerable: Kohut sees pathological narcissism on a continuum with normal, infantile narcissism, whereas Kernberg considers narcissism a distinct pathology with a structure and dynamic of its own. By analyzing pathological narcissism in connection with the broader category of borderline conditions—nearly all narcissists are borderline, but borderline conditions are not necessarily narcissistic, Kernberg reports, though both depend crucially on splitting as their basic defense mechanism—he is able to distinguish three levels of narcissistic pathology (BCPN, pp. 332–34), each level manifesting more pronounced ego-disintegration than the last: (1) the smoothly-functioning, well-adapted narcissist (who often escapes diagnosis as such), (2) the pathological narcissist with underlying borderline condition (by far the majority), and (3) the narcissist who functions overtly on a borderline level (who sometimes manifests marked anti-social traits as well, and of which Dostoyevsky's Underground Man is my favorite illustration). This continuum enables social critics and cultural historians to consider a wide range of phenomena under one rubric, "narcissism." In what follows, I use "borderline-narcissistic" in the cases of Baudelaire and Sartre to highlight within the general syndrome the extensive ego-disintegration their literary works depict; and "pathological narcissism" or simply "narcissism" to refer to less acute forms pervading society at large.

2. Christopher Lasch, *The Culture of Narcissism: American Life in an Age of Diminishing Expectations* (New York: W. W. Norton, 1978). This book has been the focus of several symposia: see *Salmagundi,* 46 (1979) and *Telos,* 44 (1980). While drawing heavily (though not exclusively) on Kernberg for his psychological theory, Lasch refers to both "narcissistic" and "borderline" personalities without distinguishing or explaining the relations between them, as Kernberg himself does with precision (see note 1). My own historical explanation of cultural narcissism emphasizes the social preconditions for the borderline condition characteristic of the modern narcissistic personality, and suggests that "the pathological grandiose self [of the narcissist] compensates for the generally 'ego-weakening' effects of the primitive defensive organization [based on splitting]" (BCPN, pp. 265, 269); see the concluding section of this chapter.

3. Lasch, *The Culture of Narcissism,* p. 47.

4. See for example Michèle Barrett and Mary McIntosh, "Narcissism and the Family: a Critique of Lasch," *New Left Review,* 135 (Sept.–Oct. 1982), 35–48, especially pp. 39 and 43.

5. Christopher Lasch, *Haven in a Heartless World: The Family Besieged* (New York: Basic Books, 1977).

6. Lasch, *The Culture of Narcissism,* pp. 33–34.

7. In addition to *Totem and Taboo, Future of an Illusion,* and *Civilization and its Discontents,* see *New Introductory Lectures* 6 and 7 for Freud's programmatic statements to this effect.

8. See Eli Zaretsky, *Capitalism, the Family and Personal Life* (New York: Harper and Row, 1976) and Mark Poster, *Critical Theory of the Family* (New York: Seabury Press, 1978).

9. René Laforgue, *The Defeat of Baudelaire,* trans. Herbert Agar (1931; rpt. London: Hogarth Press, 1932) and Leo Bersani, *Baudelaire and Freud* (Berkeley: University of California Press, 1977). Most critics use "masochism" with reference to Baudelaire in the sense of "moral masochism"—deriving satisfaction from defeat or adversity. Bersani's work is an interesting exception, dealing instead with the psychodynamics of Baudelaire's poetry and deriving therefrom a new metapsychological definition of the concept of "masochism."

10. Jean-Paul Sartre, *Baudelaire* (Paris: Gallimard, 1947) and *L'Idiot de la famille,* 3 vols. (Paris: Gallimard, 1972). The "Knights of Nothingness" include Banville, Leconte de Lisle, Mallarmé, and Villiers de L'Isle-Adam.

11. See Gilles Deleuze, *Présentation de Sacher-Masoch* (Paris: Minuit, 1967), especially pp. 6–9.

12. See Georges Blin, *Le Sadisme de Baudelaire* (Paris: José Corti, 1948).

13. Walter Benjamin, *Charles Baudelaire: Lyric Poet in the Era of High Capitalism,* trans. Harry Zohn (London: New Left Books, 1973), p. 109.

14. In a letter to Victor de Mars (secretary of the *Revue des Deux Mondes,* which published many of Baudelaire's poems), 7 April 1855 in *Correspondance Générale,* ed. J. Crépet (Paris: Louis Conard, 1947), Vol. 1, #209, pp. 330–31.

15. Cézanne to Pissarro, 15 March 1865 (in *Cézanne Letters,* trans. Marguerite Kay [London: M. B. Cassirer, 1941], pp. 68–69).

16. In addition to Bersani's short work (note 7), I refer to Barbara Johnson's studies, notably *Défigurations du langage poétique* (Paris: Flammarion, 1979).

17. *The Flowers of Evil,* trans. Richard Howard (Boston: David Godine, 1982), hereafter RH; or trans. Florence Friedman (Philadelphia: Dufour, 1966), hereafter FF.

18. See Johnson, *Défigurations,* chapters 2 and 5. The conclusion regarding "Beauty" depends on close linguistic analysis of the French, which defies translation.

19. *Paris Spleen,* trans. Louise Varèse (New York: New Directions, 1947), poem XVII, p. 31; prose poem number in roman numerals. (Copyright © 1970 by New Directions Publishing Corporation. By kind permission of the publisher.)

20. See Irving Wohlfarth, "Perte d'auréole: the Emergence of the Dandy," *Modern Language Notes,* 85:4 (May 1970), 529–71.

21. *Intimate Journals,* trans. Christopher Isherwood (New York: Stratford Press, 1947), pp. 45–46 ("Bribes" Section 17). See also Wohlfarth, "Perte d'auréole."

22. Charles Mauron, *Le Dernier Baudelaire* (Paris: José Corti, 1966); and Bersani, *Baudelaire and Freud,* chapter 12.

23. Jean Starobinski, "Sur quelques répondants allégoriques du poète," *Revue d'Histoire Littéraire,* 67:2 (1967) pp. 402–12.

24. See Kernberg, BCPN, pp. 25–30, 227–29, 64–65; and also Theodore Nadelson, "Victim, Victimizer: Interaction in the Psychotherapy of Borderline Patients," *International Journal of Psychoanalytic Psychotherapy,* 5 (1976), 115–29.

25. *Nausea,* trans. Lloyd Alexander (1938; New York: New Directions, 1964); page references to this edition follow citations in the text.

26. See David Klaas and William Offenkrantz, "Sartre's Contribution to the Understanding of Narcissism," *International Journal of Psychoanalytic Psychotherapy,* 5 (1976), pp. 547–65, for an analysis from a Kohutian perspective. It is important to note that Sartre's *later* philosophy, particularly the Marxist phase where he acknowledges the impact of history and society on human freedom, to a large extent eliminates the narcissism of early existentialism.

27. See Norman O. Brown, *Life Against Death: The Psychoanalytic Meaning of History* (Middletown, Conn.: Wesleyan University Press, 1959), especially pp. 204–5; with respect to the anality of the Protestant character, for instance, he says (p. 205) that

> orthodox psychoanalytic dogma ends in the same cul-de-sac as the neo-Freudian revisionists: adult anal character is derived from adult anal character. . . . called upon to explain a change in the character of a culture, orthodox psychoanalysis can have nothing to offer, because of the iron ring of psychological determinism it postulates. . . .

28. On this count, Kernberg (BCPN, p. 223) is not much better:

> I do not think that changes in contemporary culture have effects on patterns of object relations (where narcissists have problems). . . . This is not to say that such changes . . . could not occur over a period of several generations, if and when changes in cultural patterns affect family structure to such an extent that the earliest development in childhood would be influenced.

29. In their *Anti-Oedipus,* trans. R. Hurley, M. Seem, and H. Lane (1972; New York: Viking, 1977) Gilles Deleuze and Felix Guattari mount a devastating post-Lacanian argument against the family's being the principal determinant of the psyche: their emphasis on the social formation's determination of psychic structure is a crucial corrective to Lasch's reliance on ego-psychology.

30. See Lewis Feuer ed., *Marx and Engels: Basic Writings on Politics and Philosophy* (Garden City, N.Y.: Doubleday, 1959), pp. 6–41:

> The bourgeoisie has stripped of its halo every occupation hitherto honored and looked up to with reverent awe. It has converted the physician, the lawyer, the priest, the man of science into its paid wage laborers. . . . The bourgeoisie cannot exist without constantly revolutionizing the instruments of production, and thereby the relations of production, and with them the whole relations of society. . . . Constant revolutionizing of production, uninterrupted disturbance of all social conditions, everlasting uncertainty and agitation distinguish the bourgeois epoch from all earlier ones. All fixed, fast-frozen relations, with their train of ancient and venerable prejudices and opinions, are swept away, all new-formed ones become antiquated before they can ossify. All that is solid melts into air. . . . (p. 10)

31. In *Marx on Revolution,* ed. and trans. Saul Padover (New York: McGraw-Hill, 1971), pp. 243–328.

32. See Benjamin, *Charles Baudelaire,* passim; and Johnson, *Défigurations,* pp. 128–39.

33. Brown, *Life Against Death,* chapters 12 and 14; Deleuze, *Présentation,* pp. 50–60, 105–115 and passim; Max Weber, *The Protestant Ethic and the Spirit of Capitalism,* trans. Talcott Parsons (1905; rpt. New York: Scribner, 1958).

34. Lasch, *The Culture of Narcissism,* p. 49.

35. See E. J. Hobsbawm, *The Age of Capital* (New York: Scribner, 1975), chapter 13; and Rosalyn Williams, *Dream Worlds: Mass Consumption in Late 19th Century France* (Berkeley: University of California Press, 1982).

36. See Kernberg, BCPN, pp. 25–38; and Warren Brodey "The Dynamics of Narcissism," *Psychoanalytic Study of the Child,* 20 (1965), 165–93, especially 186–88.

37. See Kernberg, BCPN, pp. 234–35; and Nadelson, "Victim, Victimizer," p. 117.

NINE

NARCISSISM AND HISTORY: FLAUBERT'S *SENTIMENTAL EDUCATION*

Lynne Layton

Joni Mitchell ends her 1971 album, *Blue*, with a song entitled "The Last Time I Saw Richard." The first words of the song are:

> The last time I saw Richard was Detroit in '68,
> and he told me all romantics meet the same fate someday
> cynical and drunk and boring someone in some dark cafe.

It may appear odd to begin a paper on Flaubert's *Sentimental Education* with these words, but I believe they describe a point where psycho-analytic interpretation might fruitfully meet sociohistoric interpretation. Mitchell's song describes what I call the romanticism/cynicism antinomy, an insoluble conflict that I find to be at the heart of *Sentimental Education* as well. The process of conflict begins with a type of immature romanticism, which involves the projection onto reality of preconceived notions that have a strongly idealized content. Reality is cruel to our romantic; it refuses to submit to these notions or ideals. The romantic becomes disillusioned—worse, enraged—and cynicism sets in. Now the world is seen as hostile, hopeless, and no change is conceived to be possible. Perhaps our romantic, in the depths of cynical despair, meets someone who once more stirs up the romantic fantasies and desires. The cycle begins again.

The romanticism/cynicism antinomy, I believe, is a characteristic be-havioral pattern of a narcissistic personality. The cycle of idealization and devaluation, be it of others or of social possibilities, is common to those whose relationships are predominantly of the self-selfobject type. When a period in which social change or hopes for social change is succeeded by a period characterized by conservative or reactionary politics and social views, one may seek to understand how such a rapid shift in sensibility could occur. I invoke Joni Mitchell because I believe that the psychological phenomenon she describes, the romanticism/cynicism antinomy and the narcissistic personality of which it is characteristic, is the contemporary (that is, sixties/seventies) analogue of what Flaubert describes in *Sentimental Education*, the novel of post-1848 disillusionment.

In what follows, I would like first to distinguish post- from pre-1848 disillusionment. Then I will discuss *Sentimental Education* itself; here, I will focus on the narcissistic mode of relating to lovers and friends that Flaubert shows to be parallel to the mode by which his own generation, particularly radical intellectuals, relates to politics. It is my thesis that, in this novel, Flaubert condemns the bad faith of his entire generation; he explains the failure of the 1848 revolution and the acceptance of Louis-Napoléon's authoritarian regime as, in part, an outgrowth of a narcissistic mode of relating to the world. Since most of Flaubert's characters are intellectuals, and the revolution of 1848 has been called a revolution of intellectuals (see Lewis Namier), I shall also look at over-intellectualization as a defense of the narcissist. Finally, I would like to consider Flaubert's relation to his novel. Because *Sentimental Education* is strongly autobiographical, I will discuss Flaubert and the subjective neurosis that, as Sartre puts it, came to mesh with a class neurosis, thereby securing an audience for Flaubert's work. At issue is whether or not Flaubert transcends the neurosis in his novel.

Flaubert is considered by many to be the father of the modern novel. His novels are usually classified, along with those of Stendhal and Balzac, as belonging to French realism. Indeed, *Sentimental Education* and *Madame Bovary* have often been categorized as novels of disillusionment, as has Balzac's *Lost Illusions* and Stendhal's *The Red and the Black*. Yet, in *Sentimental Education*, published in 1869, Flaubert describes a different reality from that of either Stendhal or Balzac, and he displays a different understanding of disillusionment as well. In Balzac's *Lost Illusions*, for example, the economic reality of capitalism dooms the ideals of Lucien de Rubempré to failure. The ideals themselves, largely derived from those of the French Enlightenment and Revolution, are unquestioned in the novel. The main character is disillusioned by the pettiness of everyday life and gives up his ideals in order to succeed in the world. In *Sentimental Education*, the problematic is not the hero's progressive disillusionment with or abandonment of worthy ideals, but the exposition of tragic flaws in the very processes of perception, thought, and emotion that create the ideals. Flaubert thus focuses on problems in thought and perception, for he sees autonomy to be threatened from within as well as from without. Because of the way ideals such as pure love or universal freedom are formulated and sought after by the characters, they can never be realized—worse, they are doomed to turn into their repressive opposites. Thus, the reader becomes disillusioned with certain Western ideals themselves, seeing them as a product of psychopathology.

Corresponding to this different reality presented by Flaubert is a very different self, one that is not primarily rational or cohesive. *Sentimental Education* is peopled with narcissistic personalities, who, as Akhtar and Thomson (1982) have said, seem to have deficits in six areas: (1) self-concept, (2) interpersonal relationships, (3) social adaptation, (4) ethics, standards, and ideals, (5) love and sexuality, (6) cognitive style.[1]

In terms of character, themes, structure, and narrative stance, *Sentimental Education* presents a realism quite different from that of its predecessors. I believe, following Sartre, that this difference hinges on psychosocial changes that reached their height in the revolution of 1848 and its aftermath;[2] indeed, Flaubert makes this revolution the center of his novel. Sartre speaks of Flaubert's novels as post-Romantic, and post-Romantic is definitely post-1848. Flaubert, reacting to the stifling atmosphere of the militaristic, bureaucratic Second Empire, a regime that he felt was dedicated to the eradication of individual autonomy, attempts in *Sentimental Education* to understand how France made the transition from monarchy to Republic to Empire, from ennui to excitement and back to ennui, in a few years. The fault is in ourselves, he concludes, particularly in the romantic formation and illusions of the generation. In the spheres of art, love, and politics, he shows how those who were in their twenties in 1848 were lost in a world of intellectualized fantasies and systems that bore no relation to reality. In each sphere, protagonists formulate theories about life, comforting theories that they substitute for life. In my view, these theories are defenses of narcissistic personalities; they enable their formulators to avoid relationships, for the protagonists are fully engaged not with reality but with their own thoughts. Flaubert thus shows the "objective neurosis" that Sartre defines as post-1848 to have been operating well before that date.

Flaubert centers the novel on Frédéric Moreau, a young romantic born in the same year as Flaubert, 1821. The first description of Frédéric is in 1840; the narrator tells us that he is 18, his hair is long, he holds a sketch book, and, most importantly, he is immobile. The second line tells us that, at that moment, standing on a boat, he literally views things through a fog. Both the immobility and the tendency to be in a fog are quite characteristic of Frédéric, whose life from 1840 to 1868 is told in this novel. Were it not for the coherence lent by Flaubert's use of *style indirect libre*, the reader would never be able to make sense of the way Frédéric, empty and depressed, with only glimmers of creativity and purpose, goes through life. Flaubert explains his immobility as a function of his vulnerability to narcissistic injury:

> For certain people, the stronger their desire, the more impossible it is for them to act on it. They are embarrassed by their mistrust of themselves; the fear of displeasing petrifies them . . . (199; 174)[3]

Kohut would clearly find Frédéric to be a narcissist. Frédéric's frequent bouts of ennui, an empty depression at the core of which are feelings of worthlessness, and his inability to do *any* kind of work (alternately explained by the narrator as due to lack of talent, too many projects at once, and lack of ability to concentrate) are the presenting symptoms. Flaubert even gives us some hints to determine the etiology of Frédéric's problem. His father died while his mother was pregnant with him, and his mother, whom we occasionally see, is cold, unempathic, opportunistic, and very controlling (to the point of having someone spy on Frédéric when she suspects he has befriended someone whom she considers "below" him). With an absent father and an unempathic mother, we would expect that Frédéric would have difficulty constituting both poles of Kohut's self: indeed, Frédéric's depressions alternate with periods of nearly manic grandiosity, and his entire life is sacrificed to an ideal love, never consummated, with an older, married woman, whom he experiences only as a selfobject. Frédéric's depressions and periods of inability to work stand in direct relation to the vicissitudes of this ideal love relationship.

Before discussing the nature of Frédéric's love relationships, let us look at some other facets of his personality. In high school, Frédéric's interests were those of the typical romantic youth. He was fascinated by religion, the Middle Ages, memoires, the novels of Walter Scott, and Goethe's *Werther*. What these interests have in common is that they offer the subject a way to merge his self with something ideal and larger than the self. Just as Mme. Bovary consistently seeks to be overpowered by love and even turns to the church, begging it to offer her an escape from herself, so Frédéric consistently tries to evade taking responsibility for his life by merging with another. Indeed, when things go wrong, Frédéric is ready to blame others, fate, anything but himself. He often flips coins or engages in some other ritual to decide major questions in his life. When one thing goes wrong, he is apt to go into a long depression. Usually things go wrong because reality does not meet his preconceived and assiduously constructed expectations. He occasionally tries to escape from himself in projects, but this never works. His main means of escape from his emptiness is "sentimental," that is, love.

What is Frédéric's love like, in what consists his sentimental education? Overall, Frédéric's love life can be exhaustively characterized by two kinds of objectification that correspond to the romanticism/ cynicism antinomy. I speak of the mother/whore dichotomy. On the one hand, Frédéric has a long affair with a courtesan named Rosanette who he thinks is a moron. He treats her despicably, partly because he has turned to her only when his ideal love has failed, and partly as revenge for the despicable way in which she had earlier treated him. From the first time he meets her at a costume party where she is in military dress, his sexual fantasies with regard to her are permeated by masochistic imagery. He imagines her whipping him or disemboweling him with her golden spurs. Most often, when thinking of her, he dissolves her into body fragments. As he says, he desires her largely for the pleasure of conquering and dominating her (176; 153). The feeling given the reader is that Frédéric is really trying to dominate and conquer his own sexual urges, which seem to frighten him. In this novel, Frédéric's relation to Rosanette is crassly symbolized by his requisition of a grotesque painting of her by one of his "friends"—the inscription reads, "The property of M. Moreau."

As I said above, he turns to Rosanette, former mistress of Jacques Arnoux, when he fails to conquer his ideal love, Marie, the wife of Jacques Arnoux.[4] Marie, too, is an object, indeed, a selfobject. But she is the idealized mother imago, the perfect being that, as Flaubert makes crystal clear, existed in Frédéric's head years before he ever laid eyes on her.

It is as interesting to look at how this relationship begins as at how it develops, or rather fails to develop. It begins at the novel's beginning. Recall, Frédéric is eighteen and immobile. He is on a boat destined for his home in the provinces. His ennui, Flaubert says, makes time pass slowly and makes people look even more insignificant than they already do (22; 17)—our first clue that Frédéric's perceptions have more to do with himself than with the outside world. Right before the ideal comes into view, Frédéric notes that the proletarians on board are all covered with spots and stains. This disgusts Frédéric, who seeks purity. Then, as if offering salvation from the dirt of everyday existence, purity appears. Years later, in his declaration of love, he will tell her that he had been depressed in high school, but that "in his poetic heaven there shone the face of a woman, an apparition so clear that when he saw her for the first time, he recognized her immediately" (306; 270). In fact, as he gazes at her for the first time, he creates a past for her. He imagines her of Andalusian, perhaps Creole, origin; obviously, she must have brought back her Negro domestic from the islands (23–24; 19). All of this is drawn from romantic novels and poetry. He wants to know everything about her, although he seems already to have supplied all the necessary details, and he experiences a desire that is so great that mere physical desire disappears in the face of it (23; 18).

From the beginning, then, she is an extension of himself, and her characteristics are those of his own imagination. Given that Mme. Arnoux (whose first name, Marie, is rarely used by Frédéric, indicating that her unattainability is desired) is much older than Frédéric, not primarily thought of in terms of sexual desire, and, from beginning to end, is always seen and imagined in a maternal context (sewing something for a child, holding her infant), it is safe to hypothesize that she is a mother imago as well as a romantic heroine for Frédéric. After their first encounter, Frédéric, riding in a carriage and feeling "cradled" (27; 22) by the ride, notes that "she resembled the women of romantic novels. . . . She was the luminous point on which everything else converged" (27; 22). Later, the narrator says, "But bit by bit, his hopes and his memories, Nogent [where his mother lives], Choiseul St. [where Marie lives], Mme. Arnoux, his mother, all were merged in his mind" (126; 109).

Mme. Arnoux is an ideal that Frédéric hopes will save him from what he perceives to be a dirty, boring, and depressing existence. Throughout the novel, it is only in her presence that he feels alive. His desires to merge with her are sometimes expressed with oral imagery, for example, when he fantasizes a spiritual life together, where he could "gaze into her eyes and drink her soul" (91; 79). When he is out walking with her for the first time, feeling "cradled" by the wind in the middle of a cloud (89; 77), he thinks that everything, all of Paris, centers on her. Is this ideal love? Many critics have thought so and further thought that Frédéric's betrayal of this love is a betrayal of ideals.[5] But what Frédéric wants is for himself to be the center of Paris. We recognize Kohut's formulation of idealization and the selfobject in Frédéric's attempt to regain the grandiose omnipotence of the infant; in the above scene, Frédéric is really saying: You are perfect, but I am part of you.[6] It is clear that this is no more love than is the relation to the whore. In both cases, the women are experienced as part of Frédéric's self, and they never exist for him as subjects. So much for ideal love.

I began this paper by discussing the romanticism/cynicism antinomy. Given what has already been said regarding Frédéric's relation to Marie, does it not seem inevitable that this love will degenerate to hate? Since Marie is experienced as part of Frédéric, she must always meet his expectations; any indication that she has a will of her own which might not harmonize with Frédéric's needs is experienced by him as an empathic break. When the ideal refuses to do what her creator expects her to do, she is despised, and this happens often in the novel. Further, Frédéric has so prostrated himself before her, has been so willing to make himself nothing (see, for example, 107; 93), that her independent moves easily provoke the narcissistic rage that lies constantly just beneath the surface of his devotion. Let us look at a few examples.

After years of barely even seeing Mme. Arnoux, circumstances arise that make Frédéric her confidant. Her husband has been having an affair with Rosanette for a long time, and he has been engaged in several shady business deals that constantly put the family in a precarious situation. Frédéric loans Arnoux money, and, realizing that it is convenient to have his wife occupied while he is out with Rosanette, Arnoux encourages Frédéric to spend more time with Marie. She continuously talks about Arnoux's vices, and Frédéric becomes a houseboy, listening to her complaints, playing with the children (whom he despises), going shopping for her. Frédéric is quite aware that he is a slave, and he is aware of his anger. Flaubert tells us how the anger and devotion are linked: "By force of his dreams, he had placed her beyond the human condition. He felt, next to her, less important on earth than the silk scraps that fell from her scissors" (199; 174). This feeling of being nothing, of giving so much for so little in return, infuriates him.

Mme. Arnoux does eventually fall in love with him and tell him of her love, but she refuses to commit adultery. It is this independent decision of hers that Frédéric will not respect, but, to remain in her presence, he pretends to go along with it. So, whereas she can be spontaneous in expressing her love for him, he is always calculating how he can keep her and perhaps get her into bed (308; 272). After a short period of real happiness, Frédéric begins to torment her and hate her for not giving him what he wants. He demands that she prove her love by meeting him on the street. He surreptitiously rents an apartment, and, on the fated day—which happens to be the beginning of the February 1848 revolution—he waits. In the meantime, her child has a coughing attack that nearly kills him. She takes this as a sign from God and decides that she will not meet Frédéric. Frédéric's rage makes him turn to Rosanette; he takes her to the rented apartment and weeps as he simultaneously loses his virginity, and, in his view, betrays his ideal.

Does Marie play along with Frédéric's fantasies? I do not think so. Let us look at another romanticism/cynicism cycle to investigate this issue. After a period of anger at Marie, before she has admitted her love for him, she turns up at his apartment and asks a favor. He tells us that he felt "submerged by waves of infinite tenderness" (217; 191) on seeing her. He then appears one day at the country pottery factory owned by her husband. He says he wants to throw himself at her feet, but he is held back by what he describes as a kind of religious fear. Her dress, he says, appears huge, infinite, impossible to lift (229–30; 202). Unable to take any action, he passively waits for her either to encourage him or send him away. She begins to explain that she is against adultery; her principles are those of middle-class morality. Frédéric calls her a bourgeoise, and she replies angrily: "But I never pretended to be a *grand dame*" (230; 202). Marie knows herself to be quite ordinary and does not encourage his idealization. The narrator then tells us Frédéric's response to her reply:

> What he felt at first was an infinite stupefaction. This way of making him understand the ridiculousness of his hope crushed him. ["Crushed" is a word he often uses.] He felt himself as doomed as a man who has fallen to the bottom of an abyss, who knows that no help will come and that he will die. (230–31; 202)

He stumbles around as he tries to leave. One hour after arriving on the boulevards of Paris, the narrator tells us:

> He wanted to be hard, and he soothed his wounded heart by denigrating
> Mme. Arnoux with insults: "She's an imbecile, a dull woman, a brute; I
> won't think about her anymore." (231; 203)

Again he attempts to take vengeance by turning to Rosanette.

These are a few of many examples of the pathological romanticism/
cynicism antinomy in the sphere of love. The experience of the other as
an ideal selfobject inevitably leads to anger and betrayal of the ideal. As
a result of his abject slavery, Frédéric always feels that he is being used
or mocked. This perpetual fear of narcissistic injury results in rage. But,
until the end, he always comes back to the ideal, because he needs her to
stabilize his fragile self.

As I pointed out above, the sentimental events of the novel are inter-
woven with political events in France between 1848 and 1850. Just as
Frédéric always just misses relationships with women and friends, so he
always seems to miss the great turning points in French history that
happen right under his nose.

Toward the end of the novel, Mme. Arnoux flees Paris with her
husband, who is bankrupt and about to be thrown in jail. This loss
makes Frédéric feel "broken down, crushed, annihilated" (451; 400).
He feels that his whole being has been torn apart (452; 401). But worse
is yet to come. Frédéric's fiancée, a wealthy member of the haute bourgeoisie, whom he is marrying for sheer opportunistic reasons, finds out
that Frédéric had tried to save the Arnoux by borrowing money from
her and lying about where it was going. She decides to take vengeance
and has Mme. Arnoux's possessions put up for public sale. She maneuvers Frédéric to the sale, which occurs on 1 December 1851, the day
before the coup that inaugurated Flaubert's pet peeve, the Second Empire. The sale of those cherished things causes Frédéric to feel a sudden
loss of self: "It was as though the very parts of his heart went off with
those things; and the monotonous effect of the same voices, the same
gestures, numbed him with fatigue, causing a funereal torpor, a sense of
disintegration" (458; 407). The ideal woman loses her adored context
just as the Republic is destroyed.

The "love" story does not end here. It ends in 1867, when Marie
turns up to visit Frédéric, the "man of all weaknesses" (336; 298), who
has never done a thing with his life. He is at first overcome with that
same strong desire he has always had. They go for a walk, and when
they return, she takes off her hat and reveals her white hair. Frédéric is
stunned and begins to talk of his past love for her to hide his present

discomfort. The narrator tells us that he becomes drunk with his own words and begins to believe what he is saying (466; 414). Suddenly he suspects that she has come to give herself to him, and Flaubert describes his reaction as follows:

> he was overtaken by a desire stronger than ever, a furious, enraged passion. However, he felt something inexpressible, a feeling of repulsion, and something like a fear of committing incest. Another fear stopped him—that he might be disgusted later. Besides, what an encumbrance it would be! (467; 415)

Here we have final proof that Marie was a mother-image for him, and that, as desirous of her as he thought he had been, a split-off feeling of disgust and repulsion, born undoubtedly of anger, had probably always been there as well. In the final analysis, it was this ambivalence, which Frédéric did not have the capacity to tolerate, that prevented their union. For Frédéric, the education ends as Marie kisses him on the forehead—in his words—"like a mother" (467; 415). For Flaubert, this last meeting is one more example of Frédéric's impotence, symbolic of the impotence of his generation.

Frédéric fits every category of Akhtar and Thomson's narcissistic personality description. His self-concept is totally dependent on the evaluation of others; his thought shows the preference for concepts over facts that Waelder wrote about in his 1925 paper on narcissism;[7] his sexuality is blocked by ambivalent feelings toward his mother and mother imagos; he can do no work; in the course of the novel, he changes and betrays every one of his ethical principles and ideals; and he shows very little to no empathy in his relationships with others. He betrays his best friend, Deslauriers, several times, but, as with Marie, he always seems to return to him, dropping any other friends that might interfere with the dyad. This friendship, too, is a narcissistic relationship that began with Frédéric's idealization of the older, more intellectual school friend.

As I said before, Frédéric's immobility is in part explained by his fear of narcissistic injury. At several points in the novel, he is convinced that everyone is making fun of him: there is sometimes good reason for him to think so. He feels superior to others, however—even in one of his lowest moments, he says he is disgusted by people, yet happy in feeling that he is better than they (87; 75). But Flaubert's irony constantly reveals Frédéric's tragic shallowness and mediocrity—one example is where Frédéric decides to run for office in the provisional government because he is seduced by the costumes the deputies wear (335; 297). Here we have a male Mme. Bovary, but Flaubert adds a dimension to this novel that is less blatant in *Madame Bovary*, that is, the tying of individual narcissism to the fateful political narcissism of the age.

Whereas Frédéric closely fits the type of innocuous narcissist described in Kohut's writings, the two characters tied most closely to the political events of the novel, Deslauriers and Sénécal, are more aptly described using Kernberg's view of the narcissistic personality:

> These patients present an unusual degree of self-reference in their interactions with other people, a great need to be loved and admired by others, and a curious apparent contradiction between a very inflated concept of themselves and an inordinate need for tribute from others. Their emotional life is shallow. They experience little empathy for the feelings of others, they obtain very little enjoyment from life other than from the tributes they receive from others or from their own grandiose fantasies, and they feel restless and bored when external glitter wears off and no new sources feed their self-regard. They envy others, tend to idealize some people from whom they expect narcissistic supplies, and to depreciate and treat with contempt those from whom they do not expect anything (often their former idols). In general, their relationships with other people are clearly exploitative and sometimes parasitic. It is as if they feel they have the right to control and possess others and to exploit them without guilt feelings—and behind a surface which very often is charming and engaging, one senses coldness and ruthlessness.[8]

Deslauriers is Frédéric's childhood friend, and from our first view of him, we see him as an intellectual youth consumed by resentment. His mother is dead, and his father treats him cruelly, beating him and continuously cutting off his means of existence. Although he is older than Frédéric, he enjoys their relationship because Frédéric idealizes him and Frédéric has wealth. Throughout the novel, he attempts to use Frédéric to advance his career, and he betrays the friendship several times. He, like almost everyone else in the novel, is inordinately opportunistic, and, as revolutionary and conservative factions become more polarized in the 1840s, the lawyer comes to see politics as his possible means to power.

Power is clearly Deslauriers' goal; he dreams nostalgically of the French Revolution, when, unlike the ennui of the present, things were happening, and, more particularly, the down-and-out had an access to power. His fantasy of the French Revolution reveals his goal: "[It was a time when] simple lawyers commanded generals . . ." (137; 119). This same need for control is seen in his theories on women and his treatment of them: he thinks they are stupid, pure objects meant to serve him. As he reduces his girlfriend to tears because she dared to show up at his apartment unasked, he tells Frédéric: "I don't ask to be loved, but to be obeyed" (208; 183).

Deslauriers has no real political principles; believing that both popular sovereignty and divine right are fictions, he plans, with Frédéric's money, to start a journal in which he will criticize both sides. His intention is to get everyone to hate each other, so that he can fill the void and realize his old dream: "that is, the ineffable joy of controlling others . . ." (207; 182). The best thing, he tells Frédéric, is to have no opinion (206; 181). Thus, we see the same lack of responsibility and commitment in Deslauriers that we witnessed in Frédéric.

By the time of the revolution, Deslauriers is so poverty-stricken, so bitter about his circumstances, so angry that Frédéric has not shared his wealth with him, that he has come to hate the rich and he fights alongside the workers. Flaubert always makes it clear that his radicalism is directly linked to his personal feeling of powerlessness and his desire, not for justice, but for glory. Indeed, Deslauriers comes utterly to despise the workers during the period of the provisional government (1848–1851), largely because they have not recognized his genius and given him power over them (410; 364). Frédéric recognizes what such people as Deslauriers have done to the workers and counters with a statement reminiscent of Marx's *18th Brumaire*:

> You were just petty bourgeois, and the best of you ill-bred pedants! As for the workers, they have every reason to complain, for, if you except the million taken from the Civil List, which you granted with the basest toadyism, you've given them nothing but fine phrases! The wage-book remains in the hands of the bosses, and wage-earners remain the inferior of the masters (even in the courts), because their voices are not heard at all. The Republic appears to me to be jaded. (411; 365)

The workers were a means to an end for Deslauriers, and Flaubert implies that this was a general phenomenon in this period.

I will not discuss here the opportunism of the haute bourgeoisie, which always seems to remain in power no matter what the government is called. Flaubert's line on Dambreuse, their leader, is "he would have paid for the privilege of selling himself" (420; 373). They support the Republic when it is to their advantage, simultaneously working behind the scenes for its overthrow; they support the bourgeois betrayers of the Republic in June 1848, then they get rid of the betrayers and support Louis-Napoléon. Here, it is important to note that the powerlessness of Frédéric's group of friends *is not imagined* but quite real. By the 1840s in France, the upward mobility promised by the French Revolution seems to have been severely limited and even opportunism does not work for the intellectuals who have no wealth at their disposal. Thus, the resentment of the powerless is not just a product of family dynamics but of the sociohistorical situation as well.[9]

I want to discuss one more radical member of Frédéric's circle to support my statement that narcissism pervades politics as well as love in the novel. Sénécal is also an intellectual, a mathematics tutor when we first meet him, and he is not outwardly opportunistic. A confirmed socialist, he claims to speak for the people. He despises any mark of inequality and fights for universal suffrage in February 1848. But, in politics, Sénécal's way of relating is analogous to that of Frédéric in love. It is my contention that "the people" in the abstract are Sénécal's idealized selfobject and that when the people do not do what he expects of them, when they refuse to act according to his preconceived theories, he despises them. For him, "the people" serve the same narcissistic function that Marie serves for Frédéric: to stabilize a defective self.

We see a hint of this before the revolution. Frédéric has found the down-and-out Sénécal a job in Arnoux's pottery factory. Sénécal thinks this job as foreman over the workers is way beneath him, but he must take it, for he has been fired from all his tutoring jobs because he spouted revolutionary theory in the homes of his rich clients. Sénécal, who himself is extremely sensitive to praise and insult, treats his workers the way Deslauriers treats his girlfriend, and Flaubert points out the disjunction between the ideal selfobject and the real workers: "The Republican governed them harshly. Man of theories, he only respected the masses and was merciless towards individuals" (227; 199). He reprimands a worker so cruelly that Frédéric intercedes. Sénécal says:

"Democracy is not the profligacy of individualism. It means equality before the law, the division of labor, order."—"You forget humanity!," said Frédéric. (228–29; 201)

It seems that Sénécal's socialism is no less dedicated to the eradication of the individual than is bourgeois conformism. Can it be that his self-hatred, his own feeling of lacking a self—so strikingly revealed in his strict asceticism—is behind the hatred of individuals?

Sénécal has no capacity for empathy, is torn by resentment, and also has an insatiable longing for power. After the revolution, he is the head of the Club of the Intelligent, a radical "workers'" club of intellectuals, art students, unpublished authors, and teachers, all of whom see the revolution only in terms of how they can advance their own interests. The narrator tells us that Sénécal has become a Robespierre imitator, calling for the murder of the rich and idealizing the poor, who, in his words, are the repository of all virtue (345; 306). There is a yearning here for an idealized other that will make him feel powerful, perfect, and complete. Of course, the real working class does not fulfill his romantic dream, because it, like Marie, has a will of its own, and so the cycle of cynicism begins. Imprisoned in the June insurrection, Sénécal emerges as a voice for authoritarian communism. The narrator tells us: "The Republican even thundered against the insufficiency of the masses" (416; 369). Now, like the Dambreuse group, like Deslauriers, even like Frédéric (411; 365), he, too, calls for a strong man, a savior, for the authority of a dictatorship. When his own grandiosity is rebuffed, he chooses to merge with an idealized power. And so, it comes as no surprise that they all get what they wished for—Louis-Napoléon, the second Emperor of France. Indeed, the political part of the novel ends as Sénécal, in his role as policeman for the military dictatorship, kills his former friend Dussardier, who, in defending the Republic, is the only true revolutionary of the story. Dussardier is naïve, and Flaubert faults him for that, but he is the *only* person in the novel who has more of a respect and love for life and diversity than for theories about life, who can see others as separate from himself. Dussardier is the only person in the book who is, to the end, truly against hierarchy and power relations. He, incidentally, is a worker.

Deslauriers, Sénécal, and others of Frédéric's côterie are all intellectuals; Frédéric himself adopts the pretense of being one and certainly spends more of his time in thought than action. Intellectuals were at the forefront of the events of 1848, and many of those romantic intellectuals became the cynical intellectuals of the Second Empire. Here I would like to look for a moment at the relationship between narcissism and intellectual activity.

Sartre's three-volume biography of Flaubert centers on an analysis of Flaubert's neurotic self structure (lack of self, Sartre would say) and on the objective neurosis of Flaubert's reading public, that is, the intellectuals, politicians, and big businessmen of the Second Empire. Sartre's hypothesis is that the intelligentsia, filled with self-hatred and hatred of their class for having betrayed the workers in June 1848, turn this hatred against the worker as Other. The worker comes to concretize everyday life, dirty reality, whereas the upper class and intellectuals adopt a set of practices that distances them as far from living life, the worker within them, as possible. The intellectuals despise their bodies and seek refuge from life in conceptual systems; they develop an ideology that Sartre calls Black Humanism. This ideology appears in positivism, in Social Darwinism, and in the doctrine of Art for Art's Sake. It preaches the hatred of man, while it glorifies the products of man's creation, the Human Thing. It avers that all actions are doomed to failure, that everything always takes a turn for the worse, that man is by nature evil. It takes away any notion of free will from the subject. Here we certainly recognize the cynicism part of our cycle. But I think Sartre misses what Flaubert says in *Sentimental Education*, that is, that this cynicism may well be a product of the failure of an equally pathological romanticism. At the root of both is a narcissistic personality.

If we again look at the characters I have discussed above, we see that they all seek to shore themselves up by losing themselves in something, in the idealized selfobject. For Frédéric, this becomes love, love mediated, however, by romantic novels. At one point, he even asserts that the attraction for him of intellectual work is the chance it affords to escape from one's self. He begins a project that involves reading Renaissance works, and the narrator says, "In immersing himself in the personality of others, he forgot his own, which is perhaps the only way not to suffer from it" (215; 188). In high school as well, he sought escape in his romantic books.

Deslauriers, whose family life has already been discussed, read everything he could get his hands on in high school; he even stole the key to the library (31; 25). It was Plato's rationalist idealism that first attracted him, a system with the utmost contempt for the sensuous existent. His adolescent fantasy was to design a vast system of philosophy with far-reaching applications (31–32; 26). Flaubert later says of him that "Never having seen the world but through the fever of his covetous desires, he imagined it as an artificial creation, functioning in accor-

dance with mathematical laws" (102; 88). When Frédéric and Deslauriers share their dreams in high school, they exhaust themselves, and
the narrator tells us that they afterwards feel a sadness akin to what one
feels after a great debauch. It almost seems that their sexuality is all in
their intellect.

It is Sénécal who provides the clearest example of hyper-intellec-
tualization as a defense against loss of self or feelings of worthlessness.
It is he who best exemplifies the objective neurosis, as he allows systems
of thought, systems in general, to precede and subjugate his experience.[10] Flaubert introduces us to him in the following way: "Sénécal—
whose head came to a point—only valued systems" (79; 68). In Sénécal's brand of socialism, as I have already suggested, Flaubert saw the
same patterns of thought and the same hatred of life that he saw among
the opportunistic bourgeoisie. As I showed above, Sénécal's hatred of
the bourgeoisie turns to hatred of the masses, for the masses do not fit
his theoretical construct, the selfobject with which he is really engaged.
But that construct of universal freedom and a virtuous working class is
his protection against his feelings of worthlessness. Thus, I see the
objective neurosis, the domination of the concept over the lived,[11] as a
defense against an underlying lack of self-esteem. It is as much present
in the revolutionary fervor as in the postrevolutionary cynicism of the
period. The primacy of the selfobject relation for these people and their
underlying lack of a cohesive self motor the romanticism/cynicism
cycle.

But where does this lack of self-esteem come from? I have already
noted the relative powerlessness of the generation, a powerlessness resented all the more because of the rags-to-riches myths and the real
opportunities that had been promised by the French Revolution. I
believe there is yet another root, however, in psychosocial development.

Sartre would perhaps have been more correct to have focused on
Flaubert's neurosis not as a precursor of things to come, but as a typical
psychological outcome of pre-1848 reality. The central contradiction of
this reality and of Flaubert's development, as Sartre describes it, may
well be an adequate basis for a narcissistic personality. This contradiction, Sartre argues, arises from the two competing world views of the
period, mediated, in Flaubert's case, by his parents. Flaubert's mother
represented the precapitalist ideology of faith, divine inspiration, and
organic wholeness. This was also the ideology of the romantics read
avidly by Flaubert and his generation. The other ideology of the period,

that represented by Flaubert's father, was liberalism, and, more particularly, science. Science scoffs at romantic ideals and is devoted to analyzing and breaking down organic wholes. These two contradictory ideologies tore Flaubert apart from his earliest years; Sartre convincingly demonstrates this by analyzing the juvenilia. I believe it is this contradiction that fuels the romanticism/cynicism antinomy as well. Thus, along with the unempathic mother and the unavailable father that are typical psychological roots of narcissism, the above social and ideological factors would support the emergence and maintenance of narcissistic personality disorders.

In my introduction, I noted that much of *Sentimental Education* is autobiographical. Flaubert was born in the same year as Frédéric; he, too, studied law; he, too, spent many years worshipping a married, older woman, Marie Schlésinger, whom he met when he was fifteen. In Sartre's study, he shows the child Flaubert's difficulty in constituting a self. Sartre explains Flaubert's "crise de Pont-l'Évêque," the 1844 epileptic fit that kept him from having to take up the hated bourgeois profession of law, as the subjective neurosis that prefigured France's post-1848 objective neurosis. In Sartre's view, Flaubert never saw himself as an agent and refused to grow up, just like Frédéric Moreau.

As I have written elsewhere, I think Sartre is quite wrong.[12] There is a great deal of evidence to show that Flaubert was a narcissistic personality type, but, even though he lived his life alone with his mother as the "hermit of Croisset," his writings show not only an awareness of narcissistic dynamics but a furious condemnation of the bad faith spawned by such dynamics. Allow me to provide some evidence of this here.

As mentioned above, Sartre does a fascinating study of Flaubert's early works, noting their compensatory nature. Flaubert felt like the unwanted second son, the "Idiot of the Family," and he vented his destructive rage in all of his early stories. Sartre points out the break that occurs in the story "November," written in 1840–42, but I do not think he realizes the element of self-analysis that begins to emerge with this story. In "November," we have two narrators, one who suffers all the torments of the romantic hero of Flaubert's earlier works and dies of ennui, and one who looks back on the first and points out his weaknesses. Even the first narrator admits that his idealized selfobject, Marie, is quite ordinary and that he is perhaps only in love with himself. In this story, Flaubert begins to get some needed distance from himself.

After the crisis of Pont-l'Évêque, Flaubert wrote that his active life was over, dead, and that he henceforth would live a contemplative, passive life.[13] Sartre sees this as Flaubert's final capitulation to bad faith. But this conclusion is perhaps too hasty . In the works following "November," the double narrator technique is replaced by an increasing use of *style indirect libre*. As Richard Sherrington has pointed out, it is by means of this device that Flaubert resolves a literary and epistemological problem.[14] *Style indirect libre*, otherwise known as narrated thought and narrated perception, allows Flaubert to capture the process of bad faith in his characters, or, as I have termed it here, the narcissistic mode of relating to the world. Simultaneously, however, the device allows the author to be detached from this process, to criticize it, to treat it ironically, to remain a voice for free will even as the character denies it. In *Sentimental Education*, Ullmann counted the use of *style indirect libre* and found it once in every page (as compared to once in three pages in *Madame Bovary*).[15] In this text, Flaubert continues his self-criticism but extends it to a political and historical critique of the narcissism of his age. Frédéric may have done nothing with his life, but Flaubert wrote at least two great novels in his, and *Sentimental Education* is a devastating criticism of bad faith.

There is further evidence of Flaubert's central critique of narcissism in *Sentimental Education*. There is another woman in Frédéric's life, Louise Roque, the girl next door. When we first meet her she is a twelve-year-old child, wearing a white skirt covered with jelly stains (114; 99). The stain imagery here is significant, for it is repeated a bit later in the text. Frédéric reads her *Macbeth*, and she has a nightmare from which she wakes up screaming, "'The spot! The spot!', — her teeth were chattering, she trembled, and, fixing her frightened eyes on her right hand, she rubbed it, saying: 'Still a spot!'" (120; 104). If we recall, the text opened with Frédéric's repulsion at the stained and spotted proletariat on board the boat. The ideal image of Mme. Arnoux rescues him from this. It seems to me that Flaubert introduced Louise, the only woman younger than Frédéric, to give Frédéric a real opportunity for love. She is a country girl, ordinary but excitingly spontaneous, and she is very much in love with Frédéric. She has even, in part, been shaped by him, for, during one long period spent at his mother's home, he would read to her and play with her daily. Frédéric, however, can never make up his mind whether or not to marry her. Pulled sometimes by his ideal love, sometimes by his sexual urges, and sometimes by his opportunism, he betrays her love several times. After the sale of Mme.

Arnoux's things, when Frédéric dismisses Mme. Dambreuse and breaks their engagement (perhaps the only act of integrity he ever performs), he turns to Louise, whom he had neglected for months. He runs to the provinces, craving her simplicity, but, on 2 December, the day of the final sell-out of the Republic, he discovers that Louise has that very day married Deslauriers. Louise was Frédéric's chance to break the mother/whore, romanticism/cynicism cycle, to come to terms with living life, but, as always, he is too late to save himself.

Finally, I would point to the novel's end as proof, against Sartre, that Flaubert does not accept bad faith as *la condition humaine*. After the big lie, the meeting with Marie, we find Frédéric together with Deslauriers in the winter of 1868. Deslauriers is an industry lawyer; Louise ran away with a singer. Both admit their lives were failures. But the reasons they give show them still to be wrapped up in their narcissistic pathology. Deslauriers says: "I had too much logic, and you had too much feeling" (470; 418). It should by now be clear that Deslauriers' intellectualism was as empty as Frédéric's love, both defenses against feelings of worthlessness. The narrator next reports: "Then, they accused fate, circumstances, the epoch in which they were born" (470; 418). Herein lies their bad faith, for the novel shows clearly that they in fact made their epoch, that it was the passivity of their generation, their *desire* to evade responsibility, to submerge themselves in something larger than themselves in hopes of achieving power, that led to the Second Empire.

Frédéric and Deslauriers, the latter still a raving misogynist, have not learned a thing from their lives; in this regard their final reminiscence of the bordello they had visited as youths should not be read as an anomaly or as a single Golden Age incident. When they were young, Frédéric and Deslauriers decided to go to the local whorehouse for some fun. They gathered a bouquet of flowers from Frédéric's mother's garden, and they went to the bordello, which, for them, was shrouded in romantic mystery:

> Frédéric presented his [bouquet], like a lover greeting his fiancée. But the heat, the fear of the unknown, a kind of remorse, and even just the pleasure of seeing, in one eyeful, so many women at his disposal, moved him so much that he became deathly pale and stood without moving, without saying anything. Everyone laughed, tickled by his discomfiture; believing that he was being mocked, he ran away; and, as Frédéric held all the money, Deslauriers was obliged to follow. (471; 419)

Deslauriers' last line, where he hesitantly agrees with Frédéric that this was their finest moment, can only be read as ironic. Particularly with regard to Frédéric, the bordello story shows once again his inability to be in the present and to allow experience to precede reflection; it also shows his vulnerability to narcissistic injury. Thus, the incident, far from an anomaly, actually sums up their narcissistic lives of impotence, idiocy, misperceptions, resentment, passivity, and irresponsibility. Flaubert's irony is merciless; this ending parallels the assertion in his letters that, after 1848, many of his generation remained idiots for the rest of their lives. As I have argued, the novel shows that the pathology began well before 1848,[16] and that the historical events were a result not only of capitalistic economic machinations but of the narcissism of the people who made those events. Against Sartre, I thus conclude that Flaubert, at least in his art, understood and transcended his narcissism and that of his age. And I would suggest that a fruitful way to begin studying what has happened in our own time might be to look at the narcissism behind both the romantic idealism of the sixties and the cynical conservatism of the present.

NOTES

1. Salman Akhtar and J. Anderson Thomson, Jr., "Overview: Narcissistic Personality Disorder," *American Journal of Psychiatry*, 139: 1 (January 1982), 12.

2. The discussion of Sartre's views draws on his biography of Flaubert. Jean-Paul Sartre, *L'Idiot de la famille: Gustave Flaubert de 1821 à 1857*. 3 vols. I, II. (Paris: Gallimard, 1971). III. (Paris: Gallimard, 1972).

3. All quotations are taken from Gustave Flaubert, *L'Éducation sentimentale* (Paris: Gallimard, 1965). Translations are largely my own, aided on occasion by those of Robert Baldick, *Sentimental Education* (Harmondsworth, Middlesex: Penguin Books, 1964). The first page number given in parentheses is the French reference; the second is the English.

4. There is some Oedipal conflict going on here, but I do not think it is primary. He loves Marie before he knows she is Jacques' wife. Her unavailability, however, makes her all the more attractive.

5. See, for example, Victor Brombert, *The Novels of Flaubert: a Study of Themes and Techniques* (Princeton: Princeton University Press, 1966).

6. Heinz Kohut, AOS, p. 25.

7. Waelder, cited in Akhtar and Thomson, "Overview," p. 12.

8. Otto Kernberg, BCPN, p. 17.

9. For a sociological discussion of resentment, see the early work by Max Scheler, *Ressentiment*, trans. William W. Holdheim (New York: Schocken Books, 1972).

10. Pellerin does this most clearly in the realm of art. See the study of Alison Fairlie, "Pellerin et le thème de l'art dans "L'Education sentimentale," *Europe*, 485–86–87 (Sept. – Oct. – Nov. 1969), 38–50.

11. See Max Horkheimer and T. W. Adorno for an elucidation of this problem. "Dialektik der Aufklärung (Frankfurt/Main: S. Fischer, 1969).

12. Lynne Layton, "Fontane and Flaubert: The Defeat of Subjectivity?" Ph.D. Dissertation, Washington University, 1981.

13. Gustave Flaubert, *Correspondance*, I (Paris: Conard, 1926), pp. 277–78.

14. R.J. Sherrington, *Three Novels by Flaubert. A Study of Techniques* (Oxford: Clarendon Press, 1970).

15. Stephen Ullmann, "Style in the French Novel" (Oxford: Basil Blackwell, 1964), p. 115. Sherrington (*Three Novels*, p. 237) says that 70 percent of the novel is from Frédéric's point of view.

16. See Dolf Oehler, who reaches the same conclusion in his "Art-Névrose: Soziopsychoanalyse einer gescheiterten Revolution bei Flaubert und Baudelaire," *Akzente* 27: 2 (April 1980), 113–130.

TEN

THE REPRESSED GRANDIOSITY OF GREGOR SAMSA: A KOHUTIAN READING OF KAFKA'S *METAMORPHOSIS*

J. Brooks Bouson

Why is Gregor Samsa transformed into an insect? Readers have long asked this question. Does it reflect, as some critics argue, his moral or spiritual defects? his extreme alienation? his essential parasitism? his entrapment in a dehumanizing economic system? his Oedipal guilt?[1] Or is it, as others argue, ultimately unexplainable, a paradox of human existence, to quote Heinz Politzer, "knowing of neither cause nor effect"?[2] Reading *Metamorphosis*[3] in a new context—that provided by Heinz Kohut in his pioneering studies in the narcissistic personality disorder—provides a new depth-psychological insight not only into the underlying cause and meaning of Gregor's transformation, but also into the experiential core of his predicament. *Metamorphosis* provides, as Kohut himself observed, an "artistic anticipation" of the "leading psychological problem" of our time: the self-disorder.[4] In the character of Gregor Samsa, Kafka depicts Kohut's "Tragic Man,"[5] the narcissistically defective individual suffering from a fragmenting, enfeebled sense of self.

"The self," in Kohut's words, "arises in a matrix of empathy" and "strives to live within a modicum of empathic responses in order to maintain itself. . . . "[6] Gregor's predicament is not, as many critics suggest, fatal and inscrutable or a reflection of his moral and spiritual impairments. What Kafka so poignantly captures in *Metamorphosis*, as

Kohut comments, is the experience of a man "who finds himself in nonresponsive surroundings," a man whose family speaks of him coldly, in the "impersonal third pronoun" so that he becomes a "non-human monstrosity, even in his own eyes."[7] In his interactions with his family, Gregor compulsively repeats early narcissistic behavior. Lacking the intrapsychic structure of healthy narcissism, unable, as Kohut would put it, to "sufficiently supply himself with self-approval or with a sense of strength through his own inner resources,"[8] Gregor depends on others to validate his worth and provide him with an inner sense of power, strength, and vitality. Attempting to restore his defective self, he acts out his repressed grandiose needs as he tries to capture the attention of family members and extract from them the approval he needs to confirm his worth and reality. When he is thwarted in his urgent need for approving recognition of his uniqueness and both rejected and punished when he seeks to exhibit himself, he experiences self-threatening narcissistic injuries, a repetition of his early response to parental rejection, and thus feels a deep-rooted sense of abandonment, exclusion, and, underlying these, helplessness, empty depression, and rage. Pathetically vulnerable, Gregor is sensitive to what he perceives as rejecting behavior—the emotionally vacant responses of his mother and hostile, punishing behavior of his father—in all his relationships with others. Although he attempts to counteract his feelings of vulnerability through grandiose fantasies—such as his initial insect manifestation—and to repair himself by using others as selfobjects, the central defect remains. Lacking a stable cohesive self, subject to what Kohut calls "disintegration anxiety"—"dread of the loss" of the self[9]—Gregor Samsa is, to use one of Kohut's favorite descriptions, a "broken" man,[10] compelled endlessly to enact the same primitive, fixated behavior in his frustrated search for wholeness.

Critics have long argued that one of Kafka's intentions in *Metamorphosis* is to depict the dehumanization of the so-called "economic man,"[11] finding evidence for this in Gregor's recollections of being the family breadwinner. Gregor does become dehumanized, not because he is at the mercy of a self-destructive economic system but because of his underlying self-disorder and because he exists in a non-empathic milieu. After his father's business failure, Gregor, gladly claiming his father's position, becomes the sole supporter of the family, feeling a "sense of glory" when, as a successful salesman, he brings home "good round coin" for his "amazed and happy family"(110).

Behind the apparent Oedipal dynamics of this father-son situation, we find evidence of Gregor's more deeply-rooted, pre-Oedipal needs and wishes. Dominated by the repressed needs of the archaic grandiose self, Gregor becomes a successful money-maker—money being a potent symbol of power and worth—in an attempt to win his family's confirming approval, to become the center of attention, and to become dominant over them. But because he is dependent upon others to repair his defective self and patch over his underlying sense of worthlessness and powerlessness, his self-repair is only temporary. When, ultimately, the family becomes accustomed to the money he provides and accepts it without a "special uprush of warm feeling" (111), he feels devalued, deprived, and emotionally invalidated, and so his chronic low self-esteem and feelings of abject powerlessness resurface. At this point, his job becomes a meaningless, treadmill kind of existence. As a salesman, he leads a lonely life, his salesman's susceptibility to cold chills a physical response to the emotionally cold environment in which he finds himself. Further, as a salesman, he becomes subject to other people's intrusive hostility and their excluding indifference and neglect. In other words, he re-experiences his family situation in his transactions with others. Ultimately, Gregor's feelings of low self-regard are made tangible in his metamorphosis. The family's debt, which Gregor has worked hard to meet, is a psychic debt: they have been deficient in providing him with the mirroring responses he needs to verify not only his value to them but, more importantly, his humanity.

Why, then, does Gregor change into an insect? A reification of his self-state, Gregor's transformation reflects not only his inner feelings of worthlessness and powerlessness but also his repressed grandiosity, a grandiosity made distorted and grotesque because it has not been re-sponded to empathically. Like the biblical Samson (the name "Samsa," as critics have noted, is an allusion both to Samson and Kafka),[12] Gregor is at once enfeebled and imbued with secret, magical power. Both the suddenness of his metamorphosis and its magical, fantastic quality signal the eruption of what Kohut calls the "unrealistic grandiose substructure" of the self and a surfacing of archaic feelings of omnipotence.[13] Significantly, Gregor awakens a "gigantic" insect (89) and he uses the "huge brown mass" (119) of his body to frighten others away. Although one of his initial worries, as he rocks himself out of bed, is that he will make a "loud crash" and thus perhaps cause others "anxiety, if not terror" (94), unconsciously he wants to provoke just this response from those gathered outside his door. At the very outset of his

ordeal, Gregor, while disavowing his need for attention—he claims he
wants to be left "in peace" (96)—listens to the discussion about him
between the chief clerk and his parents, intent on not missing "one
word of the conversation" (96) and later, when they stop talking, he
imagines that "perhaps" they are "all leaning against" his door and
listening to the noises he makes (99). Moreover, he is "eager" (98) to
find out what they will say when they see him. As the chief clerk
complains, Gregor is "bent," albeit unconsciously, on making a "dis-
graceful exhibition" (97) of himself.

In the black comedy of his initial confrontation with the others,
Gregor's need for attention and his grandiose wish to exert magical
power over others are satisfied. For when the insect-Gregor makes his
first appearance, his father knots his fist as if to strike, then falters and
begins to weep; his mother collapses; the loathed chief clerk first backs
away "as if driven by some invisible steady pressure" (100) and then, his
right arm outstretched, approaches the staircase "as if some supernatural power were waiting there to deliver him" (102) and finally flees.
Seemingly compelled by "some secret injunction to leave the room"
(102), the chief clerk obeys Gregor's unconscious wish to get rid of him.
But Gregor's display of exhibitionistic grandiosity is short-lived. His
traumatic rejection at the moment he exhibits himself points to the
central cause of his self-disorder as it repeats and telescopes[14] both his
experience of early parental rejection and the long series of similar
rejections he has suffered throughout his life, rejections that help produce the distortion of his self-image which has become concretized in
his metamorphosis.

Significantly, one of the first things he sees when he leaves his room
is a photograph of himself dressed "as a lieutenant, hand on sword, a
carefree smile on his face, inviting one to respect his uniform and
military bearing" (101). In the photograph, he sees both a symbolic
depiction of what he lacks—a healthy grandiose self—and a depiction
of the hollowness of his former experience of self-regard, the uniform
signaling his dependency on purely *external* sources of power and respect. Punished for his self-assertiveness, Gregor is "pitilessly" (104)
driven back into his room by his father and then made a prisoner. But
Gregor's prison is also his refuge. Narcissistically damaged in each
confrontation with the external world, he retreats into the protective
isolation of both his room and his insect shell, his hard shell an externalization of his inner need to hold himself together, to be self-

cohesive. His public display rebuffed, Gregor, from the refuge/prison of his room, attempts to defend his vulnerable self and become the center of his family's attention.

Paradoxically, Gregor's metamorphosis is not only a concretization of his chronic sense of defectiveness; it also signals his attempt to assert himself and repair his distorted self. For one thing, by acting out his disavowed intentions of abandoning his family and quitting his job—he claims he has no intention of "deserting" his family (96) and that he is "loyally bound to serve the chief" (101)—Gregor affirms, in his characteristically dependent-submissive way, his independence. And while consciously thinking that the "whole future" of his family depends on his ability to detain, soothe, and win over the chief clerk (102), he scares off his superior, revealing his hidden aggression toward the family. Moreover, as an invalid, he passively exerts power over and devalues family members, for when he is no longer the breadwinner they are forced to get jobs and thus assume, with their employers, the subordinate role he once embraced. Gregor, in other words, gains active mastery over passive suffering by both rejecting and expressing his veiled hostility toward his family. More importantly, after his transformation, not only do his parents rivet their attention on him, as he learns by listening carefully at the door, but his sister takes care of him. Gregor's need for confirming attention is verified by the narrator, who serves as an extension of Gregor's consciousness, making Gregor, interestingly enough, the focal point of and dominant over the reader's perceptions. When Gregor, just after his metamorphosis, attempts to turn the key of his door, the chief clerk encourages him "but," as the narrator comments, "they should all have shouted encouragement"; Gregor, "in the belief" that they are "all following his efforts intently" (99), musters the necessary strength to complete his difficult task. Narcissistically defective, he needs external sources of approbation if he is to counteract feelings of helplessness and find the inner determination to act.

Although Gregor does eventually lose his appetite and starve to death, initially he discovers himself to be "unusually hungry" (91) and his hunger keeps awakening him the first night (107). This craving for food does not, as some critics suggest, indicate Gregor's reversion to his basic animality;[15] instead, his oral greediness symbolizes his need to obtain what Kohut calls "narcissistic sustenance or nutriment,"[16] i.e., a nurturing, mirroring response. After his transformation, Grete, the only family member he feels close to, becomes his sole source of narcissistic supplies. When Gregor rejects the milk she brings him, he symbolically rejects his sickly, asthmatic mother. Thus, the first time he displays himself, she faints—a repetition of his early relationship to an emotionally unavailable and depleted mother, who disclaims her responsibility for him, in essence abandoning him when she allows Grete to become his caretaker. After refusing the milk, Gregor, disavowing his need to be noticed, simultaneously determines he "would rather starve" than draw Grete's "attention" to his hunger and feels a "wild impulse" to "throw himself at her feet, and beg her for something to eat" (107), for narcissistic supplies. When she first brings him food, he eats "greedily" (108) for he is starved for attention, and discovers that his "wounds," narcissistic injuries, seem to have "healed completely" (108). He feels restored by his sister's attention. But the fact that what he eats is garbage—not narcissistically sustaining—reveals that his needs are not truly being met. Moreover, when Gregor greedily consumes the garbage, he not only signals his craving for an empathic, nurturing response, he also symbolically depicts his internalization of the family's negative attitudes toward him. In effect, he says, "I know that this is all that I'm worth. I'm garbage and so I'll eat garbage." Initially, he takes masochistic delight in his self-humiliation both because he is unconsciously punishing himself for his oral—narcissistic—neediness and rage and also because, in so doing, he openly indicts his family for their neglect of him.

Unable to communicate his deep-seated, preverbal needs, symbolized by his loss of the power of human speech, Gregor accepts the few scraps of attention given him by his sister. Recognizing how "repulsive" (113) she finds him, he hides under the sofa when she is in his room and fancies that he sees a "thankful glance from her eye" when he covers with a sheet the "small portion" of his body that protrudes from the sofa (114). In other words, he must hide and cover himself—efface himself and disavow his grandiose needs—to win approval and attention. Totally isolated from the others, Gregor becomes sensitive to eye glances, this hypercathexis of the visual mode, as Kohut would describe it, a signal of Gregor's unmet primitive need to be mirrored, to be the "gleam in the mother's eye."[17] While he craves attention, Gregor is however, ashamed to have others look at him; his shame is a response to his exhibitionistic wishes, his distorted grandiose self, his fear that he will be traumatically rejected and, on the family drama level, his awareness that his family is ashamed of him. Never once questioning his family's desire to keep him hidden from the world's eyes, Gregor must repress his deep-rooted need to display himself if he is to avoid bringing public shame and humiliation upon both himself and his family. Gregor's transformation, in part a defensive ploy to restore the self, serves to further the on-going process of self-dissolution.

Of perennial fascination to readers of *Metamorphosis* is Gregor's initial reaction to his transformation. What shocks the reader is passively, if not blandly, accepted by Gregor. Why this response when Gregor's initial discovery of himself in an insect's body starkly conveys the feeling-state of body-self estrangement? Instead of reacting with open anxiety, Gregor thinks at length about his job and family; he becomes anxious about the passing time and preoccupied with his new bodily sensations and his strange aches and pains. In other words, he defends himself from underlying fears of self-disintegration by focusing his attention, as Kohut would put it, on "verbalizable conflicts and anxieties" and away from an "awareness" of the "potentially crumbling self."[18]

While Gregor does this again and again to ward off feelings of diffuse, preverbal anxiety, he also signals, in other ways, his impending sense of body-self dissolution. His initial inability to control the chaotic movements of his insect legs and his later submissive turning movements before his father make manifest his inner feelings of helplessness and powerlessness; his "senseless crawling around and around" his room (117) and his increasingly disorganized appearance, his feelings of psychic disorganization; his self-mothering gestures—he rocks back and forth and tries to replicate the protective feeling of the mother's embrace by hiding under the sofa, a "half-unconscious action"[19] (106–7)—his attempts to soothe himself; his dissolving sense of clock time, his loss of an awareness of himself, to use a Kohutian description, as a cohesive "continuum" in time;[20] his lethargy and depression, his inner feelings of deadness, depletion. Suffering from a crumbling sense of self, Gregor experiences what Kohut describes as the "hollowness and insecurity" of archaic experiences of the body-self and emotions.[21] In both Gregor's hypochrondriacal preoccupations and his vague mystical feelings—he hangs suspended from the ceiling in "almost blissful absorption" (115)—there is evidence of regression to the most archaic levels of experience.[22] The description of Gregor's demise outlines, in almost clinical detail, the experience of self-dissolution: in Kohutian terms, "fragmentation of" and "estrangement from" the mind-body self.[23] Gregor's metamorphosis gives experiential immediacy not only to what Kohut calls the "devastating emotional event" referred to as a "severe drop in self-esteem"[24] but, more significantly, to the terrifying experience of the break-up of the cohesive self.

Narcissistically sensitive, Gregor is condemned to re-experience with Grete his early feelings of injury and rejection. Although initially Grete seems to be emotionally in tune with his needs, he senses behind her apparent kindness both rejection and veiled hostility. When, for example, family members first knock on his door, Grete is the only one to ask "Aren't you well? Are you needing anything?'" (92). Despite this, Gregor wonders why she does not "join the others" (96) who stand outside his door harassing him. "In the goodness of her heart" (107) Grete feeds him the garbage he craves, taking care to bring the food that "might especially please" him (125); but she also sweeps up and shovels into a bucket not only the "remains" of his meal but also the untouched, fresh food "as if" it, too, were "now of no use to anyone" (108). Gregor takes the few comments she makes about his eating as "kindly meant" or as remarks that "could be so interpreted" (109).

Although Grete tries "to make as light as possible" whatever is "disagreeable in her task" and Gregor wants to thank her for her "ministrations," "time" also brings "enlightenment" to him for when she enters his room, she rushes to the window, tears it open, and gasps for air (113). Grete, in other words, becomes a mirror image of the asthmatic—emotionally rejecting and depleted—mother. Recognizing how disgusting Grete finds him, he covers himself with a sheet even though "this curtaining and confining" of himself is not conducive to his "comfort" (113). And when Grete looks into his room for the first time and is "startled" when she catches sight of him under the sofa, Gregor's repressed, angry self comments, "well, he had to be somewhere, he couldn't have flown away, could he?" (107). From the outset, he suspects that Grete wants to get rid of him. Despite this, Gregor, at first, typically interprets Grete's behavior in a positive way both to ward off feelings of anger and rejection and because he needs an empathic response from her, for she is the only member of the family with whom he feels "intimate" (111). His very survival depends on it. Emotionally abandoned by his mother, Gregor finds a mother-surrogate figure in Grete. But tragically, when Grete becomes his sole caretaker and thus the center of Gregor's and her parents' attention, she begins to make narcissistic use of him as she asserts her own grandiose needs. Not only does she assume complete dominance over him, jealously guarding her caretaker's rights and flying into a rage when Mrs. Samsa cleans his room (an act which Grete interprets as a threat to her authority), she also begins to lose interest in him, treating him more and more as an encumbering nuisance, an object.

In a grotesque attempt to be noticed, Gregor leaves "sticky" traces of himself wherever he crawls (115) and Grete, observing this, determines to remove several pieces of furniture from his room, ostensibly to give him more crawling space. When Mrs. Samsa opposes this idea, Grete then determines to remove all the furniture "except the indispensable sofa" (117). In his characteristic way, Gregor interprets Grete's resolve as basically well-intentioned, as a sign of her "enthusiastic" but "adolescent" desire to "do all the more for him" because she has, in fact, "perceived" that he really needs "a lot of space to crawl about in." But he also senses the hidden grandiosity behind her "childish recalcitrance," for in a room where Gregor lords it "all alone over empty walls," only she is "likely ever to set foot" (117). In other words, she wants to isolate and control him. Pitifully, Gregor is compelled to hide—efface himself—when his mother comes into his room to help Grete remove the furniture. "Come in, he's out of sight," as Grete tells Mrs. Samsa (115). Despite Mrs. Samsa's at times melodramatic assertions that she wants to see Gregor, her "exclamations of joyful eagerness" die away when she approaches the door to his room (115) and she deliberately speaks in a low voice to avoid rousing him. And yet, ignoring his mother's rejecting behavior, Gregor defensively sees her as the absent, but longed for, empathic mother and he feels drawn from "the brink of forgetfulness" and back into the human circle when he hears her voice. When his mother comments that removing the furniture may show Gregor that the family has "'given up hope'" and left him "'coldly to himself'" (116), Gregor recognizes that being dispossessed of his furniture is tantamount to relinquishing the symbolic vestiges of his human identity. But he hesitates instead of immediately intervening because he is afraid that the sight of him "might sicken" (117) his mother; he is, in other words, deeply ashamed of his deformed self, afraid that his mother will again reject him and that he may in some way harm or deplete her.

Only in extremity, only when his room has been all but stripped of its furniture, does Gregor assert himself by rushing out and attempting to save something. In a pathetic act of self-preservation, he attaches himself to the picture of a woman dressed in furs which he carefully framed just before his metamorphosis. Imagining that Grete will try to "chase him down from the wall," he determines to cling to the picture and "not give it up. He would rather fly in Grete's face" (119). Although the description of Gregor pressing his insect's body against the picture suggests, as some critics maintain, Gregor's inhibited sexuality,[25] it also suggests, on a more primitive level, a telescoped memory of clinging, in both anger and longing, to a cold, detached, unresponsive mother.

Significantly, when Gregor, attempting to repair his defective self, angrily clings to the picture, his mother faints and his sister, mirroring the father, responds first with open hostility and then by isolating him, cutting him off from both herself and his mother. Similarly, on both this occasion and the first time he shows himself, Gregor's mother faints when she sees him—when he expresses his narcissistic needs and anger—and then he is narcissistically injured by his father and subsequently isolated by being locked in his room. Behind the manifest content of these repetitive incidents, which provide a mimetic recapitulation of Gregor's infantile experiences of parental unavailability and rejection, there lies an intricate cluster of archaic fantasies, fears, and defenses. The fact that the mother faints suggests at once a telescoped memory of the unresponsive mother and the infantile fantasy of the depleted mother who is harmed or destroyed through the infant's intense narcissistic neediness and rage. Gregor's hostile father and sister, moreover, simultaneously represent a telescoped memory of the angry father, warded-off aspects of the self—Gregor's projected, rageful grandiose self—and a condensed image of both the punishing Oedipal father and a split-off aspect of the primal mother, the all-powerful, rejecting "bad" mother who causes self-threatening, narcissistic injuries. Similarly, all the authority figures in the novel depict both warded-off aspects of the self and the omnipotent mother-father images. For example, the thwarting of the three lodgers, who assume power over the family only to be sent "scuttling" off, insectlike (138), expresses defensive devaluation of, projected rage against, and fantasied depletion or harming of the parental-imagoes as well as the thwarting of Gregor's grandiose self. Narcissistically fixated, Gregor exists in a strange, twilight world of resonating fears and fantasies. When Gregor, in his current situation, re-experiences his primal narcissistic traumas with his family members, his fragile sense of self-cohesion is undermined. Lacking a stable, cohesive self, he is deeply threatened by his own deeprooted needs and anger and by any behavior which he perceives as rejecting, neglectful, or hostile.

"Harassed by self-reproach and worry" when Grete cuts him off from his mother and herself and thus excludes and rejects him, Gregor acts out his feelings of disintegration anxiety as he senselessly crawls "to and fro, over everything" until, becoming enfeebled, he collapses (119). At this point, Gregor is subjected to the fury of his "angry and exultant" (120) father who, no longer lethargic, has metamorphosed into a terrifying figure of power and strength, an incarnation of the omnipotent parental-imagoes and Gregor's angry self. His fear of his father reveals both primitive fear of the punishing-rejecting parent and his fear of his own destructive impulses. "Dumbfounded at the enormous size" of his father's shoe soles—this description revealing the insect-Gregor's infantile perspective—he fears he is about to be trampled underfoot. Acting out his submissive psychic response to dominant figures, he runs before his father, "stopping when he stopped and scuttling forward again" when his father makes "any kind of move" (121). To "propitiate" his father, he wants to "disappear at once" inside his room.

During this second escape from his room, Gregor discovers, once again, how hazardous the external world is. Again his father attacks him, this time by bombarding him with apples. Sustaining a deep narcissistic injury when an apple lodges in his "armor-plated" back (89), Gregor experiences momentary self-fragmentation, a "complete derangement of all his senses" (122). Gregor's protective isolation, symbolized by his insect's shell, affords no real defense against a hostile, uncomprehending family environment or inner feelings of instability and fragility. Just before blacking out, Gregor sees his mother, in loosened clothing, embracing his father—"in complete union with him" (122)—as she begs for her son's life. Although this description of the combined parent-imago does depict, as some critics maintain, a veiled allusion to the primal scene, it also reveals Gregor's sense of exclusion and abandonment, his wish for his mother's self-confirming, life-giving attention, and his repressed desire for and fear of a symbiotic merger with an idealized, powerful figure. Merger would bring the desired fusion with the idealized imago but at the terrible cost of self-annihilation. Similarly, Gregor's punishment at the hands of his father symbolically depicts not only destructive castration but also a more basic, underlying fear: the break-up of the cohesive self through a self-threatening, narcissistic injury. Behind the apparent Oedipal dynamics of Gregor's family drama,[26] we find evidence of a richly complex, proliferating core of pre-Oedipal needs, fears, and fantasies.

Crippled by his injuries, Gregor creeps across his room "like an old invalid" (122). But he is "sufficiently compensated" for the "worsening of his condition" (123) when the door to his room is left open during the evening and he can watch and listen to the family by their "general consent as it were" (123) and thus participate, from a lonely distance, in family life. And yet often Gregor ignores the family and instead lies "in the darkest corner of his room, quite unnoticed by the family" (128), as the narrator describes it, drawing the reader's attention to Gregor. When his mother and sister, after getting his father to bed, sit close to each other and then exclude Gregor by shutting the door to his room thus leaving him in total darkness, the wound in his back begins to "nag at him afresh" (125). Succumbing to narcissistic rage, which is expressed as oral greediness, Gregor becomes deeply angered at the way the others are "neglecting him" and he fantasizes "getting into the larder to take the food" that is his "due" (125). He wants, in other words, to appropriate the narcissistic sustenance that he feels is rightfully his. Displacing his rage toward the family onto the charwoman, he angrily thinks that there is no reason for his being neglected and that the charwoman should be "ordered to clean out his room daily" (127), a wish expressing his unmet archaic need for parental attention and, on the family drama level, his inhibited desire to assume power over others and get their attention. Although unlike the family members, the charwoman does not recoil from Gregor, she does call him a "dung beetle" and subjects him to unempathic and thereby self-threatening stares (127). In a feeble act of self-defense, Gregor runs toward her once, only to retreat when she raises a chair as if to attack him. Imagining that her "strong bony frame" has allowed her to "survive the worst a long life could offer" (126), he sees in her an embodiment of what he lacks: a solid, cohesive self. More significantly, he also finds in her "gigantic" (124), terrifying figure an embodiment of not only his projected, grandiose self but also the primal, all-powerful, sadistic, and rejecting parent figures. Narcissistically experienced, the charwoman takes on deep significance in Gregor's solitary life, becoming a focal point for his primitive wishes, fears, and memories.

Increasingly neglected by his sister—twice a day she "hurriedly" pushes into his room "any food . . . available" (125)—Gregor loses his appetite, begins to shun the scraps of food, the narcissistic nutriment, that she gives him and thus slowly starves to death. When Grete becomes a mirror image of his neglectful, rejecting parents, he refuses the food she gives him just as he once refused the mother's milk given him.

Through his self-starvation, Gregor makes one last, desperate plea for attention as he masochistically complies with his sister's—and family's—wish to get rid of him and as he punishes himself for his intense narcissistic neediness and fantasied harming of the fainting, asthmatic mother and, by extension, the entire family which becomes increasingly enervated as Gregor's illness progresses. In mute protest, Gregor sits in the corner to "reproach" (126) Grete for the filthiness of his room but to no avail. Behind Gregor's silent "reproach" is repressed rage which is later voiced by the middle lodger when he gives "notice" and considers "bringing an action for damages" because of the "disgusting conditions prevailing" in the "household and family" (132). Instead of openly expressing his anger, Gregor responds in a seemingly empathic but really resentful way to his family's neglect, recognizing how difficult it is for his "overworked and tired-out" family to "find time" to "bother" about him more than is "absolutely needful" (124). Moreover, despite his mother's outrageous neglect of him, he defensively protects her against his anger through splitting: he keeps intact his conscious image of her as the unavailable (absent) but "good" mother and projects her "badness"—her rejecting, narcissistically injuring behavior—onto others.

In stark contrast to this neglect of Gregor, Grete and Mrs. Samsa do find the time to bother about, if not dote on, Mr. Samsa; and the three lodgers, who become dominant over the family, are the center of the Samsas' attention. Gregor resentfully watches while the family prepares lavish meals for the three lodgers who then stuff themselves with food while he, abandoned, is "dying of starvation." But though ignored by his family, Gregor remains the focus of the narrator's attention, the narrator acting both as an objective, factual reporter of Gregor's plight and as an extension of Gregor's consciousness. Interestingly, this dual narrative perspective invites the reader to respond to Gregor both empathically and with the emotional distance of his family.

Outcast, excluded, rejected, Gregor, when he hears his sister playing the violin, makes his final and fatal escape from his room in an attempt to repair his defective self. Although he is "filthy," covered with dust, fluff, hair, and food remnants, he feels no "shame" and "hardly any surprise at his growing lack of consideration" as he, in his desperate desire to display himself, advances over the "spotless" living room floor. Narcissistically disabled and depleted, Gregor is indifferent to "everything" but the music he hears (130). Compelled because of what he hears in the music—authentic emotional expression—Gregor wants Grete's eyes to meet his: he craves a confirming, healing gaze. Feeling as if the "way" is "opening before him to the unknown nourishment" he craves (130–31)—narcissistic gratification—he wants to take Grete into his room and never let her out so long as he lives (131). Gregor's desire exclusively to possess Grete signals not only his unmet, archaic need for symbiotic merger with and exclusive possession of the idealized parent imago, but also his need for parental nourishment, protection, and self-validating empathy. Attempting to restore his disabled, defective self, Gregor wants to use Grete as a selfobject and fulfill, through her, his primitive needs. He wants to extract praise from her (he imagines she will be touched and admire him when he tells her how he had meant to send her to the Conservatory); he wants to dominate her (he disavows this need, imagining that she will stay with him of "her own free will" (131); and he wants to merge with her power and strength). Not only does Gregor's plan fail miserably, he is both subject to the unempathic stares of the three lodgers and made aware of how ashamed his family is of him when his father tries to "block" the lodgers' view of him (131).

At this point, Gregor, disappointed and weak "from extreme hunger" (132)—depleted from a lack of narcissistic sustenance—fears that there will be a "combined attack on him" (133), that he will sustain traumatic narcissistic injury. And he does when his sister pronounces judgment on him: "I won't utter my brother's name in the presence of this crea-ture," as she tells her parents, "and so all I say is: we must try to get rid of it. We've tried to look after it and to put up with it as far as is humanly possible, and I don't think anyone could reproach us in the slightest" (133). When she complains that Gregor "persecutes" the fam-ily, "drives away" the lodgers, "wants the whole apartment to himself" and would have the family "sleep in the gutter" (134), she both projects her own hostility onto Gregor and voices his hidden wishes. This makes her judgment against him doubly deadly: her desire to punish him is compounded by his masochistic desire to punish himself for his repressed grandiose needs and anger. When Grete invalidates him by refusing to recognize him as her brother, he, in effect, suffers a repeti-tion of his primal, self-fragmenting experiences of parental rejection. Impaired, enfeebled, he crawls back to his room, his last glance falling on his impassive mother who is "not quite overcome by sleep" (135). Again, when Gregor displays himself, his depleted mother becomes non-responsive, he is punished, then locked in his room and, on this final occasion, left to die. Disavowing his anger and disappointment, Gregor, just before his death, thinks of his family with "tenderness and love" (135). To the end, his needs for love and confirming attention are unrequited. When Gregor agrees with his sister's "decision" that he must "disappear" (135), he expresses, on the family drama level, his feeling that his family is better off without him. This feeling is corroborated by the narrator's description of the family's cold, uncaring response to his death, a description which invites the reader to feel Gregor's disavowed anger. "Now thanks be to God" (136), Mr. Samsa pronounces when the family gathers around Gregor's emaciated body. "Let bygones be bygones," Mr. Samsa further comments (139) as the family members quickly leave off mourning and rejuvenate as they begin to celebrate their liberation from the insect-Gregor, their release from a shameful, secret family burden.

Agreeing to "disappear," Gregor also expresses, on the depth-psychological level, his extreme self-rejection and masochistic desire to remedy his situation by effacing himself and thus nullifying his unendurable sense of worthlessness, shame, failure, and defectiveness. Moreover, in dying he both punishes himself for his hidden aggression against the family and magically undoes his hidden crime against them—his fantasied depletion of and retaliatory devaluation of family members through his intense neediness and anger—and thus revitalizes them. The description of Grete's metamorphosis—she has blossomed into "a pretty girl with a good figure" (139)—symbolizes, at once, Grete's development of a cohesive self and the revitalization of the depleted mother. In stark contrast to his sister's transformation, Gregor has been reduced to a thing, an "it," his "flat and dry" carcass (137) imaging his empty, depleted, hollow self. It is appropriate that the charwoman, an embodiment of the neglectful, hostile aspects of the family, is the one to dispose of his body. Desperately seeking but never receiving the self-confirming attention, that "matrix of empathy" which Kohut feels the individual needs to form and sustain a cohesive sense of self, Gregor, in the end, is destroyed. His fragile, exquisitely sensitive self has been eroded, bit by bit, by the emotionally invalidating responses of his family.

The "deepest horror man can experience," as Kohut comments, "is that of feeling that he is exposed to circumstances in which he is no longer regarded as human by others, in a milieu that does not even respond with faulty or distorted empathy to his presence."[27] In

Metamorphosis, Kafka conveys, in exacting detail, the horror of such a situation. Essentially a family story, *Metamorphosis* reflects, as many critics have noted, aspects of Kafka's life: his submissive relationship to his father, his alienation from his mother, his hidden anger and resentment, his hypochondria, depression, feelings of worthlessness, powerlessness, physical imperfection, loneliness, isolation. Although most discussions of the autobiographical elements of Kafka's fiction focus on his relationship with his insensitive, domineering father, which is well documented in his "Letter to His Father," Margarete Mitscherlich-Nielsen, in her "Psychoanalytic Notes" on Kafka, offers an interesting speculation on Kafka's early relationship with his mother, pointing to a disturbance in the early mother-child relationship. "The early death of Kafka's brothers and his mother's reaction to their loss— probably warding off emotion on the surface but deeply depressed beneath—," she writes, "must have had a profound effect on Kafka."[28] Equally suggestive are recent discussions of Kafka's narcissistic relationships with both Felice and Milena.[29]

In his letters, diaries, and conversations, Kafka gave compelling testimony to his inner feelings, fears, and needs. Expressing his deep self-rejection and depressive, suicidal feelings in a conversation, he said, "Every day I wish myself off the earth."[30] "The present is a phantom state for me," he said in his diary, "Nothing, nothing . . . merely emptiness, meaninglessness, weakness."[31] "[I]f," he wrote, revealing his deep-rooted feelings of defectiveness, "I lacked an upper lip here, there an ear, here a rib, there a finger, if I had hairless spots on my head and pockmarks on my face, this would still be no adequate counterpart to my inner imperfection."[32] Describing an experience of momentary self-fragmentation, he recalled how, during an "attack of madness" the "images became uncontrollable, everything flew apart until, in my extremity, the notion of a Napoleonic field marshal's black hat came to my rescue, descending on my consciousness and holding it together by force."[33]

While Kafka, in a deep-rooted way, experienced his family members as "strangers"—"you are all strangers to me, we are related only by blood, but that never shows itself"[34]—he formed deep narcissistic attachments to the women in his life, especially Felice and Milena. The first time he saw Felice he was struck by her "Bony, empty face that wore its emptiness openly."[35] When they began what turned out to be a prolonged correspondence, he insisted that she share with him every detail of her life: he wanted totally to possess her in fantasy and in writing but not in the flesh. "You are my own self"; "you belong to me"; "I belong to you",[36] he wrote her. "I wish you were not on this earth, but entirely within me, or rather that I were not on this earth, but entirely within you; I feel there is one too many of us; the separation into two people is unbearable."[37] But in his diary, he confided his "Anxiety about being a couple, flowing into the other person."[38] Similarly, Kafka told Milena that she belonged to him and described how he felt "dissolved" in her and how, in a dream, he envisioned them "merging into one another, I was you, you were me."[39] And yet, despite the imaginative intensity of these relationships, he could never assuage his inner feelings of alienation, aloneness. "I am capable of enjoying human relationships," as he once described it, "but not experiencing them."[40] To be fully understood by one person, Kafka felt, "would be to have a foothold on every side, to have God."[41]

Having only a precarious foothold on such feelings, Kafka, as biographer Ronald Hayman puts it, used writing to "give him the illusion of inching his way towards his objective of being understood, of bringing the reader to know him as well as he knew himself."[42] In *Metamorphosis,* Hayman comments, Kafka allegorized his "relationship with the family, building out from his sense of being a disappointment, a burden."[43] That Kafka was thinking of his own family situation when he wrote *Metamorphosis* is revealed in the few recorded comments he made about the story. After its publication, he remarked to an acquaintance, "What do you have to say about the dreadful things happening in our house?"[44] In a conversation with Gustav Janouch, he described the story as an "indiscretion." Is it perhaps delicate and discreet," he asked, "to talk about the bugs in one's own family?" When Janouch described the story as a "terrible dream, a terrible conception," Kafka responded, "The dream reveals the reality, which conception lags behind. That is the horror of life—the terror of art."[45] Verbalizing in his art his preverbal fears, needs, and fantasies, Kafka confronted and gave artistic expression to the twilight world of "Tragic Man."

Kafka was one of those writers who felt compelled to write. At times, in the actual process of writing, he felt a sense of perfection and self-approval which he rarely experienced in his daily life. "If I indiscriminately write down a sentence," he once wrote in his diary, "it is perfect."[46] "Not to write," as he commented in a letter, "was already to be lying on the floor, deserving to be swept out."[47] Through art, Kafka could express, distill, and distance himself from the "horror of life" and thus gain temporary mastery over his deep-rooted feelings of vulnerability, impotent rage, and inadequacy. Critics have long commented on the repetitive nature of Kafka's fiction. The "form" of Kafka's fiction, as one critic puts it, is "circular"; the "basic situation" of a given narrative "emerges again and again" like the repetition of a "trauma."[48] Reading *Metamorphosis* through a Kohutian lens, we can understand, in greater depth, both the source and experiential core of that central, narcissistic trauma.

NOTES

1. For an overview of the critical response to *The Metamorphosis* up to 1972, see Stanley Corngold's critical bibliography, *The Commentators' Despair: The Interpretation of Kafka's Metamorphosis* (Port Washington, N.Y.: Kennikat Press, 1973). Corngold's bibliography includes the work of American, English, Spanish, French, German, and Italian critics.

2. Heinz Politzer, *Franz Kafka: Parable and Paradox* (Ithaca, N.Y.: Cornell University Press, 1962), p. 78.

3. *The Metamorphosis,* trans. Edwin and Willa Muir, in *Kafka: The Complete Stories* (New York: Schocken Books, 1971), pp. 89–139. Page references to *The Metamorphosis,* indicated parenthetically in the text, are to this edition.

4. Kohut, ROS, pp. 285–88. See also Ornstein, SFS, vol. 2, pp. 680–81, 780 and Goldberg, ASP, pp. 518–19.

5. See, e.g., ROS pp. 132–33, 206–7, 224–25, 238–39; SFS, 757–61; ASP, 539–40, 543, 545–46.

6. SFS, fn. 5, p. 752.

7. See, respectively, SFS, pp. 718, 680 and ROS, 287.

8. SFS, p. 846.

9. ROS, pp. 104–5.

10. "[N]owhere in art," states Kohut, "have I encountered a more accurately pointed description of man's yearning to achieve the restoration of his self than that contained in three terse sentences in O'Neill's play *The Great God Brown.* . . 'Man is born broken. He lives by mending. The grace of God is glue.' Could the essence of the pathology of modern man's self be stated more impressively?" (ROS, p. 287).

11. For example, Franz Kuna (in *Franz Kafka: Literature as Corrective Punishment* [Bloomington, Ind.: Indiana University Press, 1974], p. 51) states: "The main aspects of economic man debased to a functional role, as they were amply analysed by early twentieth-century philosophers and sociologists, emerge in Kafka's story in paradigmatic fashion."

12. The Samson allusion, e.g., has been noted by Norman Holland in "Real-

ism and Unrealism, Kafka's 'Metamorphosis,'" *Modern Fiction Studies,* 4 (Summer 1958), 148–49 and by Jean Jofen in *"Metamorphosis,"* *American Imago,* 35 (Winter 1978), 349. In a conversation with Kafka, Gustav Janouch commented that the name Samsa sounded "like a cryptogram for Kafka. Five letters in each word. The S in the word Samsa has the same position as the K in the word Kafka. the A . . ." To this, Kafka replied: "It is not a cryptogram. Samsa is not merely Kafka, and nothing else." (Gustav Janouch, *Conversations with Kafka,* rev. ed., trans. Goronwy Rees [New York: New Directions, 1968], p. 32).

13. See "The Therapeutic Activation of the Grandiose Self," in AOS, pp. 105–99. Archaic grandiose fantasies of omnipotence and magical power (such as superman fantasies) often emerge when the narcissistically disturbed individual feels powerless, disappointed, lonely, and/or abandoned. This also happens in the case of Gregor Samsa. See also the casebook, Arnold Goldberg ed., *The Psychology of The Self* (New York: International Universities Press, 1978), pp. 281, 284, 291–92, 308–9, 321–24, and passim.

14. "Telescoping," i.e., "the recall of memories of analogous later experiences which correspond to the archaic ones" (AOS, p. 39) according to Kohut, signals the psyche's attempt to "express the early trauma through the medium of analogous psychic contents that are closer to the secondary processes and to verbal communication" (AOS, p. 53).

15. See, e.g., Irving Howe's "Introduction" to *Metamorphosis* in *Classics of Modern Fiction,* 2nd ed. (New York: Harcourt Brace Jovanovich, 1968), p. 405.

16. If the grandiose self is repressed too early, according to Kohut, the "reality ego" is deprived of "narcissistic nutriment" from the "deep sources of narcissistic energy" resulting in the "symptomatology" of "narcissistic deficiency": "diminished self-confidence, vague depressions, absence of zest for work, lack of initiative, etc." (AOS, p. 177). Because Gregor lacks an inner sense of sustaining self-esteem, he depends upon external approbation to supply him with narcissistic nutriment.

17. See, e.g., AOS, pp. 117–18.

18. ROS, pp. 106, 108.

19. Gregor's hiding under the couch recalls the behavior of one of the infants observed by Margaret Mahler and her collaborators. "[W]hen in distress," writes Mahler, "she would lie flat against the surface of the floor, or on the mattress on the floor, or would squeeze herself into a narrow space; it was as if she wanted to be enclosed (held together) in this way, which would afford her some of the sense of coherence and security that she was missing in the relationship with her mother." (*The Psychological Birth of the Human Infant* [New York: Basic Books, 1975], p. 94).

20. ROS, p. 177.

21. Ibid., p. 20.

22. See AOS, pp. 9, 29–30, 86, 214–17, and passim.

23. ROS, p. 105.

24. ASP, p. 503.

25. See, e.g., Politzer, *Franz Kafka,* p. 72.

26. See, e.g., Hellmuth Kaiser's Freudian interpretation of the text: "Franz

Kafka's Inferno," *Imago,* 17: 1 (1931), 41–104. See also Corngold, *The Commentators' Despair,* (pp. 148–51) for a summary and discussion of Kaiser's analysis.

27. ASP, pp. 486–87.

28. Margarete Mitscherlich-Nielsen, "Psychoanalytic Notes on Franz Kafka," *Psychocultural Review,* 3 (Winter 1979), 5.

29. For a discussion of Kafka's relationship to his mother and to Felice and an interesting analysis of the *pavlatche* incident described in Kafka's "Letter to His Father", see Charles Bernheimer's *Flaubert and Kafka: Studies in Psychopoetic Structure* (New Haven, Conn.: Yale University Press, 1982), pp. 149–61, and passim. For a discussion of Kafka's relationship with Milena, see Harmut Böhme's "Mother Milena: On Kafka's Narcissism," trans. John Winkelman, in Angel Flores ed., *The Kafka Debate* (New York: Gordian Press, 1977), pp. 80–99.

30. Max Brod, *Franz Kafka: A Biography* (New York: Schocken Books, 1960), p. 75.

31. Diary entry, 3 May 1915 in *The Diaries of Franz Kafka, 1914–23,* trans. Martin Greenberg, ed. Max Brod (New York: Schocken Books, 1949), p. 126. Hereafter cited as DII.

32. *The Diaries of Franz Kafka, 1910–13,* trans. Joseph Kresh, ed. Max Brod (New York: Schocken Books, 1965), p. 19. Hereafter cited as DI.

33. Letter to Felice, 6 August 1913, in *Letters to Felice,* trans. James Stern and Elisabeth Duckworth, eds. Erich Heller and Jürgen Born (New York: Schocken Books, 1973), p. 298. Hereafter cited as LF.

34. Diary entry, 15 August 1913, in DI, p. 297.

35. Diary entry, 20 August 1912, DI, p. 268.

36. LF, 4 Dec. 1912, p. 85; 19 October 1916, p. 525; 11 Nov. 1912, p. 37.

37. Ibid., 13 May 1913, p. 256.

38. Diary entry, 21 or 22 July 1913, cited and translated by Ronald Hayman in *Kafka: A Biography* (New York: Oxford University Press, 1982), p. 163; from *Tagebücher 1910–23* (New York: Schocken Books, 1951), p. 195. See also DI, #5, p. 292.

39. *Letters to Milena,* trans. Tania and James Stern, ed. Willi Haas (New York: Schocken Books, 1953), pp. 71, 79, 207.

40. Letter to Grete Bloch, 6 Nov. 1913, in LF, p. 326.

41. Diary entry, 4 May 1915, cited and translated by Hayman, *Kafka,* p. 256 from *Tagebücher,* p. 296. See also DII, p. 126.

42. Hayman, *Kafka,* p. 198.

43. Ibid., p. 151.

44. Johannes Urzidil, *There Goes Kafka,* trans. Harold A. Basilius (Detroit: Wayne State University Press, 1968), pp. 18–19.

45. Janouch, *Conversations with Kafka,* p. 32.

46. Diary entry, 19 Feb. 1911, cited and translated by Hayman, *Kafka,* p. 92 from *Tagebücher,* p. 29. See also DI, p. 45.

47. Letter to Felice, 1 Nov. 1912, cited and translated by Corngold, *The Commentators' Despair,* p. 24 from *Briefe an Felice,* eds. Erich Heller and Jürgen Born (Frankfurt am Main: S. Fischer Lizenzausgabe, 1967), p. 65. See also LF, p. 20.

48. Günter Anders, *Franz Kafka,* trans. A. Steer and A. K. Thorlby (London: Bowes and Bowes, 1960), p. 37.

ELEVEN

SWEET ARE THE USES OF ADVERSITY: REGRESSION AND STYLE IN THE LIFE AND WORKS OF HENRY JAMES

JOSEPH D. LICHTENBERG

Summing up his childhood, Henry James remarked, "We wholesomely breathed inconsistency and ate and drank contradictions" (UY, 47).[1] The paradoxical use of the word "wholesome" cannot be understood as a simple, direct approbation of the perversely ambiguous world of his childhood. The inconsistency he breathed and the contradictions he ate and drank became wholesome through the unique uses he put them to in the creation of his personal style and in the changing styles of his work. My premises are:

(1) Henry James became the unique individual he was as a result of responding to adversity by a series of developmental choices. These choices involved, first, a remarkable progression in the line of development of narcissism; second, a relative regression in the line of development that leads through well-differentiated separation and individuation to mature sexual and aggressive functioning; third, a great vulnerability in the line of development of cohesiveness of the body self because of a back-and-forth pull between progressive and regressive tendencies.

(2) As an adult artist, his responses to adversity involved regression, often severe, from which he would rebound by a progressive thrust into an increasingly mature creative output.

(3) In mid-life he responded to his most severe adversity by a creative rebound that not only resulted in a progressive thrust in creative output, but in a remarkable creation of a major stylistic revision. In each movement forward, Henry James used regression much as a patient in analysis does, to reopen and renegotiate an unresolved conflict. Like the solutions of his childhood responses to adversity, his adult restitutions were forward movements primarily in the developmental line of narcissism. This left him with a degree of restrictiveness in personal life style and in creative stylistic range, and a vulnerability to collapse in the face of further adversity.

Some of these adjustments can be seen in the life and problems of the main character in James' tale, "The Altar of the Dead" (1895).[2] The hero, George Stransom, at age 55, works out for himself a very satisfying life style. He carries out a formal life appropriate to his position and wealth, but lives out his passion in a remote church where he beautifully furbishes a private altar. There, by a happy accident of fate, he is joined by a fellow worshipper of the dead. His silent communion with her constitutes a central relationship in his life. This fortuitous relationship continues for many years, augmented by occasional contacts outside the church. He comes to know that while the many candles he has set on the altar signify his many exalted dead, her worship is confined to a single loss. Then, dramatically, his bliss is shattered. He discovers "that the shrine he himself had reared had been passionately converted" by her into a consecration for Acton Hague, the one man whose closeness had meant the most to him at one time and whose unspecified "unforgettable wrong" (274) had left "without an occupant" (258) the place of nearest friend. In his astonishment at this revelation, he identifies Hague in this way; "He was the friend of all my youth—my early manhood" (273). The rent in Stransom's relationship with his fellow worshipper of the dead is severe and only repaired at his moment of death. She mutely but powerfully pleads with him to add to his extensive altar a candle for "one more, one more—only just one" (284), but he cannot and will not. He is determined not to add a candle for Hague despite the fact that his refusal costs him not only contact with the one person who shares his altar, but with the survivor to whom he had planned to entrust the service for his own death.

How is Stransom's intransigence to be understood? Is there an analogous situation in James' life that could be a prototype for a failing of compassion directed at a single individual? The omnipresent friend of all Henry's youth was his older brother, William—the man of "action." Henry viewed the adversity of his early life as a result of William's effect on him. William "had gained such an advantage of me in his sixteen months' experience of the world before mine began that I never for all the time of childhood and youth in the least caught up with him" (UY, 59). In taking this view of the source of his problem, Henry defensively denied inconsistencies and contradictions of parenting that seemed to constitute the background for this disturbing dominance pairing. Instead, William's elder-brother overlordship was seen as the sole source of the adversity, and the parents' childrearing failures were viewed as the wholesome source of the unique adaptation in personality style that Henry accomplished.

Edel writes:

> William could be impulsive, filling each moment with imagination translated into action. Henry, possessing equal capacity for action, translated it into imagination; he discovered that there was a virtue to immobility: if he could not participate in William's adventures he could actively employ his mental resources: he could observe, and his memory clung tenaciously to all that it absorbed. They might urge upon him greater activity; he sat back and looked, looked at everything with the calm yet hungry eyes of childhood and the aid of his fostered and stimulated imagination. . . . The small boy cultivated a quiet aloofness; nothing would happen to him if he withdrew and used his eyes and his mind in that turbulent family. Inside the little mind great worlds were created, great achievements, great aggressions planned. For frustration, engendering aloofness, engendered also rebellion, and rebellion in turn had to be smothered to maintain his facade of passivity. . . . [I]n this fashion, by controlling his environment, suppressing his hostilities, electing the observer's role, rather than the actor's, he was able to act in his own highly personal way and conquer. He came to be his mother's favorite son. He was called "angel" in the family circle. (UY, 64–66)

Let us note how this personality or character style reflects progression and regression on differing lines of development. The line of development of narcissism reflects the transition from archaic forms of grandiosity and idealization to adult forms of self-esteem regulation, of creativity and wit, and of ideals. It is in this sector of the personality that Henry James' development centered. As the "angel" in the family circle, he consolidated a form of love of self that served as a core conviction of his value. It is this core that he transferred to the image of himself as a writer. It is this conviction of his value that allowed him, as a young man of 22, to write an authoritative treatise on the novel— before he had himself written one. The core conviction of his specialness, transferred to his role as writer, permitted him to establish himself as a self-assured critic of all other writers. But it meant that his self-esteem was to be regulated by his productivity and success as a writer—and therein lay a great vulnerability and a great impetus for restitutive efforts through writing.

Self-love is only one of the developmental outgrowths of grandiosity. Exhibitionism and omnipotence are two others. In Henry James, exhibitionism was severely restricted and remained a principal source of vulnerability. In a compensatory way, voyeurism was heavily invested and omnipotence became his central mode of functioning. What we would call the world of omnipotent fantasying, the activity of the mind by which images of the self and of others are created, altered, and manipulated in self-serving ways (defensive, preservative, and creative) became for Henry James the meaning of "imagination"—his most valued of human qualities. Imagination, for James, differentiated the pathological egotist from the man of sensibility that he himself was and the men and women of sensibility that he admired. In his short story, "Julia Bride," (1908)[3] James describes an egotist, a man of surface, seductive charm:

> He had affirmed himself, and his character, and his temper, and his health, and his appetite, and his ignorance, and his obstinacy, and his whole charming, coarse, heartless personality . . . by twenty forms of natural emphasis, but never by emphasis of interest. How in fact could you feel interest unless you should know, within you, some dim stir of imagination? There was nothing in the world of which Murray Brush was less capable than of such a dim stir; because you only began to imagine when you felt some approach to a need to understand. *He* had never felt it, for hadn't he been born, to his personal vision, with that perfect intuition of everything which reduces all the suggested preliminaries of judgment to . . . impertinence. . . ? He had had, in short, neither to imagine nor to perceive, because he had, from the first pulse of his intelligence, simply and supremely known. (348)

To "know" without interest, curiosity, and observation was empty, omnipotent posing—a mere "brush" with life. Vision and visualizing became the replacements for exhibiting and acting. They became activities of the mind, ruthlessly pursued. All people, himself especially, became James' source materials. His and their lives, his and their stories, and, above all, his and their minds became an open window into which he peered. He probed into what he saw and rearranged it for his own purposes, thereby transforming people from their live selves to his own character creations. He wrote that, as a school boy, he made

> all pastors and masters, and especially all fellow-occupants of benches and desks, all elbowing and kicking presences within touch or view, so many monsters and horrors, so many wonders and splendors and mysteries, but never . . . realities of relation . . . . They were something better . . . they were so thoroughly figures and characters, divinities or demons, and endowed in this light with a vividness that the mere reality of relation, a commoner directness of contact, would have made comparatively poor. (UY, 117)

Suppressing action and exhibitionism, and developing compensatory voyeuristic tendencies in the service of omnipotence, Henry James completed his progression on the line of development of narcissism by the exploitation of the openness of boundaries of the self and by the maintenance of an exaggerated egocentricity of view. In any child's efforts to comfort himself, to stabilize himself in the transitional moments of life that demand new or difficult adaptive solutions, and especially in the moment-to-moment evaluations of self, he remains interdependent with his idealized parental objects long after infancy is past. The object is then re-experienced or regressively recreated (in his or her absence), not as a separate individual but as having qualities communally shared between the self and the other. It is this common, automatic, preconscious activity of everyday life that Henry James made a conscious tour de force. As an old man he wrote that in boyhood he wished to live if only "by the imagination, in William's adaptive skin" (UY, 63). The skill to live within the skin of countless others was, in childhood and in later life, his most unique attribute. This is, I would say, especially true of his ability to live equally well in the skin of men and women, and of the young and the old, and it gives his work considerable range.

Self-centered observer that James was, he knew how significant was the point of view, the focus that each individual forms for the conclusions he draws and the evaluations he makes. Subjectivity and objectivity are dynamisms around which his stories unfold, with subjectivity predominating. Since, in his stories, the importance of objectivity is diminished and the significance of facts is confined to their psychological impact, a tilt occurs in the reality that is so constructed. Thus Henry James could fit himself into the skin of men and women of all ages—but he was most comfortable when the interior of their mental and physical milieu most closely resembled his. It is to be expected then, that in his life and in his characters we find expanding refinements of narcissistic potentialities—a progression from archaic grandiosity to mature forms of creativity and intelligence. But while he could penetrate deeply into a world characterized by egotistical clashes of will, and could sometimes stretch his empathic-intuitive capacities widely into mankind's sociological struggles (as in *The Princess Casamassima,* and in his effective contact with the wounded soldiers of World War I), his flexibility to do so was limited by his relative lack of progression in the other lines of development.

Henry James said that he envied orphans and wished to experience homesickness (UY). I understand his wish to be less well parented as a wish to be able to feel separate—not imbedded among father, mother, aunt, brothers, sister, and innumerable other Jameses, as the observant, inactive, dutiful angel. To be homesick, I take as his wish to have a home, to feel rooted—to go away like a toddler for an excursion of his own choosing, and then to feel the distance and the yearning to return—the rapprochement that Mahler describes. Henry was well travelled and was placed in school after school but never as a separate individual making his own choices, or even his own path as distinct from William. Thus, people in his life and in his stories often seem to lack a distinctive center of gravity. They exist in a peculiarly unbalanced way as extensions or mental representatives of others. The manipulation of one character by another is unending and it is a rare Henry James character that can seem to withstand this partial or total engulfment. In *The Wings of the Dove* (1902),[4] Milly Theale lives out her tragic last days engulfed in the plots of others. Kate Croy, strong as she is, cannot disengage herself from her past entrapments and determine her own future. Merton Densher chooses to live in the theater of his mind with the dead Milly, rather than with the live Kate. Only the heroine of the final great novel, James' work at the height of his maturity and final style, *The Golden Bowl* (1904),[5] makes the heroic choice to eschew the "depth" of narcissistic mortification as her guide to behavior. She refuses to be trapped into a regressive abandonment of the potential for intimacy with her individualistic and imperfect husband.

> She might fairly . . . have yearned for it, for the straight vindictive view, the rights of resentment, the rage of jealousy, the protests of passion, as for something she had been cheated of not least; a range of feeling which

for many women would have meant so much, but which for *her* husband's wife, for *her* father's daughter, figured nothing nearer to experience than a wild eastern caravan, looming into view with crude colours in sun, fierce pipes in the air, high spears against the sky, all a thrill, a natural joy to mingle with, but turning short before it reached her and plunging into other depths. (vol. 2, 243)

To be the wife and daughter she wanted to be—and the order is significant (wife first, daughter second)—Maggie had to resist the natural joy of mingling with the wild caravan of narcissistically self-expansive affects of vindictive rage. To be the wife, she had to separate from her father, however belatedly, and to choose, instead, a mature love relationship that included the experience of realistic, effective anger—an implication that James at least suggests even if he does not state it explicitly.

In appraising the two-sidedness of James' genius, we can say that he took narcissistic preoccupations, their imagery and feeling states, and developed and depicted them to a remarkable degree with great aesthetic skill—creating the modern psychological novel. Or we can say that he left out of his works the imagery and feeling states of full-blooded sensual love, anger, assertive action, and guilt that are experienced by separate and distinct people making individualistic choices about career, marriage, and pregnancy. Throughout his writing career, he utilized the formal aspects of triangular Oedipal relationships as themes in his tales and novels. On close examination, the issues between his characters are generally not sensual love and jealousy, but struggles about dependence, possessiveness, and control. Only in the works of the final period do the triangles (such as exist in all possible variations in *The Golden Bowl*) stimulate in the reader a feeling of romantic passion—restrained or actual.

How much Henry James, in his personal life, missed being a more separated and individuated person is difficult to say. He compensated by having a vast array of acquaintances to people his free hours and to supply his storehouse of plots and characters. A person who tried to get too close, such as Edith Wharton, his most devoted of admirers and supporters, was regarded by him as an "Angel of Devastation".[6] His truly dearest friend was the muse of his writing table, whom he addressed aloud and in writing as "Mon Bon." The last dear friend of his old age, after he had suffered through often depressing efforts to be the master to a brood of creative artists, was an unintellectual man of gen-

tlemanly activity whose comings and goings were intimate enough to
show he cared, and distant enough not to be an intrusion.

Henry James' failure to progress to a mature, cohesive sense of body
integrity did cause him repeated pain. It was as if the interior of his
body and its functioning did not exist as a distinct part of himself
subject to his definition of its state of need and of capacity. Rather, his
sense of bodily security seemed dependent on the benevolent approval
of his mother and the absence of his older brother. A critical word from
his mother could lead to constipation. A critical campaign by her about
his expenditures in his early adult life could lead to episodes of such
prolonged bowel dysfunction that he was forced to make lengthy visits
to health spas. The worst aspects of this symptom happily ended when
his mother's death seemed to release her handhold on his bowels.

William's influence seemed even stronger. A criticism, or the threat of
a visit by him, could lead Henry to a weeklong headache. William's full
physical presence would paralyze Henry's creative output. For example,
at the age of twenty-five Henry was living with his parents and pro-
ductively developing his writing skills when William returned after an
eighteen-month absence. "Henry promptly ceased to publish. His
back-ache revived and he could bring himself neither to read nor write"
(UY, 243). In his quest for approval, Henry could never seem to refrain
from offering himself up to William, who would invariably, it seemed,
apply another turn of the screw. I believe this pattern of disturbed
bodily integrity became pathologically consolidated after Henry's un-
diagnosed back ailment during adolescence. It was as though Henry
viewed his injured self and his injured father (amputated leg) as the
victims of some obscure unspeakably malign force that could leap out at
them at any time. When it did, it could crush body and spirit in a unity
of catastrophic effect. This was to happen to Henry James in small and
large episodes throughout his life. But, as with his positive reaction to
other developmental adversities, James was able to portray this "ineffable state" with unique brilliance in his description of the present terror
in *The Turn of the Screw* (1898) and "The Jolly Corner" (1909), and in
the suggestion of terrors ominously awaited in *The Beast in the Jungle*
(1903).[7]

But in James' works, the highly developed is paid for by the absent.
No character in a James story has real bodily feeling. The dying Milly
has no specified illness and, as far as the reader knows, no physical pain.
The narcissistic injury of not being in control of life, by virtue of the

pre-knowledge of death, she bears nobly. But no one hurts from his stomach, or enjoys physical joy from running, leaping, or having an orgasm. People are appalled by terror and can suddenly and mysteriously die, like the boy in *The Turn of the Screw*. Like James himself, they can experience narcissistic shock that paralyzes mind and body alike. In "The Altar of the Dead" (1895), when Stransom perceives his friend's devotion to the wicked Acton Hague "the room heaved like the cabin of a ship. . . . The revelation seemed to smite our friend in the face, and he dropped into a seat and sat silent" (p. 223).

In Henry James' late style, he began to deal with aspects of human experience he had previously avoided. To better understand this change, let us turn now to two of the traumatic events of Henry James' later life: first, the death of his female friend, Fenimore, and second, his failure as a dramatist with the accompanying assault on his exhibitionistic self by a hooting audience.

As 1894 began, Henry James, at the age of 50, a famous, well-established writer, was in the midst of his five-year venture as a dramatist. He continued to write an occasional short story, but his main investment—emotional and artistic—was in making what he referred to as a reasonable show of fame and perhaps a modest show of fortune. He was jolted out of his troubled but steadily pursued assault on the theater with the news of the unexpected death of Fenimore Woolfson, his friend, fellow writer, and sometime close companion of many years. Shocked and horrified, he assumed her death to be of natural causes and immediately prepared to journey to Venice to meet her sister and assist in funeral arrangements. But a second and more profound jolt awaited him—the discovery that Fenimore, in a moment of physical illness and persisting depression, had flung herself out of the window of her Venetian apartment. This knowledge precipitated a typical Henry James regression into stunned inactivity. He cancelled his travel plans, writing to his diplomat friend John Hay that, before the "horror and pity" of the news,

> I have utterly collapsed. I have let everything go . . . with the dreadful *image* before me. I feel a real personal indebtedness to you in the assurance I have of your beneficent action. . . . I feel an intense nearness of participation in every circumstance of her tragic end and in every detail of the sequel. But it is just this nearness of emotion that has made—since yesterday—the immediate horrified rush to personally *meet* these things impossible to me.[8]

Henry's regression was relatively short-lived. He wrote to many friends about being sickened and overwhelmed. He continued to be haunted with the image of the act. On the day of the funeral, he found it "all unspeakably wretched and obscure"[9] that someone with whom he had been "extremely intimate" and "greatly attached"[10] should have acted in such a gruesome way and he felt vaguely implicated. He rationalized that her action was caused by her mental illness and that without his kindness and friendship her suicide might have occurred sooner.

He gradually accustomed himself to Fenimore's death and by the end of March prepared to travel to Venice. Ostensibly his trip was to assist her family in settling her affairs. More personally, he hoped to rescue and destroy his correspondence, fearing, as he always did, the exposure of his personal life to public view. He carried out his trip effectively, visited friends, and fortified himself by maintaining a questionable theory of Fenimore's having suffered a sudden derangement because of a cerebral accident. By early May, still in Venice, he was actively writing a short story, a continuation of his tales of the literary life. He went to Rome, visited Fenimore's grave and returned to England. In Oxford, where he had last spent time with Fenimore, he set down the title and idea for "The Altar of the Dead." On his return to London, he completed it with remarkable rapidity.

James wrote "The Altar of the Dead" before the full impact of Fenimore's death had set in. He was still at the height of his powers as a novelist who portrayed with remarkable skill the engagement of narcissistic characters. In contrast to his final style, which I shall describe later, elements of this style of his mature middle period are:

(1) The reverberating metaphor between person and scene with affect embedded in both:

> He was arrested . . . by the particular effect of a shopfront which lighted the dull brown air with its mercenary grin. . . . It was the window of a jeweler whose diamonds and sapphires seemed to laugh, in flashes like high notes of sound. . . . [Creston's new wife] had a face that shone as publicly as the jeweler's window, and in the happy candor with which she wore her monstrous character there was an effect of gross immodesty. . . . The happy pair had just arrived from America, and Stransom had not needed to be told this to divine the nationality of the lady. . . . he had heard of poor Creston's having, while his bereavement was still fresh, gone

to the United States for what people in such predicaments call a little change. He had found the little change, indeed he had brought the little change back; it was the little change that stood there. (255–56)

(2) The action as a suspended, sustained clash of wills between self-centered characters:

She let him [Stransom] press her with his somber eyes, only smiling at him with an exquisite mercy. . . . She told nothing, she judged nothing; she accepted everything but the possibility of her return to the old symbols. . . . To the voice of impersonal generosity he felt sure he would have listened; he would have deferred to an advocate who, speaking from abstract justice . . . should have had the imagination to say: "Oh, remember only the best of him; pity him; provide for him!" To provide for him on the very ground of having discovered another of [Hague's] turpitudes was not to pity him, but to glorify him. . . . In one way or another the poor woman had been coldly sacrificed. That was why, at the last as well as the first, he must still leave him out. (282–83)

(3) Stylistic shifts between resonating tones of high-mindedness and ironic humor with even a bit of playfulness thrown in:

She lived . . . in a mere slum, with an old aunt, a person in connection with whom she spoke of the engrossment of humdrum duties and regular occupations. She was not, the mourning niece, in her first youth, and her vanished freshness had left something behind which, for Stransom, represented the proof that it had been tragically sacrificed. Whatever she gave him the assurance of she gave it without references. She might in fact have been a divorced duchess, and she might have been an old maid who taught her harp. (267)

(4) Symbolism that shifts between universal questions of values and ethics (such as the general problems of mourning) and personal questions of guilt and responsibility:

By this time he had survived all his friends; the last straight flame was three years old; there was no one to add to the list. Over and over he called his roll, and it appeared to him compact and complete. . . . More and more . . . face to face with his little legion, reading over endless histories, handling the empty shells and playing with the silence—more and more he could see that he had never introduced an alien. He had had his great compassions, his indulgences—there were cases in which they had been immense: but what had his devotion after all been, if it hadn't been fundamentally a respect? He was, however, himself surprised at his stiffness, by the end of the winter the responsibility of it was what was uppermost in his thoughts. The refrain had grown old to them, the plea for just one more. (286)

(5) Thinly veiled themes of autobiographic conflict transformed by unconscious defense and art into an idiosyncratic solution that could be shared by a reasonably wide audience:

He had a mortal dislike, poor Stransom, to lean anniversaries, and he disliked them still more when they made a pretense of a figure. Celebrations and suppressions were equally painful to him and there was only one of the former that found a place in his life. Again and again he had kept in his own fashion the day of the year on which Mary Antrim had died. It would be more to the point perhaps to say that the day kept him: it kept him at least, effectually from doing anything else. (252)

There was never a word he had said to her that she had not beautifully understood. For long ages he never knew her name, any more than she had ever pronounced his own; but it was not their names that mattered, it was only their perfect practice and their common need.
These things made their whole relation so impersonal that they had not the rules or reasons people found in ordinary friendships. They didn't care for the things it was supposed necessary to care for in the intercourse of the world. They ended one day . . . by throwing out the idea that they didn't care for each other. Over this idea they grew quite intimate; they rallied to it in a way that marked a fresh start in their confidence. If to feel deeply together about certain things wholly distinct from themselves didn't constitute a safety, where was safety to be looked for? (267–68)

These passages indicate how James had taken his adolescent idealization of his spirited cousin Minny Temple, had defensively reacted to her early death by incorporating her into a character in the theater of his mind, and through his art, had immortalized her as a flame that went out young but could be rekindled at his will on the altar of the dead. He then had reacted to Fenimore's death by having a serious conflict— should the suicide join the beautifully, charmingly, or even piteously dead on his altar? What they had together during her life was indeed valuable. It was something that he could salvage in the theater of his mind and create a character to reveal and share it. The good thing had been their shared "perfect practices," their feeling deeply "together about certain things wholly distinct from themselves"—their shared interest in writing, in values, and in life. If not safety in that, then in what? But there had not been safety in it. Wills had clashed and an action had been taken to interrupt the long period of their perfect practices. She had committed suicide and that act left him to deal with his affective response. First came the paralysis, then the personal recovery, and then months later, the aesthetic recovery. He would write the emotional catastrophe into the story. His hero would be smitten in the face, drop into a seat, and remain in a state of shock. Furthermore, the story would deal from beginning to end with all the emotions related to mourning and death and dying—with the mysterious and ghostly, almost ghoulish, relationship of the dead to the living. But he would alter the cause—and, simultaneously and parsimoniously, deal with his other conflict. The cause of Stransom's shock was not a suicide but the sudden re-intrusion into his life of the evil man of action and the inexplicable attachment of the heroine to him. In this tale, Henry James, I think, implicates several individuals as moral villains: (1) William; (2) Fenimore, who took an action that, like Acton Hague, betrayed her loyal friend Henry; (3) the otherwise innocent John Hay, who was capable of action when Henry was not, and who, because of that, may have given the character his last name; and (4) unconsciously Henry James himself. The self-image is tied up in the construction James gives to Acton Hague's "infamy" to the "mourning niece." All she herself is quoted as saying is that she had loved even where she too suffered. Stransom concludes: "He had ruthlessly abandoned her—that, of course, was what he had done" (278). "In one way or another the poor woman had been coldly sacrificed" (283). Why "of course"? Why such certitude? Here there is a similarity to many of James' ghost stories—what exists in the imagination is what is real; it is what governs the outcome. So Stransom acts for Henry as the one who sounds the high moral note and Acton takes care of Henry's nagging question: What responsibility did he have for Fenimore's suicide? Had he ruthlessly abandoned her? The artistic conception is exquisite in its "moral" solution—Acton was responsible for harm to them both—Stransom, who had been his friend, had been betrayed by him, and the niece had been abandoned by him. The two innocent victims, male and female aspects of Henry, could quarrel then over which was the nobler—the one who forgave all, or the one who maintained an implacable righteous indignation. Thus did Henry mourn his dead—not like a person who separates from them through the process of mourning that Freud described, but as a person who retains them in his mind. He manipulates them for his own omnipotent purposes and then shares them in their reconstituted form with his readers, as one would share a candle's luster "as dazzling as the vision of heaven in the mind of a child" (286). Henry James in doing this was not naive. He knew the irony of it: Antrim is antrum—a cavity or sinus; Stransom is transom—an opening or window above a door; the heroine's name is left unspecified, empty. His summary statement about the folly of both his characters, the niece and Stransom, is stated in two sentences: Hers was "a life in which a single experience had reduced all others to naught. His own life, round its central hollow, had been packed close enough" (269).

It is my belief that Henry dealt with the affective response of his reaction to Fenimore's death through his story, with its imagery of stunned shock, its organ tones of moral incredulity, and its ghoulish characters with their monomania and central hollowness. Having worked through his regressive emotional reaction, he was free to plan a second and different effort to treat the theme of death. Shortly after completing "The Altar of the Dead," he jotted down the plot for *The Wings of the Dove*—a novel in which the heroine, unlike Fenimore, was to be portrayed as a master of the art of dying graciously. When James wrote the novel some years later, the macabre was removed entirely and the characters were given more substance, even if the substance remained self-centered in its portrayal of the clash of wills.

Fenimore's suicide was a blow to Henry James' sensibilities and to the code of moral and ethical behavior that he expected from his intimate friends. A more direct blow to his person was shortly to come, and its effect was more profound.

The devastating culmination of his attempt to produce dramas for the theater—to him, a demeaning quest for popular success—ended with his allowing himself to be pushed onto the stage at the end of the performance of his play, *Guy Domville*. The rowdies in the gallery hooted at him. Henry, the shy "angel" who had avoided exhibitionistic tension since early childhood, was exposed to an inner torment for which he was woefully unprepared. He tried for a time to hide with a good face the effect of this major narcissistic hurt. For some time he went about his schedule. He began to formulate plans. Mostly they were for novels and stories he would write. Some even were for plays. He wrote in his notebook: "I have my head, thank God, full of visions" (TY, 109).[11] The protective self-expansiveness of these lines indicates the reassurance to himself of his mental functioning—the cornerstone of his self-esteem. What they omitted were his emotions. These he was months away from even beginning to cope with. Edel explains James' mood of despair in these telling words: It was "as if some remote little being within James himself had been killed by the audience during that crucial night . . . and he had been left open to the world's indifference" (TY, 168).

As a young man, he had studied the novel as a critical form, creating for himself a confidence built on a mixture of pretensiousness and solid intellectual mastery. This had enabled him to emerge from a somewhat chaotic adolescence and fight off the regressive pull of life among the James family, freeing his own identity as novelist. Now, again struggling to restore his confidence and resist the fragmenting pull of regression, he resumed his intellectual attack on the meaning, the structure, and the form of the novel. He would reorganize his life's work. His defeat and his pain would lead to an eventual restoration of his artist self. It would be transmuted through the resolution of the disappointment over his "wasted passion and squandered time" (TY, 111) into a new sense of self as an artist who had discovered the "key that . . . fits the complicated chambers of both the dramatic and the narrative lock." Through what he had learned from writing for the theater, the techniques of scenario and scene creation, he believed his "infinite little loss is converted into an almost infinite gain" (TY, 111). In his notebook James wrote, "Compensation and solutions seem to stand there with open arms for me—and something of the 'meaning' to come to me of past bitterness, of recent bitterness that otherwise has seemed a mere sickening, unflavored draught" (TY, 111).

Although he could formulate his plans in his mind and restructure his approach to method, he could not write. His mastery through intellect could restore his self-esteem enough to permit daily life to proceed, but his writing required his emotional recovery and that took a great deal longer. In the meantime, a measure of grandiosity served as a protective armor. Henry sat down over elaborate outlines and demanded of himself levels of originality that paralyzed his effort. Finally, he began again to write a group of four tales, published in a volume entitled *Embarrassments*. After this beginning, he dealt with his emotions by writing about the responses of a series of little girls and young female adults "who want to know—who try to probe the secrets of the world around them, but who do not possess enough facts" (TY, 150). They exist in a world of confusion, ranging from perplexity to the horror and death found in *The Turn of the Screw*. The sense of the ghastly, the painfully enigmatic, the appallingly evil pervades these stories and evolves from the author's inner turmoil. "In all these tales James seems to have worked toward a single conclusion: the facts of life were crude and raw; art colored and gilded them, and suffused them with eternal truth. The human imagination brings life into existence" (TY, 150).

At the end of this period, Henry James entered into the most productive phase of his life. How he mastered his crisis is poignantly described by Edel:

> In his deep well of unconscious cerebration, Henry James had moved slowly from sickness to health. He had taken backward steps into the black abyss in order to discover his power of self-creation, and now he had emerged again a whole man in spite of assaults and misfortunes. Step by step, James' imagination had found, had wrought, the healing substance of his art—the strange, bewildering and ambiguous novels in which somehow he had recovered his identity, so that he might be again a strong and functioning artist. In this process he had opened himself up—life aiding—to feeling and to love. He had taught himself to accept middle age, and to face great loneliness, and had turned again and again for solace to the discipline and difficulty of his craft. . . . In this indirect soothing of his soul, the frigid wall of his egotism had been breached to an enlarged vision of the world, and a feeling at last of the world's human warmth. (TY, 354–55)

This was, I suggest, a double process of soothing of the soul. It involved the step-by-step externalization of the disappointments into the themes and styles of the creative work. Simultaneously, it involved the step-by-step internalization of the renewed self-affirmation of "his identity so that he might be again a strong and functioning artist" (TY, 354), only now one altered by his experience. Both in his work and in his life he was to become more open to the emotional intimacies life offered.

In the uses he made of his adversity, Henry James illustrated, I believe, the unique gift of all human beings to soothe their souls during the transitional and traumatic moments of life by the constructive use of regression, the creation of illusion, and the internalization of the benevolent and the highly esteemed. Furthermore, he illustrated the even more unique gift of the creative artist to broaden this human resource for meeting disappointments into both an internal transformation and an external transformation—the creative work.

Let us examine the details of the transformation that took place in Henry James' work after his recovery.

(1) The incorporation into the novel of major stylistic elements from the drama—the unities of setting, time interval, character, and action. Henry James now planned his novels as a series of scenarios similar to the scenes and acts of a play. This increased the dramatic tension in each and the full impact of the whole when the proper balance between the parts was achieved. It gave Henry James, as writer, a heightened sense of control over his craft—a mastery to go with his public and personal image as the Master.

(2) The inclusion of more sensual and emotive touching in the interaction between people. The psychological emphasis was retained, but the range was expanded to include sexual intercourse, physical holding, and more mature elements of love. This change in the stories paralleled a comparable trend in Henry James' life toward sensual and emotive touching—albeit highly restrained—first with Hendrick Anderson in an idealized, unsatisfactory relationship, then with Jocelyn Persse in a more realistic shared affection.

(3) At the same time as he treated sensuality and emotion more freely, his sentence structure and the use of metaphor became more idiosyncratic. The effect was one of controlling and manipulating the reader into the closest possible attention. I believe the effect on the reader was to give expression, through the sentence structure itself, to James' struggle with values, the mundane, the sensual, and the emotional. By his interruptions in the flow of the sentence, he appears to be saying (a) I assert "this" but it cannot be unqualified; (b) I know the vernacular people use, the simple, the common, the earthy, but I cannot say it straight out any more than I can refer to the unadorned bathroom function; and (c) the sensual and emotional are to me never straight out—they are always complex, requiring analysis to deal with the multiple determinants in each.

(4) In the great revision of style that followed his severe regression, James was selective in what he included and excluded. For the first time, he opened his mind to the significance of symbolism as a unifying device. Thus, his dove and her wings can be compared to Ibsen's wild duck in its evocation of a set of related but rich and shifting metaphoric usages. He remained closed to the use of writing for political or social purposes. He wished to explore values through the careful analysis of their effect on characters, each of whom makes value judgments while the author suspends his. He developed still further his dual approach to the expression of emotions. Strong emotion, especially shock, awe, dread, and terror were expressed through the eyes of characters, especially children, when confronted with "the apparitional world" ("The Jolly Corner," 620) of the monstrous, the ineffable, and the bestial. When Henry James successfully converted his own sense of paralyzed

dread into the fabric of his story, he was then able to write of less violent affects with increasing control. He could more deeply explore love and grief, but continued to use irony as the principal buffer against too great a personal involvement or sentiment.

(5) By combining the suspense of the ghost story with the tension of the psychological interaction between subjective and objective reality, he perfected the new climax of the psychological novel. The climax does not occur when something happens in the form of action, although that may incidentally be true. Rather, it occurs when something is discovered—when insight is obtained by the confluence of psychic recognition by two or more of the characters who have the stir of imagination to want to "know," in spite of the consequences of knowledge. When successful, he created an experience in which the characters, the readers, and even the author suddenly share awareness. Whereas, before, awareness almost always made the characters withdraw, now, in *The Golden Bowl* and in "The Jolly Corner," the shared vision cements the intimacy. In his work, James had come to terms with that special amalgam of mind and body that allows "narcissistic" intellectual people, who are much given to the omnipotence of the mind, also to want the warmth, the invigoration, and the pain of caring deeply about a separate and distinct other person. Life then includes loving, and death with mourning and grief—not the narcissistic manipulation of people in one's own private theater of the mind. Let me illustrate this final point by quoting from "The Beast in the Jungle." Bear in mind the comparison with "The Altar of the Dead."

> [A]n accident, superficially slight . . . moved him . . . with a force beyond any impression of Egypt or of India. It was a thing of the merest chance—the turn, as he afterwards felt, of a hair, though he was indeed to live to believe that if light hadn't come to him in this particular fashion it would still come in another. . . . The incident of an autumn day had put the match to the train laid from of old by his misery. With the light before him he knew that even of late his ache had only been smothered. It was strangely drugged, but it throbbed; at the touch it began to bleed. And the touch, in the event, was the face of a fellow mortal. This face, one gray afternoon when the leaves were thick in the alleys, looked into Marcher's own, at the cemetery, with an expression like the cut of a blade. He felt it, that is, so deep down that he winced at the steady thrust. The person who so mutely assaulted him was a figure he had noticed, on reaching his own goal, absorbed by a grave a short distance away, a grave apparently fresh, so that the emotion of the visitor would probably match it for frankness. . . . Marcher knew him at once for one of the deeply stricken—a perception so sharp that nothing else in the picture comparatively lived,

neither his dress, his age, nor his presumable character and class; nothing lived but the deep ravages of the features he showed. He *showed* them— that was the point. . . . The stranger passed, but the raw glare of his grief remained, making our friend wonder in pity what was wrong, what wound it expressed, what injury not to be healed. What had the man had, to make him by the loss of it so bleed and yet live?

Something—and this reached him with a pang— that *he,* John Marcher, hadn't; the proof of which was precisely John Marcher's arid end. No passion had even touched him, for that was what passion meant; he had survived and maundered and pined, but where had been *his* deep ravage? . . . He had seen *outside* of his life, not learned it within, the way a woman was mourned when she had been loved for herself. . . . Everything fell together, confessed, explained, overwhelmed; leaving him most of all stupified at the blindness he had cherished. The fate he had been marked for he had met with a vengeance—he had emptied the cup to the lees; he had been the man of his time, *the* man, to whom nothing on earth was to have happened. That was the rare stroke—that was his visitation. . . . The escape would have been to love her [May Bartram], then, *then* he would have lived. She had lived—who could say now with what passion?—since she had loved him for himself; whereas he had never thought of her (ah, how it hugely glared at him) but in the chill of his egotism and the light of her use. (593–597)

Thus Henry James concluded from the personal adversity he had suffered, and the criticism—external, and more significantly, internal— he had received, that, for a believable character in a tale or novel, life includes loving and death is responded to by grief. In his personal life, James made some tentative, mostly unsuccessful, efforts to achieve greater physical closeness. In the main, James remained true to his lifelong dedication to the creative act as his principal mode of expression, and in his late work, he was able as a novelist to transcend the limitations of personal experience. In response to the betrayal, hostility, and piercing criticism of H. G. Wells, James, at the age of seventy-two, rose to the occasion to express with dignity his creed: "I live, live intensely and am fed by life, and my value, whatever it may be, is in my own kind of expression of that. Art *makes* life, makes interest, makes importance."[12] I would add that this study of Henry James indicates that, if we take his life as an example, when the creative capacity is genetically present, art makes life, adversity feeds art, and regression into the depths of the artist's lifelong yearning and unresolved conflicts gives the art its significance as an evocative expression to be shared with the reader.

NOTES

1. Leon Edel, *Henry James: The Untried Years (1843–1870)* (New York: J. B. Lippincott, 1953), hereafter referred to as UY.

2. Henry James, "The Altar of the Dead," in *The Turn of the Screw and other Short Novels* (New York: Signet Classics, 1962), pp. 252–90.

3. Henry James, "Julia Bride," in *The Marriages and Other Stories* (New York: Signet Classics, 1961), pp. 324–60.

4. Henry James, *The Wings of the Dove* (Baltimore: Penguin Books, 1976).

5. Henry James, *The Golden Bowl*, 2 vols. (New York: Grove Press, 1952).

6. Leon Edel, *Henry James: The Master (1901–1916)* (New York: J. B. Lippincott, 1972), p. 207.

7. Henry James, *The Turn of the Screw,* in *The Turn of the Screw and Other Short Novels* (New York: Signet Classics, 1962), pp. 291–403; "The Jolly Corner," in *The Short Stories of Henry James* (New York: The Modern Library, 1945), pp. 603–41; *The Beast in the Jungle,* in *The Turn of the Screw and Other Short Novels* (New York: Signet Classics, 1962), pp. 404–51.

8. Leon Edel, *Henry James: The Middle Years (1882–1895)* (New York: J. B. Lippincott, 1962), p. 358.

9. Ibid., p. 361.

10. Ibid., p. 360.

11. Leon Edel, *Henry James: The Treacherous Years (1895–1901)* (New York: J. B. Lippincott, 1969), hereafter referred to as TY.

12. Edel, *Henry James: The Master,* p. 536.

TWELVE

THE FAITHLESS MOTHER: AN ASPECT OF THE NOVELS OF E. M. FORSTER

PEER HULTBERG

The evolution of character in the works of E. M. Forster has much to do with the author's continued attempts to work through his relationship with his mother.

Forster's mother was the third child and the first daughter of a poor and socially low-ranking family with ten children in all.[1] Very early in life her overtaxed mother seems to have forced her to take care of her seven younger siblings; and when her father died her mother appears to have relied heavily on her for practical and moral support. The girl was then twelve, the mother had just given birth to her tenth child, and they had hardly a penny to their name. Forster's mother seems to have been intelligent, quick-witted, tenacious, and known for her sharp tongue. At the age of seventeen she describes herself as "a great heroine . . . manners 71 years of age, from her infancy always very old for her age"[2]—in other words she sees herself as the typical precocious child displaying a good deal of infantile grandiosity. About the time of her father's death a rich woman took an interest in her and virtually adopted her into her household, very much, however, insisting that she should act the role of the poor relation. Her own mother seems to have given her up only too readily: "Lily is your child, Miss Thornton, now," she told the benefactress, "—never ask me about her. I only feel thankful that it is so."[3] In other words, despite the sacrifice of her childhood for the sake of her mother and her siblings, she seemed rather easily dispensed with. In her new surroundings she met the nephew of her benefactress, an architect, and married him when she was twenty-two and he thirty. She soon became pregnant but her first baby died at birth. Less than a year later, on 1 January 1879, she gave birth to E.M. Forster. Soon afterwards Forster's father began to ail and within two years died of consumption. His family seems to have been very critical of the unsympathetic way in which Forster's mother treated him during his illness: she seems hardly to have been aware of the seriousness of his state, appearing to have met his suffering with impatience and lack of understanding, and the family in the end secretly blamed her for his death.

After the death of her husband, Forster's mother, then twenty-five years old, seems to have fallen into a somewhat restless depressive state. She was able in a modest way to support herself and her child and traveled on and off alone, without her son, staying with friends and relations for about a year and a half in search of a place to settle down. Her chances of remarrying were obviously slight because of the child, and consequently she made a virtue out of necessity and was praised for her independence: "She is the most self-contained woman I ever met with, but to be sure she's been brought up to independence," her bene-factress remarked.[4] She seems to have left her son in the care of various relatives, especially her former benefactress, but she refused to share house with any of them and jealously guarded her first right to her child. Her reunions with him were highly demonstrative affairs, espe-cially on the part of the son: "The moment he saw her he ran to her in a sort of ecstasy as tho' they had been separated for years, and half stifling her with kisses as she carried him off."[5] It is interesting to note that there is never any mention of the reactions of resentment, sadness or, indeed, rage which are usually met with in children who are abandoned by their mothers. One wonders whether this was because Forster as a baby fully realized the fatal consequences of such unwanted reactions. He seems very early to have adapted to the role of the happy, contented, and demonstratively loving boy and to have repressed any negative feelings toward his mother at her neglect and possibly unempathic behavior toward him. He quickly accepted the role of being her only support and comfort. Hence he was referred to in the family as the "Important One." Again one wonders what might have lain behind this expression. Its absolute and somewhat demonstrative nature makes one suspect that it might represent a case of "transformation into the opposite." In other words, it might very well cover the unconscious statement, the "Not-So-Important-One." Or perhaps the expression might have meant: "You are the Important One as long as you behave as the Important One and repress everything that does not conform to your mother's idea of what makes an Important One. If, however, you do not conform to this notion you become the Un-Important One, and your mother has no use for you at all."

The way in which Forster's mother brought up her son seems to have been based on the principle of emotional abandonment and withdrawal of affection. In this connection one should not forget that in spite of having only this child she was far from inexperienced in the bringing up of children. In fact, she probably knew it all too well, having been in charge of seven younger siblings. One gets the impression that she went about the upbringing of her own son in the rather brisk, unempathic, no-nonsense manner with which an older sister may treat a younger brother. Again the words of her benefactress:

> There is a sort of firmness which Emmy said amounted to sternness in the way in which she let him scream and go into a violent passion when refused anything on which he had set his mind. — And it was piteous to behold him trying to get over her and make her kiss him, which she professed she never would the days he beat and kicked Morris and scratched her face when taken out of bed forcibly to be washed and dressed. Tho' he tried so hard, I never saw her give way about this.[6]

There can be little doubt of the efficacy of this kind of upbringing on a small, sensitive boy whose situation in life has been made very uncertain by his father's early death as well as the death at birth of an older sibling, and who unconsciously senses his mother's own uncertainty, dejection, and perhaps even resentment of him. However, this mother was also his only real point of reference in his life, although elderly female admirers, including his grandmother, certainly played an important and probably soothing part. It would therefore not be surprising if from the outset he should unconsciously repress every impulse of his own that went against her wishes and desires, and conform to her ideas of how an "Important One" was supposed to feel and behave. His vigorous but also overtaxed and probably somewhat depressed mother seems to have made him well aware of her ideal of a son. And through his great gifts of empathy and sensitivity he was able to introject this ideal and adapt almost fully to it. As a result, at the age of about four he could settle down with his mother to a "radiantly happy" childhood[7] and a subsequent close relationship which was to last nearly sixty-five years.

Summing up one may put forward the following hypothesis about Forster's early childhood. Forster's mother probably experienced little warm maternal feelings herself in her own childhood. In spite of her sacrifices for the family, her mother abandoned her with relief to her benefactress, ostensibly for the sake of her own good, although the girl might unconsciously have felt this as a severe rejection. She had by then learned how to deal with small children in an energetic, matter-of-fact, rather non-committal manner. She had firm ideas of what a well-behaved child ought to be like, and could probably only relate to a child who conformed to this ideal. Her first child died at birth, and Forster thus was probably not only a wished-for child but also a child who had to make up for the loss of an unknown sibling. Immediately after his birth Forster's life was overshadowed by his father's fatal illness, which lasted until he was twenty-two months old. His mother seemed quite unable to cope with the situation of a dying husband and a living infant and hence was unable to offer herself to her son as a "good-enough mother" or to present him with "optimal frustrations." She did not have the qualities enabling her to be a "holding mother," and he thus lived in permanent fear of her "letting him fall." Hence the highly sensitive and extremely empathic child had early on to take over the role of comforting and supporting the mother under the threat of abandonment and annihilation if he did not do so, as well as having to conform to her rigid ideals of a well-behaved baby. The reward for this, however, was that he became the "Important One" and later probably also a replacement for the father, whose Christian name he bore. He did accomplish this very difficult task set him by his mother. It would be impossible as well as presumptuous and irrelevant in the present context to calculate the cost of his doing so. The positive outcome, however, was no doubt a steady further differentiation of his life-saving empathy, which eventually reached exceptional heights as expressed in his literary work. He developed a capacity for extraordinary empathy with his surroundings but seemed rather deaf to his own needs.

In the language of narcissism theories, one may briefly say that Forster suffered deprivation in both areas of the bipolar self, in the area of the grandiose self because of inadequate mirroring on the part of the mother, and in the area of the idealized selfobject because of the lack of a father or of a human being whom he could idealize unconditionally. However, it is also certain that he eventually achieved some narcissistic fulfillment through his literary work which, at least in his early years, seems to have taken priority over relationships. He seems above all to have been deprived of the unconditional "gleam in the mother's eyes," in the sense that he could only perceive it when he fulfilled specific conditions. In other words, he had to call this "gleam" forth by his own efforts and by his own ever-increasing empathy. If he did not manage to do so he was punished by "deadness of the eyes" in the first place and subsequently by emotional abandonment with the inherent risk of annihilation. This situation might have been exacerbated by what were to him the mother's inexplicable absences while house-hunting after the father's death, which he no doubt understood as punishment for disobediences which he had himself to detect and which he had to make good by adapting further to his mother's ideal of a child. Hence he learned by empathy how to bring about the "gleam in the mother's eyes." When the need came for an idealized imago his mother readily offered herself, and could also be accepted for this purpose. However, what he above all idealized in her was probably not his mother as a human being but the image he found in her of the ideal figure of a boy and a man. This was the ideal for which he had already suppressed aspects of his own personality or his own self, and he now through idealization continued this process. However, because it had the quality of an ideal rather than a human being, this figure was so rigid that it could not under any circumstances be modified by optimal frustration and viewed in a realistic light. It acquired the nature of an implacable force which he could never appease and seems eventually to have turned into a highly severe superego. One might thus surmise that Forster, in any event in his childhood, lived in a state of latent fear that he might on the one hand be unexpectedly rejected by his mother for not adapting to ideals she had set up for him; on the other that he might suddenly be overwhelmed by crushing feelings of inferiority vis-à-vis the idealized imago and later superego. And both these dangers might have provoked unconscious anxieties that he might be punished with rejection and abandonment, if not directly by death, which, through the fate of his father and his older sibling, had become a reality in his life. Such might have been the permanent trauma of his early childhood.

This psychic situation seems reflected in various ways in Forster's fictional work and is most likely the main reason for his eventual silence as a writer of fiction. In his novels it is, for instance, illustrated by the general lack of genuine father-figures, by the negative representation of the so-called masculine world as illustrated, for example, in *Howards End,* and by the almost hateful description of the Anglo-Indians in *A Passage to India*. However, it appears that Forster's childhood trauma found strongest expression in the theme of abandonment, rejection, and direct betrayal on the part of motherly figures or mother substitutes, which seems to run as a leitmotif throughout his whole fictional work. From the point of view of the theories of narcissism, it appears that the well-known compensatory mechanisms, the grandiose self and the idealized selfobject, are not a prominent component of Forster's fictional work, except perhaps in a few of the very early short stories. They are in his case probably rather to be seen in certain aspects of his personal life. In his novels one appears above all to be confronted with the underlying anxieties against which these above-mentioned compensatory or defence mechanisms protect the ego. In other words, his work seems to go behind the defence mechanisms and depict a deep, almost persecutory experience of the world, against which the so-called false self guards a fragile ego and a rudimentary self. His work thus reaches layers of the psyche dominated by archaic fears, which above all are fears of betrayal and rejection, all entailing annihilation.

As a leitmotif, these anxieties are clearly illustrated as early as 1905 in Forster's first novel, *Where Angels Fear to Tread*—Forster was only twenty-four when it was published. Lilia, the main protagonist (her name, incidentally, is almost identical with Lily, the name of Forster's mother), entirely rejects her small daughter Irma in her infatuation with Gino, her Italian lover and, later, husband. He in turn abandons Lilia by treating her according to the conventional way in which women are treated in his sphere of society. And subsequently, after the death of Lilia, he himself is betrayed by having his beloved son abducted by Lilia's relatives. During this adventure the baby dies, and the novel ends on a note of deep resignation. Everyone seems poorer than at the outset of the action, and neither the flimsy friendship between Gino and Lilia's brother-in-law, nor the profound insights into Lilia's life situation by her woman friend can make up for the feeling that powerful, negative female characters triumph in the end and have come to do so through a series of betrayals. The world has been put into order after chaos and upheavals, but it is the order of stagnation.

The theme of betrayal is even more pronounced in Forster's second and in many ways most personal and perhaps most profound novel *The Longest Journey*. This novel contains perhaps the most negative and blatantly treacherous female main characters in Forster's novels, Rickie's wife Agnes and his aunt Emily Filing. Moreover, two new aspects of the motif of betrayal emerge—abandonment by sudden death and betrayal by life itself. Death is known very often to be experienced as rejection. An important part of the mourning process consists generally of making conscious the resentment and aggression toward the dead person at his seemingly groundless abandonment of the living. This rejection, in the form of death, is found at various points in *The Longest Journey*. What is probably the most striking instance occurs in the adolescence of Rickie, whose life is the subject of the novel. After his father's death following a protracted illness, his mother suddenly dies, eleven days after her husband, just as she and her son were planning to settle down to a blissful life together. Forster does not go into detail as regards Rickie's reaction to this case of severe rejection. One of the reasons for this might be that it would have involved the disentanglement of painful and highly complex feelings, especially ambivalence. However, from a biographical point of view, one cannot help feeling that this represents an echo of Forster's own possible childhood fears that his mother might suddenly die leaving him an orphan; such anxieties might well have contributed even further to his overadaptation to maternal expectations. Another case of sudden death occurs to Agnes, Rickie's future wife, who is unexpectedly confronted with the fatal accident of her first fiancé. Rickie is here presented as a mature person who encourages her to mourn, whereas her relatives exhort her to suppress her grief and thus not work through her loss. As her brother proclaims, "one must not court sorrow." In other words, the feeling of rejection through death is here repressed; and this may well be the reason for Agnes' later rejection of Rickie and also for the unconscious murder of their one-week-old crippled baby. Agnes is herself betrayed not only by sudden death but also by being prevented from mourning; the betrayed thus turns betrayer.

The main theme of the novel, however, seems to be rejection and betrayal by life itself. Rickie's fate is characterized by rejection and abandonment, by friends, by relatives, and above all by his wife. Even his hereditary crippled foot may be seen in this light. It is a betrayal which finally costs him his life, since his half-brother breaks his word to him, gets drunk and lies semi-conscious over a railway line. Rickie manages to pull him away from an oncoming train just in time but is himself run over and killed. His posthumous literary fame merely underlines the tragedy and the irony of his fate: during his life he never seemed to have been able to extract any real narcissistic sustenance from his creative writing. Hence after his death it can be seen only as a means of income to greedy relatives.

The theme of rejection is prominent also in Forster's most lighthearted, almost "Mozartian" novel, *A Room with a View,* although the bitterness is perhaps not so pronounced here as in his other novels. However, to give just one example, when they eventually do get married, the two main characters are ostracized by everyone, even by the benevolent pastor Beebe, who practices the rather subtle kind of abandonment known as "loss of interest." The novel thus links up with the later work *Maurice,* which also ends with the lovers being rejected by society. Furthermore, in both novels they are finally forced by society into a relationship very much akin to the twinship merger, with its inherent threat of total deadlock in mutual projective and introjective identifications.

In *Howards End,* which is considered by many Forster's most important early novel, rejection and betrayal play a prominent part. Leonard Bast, for example, a man whose fate is dominated by treachery, immediately springs to mind. He seems to be a clear parallel to Rickie from *The Longest Journey,* albeit on a different social level. Both characters are depicted as having been betrayed by all facets of life and both meet with a violent death at the moment when they attain some degree of reconciliation to their fate, be it positive or negative.

From the point of view of treachery on the part of maternal figures, however, the highly enigmatic figure of Mrs. Wilcox seems to be of special interest. She is introduced as an almost saintly woman with an uncanny intuition bordering on the supernatural in her knowledge of people's minds and in her grasp of relations between people. She is built up to represent true values as opposed to intellectual cleverness and urban snobbishness. In her encounter with Margaret's bright and "delightful" friends, for example, she shows them up as "gibbering monkeys" in her unassuming and modest manner.[8] She is truly conservative, but her conservatism is described as an expression of inner wisdom and adherence to the profoundest traditional values, in contrast to her husband's and her children's adoration of the motorcar, the symbol of the shallowness of the modern age.

However, in one of the few scenes where she is extensively portrayed, in the brilliantly written chapter ten, Forster clearly reveals the rejecting and disparaging, if not downright treacherous, aspect of her character. After a heavy day of Christmas shopping when she has twice treated Margaret slightingly as a small girl, Mrs. Wilcox on the spur of the moment suddenly invites her to come down with her to her beloved house Howards End. For practical and very sensible reasons Margaret asks for permission to postpone the visit, not realizing the extent to which Mrs. Wilcox narcissistically identifies with her house. Mrs. Wilcox reacts by taking offence in the typical infantile manner of persons whose grandiosity has been hurt. Margaret subsequently realizes the nature of the situation, at the same time letting herself be infected by Mrs. Wilcox's grandiose and unrealistic overestimation of her house. She changes her decision, characteristically taking all the blame for the misunderstanding, which is often the only manner of dealing with a narcissistically slighted person if any relationship is to be upheld at all. She rushes after Mrs. Wilcox, catching up with her at King's Cross Station five minutes before their train is due to leave:

'I will come if I still may,' said Margaret, laughing nervously.

'You are coming to sleep, dear, too. It is in the morning that my house is most beautiful. You are coming to stop. I cannot show you my meadow properly except at sunrise. These fogs'—she pointed at the station roof—'never spread far. I dare say they are sitting in the sun in Hertfordshire, and you will never repent joining them.'

'I shall never repent joining you.'

'It is the same.'

They began the walk up the long platform. Far at its end stood the train, breasting the darkness without. They never reached it. Before imagination could triumph, there were cries of 'Mother! Mother!' and a heavy-browed girl darted out of the cloakroom and seized Mrs Wilcox by the arm.

'Evie!' she gasped. 'Evie, my pet —'

The girl called: 'Father! I say! Look who's here.'

'Evie, dearest girl, why aren't you in Yorkshire?'

'No—motor smash—changed plans—father's coming.'

'Why, Ruth!' cried Mr. Wilcox, joining them. 'What in the name of all that's wonderful are you doing here, Ruth?'

Mrs. Wilcox had recovered herself.

'Oh, Henry dear!—here's a lovely surprise—but let me introduce—but I think you know Miss Schlegel.'

'Oh yes,' he replied, not greatly interested. 'But how's yourself, Ruth?'

'Fit as a fiddle,' she answered gaily.

'So are we, and so was our car, which ran Al as far as Ripon, but there a wretched horse and cart which a fool of a driver—'

'Miss Schlegel, our little outing must be for another day.'

'I was saying that this fool of a driver, as the policeman himself admits—'

'Another day, Mrs. Wilcox. Of course.'

'—But as we're insured against third-party risks, it won't so much matter—'

'—Cart and car being practically at right angles—'

The voices of the happy family rose high. Margaret was left alone. No one wanted her. Mrs. Wilcox walked out of King's Cross between her husband and her daughter, listening to both of them.[9]

This scene might be seen as a rendering of the manner in which parents often narcissistically insult their children and hurt their self-esteem. Here one has a maternal figure who, by a mixture of subtle moral blackmail and promises of an extraordinary experience, as well as by the intimation that she has herself been narcissistically slighted, induces someone else to conform to her whim of the moment. Then all of a sudden people turn up who seem more important than the person who previously appeared so essential and was so urgently needed to provide narcissistic sustenance, and this person is consequently dropped without further ado. In other words, here is a picture of a typical childhood situation where a child and its interests at one moment are considered of paramount interest and the next moment are discarded as being merely childish matters. This is one of the severest insults to a child's self-esteem. It happens especially often to precocious children and makes a particularly strong impact on such children. One can well imagine Forster having experienced many such snubs from his mother at moments when, from being the absolute centre of her attention as the "Important One," he was suddenly dropped and relegated to being "a mere child," whom "no one wants," when so-called grown-up affairs suddenly claimed the mother's interest.

It is also interesting to note that Margaret does not take offence at being snubbed so severely and having her own refusal, 'another day,' flung back at her in an almost impolite manner without even an attempt at an apology from Mrs. Wilcox. This is probably less an intimation of social grace and comprehension of the family situation on Margaret's part than an indication that she is by now firmly embedded in Mrs. Wilcox's narcissistic universe with its pronounced overrating of

Howards End. The two women are now so narcissistically entangled that they can feel above petty conventionality. They both experience themselves as part of something greater and have merged with it, thus arriving at a state of identity with each other. Although Margaret has never seen Howards End she is, in other words, by now the rightful spiritual heir to the house.

Mrs. Wilcox's unexpected death immediately after the above scene seems to underline this. Margaret appears willingly to have accepted the role she has assigned to her and so Mrs. Wilcox can presumably die in peace. Her death as such is quite clearly felt as an act of rejection and treachery by her family, and the feeling of having been deceived is further increased since she has told no one about the gravity of her state and has thus made them go about their everyday business rather like fools. She rationalizes this action as not wishing to cause undue alarm. However, it does leave the family with deep resentment toward her: "Without fully explaining, she had died. It was a fault on her part, and—tears rushed into his eyes—what a little fault! It was the only time she had deceived him in those thirty years."[10]

This feeling of having been betrayed is further aggravated when the family learns that Mrs. Wilcox in a last will scribbled on a piece of paper has intended to leave her only dowry and hence her only genuine personal possession, Howards End, to Margaret. The message causes a great shock to the family: to them Margaret is an unknown person and in addition they are to some extent financially dependent upon the house, especially Charles Wilcox, the oldest son, who was supposed eventually to inherit it. For the first and only time the word treachery is directly applied to Mrs. Wilcox. However, in an authorial comment Forster reverses the situation and blames the family for not understanding her and accepting her wish to make Margaret her spiritual heir in this highly concrete manner of handing her only and most treasured possession over to her: "Today they thought: 'She was not as true, as dear, as we supposed.' The desire for a more inward light had found expression at last, the unseen had impacted on the seen, and all that they could say was 'Treachery.'"[11]

The question arises why such a misunderstanding could take place and why Mrs. Wilcox was unable to impart any of her spiritual values to her family. In spite of having been married for thirty years, this almost saintly woman is depicted as having exerted no saintly influence at all upon her husband and she has raised three rather unsaintly children. In the first place it seems that this lack of influence stems from a tendency in her to expect to be understood without imparting any information, as is clearly illustrated in the above-mentioned scene where she invites Margaret to come down to Howards End, and also when she abstains from informing her family about her grave illness. This is a well-known, typical feature of so-called narcissistic people. It is probably in part based on an archaic symbiotic concept of relationships where "my thoughts are your thoughts," and seems in part to be a manifestation of grandiosity: the person feels so great and important that he does not need to explain himself; his thoughts should be gathered without his having to express them. In the second place the failing influence may also stem from the exaggerated importance itself which Howards End has for Mrs. Wilcox. As she is reflecting upon Mrs. Wilcox's spontaneous invitation to the house, Margaret, for example, realizes "that Mrs. Wilcox, though a loving wife and mother, had only one passion in life— her house—and that moment was solemn when she invited a friend to share this passion with her. . . . 'Another day' will do for bricks and mortar, but not for the Holy of Holies into which Howards End has been transfigured."[12]

Howards End, in other words, takes precedence for Mrs. Wilcox over her relationship with her family. It becomes an idealized selfobject and thus an extension of her own grandiosity. The cathexis of the house, however, is so strong that this in itself precludes her from imparting to her family the symbiosis, let alone making at least one of them her spiritual heir. This may well be caused by feelings of guilt toward the family, or fears of an overwhelming reaction of shame should this symbiosis be revealed. Only a person outside the family may be able to accept such a state of affairs. Mrs. Wilcox has thus, in fact, been living a secret life in a world apart from her family. And her death thus might not be said to be the first time she has deceived her family in those thirty years; they have been deceived throughout the thirty years.

The theme of treachery and deception seems also very important when it comes to the highly ambivalent ending of *Howards End*. On the surface Forster appears to have intended it to be a happy ending, even in the profound sense, insofar as Mr. Wilcox finally comes to realize the genuine values of life and abandons the modern, aggressive "masculine" mode of existence symbolized by the motorcar. However, the reality of the novel seems somewhat different. Mr. Wilcox, a highly active man, has broken down entirely after the conviction of his son Charles for manslaughter. Margaret, now his wife, takes things in hand and persuades him to give up all his former activities and his former identity and come to live permanently at Howards End together with her sister Helen and Helen's illegitimate baby. The drawback for Mr. Wilcox is his severe suffering from hay fever. In fact, in the last scene of the novel he is depicted almost incapacitated by this, having to live during the hay season in a darkish room which cannot be aired. Furthermore, the very last passage of the novel reads:

'The field's cut!' Helen cried excitedly— 'The big meadow! We've seen to the very end, and it'll be such a crop of hay as never!'[13]

Which, in fact, could also be transcribed as: "The field's cut!" Helen cried excitedly— "and it'll be such a bout of hay fever as never!" In other words, the novel ends on rather a sadistic note. And there is no indication that the sisters are at pains to help Mr. Wilcox in any other way than keeping him imprisoned in his darkish and airless room. Hence it seems that the solution to Mr. Wilcox's problem offered by his wife is regression. Margaret appears to infantilize him; and the novel ends with the two sisters each having their baby, one of which is a grown man. At the outset, Mr. Wilcox has been shown to suffer from a lack of human warmth. As a compensation for this or rather for his lack of unconscious self-esteem as a person who cannot establish deep personal relationships, he has managed to make a career as a successful businessman. However, when this grandiose compensation breaks down and he manages to give up further ambitious plans, his wife does not seem able to furnish him with a constructive possibility of building up the new and true self. Hence on a deep level Margaret might be said to betray her husband by infantilizing him and by driving him into a regression rather than by actively helping him find his true self.

There seems little doubt that the reason for this betrayal is Margaret's own symbiotic relationship with Howards End. By establishing Margaret as the rightful spiritual heir to Howards End, Mrs. Wilcox has ensured that the chain of narcissistic cathexes of the house is not interrupted. Through this house, which she conceived of as part of herself, she can thus exert an influence even after her death, a goal which is typical of many narcissistically disturbed people. The aim of Mrs. Wilcox and later of her spiritual heir is to be able to enjoy fully the symbiosis with the house. In order to do so they have to pacify Henry

Wilcox by preventing his further development. This is rationalized by reference to the attainment of so-called true values. However, behind this defensive maneuver of depriving Henry Wilcox of his autonomy lies the deep dread of the modern world, which in the last chapter is symbolized by the threatening approach of the city of London. Hence, in the last instance, the narcissistic cathexis of Howards End serves to create a shelter not only for Henry Wilcox but also for Margaret, her sister, and her nephew. Like four small children they huddle together in the idyl of the grandiosity of the highly overestimated house, obviously a symbol of something maternal. Through the idealization of Mrs. Wilcox and of her house, they experience the feeling of being part of something great and grandiose and hence they may feel defended against the frightening masculine world of London and competition and motorcars. At this point one might draw a brief parallel to Forster's biography. *Howards End* is a homage to Rooksnest, the house where he finally settled down alone with his mother to the bliss of his childhood. He was then between three and four years old, the age of psychological birth and the first development of real consciousness of being an individual, and the subsequent breaking up of the symbiosis with the mother. It seems likely that this break never really took place. Not only did the involvement with the personal mother persist, but mother and son were probably united in a symbiosis with a greater maternal instance, symbolized by the house. Forster seems all through his life to have strongly cathected certain houses where he lived. One is here reminded of his irrational reaction and his great despair when he had to leave West Hackhurst in 1946.[14] And it seems a very natural consequence that he should finally find peace of mind in his rooms in King's College Cambridge, the alma mater which he had idealized ever since his days as an undergraduate.

In the context of rejection and betrayal in *Howards End,* one other aspect of the problem deserves briefly to be pointed out—betrayal by a sin of omission. This is, for example, well illustrated when Charles, the Wilcox's eldest son, is convicted of manslaughter and has to go to prison for three years. His rather infantile wife remains curiously unperturbed by this and only thinks of how to save the family's reputation in a very conventional way. In view of Forster's deep admiration for Dostoyevsky as professed in *Aspects of the Novel*[15] it may seem odd that he has not let Charles' wife rise to the occasion and support her husband morally and ethically as do, for example, the heroines of *Crime and Punishment* and *The Brothers Karamazov* when faced with similar situations. This contrast to Dostoyevsky seems very significant and points to Forster's deeply pessimistic if not downright paranoid attitude. The characters in Forster's novels seem to display little of the innate human loyalty and mutual compassion which is such a typical feature of Dostoyevsky's writing. Forster seems always to be expecting basic distrust, whereas Dostoyevsky often reveals a surprising basic trust.

With the exception of Mr. Beebe in *A Room with a View,* the problem of abandonment, rejection, and betrayal has until this point mainly been discussed in relation to female, and especially to motherly, characters. It is, however, important to underline that the problem is not at all exclusively connected with women. A close reading of *The Longest Journey,* for example, will clearly reveal that men are just as liable to reject and betray as women. Rickie's mother, for instance, is betrayed by her husband in general terms as well as by her lover through his sudden death by drowning. Abandonment on the part of a man is, however, seen most prominently in *Maurice,* which presents perhaps the most painful and clear-cut case of rejection and betrayal in Forster's novels. As an undergraduate at Cambridge Maurice is seduced by his fellow student Clive, or perhaps rather Clive awakens the latent homosexuality in Maurice. The two become lovers and carry on their relationship after leaving Cambridge. It becomes the stable and fixed point in their lives. Then all of a sudden Clive changes his attitude toward his sexuality, and Maurice, hardly able to believe or understand his friend, is plunged into a severe crisis. It is interesting to note that Forster himself does not seem to understand Clive either. He who in general is the master of analyzing people's motivation is silent when it comes to giving the underlying reason for Clive's change. He merely contents himself with registering it, and only later intimates that it might represent a surrender on Clive's part to the pressure of conventionality—a somewhat superficial argument, which seems hardly convincing considering the character as initially described. In other words, here too Forster introduces a case of sudden inexplicable abandonment, where a person is let down or even betrayed by someone intimately connected with him, without being given the possibility of understanding the reason behind the rejection. It seems significant in two ways that the strongly rejecting person here is a man. In the first instance, it shows that a homosexual relationship as described by Forster offers no protection against rejection; homosexuality is in other words, not seen in the novel as a neurotic defense against archaic fears of abandonment.

Furthermore, it appears that the fears of abandonment which pervade all Forster's novels are grounded in layers of the psyche which reflect a state which is so early that the environment is not differentiated into male or female. The environment is simply hostile, persecutory, and punitive; it bans and supresses any healthy individual growth. Hence the rejection and betrayal in Forster's novels are never instances of a *felix culpa*. As is illustrated, for example, by the case of Charles Wilcox, abandonment never seems to lead to further growth or development of the individual. On the contrary, all the novels with the exception of the deliberately appended happy ending of *Maurice,* finish on a note of resignation and even stagnation. The persecutory, destructive, rejecting, and betraying element has the upper hand. One might here make a reference to Forster's biography. In view of his deep-seated pessimistic view of life, one might say that it is not astonishing that he "dried up" as a writer; the astonishing thing is that he managed to write six major novels at all. One might consider this a demonstration of the extraordinary strength of what is generally referred to as the true self.

The problem of treachery and deception on the part of maternal figures seems to be summed up in the figure of Mrs. Moore in *A Passage to India*. And here Forster also seems to indicate, if not directly a solution, then at least an explanation of the phenomenon. Like Mrs. Wilcox, Mrs. Moore is introduced as an almost saintly figure who seems rather too good for the world of the novel and hence apparently has to drop out of the action, to die, and to be nearly deified by the Indians. She seems to be one of the few, if not the only, unquestionably positive English characters in the novel. She is the first English person to be introduced into the plot when she meets Aziz in a mosque at night a few days after she has arrived in India. The two are immediately able to communicate across the cultural barrier because of mutual spontaneous sympathy and depth of soul. Later Mrs. Moore is invited by Aziz to the fateful excursion to the Marabar Caves which ends with Aziz' being accused of having accosted her future daughter-in-law, Miss Quested. Both to Miss Quested and to Aziz, Mrs. Moore seems a guarantee of goodness and moral justice in the face of evil. She seems their only fixed point in a world gone mad, where one can no longer trust one's perceptions. Then all of a sudden, in the last scene where Mrs. Moore is fully described, in the psychologically very profound and masterly twenty-second chapter of the novel, she turns mean, unfair, selfish, and even malicious. She seems to refuse to do anything to help clear things up and support Miss Quested in her wish to withdraw the case before it is too late and thus to save Aziz, a man who considers her his friend. Although both persons are in deepest need of her, and although it would be fully in her power to come to the rescue of them, she just abandons them with an almost brutal lack of consideration, entirely neglecting what could be regarded as her elementary moral responsibility towards them.

Immediately after this scene, Mrs. Moore is dispatched back to England and dies at sea. After the treacherous and deceiving aspect of her character has been revealed, she seems unnecessary for the action, as was also Mrs. Wilcox after the above-quoted scene at King's Cross Station. However, like Mrs. Wilcox, she does exert a certain positive influence after her death. But this seems merely because the characters whom she influences practice the defensive maneuver of splitting, in the sense that they divide their internalized image of her into a good and bad figure and subsequently repress the bad part, either entirely or as regards its all-important emotionally negative impact. As Aziz, for example, remarks toward the end of the novel:

'Yes, your mother was my best friend in all the world.' He was silent, puzzled by his own great gratitude. What did this eternal goodness of Mrs. Moore amount to? To nothing, if brought to the test of thought. She had not borne witness in his favour, not visited him in prison, yet she had stolen to the depths of his heart, and he always adored her.[16]

One notices here the clear parallel to the reaction of the Wilcox family to Mrs. Wilcox's last will. In both cases feelings of evident treachery are suppressed, in the latter case by the character in question himself, in the first case by a parental author who, in fact, challenges the family's right to feelings of resentment. The Wilcox family is still too young to understand the profundity of the action of the mature and wise Mrs. Wilcox, hence their geniune feeling of having been deceived is not to be taken seriously but merely to be treated as the reaction of immature children.

In contrast to *Howards End* and his previous novels, however, in *A Passage to India* Forster does offer an explanation of Mrs. Moore's sudden change of behavior from positive to negative. This explanation is

Mrs. Moore's own experience in the Marabar Caves. Forster describes this as a case of utter abandoment and rejection by existential forces. These are not personified. Apparently they too belong to very deep layers of the psyche. They are represented only by a terrible haunting echo—the symbol of the utter emptiness and futility of human existence:

> Her eyes rose . . . to the entrance tunnel. No, she did not wish to repeat that experience . . . . The crush and the smells she could forget, but the echo began in some indescribable way to undermine her hold on life . . . . It had managed to murmur, 'Pathos, piety, courage—they exist, but are identical, and so is filth. Everything exists, nothing has value.' If one had spoken vileness in that place, or quoted lofty poetry, the comment would have been the same— 'ouboum.' If one had spoken with the tongues of angels and pleaded for all the unhappiness and misunderstanding in the world, past, present and to come . . . it would amount to the same . . . . Suddenly, at the edge of her mind, Religion appeared, poor little talkative Christianity, and she knew that all its divine words from 'Let there be Light' to 'It is finished' only amounted to 'boum' . . . . She realized that she didn't want to communicate with anyone, not even with God. She sat motionless with horror . . . . She lost all interest, even in Aziz, and the affectionate and sincere words that she had spoken to him seemed no longer hers but the air's . . .[17]

And:

> She had come to that state where the horror of the universe and its smallness are both visible at the same time . . . but in the twilight of the double vision, a spiritual muddledom is set up for which no high-sounding words can be found; we can neither act nor refrain from action, we can neither ignore nor respect Infinity . . . . What had spoken to her in the scoured-out cavity of the granite? What dwelt in the first of caves? Something very old and very small. Before time, it was before space also. Something snub-nosed, incapable of generosity—the undying worm itself.[18]

The existential abandonment and rejection which Mrs. Moore experiences in the cave is thus directly responsible for her own betrayal of the people who have relied upon her. Her world has broken down; there are no values to be relied upon any longer. Religion, the belief in the community of man, in compassion, has been destroyed, and even the vague faith in something greater than man, in Infinity, is obliterated. Mrs. Moore thus has become the victim of the cruellest form of rejection and abandonment that a human being can experience. She is faced with only horror and smallness, as the basis on which she has built her life is crushed. In the language of the theories of narcissism one might say that she is suddenly confronted with the fact that all the values she has cherished, however high and noble these might have seemed, are only values of the ego or of the false self. What has happened to her in the cave is that both her grandiosity and her idealized values have crumbled. The only thing left is the "undying worm itself, incapable of generosity." Mrs. Moore, in other words, has nothing to fall back on when faced with this betrayal. And again it is typical of Forster's deep pessimism that there is no positive aspect at all to this unmasking of a life-long deception. Hence there is no other way ahead for Mrs. Moore than death and burial at sea. She has been rejected by life itself, the falsehood of her life has been unveiled, but this cannot spur her on to further and higher inner development.

Looked at from a symbolic point of view, the cave is one of the oldest symbols of the mother. Hence, one might put forward the assumption that what Mrs. Moore experiences in the cave is connected with something maternal. She is rejected and betrayed by a force which has motherly qualities, or one might say that the false self which is revealed to her has the features of the mother. This is, in fact, consistent with the character of Mrs. Moore as presented in the novel. She is above all described as the mother, or rather as a human being who has lived her motherly side to the exclusion of everything else. In the crucial scene in chapter twenty-two she concludes:

> 'I am not good, no, bad . . . . A bad old woman, bad, bad, detestable. I used to be good with the children growing up, also I meet this young man in his mosque, I wanted him to be happy. Good, happy, small people. They do not exist, they were a dream.'[19]

Her true self has thus never come to be experienced by her nor has it been developed or differentiated; it has her whole life been overshadowed and pressed aside by a maternal false self. Mrs. Moore, the betrayer, has thus, in fact, been betrayed just as cruelly and mercilessly as the people whom she herself rejects and abandons.

There is here a striking difference from the situation in *Howards End*. Howards End remains a narcissistic extension both of Mrs. Wilcox and of Margaret. Their symbiosis with the house, which, like the cave, is also a mother symbol, is never broken; hence, in contrast to Mrs. Moore, they remain blissfully ignorant children who experience the mother as exclusively positive and perfect and attribute everything negative to the outer "masculine" world. It is further interesting to note that like the cave with its "undying worm," the symbol of an undifferentiated archetypal mother, Howards End as a house harbors two aspects of the archetypal mother. The one is the highly enigmatic figure of Miss Avery, who seems to conform to almost supernatural laws, and finally, after the murder of Leonard Bast, emerges from the house like a goddess of fate. The other is the old sacred tree, the wych-elm, which stands in the garden of Howards End and for generations has had a soothing and healing function by curing people of their toothache. Hence from the point of view of composition and inner logic it seems apposite that both novels should begin with a symbolic description of an aspect of the treacherous mother—Howards End, the deceitful mother who never lets go of her child, and the Marabar Caves, the inexorable mother who rejects it.

The theme of betrayal thus reaches very deep levels in Forster's novels. And not only Mrs. Moore but also other main characters as for example, Agnes in *The Longest Journey* and Margaret in *Howards End,* may, in fact, be considered "betrayed betrayers." If one draws a biographical parallel to Forster's life, his mother's existential situation immediately springs to mind. Hence the predominance of the theme of "double betrayal" seems to indicate that Forster, at any rate unconsciously, was well aware of his mother's predicament of having been rejected, and perhaps even more cruelly rejected than he himself had been. Such insight might have prepared the way for a possible healing of his childhood trauma, since it would lead to a view of the mother as a fellow human being with her own fate. She would no longer merely be experienced as a mirror for grandiosity or as an object of idealization. She might then be accepted as an independent individual in her own right and with her own, perhaps tragic, fate, which might have forced her to act in a traumatic way toward her son. And as a consequence of this liberation of the mother from functioning as a mirror, Forster himself might also have been set free. He might then have been able to relate to his mother with full ambivalence, which would have entailed disappointment and resentment at her failure as well as grateful devotion. And this might further have enabled him to see the world, or at least in part, without projections. He might then have arrived at a point where he experienced the world with the freedom of ambivalence, which is the opposite of the rigid compulsion to see the world as split into good and bad. It is difficult to determine whether Forster did attain such freedom and whether he was able to work through his childhood trauma. It appears, however, that through his creative writing he came a long way toward a solution to his particular predicament, even if the knowledge which he acquired might have been only unconscious. However, it is very difficult to say whether he, like many other characters, for example in *A Passage to India,* did not also, to some extent at least, apply the defensive maneuver of splitting, deifying the good, and repressing the bad image of the mother.

It is possible that an indication of a solution to the childhood trauma, be this through conscious insight or unconscious knowledge, is reflected in the strangely haunting end of *A Passage to India.* Here the two friends, the Indian Aziz and the Englishman Fielding, realize that, as their worlds are at the present moment, they cannot remain friends. Both reluctantly and with pain acquiesce to the reality in which they live. They come to see the world as realistically as is possible for them, and they seem to come to terms with this reality without having to take recourse either to grandiosity or to idealization. In other words, they seem finally to be able to resign themselves to the inevitability of abandonment, rejection, loss, and even treachery and betrayal as part of the human predicament. And such ultimate acceptance of one's fate and reconciliation to one's destiny might be said to be a sign of psychic maturity and to be the true aim of any analysis of the unconscious psyche.

NOTES

1. The material for this survey of Forster's childhood has been collected from P.N. Furbank's authoritative biography *E.M. Forster: A Life,* vols. 1 and 2 (New York: Harcourt Brace Jovanovich, 1977 & 1978). In a personal message P.N. Furbank has assured me that there is hardly any more material concerning Forster's childhood than what is quoted in his work.

2. Ibid., vol. 1, p.3.

3. Ibid., p. 4.

4. Ibid., p. 14.

5. Ibid., p. 14.

6. Ibid., p. 15.

7. Ibid., p. 21.

8. E.M. Forster, *Howards End* (Harmondsworth, Middlesex: Penguin Books, 1973), p. 88.

9. Ibid., pp. 96f.

10. Ibid., p. 99.

11. Ibid., p. 108.

12. Ibid., p. 95.

13. Ibid., p. 332.

14. P.N. Furbank, *E.M. Forster: A Life,* vol. 2, pp. 263ff.

15. E.M. Forster, *Aspects of the Novel* (Harmondsworth, Middlesex: Penguin Books, 1962, p. 15 and pp. 131-41.

16. E.M. Forster, *A Passage to India* (Harmondsworth, Middlesex: Penguin Books, 1967), p. 307

17. Ibid., pp. 147f.

18. Ibid., pp. 202f.

19. Ibid., p. 200.

THIRTEEN

"WE PERISHED, EACH ALONE": A PSYCHOANALYTIC COMMENTARY ON VIRGINIA WOOLF'S *TO THE LIGHTHOUSE*

ERNEST S. WOLF AND INA WOLF

Two years before the publication of *To The Lighthouse,* Virginia Woolf announced in her diary[1] the project for its creation: "This is going to be fairly short; to have father's character done complete in it; and mother's; and St. Ives; and childhood; and all the usual things I try to put in— life, death, etc. But the centre is father's character, sitting in a boat, reciting We Perished, Each Alone" (Diary, 14 May 1925). *To The Lighthouse* is indeed a realization of the plan announced in the diary. The book has also become one of the more warmly received as well as critically acclaimed of Virginia Woolf's novels. The proposed central role of her father turned out to be peripheral to the pivotal theme of the book which was constructed around her mother. This chapter, however, is not focused on psychobiographical questions, and we shall be interested in the biographical and autobiographical aspects of this novel only as much as they throw light upon what we think to be the main theme: "We Perished, Each Alone." And it is to this theme that we are addressing our psychoanalytic commentary.

Let us, very briefly, indicate the context of Virginia Woolf's writings. Independently of, but parallel to, the revolutionary modernism of the arts of the twentieth century—one thinks of the Picassos and Stravinskys—the literary landscape has been transformed by tradition-shattering upheavals. Virginia Woolf, as well as Proust and Joyce, is one of the pioneering creators who speak to us from within the new sensibility, a sensibility that psychoanalytically we might characterize as being grounded more in the perception of psychic reality than in the facts of external reality. Psychoanalysis, as a science, represents a similar shift in the major focus of attention away from the older psychologies of externally observable behaviour to the introspectively graspable data of a psychology of inner experience. Virginia Woolf is the writer *par excellence* of introspective reality. She knows, however, that many people prefer to look upon life as happening out there in external reality. In *To The Lighthouse* it is Mr. Ramsay, modelled after her father, who looks upon the world with scientific objectivity: "he was incapable of untruth; never tampered with a fact; never altered a disagreeable word to suit the pleasure or convenience of any mortal being, least of all his own children . . . facts uncompromising . . . above all courage, truth, and the power to endure" (13).[2] Mr. Ramsay reminds us of Sigmund Freud who taught us to look upon inner psychic reality with the objectivity that the natural scientist had thought possible only when looking at external reality.

To The Lighthouse was Virginia Woolf's third major novel, coming after *Jacob's Room* and *Mrs. Dalloway*, and it is of particular interest to us not only because it exemplifies the writer's methods and style but also because it is acknowledged by Woolf to have been of the greatest psychological significance to her. The characteristic literary sensibility that distinguishes Woolf's writing had already crystallized by the time she wrote *Jacob's Room*. Her earlier novels, *The Voyage Out* and *Night and Day*, were still in the traditional mode though the innovations of the future could be sensed by the discerning reader.

The critical literature that has developed since the publication of *To The Lighthouse* in 1927 has been growing voluminously. In contrast, there has been relatively little psychoanalytic interest in either Virginia Woolf or her *oeuvre*, to judge by the scarcity of references in the psychoanalytic literature. This neglect seems all the more surprising in view of the importance that Virginia Woolf—together with her husband Leonard Woolf—had for the development of psychoanalysis in the English-speaking world. For it was the Woolfs who founded the Hogarth Press in 1917 and in 1924 became Freud's publisher in England, a publishing venture that resulted in the *Standard Edition*[3] and numerous other psychoanalytic publications. Nor should it be forgotten that Virginia Woolf's youngest brother Adrian Stephen (he was one and a half years younger than Virginia and appears in *To The Lighthouse* as James) and his wife, Karin Costelloe Stephen, were among England's earliest and leading psychoanalysts. In the face of these close connections one wonders about the mutual caution with which Virginia Woolf and psychoanalysts have approached each other. For her part Virginia Woolf did not seek psychoanalytic consultation for her recurrent episodes of severe mental illness. Her nephew and biographer, Quentin Bell, states that her symptoms were of a manic-depressive character and that in her later years she showed little enthusiasm for the discoveries of Freud nor could she have been persuaded to consult a psychiatrist.[4] Nevertheless, during the war-time shortage, the Woolfs' Hogarth Press gave the highest priority in allotting their small supply of printing paper, next to Virginia's own books, to the works of Sigmund Freud.[5]

The complexity of the Woolfs' response to Freud has been ably discussed by Goldstein[6] who documents Virginia Woolf's denial of conflict and repression, her avoidance of conflicted sexuality and her fear that an emotional numbness that might interfere with her artistic perceptivity would be a consequence of psychoanalytic treatment. Goldstein compares the Bloomsbury attitude toward the depth of the psyche to a water spider's skimming on the surface of a pool. While essentially correct in her judgments regarding some of the reasons for the Woolfs' coolness concerning psychoanalytic treatment, Goldstein may not be quite fair to them. For Virginia Woolf might have been correct if she surmised that the aetiology of her psychopathology was rooted neither in infantile sexuality nor in unconscious conflict. By the light of contemporary psychopathology we would speculate that Virginia Woolf's illness was the result of a pre-structural defect of her psychic apparatus, i.e., a narcissistic disorder. Though the Woolfs in general accepted the theories of Freud, we would suggest that Virginia Woolf's specific rejection of psychoanalytic treatment for herself was also influenced by the ambivalence of her relationship to her brother Adrian who had become a psychoanalyst. Adrian had been her mother's favourite, he had been cherished separately, he had been her mother's joy, as Virginia clearly recalled.[7]

The relative infrequency with which psychoanalysts have written about Virginia Woolf could be explained either by the novelty of her work or by their unfamiliarity with it. When applying psychoanalysis outside the clinical situation, psychoanalysts have been interested mostly in the classics and little in more contemporary art, a fact that might be expected as the consequence of their education. Yet, other reasons seem to us more weighty. Virginia Woolf's novels appear, in general, to be almost void of the themes with which psychoanalysis, especially in its application to literature and the arts, has been most concerned. The near absence of recognizably Oedipal and other instinctual derivatives might have discouraged some analytic interpreters. This apparent absence thus might cause the novels to lack even that minimum of discernible neurotic conflict which would make them interetsing to the psychoanalytic scholar. However, this is not the case in *To The Lighthouse*. Here we do find a clearly Oedipal theme in the bluntly stated animosity between Mr. Ramsay and his son James. Ramsay comes equipped with a "beak of brass," and "arid scimitar" which plunges into "delicious female fecundity" (62). James, to whom his mother had transferred the affection she felt for her husband (52), hates him, would like to kill him with an axe or a knife (12, 282 and 287), this father who never praised him (314). And yet, this conflict serves merely as a gloss upon the intricacies of the marital relationship and is in no way central to the theme of the novel. We suggest that the relative infrequency of psychoanalytic concern with the novelist of modern sensibility, of which Virginia Woolf is a leading proponent, is at least partially the result of the inability of classical drive-and-defence psychology to throw much light upon the main themes of these modern novels, that is, upon those themes which make them interesting as novels.

What is the theme of *To The Lighthouse*? There is little plot. In the first part of the novel we watch a day in the life of the Ramsay family as they vacation in their summer house by the sea. Not much happens. The youngest of the eight children, James, is longing to visit the lighthouse but is frustrated by his father and by the weather. A visiting couple decide to marry. The day culminates in a grand dinner. Throughout, Mrs. Ramsay is, more or less, in communication with all, husband, children, guests. In the brief second part, the house, neglected for ten years after the death of Mrs. Ramsay and two of her children, is restored to its former appearance. In the third, and last part of the novel, Mr.

Ramsay, James, and daughter Cam finally make the trip to the light-house. Even if one were to add every detail of event and action to this barebones description one would be no nearer to the theme of the novel. For this resides in the *inner* experience of the main protagonists, and, particularly, that of Mrs. Ramsay.

Mrs. Ramsay's day, from the opening page to the final drawing to-gether with her husband (189) is a continuous and near frantic quest for involvement, for relationship with the people and objects around her: precipitated by her intercourse with the present are memories of the past and hopes and fears for what the future might hold. When at the beginning she tries to soothe her disappointed son James she (or the narrator, the distinction is often not clear) is reminded that in earliest childhood sensations occur that fix the moment in memory, in either its gloom or its radiance (11). It seems that the lasting beneficial or traumatic potential of intensely experienced childhood events was familiar to Virginia Woolf.

Mrs. Ramsay's thoughts enclose the inhabitants of the lighthouse as—'how would you like to be there?' she addresses her children—she imagines their loneliness and exposure to the storming elements (14). In this vignette the reader already feels the vagueness of individual boundaries: probably Mrs. Ramsay is really soothing herself vicariously as she holds her six-year-old son. A few pages on, still holding James' hand, she deplores all differences of opinion and especially critical ones (19) and then, still holding James, invites an odious, ill-mannered guest, Mr. Tansley, to join her on an errand in town because he is so awkward, feeling so out of things (20). It seems as if no one should be allowed to remain feeling solitary for she now immediately turns to another guest, Mr. Carmichael; he, however, refuses her blandishments since he is already sunk in a drug-induced, somnolent, all-embracing lethargy. And on she goes, "moving with an indescribable air of expec-tation, as if she were going to meet someone round the corner" (22). And while she pities poor Tansley and just as he is about to open up to her, about to feel responded to and ready to become responsive to her concern, she espies an advertisement for a circus which wrings from her the immediate excitement of "Let us all go!" (23), leaving Tansley sud-denly cut off in mid-thought and bewildered: "what was she looking at?" Her attention never stays long enough with anyone to give that other person a feeling of importance, a confirmation of his self.

Mrs. Ramsay's restless but fleeting involvements, born out of her own vulnerable self's neediness, are too shallow and inconstant to give others much narcissistic nutriment. We strongly suspect that Virginia Woolf has endowed Mrs. Ramsay with particularly those deficiencies of Virginia's mother that were decisive in leaving their pathogenic mark on Virginia's personality. Enmeshment into a tangle of elusive connections is no substitute for the solid bond of an empathic relationship. The unhealthy personality of the parent rather than the traumatic events in a child's life is the most toxic ingredient that injures the child's psyche.

Such is the microscopic texture of this novel as Virginia Woolf takes us from moment to moment, intricately and delicately. The psycho-analytically trained and attuned reader senses in this frantic woman, Mrs. Ramsay, outwardly appearing so calm, firm, direct, as she diffuses her presence over and into everyone, that she is trying to weave them into the web of her own defective personality. She cannot bear to see loneliness nor can she bear it herself as she fills the defect in her own self by this encompassing enmeshment with others.

How necessary for Mrs. Ramsay is this continuous and diffuse in-volvement? A gruff murmur of men happily talking, like the monoto-nous sound of waves on the beach, assures her, and consoles her as if she were a child being sung to at the cradle; the sounds beat a measured and soothing tattoo to her thoughts until suddenly her fantasies veer to-ward destructiveness. She looks up with an impulse of terror. They had ceased to talk (30). Then, waiting for some habitual, regular, rhyth-mical sound she hears her husband "beat up and down the terrace" and is soothed once more. All is well (31). During rare moments she knew that all her desire to give and to help was vanity, that it was for her own self-satisfaction. When no longer being looked at with admiration, she felt snubbed, despicable and self-seeking; she began to feel shabby, worn out and no longer a sight that filled the eyes with joy (68–69). These lines by Virginia Woolf illustrate the experience of beginning fragmentation of the self and lowered self-esteem with which psycho-analysts are becoming increasingly familiar.

People like Mrs. Ramsay are met with frequently in contemporary psychoanalytic practice, people who psychologically exhaust themselves in a frenzy of involvements until there is scarcely a shell of themselves left (63). They tell us that they lead a life of furious activity because the moment they stand still, alone, they become aware of the ever-present, unbearable empty depression. Recent advances in psychoanalysis en-able us to understand these people better.

There have probably always been some psychoanalysts whose empathic perceptiveness and sensitivity allowed them to work successfully with people suffering from narcissistic pathology. Most psychoanalysts, however, are able to expand the range of their psychoanalytic treatment only as a consequence of expanding the theoretical underpinnings for their clinical work. The addition of a psychology of the self to the drive-and-defence psychology of classical psychoanalysis has allowed us to enlarge our *clinical* scope and effectiveness. As a result we also can now approach *literary material* such as *To The Lighthouse* with new insights derived as much from the deepened resonant responsiveness evoked within us as from the complementary theoretical framework through which we can give expression to the new insights.

The conceptual framework which has proved itself most useful to us in making sense of the subjective experience of Mrs. Ramsay is the psychology of the self as developed by Kohut (1966, 1968, 1971, 1972, 1977).[8] The vicissitudes of Mrs. Ramsay's day begin to fall into an understandable pattern when we recognize in her experiences the anxiety-driven feelings, thoughts and actions of a vulnerable fragmentation-prone self which tries to bolster its cohesion by filling the emptiness inside, the structural defect, through merging with any number of selfobjects in her surround. These selfobjects—they are objects that through psychological merger come to be experienced as part of the self—by filling the empty self provide Mrs. Ramsay with a feeling of wholeness and substance, and thus by lending cohesion to her self confirm her feeling of being alive: "how life, from being made up of little separate incidents which one by one, became curled and whole like a wave" (76). Above, we have already called attention to her empathic closeness to James, her vicarious identification with the people of the lighthouse, and with her need to pull Mr. Tansley and Mr. Carmichael into her orbit. We also examined the disintegration of her sense of well-being when the sound of people talking suddenly ceased or when she no longer felt herself looked at with admiration. The novel contains many such illustrations of the ups-and-downs of a struggling self. We will add here now the culmination of this all-day, exhausting effort to keep herself together in the grand finale of a dinner. It is interesting to note that Clarissa's travail in *Mrs. Dalloway* culminates in a similar grand finale, a party.[9]

At the beginning of the dinner Mrs. Ramsay had a sense of being out of everything, being out of it (130). As she assigned places around the dinner table everything still felt shabby without beauty anywhere, a sign that she was suffering a partially fragmented, empty self. "Nothing seemed to have merged. They all sat separate. And the whole of the effort of merging and flowing and creating rested on her" (130–31). The word "creating" is significant; it indicates that Mrs. Ramsay, every day, through laborious yet inspired activities, created her self over and over again. So, one by one, at the dinner, she pulled the separate guests into relationship. She turned to Mr. Bankes, imagining him to be in a pitiable state although in fact he did not need her ministrations and would have preferred to dine alone (138). She involved herself with Mr. Tansley and then involved a reluctant Lily Briscoe with him. She talked about people that she had not seen for twenty years yet she could remember "as if it were yesterday" (136)—if one is a Mrs. Ramsay one can never let go of relationships because they all are needed to sustain life. To Mrs. Ramsay, therefore, it appeared extraordinary that these people "had been capable of going on living all these years when she had not thought of them more than once all that time" (137). Eventually Mrs. Ramsay's efforts were successful. Eight candles were lit which drew the whole table into visibility for everyone and "looking together united them." The light brought the faces together and composed them into a party around the table. "Some change at once went through them all . . . they were all conscious of making a party together . . . common cause against the fluidity out there" (152). She experienced herself gaining a new cohesion, a new well-being through the merger with all of her family and guests around the dinner table. "Like a smoke . . . holding them safe together . . . all around them . . . there is a coherence in things, a stability" (163).

Mrs. Ramsay illustrates the sometimes insidious nature of narcissistically traumatizing relationships. To an outside observer Mrs. Ramsay may well appear as a vigorous, active, involved mother. Yet the children sense that their mother's involvement with them is superficial. Mrs. Ramsay's activity is, in essence, the enactment of a need to use everyone around her in order to keep herself together.

There is, of course, much more to this novel than Mrs. Ramsay and her need for selfobjects. Virginia Woolf gives us in the character of Lily Briscoe a text on creative activity. Lily Briscoe is a painter who attempts to make connections that enclose a space (244), in other words to reconstitute a lost whole, which suggests, in terms of Kohut's psychology of the self, that this type of artistic creativity is the creation of a self by completing it with the artistic product as a selfobject.

Lily Briscoe probably represents a mature Virginia Woolf as an observing artist who is seeking to fill her need for selfobjects through her artistic creativity. In addition, Lily also has a need to merge into Mrs. Ramsay, who had become for her a mother-like person: "like waters poured into one jar, inextricably the same, one with the object one adored" (82). Lily sublimated this need into her art and eventually even into an inner vision which sufficed to give cohesion to her self by becoming part of it. Some people, especially during times of stress and fragmentation, attempt a sexualized route into the merger. We only get a hint of this here when Lily briefly fantasizes penetrating into a sanctuary as she leans her head on Mrs. Ramsay's knee.

In contrast to Lily Briscoe the therapeutic efficacy of Virginia Woolf's creative activity was unfortunately only evanescent. The completion of her novels was usually accompanied by serious depression as she anticipated and suffered the trauma of seeing her 'offspring' rejected by friends or critics. She poured all of her self into her books, which thus became proxies for her vulnerable self and exposed her to the most excruciating experiences of mortification. In her diary she wrote: "after *Lighthouse* I was, I remember, nearer suicide, seriously, than since 1913" (16 October 1934). It was her husband, Leonard Woolf, who, time and again, provided a healing selfobject milieu and who thus lent her the structure she needed to write and to publish. One is reminded of Mrs. Ramsay as she drew strength from her husband: "She let it uphold her and sustain her, this admirable fabric of the masculine intelligence, which ran up and down crossed this way and that, like iron girders spanning the swaying fabric, upholding the world" (164).

Virginia Woolf also delineates the character of Mr. Ramsay, whose vulnerable self needs constant confirmation of its greatness from the admiration by wife, children, students, guests, anybody. Mr. Ramsay "had the other temperament, which must have praise, which must have encouragement." This contrasts with Mr. Bankes "who was entirely free from such vanity" because, we would add, he 'had his work,'—in other words, the ideas expressed in his work had become for him the internalized selfobject (166).

As already mentioned, Virginia Woolf outlined in her diary the biographical nature of this novel. Mr. and Mrs. Ramsay are representative of her parents and apparently recognizably so in spite of the distortions introduced for various reasons, including artistic ones. The family constellation, eight children, aspects of their fate (the death of a sister and a brother), the summer house by the sea (displaced from St. Ives to the Scottish coast)—all find their place in the novel. Nevertheless, it is wise to remain cautiously sceptical in treating such fictional material based on biographical events as if it were truly biographical in the historical sense of that term. Mr. Ramsay undoubtedly portrays some aspects of the character of Sir Leslie Stephen, Virginia Woolf's father. Similarly, Mrs. Ramsay depicts Julia Stephen, Virginia Woolf's mother, as she was experienced by the author. Virginia's sister Vanessa called it an amazing portrayal of mother (Diary, 16 May 1927). But a novelist as skilled, competent, and creative as Virginia Woolf fashions complex personages who combine aspects of multiple historical models, not least of which are aspects of the author's own personality. To her diary, however, Virginia Woolf confided, "this is not made up; it is the literal fact" (30 April 1926).

A reasonable yet still speculative conclusion is our belief that Julia Stephen was a narcissistically vulnerable and over-burdened mother who enmeshed her children into her psychological needs, often using them to maintain her own self-esteem in the face of threatening exhaustion and depression. To the children she must have been an image of beauty and activity, but restlessly inconstant as the focus of her interest rapidly shifted to someone else so that the child could hardly ever have felt really at the centre of the mother's concern and understanding.

Elizabeth Robins, an American actress and writer who knew the Stephen family when Virginia and Vanessa were children, described Julia Stephen as very different from the saintly picture in Leslie Stephen's memoirs. Miss Robins noted that Julia would suddenly say something so unexpected that one would think it vicious.[10] Virginia Woolf described her mother as "of a quick temper, and least of all inclined to spare her children . . . she was impetuous and also a little imperious . . . her mark on [those years] is ineffaceable, as though branded by the naked steel, the sharp, the pure".[11] That's how one senses that Virginia experienced her mother, hardly an image of warmth or empathy, and it accounts for Virginia's vulnerable self. Certainly there were other pathogenic influences, such as the death of her mother—"the greatest disaster that could happen"[12]—when Virginia was an early adolescent, and perhaps also possible seductions by her half-brother, and the tyrannical outbursts of an admired father.

In an autobiographical sketch she explains "a little of my own psychology; even of other people's. Often when I have been writing one of my so-called novels I've been baffled by the same problem; that is, how to describe what I call in my private shorthand—'non-being'." Every day includes much more non-being than being. In this sketch Virginia Woolf writes about three instances of exceptional moments she has experienced, three "moments of being." One of these ended in a state of satisfaction when she suddenly realized that a flower is merged with the surrounding earth into a whole; "that is the whole," she said, and felt that she had made a discovery. The other two moments she recalls with despair: "I was quite unable to deal with the pain of discovering that people hurt each other." In such "moments of being" she described and experienced much of her life. This experience of discontinuity gives support to our view that Virginia Woolf continuously struggled in her attempt to give cohesion to her self through her artistic creativity. Rather than cohesion these exceptional moments often brought with them a horror and a physical collapse. Yet she constantly fought to maintain cohesion by extracting from the threatened collapse the elements for a creative synthesis:

> [The exceptional moments] seemed dominant; my self passive. This suggests that as one gets older one has a greater power through reason to provide an explanation; and that this explanation blunts the sledge-hammer force of the blow. I think this is true, because though I still have the peculiarity that I receive these sudden shocks, they are now always welcome; after the first surprise, I always feel instantly that they are particularly valuable. And so I go on to suppose that the shock-receiving capacity is what makes me a writer.[13]

Did Virginia Woolf sense the curative power of insight, of reasoned explanations within a context of controlled emotionality?

In the following we shall discuss some of the reverberations of the act of writing *To The Lighthouse* on Virginia Woolf's psychology. Virginia Woolf herself ventured the opinion that in writing *To The Lighthouse* she did for herself what psychoanalysts do for their patients.[14] Until Virginia Woolf was forty-four, she was obsessed by her mother, every day, apparently constantly obsessed by her mother's image and voice (Diary, 28 November 1928). Then one day, in an apparently involuntary rush, she began to make up *To The Lighthouse* and when it was written she ceased to be obsessed by her mother, could no longer hear her voice nor see her. In the book, she expressed some deeply felt emotions and in expressing them, "explained" them, thus laying them to rest. "Why," she asked, "because I described her and my feeling for her in that book, should my vision of her and my feeling for her become so much dimmer and weaker? Perhaps one of these days I shall hit on the reason." Her question is, of course, a psychological one and one to which psychoanalysis may offer some answers. It has long been one of the tenets of clinical psychoanalysis that it is necessary to verbalize memories and insights in order to make them therapeutically effective. The assumption is that without verbalization the content of these thoughts will again be repressed and lost to the conscious mastery of the ego. The experience reported by Virginia Woolf suggests that writing down thoughts, memories, fantasies, etc., may have an effect similar to verbalization in fixing them in consciousness. Virginia Woolf usually wrote in a high state of emotional tension and one can surmise that she experienced much affect. Her husband commented on the passion and excitement during her writing.[15] Though probably at times these emotions were of disruptive intensity, one must also assume that sometimes she was able to cope more adequately with her feelings so that some transmuting internalization could take place. As a result, her self gained some additional structure which ameliorated the continuous longing for merger with the mother. This may be the main reason that her obsessions with her childhood mother and father were modulated into a dimmer vision. In her diary Virginia Woolf states "I used to think of him [father] and mother daily; but writing the *Lighthouse* laid them in my mind. And now he comes back sometimes, but differently. (I believe this to be true—that I was obsessed by them both, unhealthily; and writing of them was a necessary act.) He comes back now more as a contemporary" (Diary, 28 November 1928). We would add that coming back as a contemporary means she can now see her father as an external reality from an adult point of view, rather than as a childhood psychic reality. For, as she says, "I have been dipping into old letters and father's memoirs . . . but if I read as a contemporary I shall lose my child's vision and so must stop" (Diary, 22 December 1940). Here again we can discern Virginia Woolf's old fear that too much insight will rob her of her unique vision, a vision which she considers the fountain of her artistic creativity in spite of its archaic and painful qualities.

Why, then, we might ask, was her self-analysis, if one might call it that, so spectacularly unsuccessful that she continued to have repeated psychotic or near psychotic episodes and eventually escaped the pain of

her traumatized state through a suicide which also was an attempt to merge with her mother by wading into the boundaryless waters of the Ouse? Perhaps the severity of her illness was such that no psychological approach, whether self-analytic or treatment by a psychoanalyst, could have provided a cure. Furthermore, the self-analysis of a gifted writer may provide brilliant insights, but without the ongoing transference vicissitudes and their interpretation in a psychoanalytic treatment such efforts are devoid of the beneficial effects of working through. We suspect that a psychoanalytic treatment informed by the insights of a psychoanalytic psychology of the self (which was not available to Virginia Woolf) might well have been therapeutically effective. A well-conducted analysis would have clarified her resistance to a full re-experience of her traumatic memories. In her diary, Virginia Woolf speaks of her father coming back to her as a contemporary after her writing to *To The Lighthouse* had laid the obsession to rest. But she was afraid of losing her child's vision if she read her parents' letters and memoirs as a contemporary, and to hold on to the child's vision was important to her as a writer. Would, then, a well-conducted psychoanalysis have laid to rest, perhaps permanently, her child's vision and impaired her inspiration as a writer? We do not want to answer this dogmatically but our experience in the psychoanalytic treatment of creative individuals leads us to believe that, far from impeding creativity, analytic working through weakens the inhibitions and fears that prevent a self from allowing its creative potential full reign. In particular, those analysands whose primary psychopathology is rooted in the realm of the self, in narcissistic fixations, experience in the course of their therapeutic analyses a resumption of the arrested development of their archaic ambitions and ideals into more mature forms that may find appropriate expression in artistic or other creativity.

Earlier in this chapter we illustrated with a number of quotations from *To The Lighthouse* the central role of Mrs. Ramsay in the novel and suggested Kohut's self-selfobject model as most fruitful in the interpretation of Mrs. Ramsay's character and her need for constant enmeshment with selfobjects. We dealt with other characters in *To The Lighthouse* only briefly, and we now want to conclude our discussion by elaborating on the theme of the novel.

To The Lighthouse is Virginia Woolf's statement of the human condition in its most poignant form, the condition of essential psychological incompleteness of each individual's human psyche. For the necessity to have selfobjects in order to achieve an optimal level of cohesion transcends the pathological intensity of Mrs. Ramsay's need to incorporate and enmesh her selfobjects and also goes beyond the equally pathological demands of Mr. Ramsay for constant admiration from his selfobjects. At best one can achieve a certain optimal distance from one's selfobjects and gradually begin to substitute created selfobjects for the personages in one's family who perform the mirroring and idealizable functions which soothingly give cohesion to one's slowly maturing self. In *To The Lighthouse* the children or Mr. Tansley or Lily Briscoe may appear less needy than the Ramsays but that is only a quantitative difference. Mr. Bankes through his work and eventually Lily Briscoe through her art were able to give cohesion to their selves by incorporating the products of their creativity into the psychological fabric of their self-being. But even Mr. Bankes, relatively self-sufficient as he was, gained something from closeness to Mrs. Ramsay: the sight of Mrs. Ramsay sitting at the window, reading to James, had on Mr. Bankes precisely the same effect as the solution of a scientific problem: "chaos subdued" (77). And Mr. Carmichael's apparent self-sufficiency was a sham and delusion bought, apparently, with drugs until he also could turn to creativity, to writing poetry.

Virginia Woolf places at the center of her novel this paradox of a universal need to merge, in order to establish one's self as a cohesive individuality. It determines her stylistic ambition, a style which she calls so fluid that it runs through the mind like water (Diary, 7 November 1928). It determines the image of a "window" which captions the first part, Mrs. Ramsay's part of the book. And it determines the symbolic value of the image of the Lighthouse, the goal of everyone's longing. The Lighthouse becomes symbolic for everyone's selfobject, with merger symbolized by the radiating light beam. The long steady stroke of the Lighthouse was Mrs. Ramsay's stroke, she felt that she "became the thing she looked at, the light," and "it seemed to her like her own eyes meeting her own eyes . . . she was beautiful like that light" (101). In the merger with the light, eyes meeting eyes, Virginia Woolf recreates the cohesion-facilitating experience of the child's merger with the empathic-responsive mother, eyes meeting eyes. We are reminded of the myth of Narcissus who similarly mirrored himself in the cool waters of the shady pond. The Lighthouse also becomes a symbol for the distant, unreachable, and untouchable person who is only visually available.

Drowning may become the final merger in an attempt to experience the longed-for sensation of tactile closeness.

This central theme of longing for the selfobject was also apparent in the first hint that Virginia Woolf gave of her ideas about this novel in the diary entry quoted at the beginning of this essay: "We Perished, Each Alone." This line from the poem, *The Castaway* by William Cowper, is the same theme, the need for selfobjects, stated negatively. The lines, "We Perished, Each Alone" are quoted seven times in *To The Lighthouse* (227, 228, 256, 258, 262, 293, 318). Such emphasis in a careful writer like Mrs. Woolf cannot be a mere accident. For various reasons William Cowper and the poem *The Castaway* may have been of special interest to Virginia Woolf. Like her, he had lost his mother in childhood (when he was six years old). Throughout his adult life he was, like Virginia Woolf, always threatened with madness and suffered a number of depressive episodes of psychotic proportions. He was a widely read English poet and through his mother was related to the family of the great John Donne. Virginia Woolf wrote about William Cowper that "there lurked beneath that levity and perhaps inspired it a morbidity that sprang from some defect of person".[16] Perhaps her interest had been stimulated by her father, Sir Leslie Stephen, who had mentioned that Cowper gave interest to the flat meadows of the Ouse.[17] One wonders whether Virginia's identification with Cowper was facilitated by her father's moving tribute to the poet: "[Cowper] escapes to quiet fields and brooks from the torture of his own excited imagination, and from agonies inflicted upon a morbidly sensitive character by the conflict with his coarser fellows . . . his intense love of scenery . . . scattered through his pages vignettes of enduring beauty".[18] To Lytton Strachey she wrote in January 1909, "Now I must go to bed, and read some of my exquisite Cowper,"[19] and to Vita Sackville-West she wrote, "He [Cowper] had a dash of white fire in him . . . what I call central transparency".[20] Thus she both compared and contrasted Cowper to herself, for she was in constant fear about her wish to lose herself, to lose her personality, to find rest, peace, eternity, as a wedge of darkness (99–100).

Cowper's last poem, *The Castaway,* was the work of despair after he had fallen into a hopeless melancholia following the death of his friend of many years, Mrs. Unwin. *The Castaway* is the sad story of a shipwreck, and in the last stanza it becomes a self portrait:

> No voice divine the storm allay'd,

No light propitious shone;
When, snatch'd from all effectual aid,
We perished, each alone:
But I beneath a rougher sea,
And whelm'd in deeper gulphs than he.

Virginia Woolf knew this portrait all too well.

NOTES

1. Virginia Woolf, *A Writer's Diary*, ed. L. Woolf (London: Hogarth Press, 1953).

2. In this chapter we shall indicate page references to *To The Lighthouse* (1927; rpt. London: Hogarth Press, 1967) by numbers in parentheses in the text.

3. Sigmund Freud, *The Complete Psychological Works of Sigmund Freud*, Standard Edition (1886–1939; London: Hogarth Press, 1953–1974).

4. Quentin Bell, *Virginia Woolf: A Biography*, vol. 2 (London: Hogarth Press, 1972), p. 19 fn.

5. J. Lehmann, *I Am My Brother: Autobiography II* (London: Longmans, Green, 1960), p. 153.

6. J. Goldstein, "The Woolfs' Response to Freud," *Psychoanalytic Quarterly*, 43 (1974), 438–76.

7. Virginia Woolf, *Moments of Being. Unpublished Autobiographical Writings*, ed. J. Schulkind (London: Chatto & Windus / Sussex University Press, 1976), p. 83.

8. See Heinz Kohut, "Forms and Transformations of Narcissism," *Journal of the American Psychoanalytic Association*, 14 (1966), 243–72; "The Psychoanalytic Treatment of Narcissistic Personality Disorders," *Psychoanalytic Study of the Child*, 23 (1968); AOS (1971); "Thoughts on Narcissism and Narcissistic Rage," *Psychoanalytic Study of the Child*, 27 (1972); ROS (1977).

The fact that our immersion into *To The Lighthouse* evokes in us introspective perceptions that are most like those evoked clinically during the analysis of narcissistic personality disorders makes the psychology of the self (see especially Kohut, ROS) the most useful framework for ordering our data at this time. By doing this we make sense of our experience, or, in other words, we discern meanings. Insights into the novel and clinical insights become mutually enriching. Vignettes from the novel, like clinical vignettes, illustrate theoretical constructs; they do not constitute proof for the correctness of the theory, nor do they rule out the possibility that deeper immersion or more encompassing conceptual frameworks may some day bear fruit in deeper insights and new meanings.

9. See Ernest S. Wolf, "The Disconnected Self," in A. Roland ed., *Psychoanalysis, Creativity and Literature: A French-American Inquiry* (New York: Columbia University Press, 1978).

10. Leonard Woolf, *The Journey Not the Arrival Matters* (London: Hogarth Press, 1969), p. 81.

11. Virginia Woolf, *Moments of Being,* p. 36.

12. Ibid., p. 40.

13. Ibid., pp. 70–72.

14. Ibid., p. 81.

15. Leonard Woolf, *Downhill All the Way* (London: Hogarth Press, 1967), pp. 53–54.

16. Virginia Woolf, "Cowper and Lady Austen," in *The Common Reader,* second series (London: Hogarth Press, 1932), p. 140.

17. L. Stephen, *English Literature and Society in the 18th Century* (London: Duckworth, 1904), p. 208.

18. L. Stephen, *History of English Thought in the 18th Century,* vol. 2 (1876; rpt. New York: Harcourt, Brace & World, 1962), p. 385.

19. Virginia Woolf, *The Letters of Virginia Woolf,* vol. 1, 1888–1912, ed. N. Nicholson (London: Hogarth Press, 1975), p. 378.

20. A. Pippett, *The Moth and the Star: A Biography of Virginia Woolf* (Boston: Little, Brown, 1953), p. 338.

FOURTEEN

THE DISSOCIATION OF SELF IN JOAN DIDION'S *PLAY IT AS IT LAYS*

Rodney Simard

Although Joan Didion's *Play It As It Lays* (1970) is unquestionably a study of the modern malaise and an exploration of the futility of existence in a crumbling and decadent society, one must be careful not to assume that Maria Wyeth is an existential Everyman.[1] She is a victim of absurdity, but hers is a very specialized case; she is an intelligent and sensitive woman, a type of human being who is quickly aware of the complexities and metaphysics of ordinary existence. Moreover, her victimization is not due to society, but to herself. She is primarily the victim of her own ego weakness and her suffering is largely self-inflicted; she is, in terms of contemporary psychoanalytic practice, a narcissistic personality. She has so objectified everything around her that she reacts reductively, comprehending the general nature of the people and events of her life, but not their individuality and uniqueness. Everything she encounters she deals with as if it were an archetype, dismissing its "otherness," its existence as an entity independent of her for significance. The trappings of her life and the people she is surrounded by are selfobjects, props she experiences as part of herself.[2] Her disintegration in the novel finally reaches the point where she reduces herself to a mere concept, a point where she does not exist even for herself.[3]

In Maria's defense, her environment provides her with few reference points for healthy, integrated existence, a condition which augments her descent into "nothingness." *Play It As It Lays* clearly belongs to the subgenre of Hollywood novels, and as such, the world it portrays is governed by the metaphor of the cinematic image: romantic illusion in surface representations with an almost total devaluation of integrity, depth, and substance. Maria is an actress, surrounded by film people and their retinues. In this illusory setting, the people who form the cast of the metaphoric movie of her life are themselves all vacuous narcissists, solely concerned with their individual roles. Maria's challenge in this world is to function as wife and mother, a role dictated to her by her director-husband, Carter, but due to her lack of a sense of self, she founders in these roles. By extension, her problem becomes one of direction and control: lacking a formal "director," she lacks control, both internal, or subjective, and external, or objective. Unscripted, her life becomes a paradigm of aimlessness.

In structure as well, the novel is suggestive of a screenplay, a juxtaposition of brief scenes that often end in a static tableau. Four "camera-views" are involved in the novel's 87 scenes, beginning with the longest, a first-person account in the voice of Maria after she has survived the events of the main narrative. Two brief narratives are next presented by Helene, ostensibly her best friend, and by Carter, in which the reader is invited to contrast the position of the institutionalized protagonist with the supposedly healthy people who had been closest to her. By their contrast, these opening scenes reveal Maria coming to grips with a new awareness of self, beginning a positive reassessment of her life, while her supporting cast evinces only bitterness and unaffected narcissism. The first 67 scenes of the body of the novel retrace the previous year of her life and chronicle the events that led to Maria's breakdown, presented in third-person narration. With scene 68, the voice of Maria that opens the novel reemerges, continuing in seven interspersed scenes to close the narrative in scene 84, completing the circularity of the novel in the symbol of her new objective—to live in the present, to "*watch the hummingbird.*"[4]

The principal events in her life begin in the action antecedent to the autumnal, infernal atmosphere of scene 1. Raised in the desert village of Silver Wells, Nevada (now part of a military installation), Maria fled her gambling father and her frustrated mother to become a model in New York. Dominated there by her lover, Ivan Costello, she had a breakdown when she learned of her mother's death, a probable suicide in an automobile on a lonely stretch of desert highway. Guilty at not having responded to her mother's depression at their last meeting, she wanders New York until she meets and marries Carter, who gains his reputation by filming *Maria,* a docudrama of her life. Transplanted to California, Maria has a child, Kate, who is born retarded, the victim of "an aberrant chemical in her brain" (3). Apparently at Carter's insistence, Kate is institutionalized and the marriage begins to fragment along lines parallel with Maria's personal disintegration.

The main narrative of the novel opens in September, after the summer of her separation from Carter, and Maria is again pregnant. However, she is unsure of the father, who may be either Carter or Les Goodwin, a screenwriter with whom she has apparently had a brief affair. The novel then elliptically describes her abortion (at Carter's direction), her divorce, and the fragmentation that results in her confinement in a clinic.

In treatment, Maria announces that "from my father I inherited an optimism which did not leave me until recently" (3), and what the novel explores is the failure of her belief in cause and effect relationships, her faith in purpose. She is a woman who wanted to believe in reward and punishment, in an external controlling factor to her life that would be both predictable and just. But when confronted with her mother's suicide, Kate's retardation, and her pregnancy, she begins to realize—if not to understand—that the external plan in which she had placed her faith has failed. But Maria is not so much a character suddenly cast adrift in a chaotic world as she is a woman who resents a world that she realizes has no inherent meaning.[5] Her tone is less despair than resentment, for she seems to assume that there should be a pattern of order and that she is being deprived of a natural right. She assumes, because she holds no system of belief, that the systems of all the people she encounters must be false and that others are deluding themselves; only she is aware of absurdity and it is her special province, her private pain. Didion constantly juxtaposes her against others who suffer their own kinds of despair, such as "the thin beautiful girl with the pelvic abscess" (120), but Maria feels no sense of camaraderie, and, in fact, tries to avoid her fellow humans. Her only companion in despair is BZ, Helene's homosexual husband, but she refuses to grant even to him her stature of seriousness and shows him little true compassion. Again to Maria's credit, however, BZ is hardly a worthy candidate for her empathy. In his narcissistic glee at having discovered the "nothingness" of his own life, he is often sadistic in taunting her with the emptiness she feels, but she is quick to dismiss his life with, "I'm sick of everybody's sick arrangements" (48).

This sort of reductive intellectual snobbery, or "narcissistic home-ostasis,"[6] is characteristic of her relationship with BZ. On their first meeting, he is intensely attracted to her, presumably intellectually be-cause of his sexual orientation and his topics of conversation. His inter-est in her is genuine, and he is drawn to her because he senses an emotional companion for his despair; however, she has little more than tolerance for him. He believes he knows her griefs, and probably does, but never realizes that her passivity and lack of control have thrown her into isolation and are the source of the depth of her indifference to him. He tells her, "You're getting there," but she must ask where, to which he responds, "Where I am." His condescension sparks her need to feel differently, to reject despair; nonetheless, her reply is the emptiness of a truncated chapter (191). While she feels her own pain intensely, she cannot empathize with such intensity of feeling in others, which is most clear in the episode of BZ's suicide. He tells her, albeit elliptically, that he plans to overdose, and her comment is a flippant, "That's a queen's way of doing it." With their knowledge of Helene's affair with Carter, their bond has a renewed immediacy. When she asks why he came to her, he says, "Because you and I, we *know* something. Because we've been out there where nothing is. Because I wanted—you know why." Maria replies, "Just go to sleep," and even after she realizes that he has taken the pills, she does nothing (211). This is the behavior of an anesthetized sensibility; it is the apathy of the narcissistic personality.[7]

Maria's empathic reaction to BZ's suicide, if not to BZ himself, is the culmination of another form of death-wish that permeates the novel: her highway driving. In an attempt to superimpose a purpose on her life, an artificial sense of direction, she begins the novel with ritualized driving on freeways. Heinz Kohut observes that the narcissistic person-ality, "sensing the rapid and dangerously increasing fragmentation of the self which precedes the overt outbreak of the psychosis, attempts to counteract it by frantic activity."[8] Sensing her own fragmentation in the month following her separation from Carter, Maria attempts to create form from her chaos: "to pause was to throw herself into un-speakable peril" (13). Only when she realizes that her driving is a mani-festation of her attempts to get back to Carter does she abandon it; "after that Maria did not go back to the freeway except as a way of getting somewhere" (33).

Representative of the automobile culture to which Maria belongs and suggestive of her role as a traveler and questor, driving also has other implications in the novel. Delighted in her ability to negotiate difficult and dangerous maneuvers behind the wheel, Maria is obviously manifesting an overt form of a death-wish, but she may be signaling an even deeper subconscious desire for destruction. Guilty at having failed to respond to her mother's self-destructive signals, her driving might represent a desire for a reunion with the mother, since her mother's suicide was in an automobile. In her attempt to alleviate her own guilt at her treatment of her mother, Maria overcompensates in her reactions to Kate, self-deceptively believing that the child is capable of functioning in and completing Maria's idealized notion of domesticity. She attempts to bury her feelings for her mother in her attentions toward her child, but she can only feel frustration and generate more guilt in herself: vainly attempting to believe in cause and effect relationships, she seeks justification for having been punished with the child's affliction. Only at the end, in treatment, does she begin simply to accept Kate for what she is and begin to unburden herself of her double sense of maternal guilt.

In her other relationships, although few candidates are worthy, Maria never admits the possibility of finding security or meaning in friendship, and she dismisses everyone who does not offer to complete a conventionally romantic scenario. Her affair with Les Goodwin seems to have been tentative in the past, but the idea of an idealized relationship attracts her. She arranges an assignation in Oxnard (ironically prosaic as a setting) and busies herself with the usual trappings of illicit behavior. But the incident holds no romance and is a failure (131–34). She tries to resume the exaggerated role of Ivan Costello's lover because of the artificial security she remembers (141), only to be disillusioned by the ugly reality and the pathetic silliness of the pose (179). But without voicing her feelings, Maria seems to feel that the men have somehow failed her, without recognizing the burden her distorted idealization has placed on them. Her romantic grasping is in sharp contrast to the reality they offer; her impetuous calls meet with what she realistically should expect: to "Take me somewhere," Goodwin replies, "You got a map of Peru?" (180), and Costello asks, "You want to know what I think of your life?" (145).

Her abandoned attempts at achieving a romantic state are perfectly understandable in the context of her accelerating disillusionment, but she cannot be excused for the opacity of her escapism. Twice she tries to choreograph the same situation, twice fails, and twice flees the failure rather than admit defeat. Her romantic concept of herself as validated by being another's lover is still intact; she gains no insight into herself from these experiences.

Her attempt to reconstruct her affair with Costello also suggests another of Maria's romantic self-indulgences: a retreat from the present and a reconstruction of the past, for as she admits while in treatment, "I might as well lay it on the line, I have trouble with *as it was*" (5). (In fact, her treatment seems to require her to deal with this, for as she begins her history, she says, "So they suggested that I set down the facts, and the facts are these: My name is Maria Wyeth" [2]. Indicating a positive reassessment, she begins with an assertion of self.) In times of stress, she dwells on the experiences, or rather, sensations, of her childhood. These attempts at achieving a naïve simplicity and sense of order collapse, however, when she realizes she was not even aware of her mother's death and that she is the only one who remembers, much less values, the details of her home life. She rejects Benny Austin, an old friend of the family, because he reminds her of the illusory nature of her escapist memories, and when she guiltily realizes she has probably hurt him, she tries to repent. But even here she fails, for characteristically, her information is wrong and he is lost to her. Again, Maria simply moves on.

Because she offers nothing of herself to people, Maria receives nothing, cultivating emptiness as a defense. Because of her inability to see other people as individuals, Maria feels no need to share her life, feelings, or behavior. These elements combine to underscore the reader's perception of her isolation and how much of it is self-imposed. The most outstanding quality of this retreat is its tone of superiority, an intellectual egotism that superficially scans, classifies, and dismisses anything Maria feels is "not-I." For example, when racked with guilt over her abortion and looking for comfort, Maria recalls an abortion story told to her by a fellow model, whom she names only incidentally. She dismisses the story, however, for she finds no possible connection between the two of them: "In the end it was just a New York story" (117), foreign and unrelated to her. Likewise, Maria buys huge quantities of unneeded food to avoid seeming to be one of "them": young, single women in circumstances identical to hers (121–22). In attempting to validate her individuality, she refuses to accept who she really is; to defend against emptiness, she becomes grandiose: her perceptions must be superior to everyone else's, and she belongs to no one or no group. She voyeuristically participates in parties and gatherings, watching others involved in a spectrum of emotional response, never extending herself, resenting their presence on the stage of *her* life, and barely suppressing the nausea she continually feels in the presence of others. The slightest human contact, if it holds any promise for self-revelation, sends her retreating to the bathroom with dry heaves. To remain cohesive, she must affect a stance of distinct superiority—her perceptions are more delicate, her emotions more valid, and her life more important.

Manifesting what Freud calls "the narcissism of minor differences,"[9] or the inability to recognize sameness in those one is closest to, Maria is bored and unempathetic with the small fragmentations of Helene, with whom she maintains a superficially close relationship. When Helene shows a rare crack in her polished facade, using the absence of her hairdresser, Leonard, as a tangible symbol for her own despair, Maria makes only a languid gesture toward soothing her before the vacuum of another chapter ending again signals Maria's lack of response, her inability to empathize (126–27). If Maria realizes that Helene's reaction to Leonard's absence is very little different from her own neurotic fixation on plumbing, she fails to indicate that perception.

The level of repression evident in Helene's fragmentation, representative of a partially conscious awareness of the lack of a virile man in her life and her compromised marriage of convenience, parallels Maria's repressed feelings about her abortion. Aware of the bland domesticity of the house in Encino where she has the operation, Maria comes to associate the doctor's flushing of her fetus with all plumbing and begins to have nightmares about stopped up pipes. When the sink backs up in her Beverly Hills home, she makes a futile attempt to regain the control over herself that she sacrificed in passively allowing the operation by moving to a furnished apartment on Fountain Avenue. She tries to assuage her guilt by turning toward Kate; self-deluded, but with genuine emotion, she fails miserably in trying to stage a conventional Christmas dinner with the Goodwins (98). Attempting to recreate herself in the apartment, rejecting her immediate past, she becomes obsessed with "the peril, the unspeakable peril, in the everyday" (99). But this denial of reality is also a failure, for one morning, she thinks the shower is slow to drain and her repressed guilt overwhelms her. She returns to Beverly Hills, aware that "There would be plumbing anywhere she went" (103); she knows she cannot escape her guilt through pretense and simple flight.

As with Maria's addresses, Didion's selection of physical details signals the superficiality and isolation of her central character: the scene is Hollywood, the *milieu* is the movies, and Maria is a professional *poseur*. She is trained in role-playing, in containing and masking expression of the true self, and the aesthetic distance she employs in her work is also the substance of her private life. Kernberg observes that:

> highly intelligent patients . . . may appear as quite creative in their fields: narcissistic personalities can often be found as . . . outstanding performers in some artistic domain. Careful observation, however, of their productivity over a long period of time will give evidence of superficiality and flightiness in their work, of a lack of depth which eventually reveals the emptiness behind the glitter. Quite frequently these are the "promising" geniuses who then surprise other people by the banality of their development.[10]

In her profession, Maria manifests the grandiosity of her false self, but in the course of the novel, the promise she once held dissipates. She works only once, on a television segment of *Interstate 80,* and performs only adequately. Although she wants to believe in the validity of work, even her professional self is beginning to fade; she begins to lose yet another self by which she can identify herself, although she still wants to believe herself to be an actress.

In this setting, stereotypical for its superficiality, Maria allows herself to be sucked into ritual action and response, as if following a script, jealously guarding self from what she feels would be exposure. That she refuses to acknowledge the substance of the society and values that surround her, including the people closest to her, comes as no surprise in these circumstances, but her seemingly conscious relegation of herself to the same level is surprising, especially since she is aware of the narcissistic superficiality of her environment. Only when she relaxes her pose is she aware that she is "watching the dead still center of the world, the quintessential intersection of nothing" (66).

To her, Carter is no more than "husband," even though she feels an emotional longing that defies such a categorization. He cannot emerge as a vital human being to her (perhaps largely due to his own inadequacy, as revealed in his opening section [11–12]), but remains what his role dictates. She objectifies and abstracts him to the degree that they cannot have conversations, even about the things she feels most deeply; she enacts internal scenes that have prescribed dialogue. Before her penultimate resignation, when she meets Carter in the desert, Maria is fully aware, if somewhat opaquely, of the nature of their relationship, even if she tries not to understand it. When she first contemplates going to him, she kills the desire by experiencing what she knows would happen:

> Whatever he began by saying he would end by saying nothing. He would say something and she would say something and before either of them knew it they would be playing out a dialogue so familiar that it drained the imagination, blocked the will, allowed them to drop words and whole sentences and still arrive at the cold conclusion. "Oh Christ," he would say, "I felt good today, really good for a change, you fixed that, you really pricked the balloon."
> "How did I fix that."
> "You know how."
> "I don't know how." (31)

The incident would end by her trying to "shake him out of what she could not see as other than an elaborate pose" (32), their meeting would degenerate into unattractive and noncommunicative posing on both their parts, and the encounter never even takes place. Maria is aware, at least, of the formulaic quality of their interaction but somehow still feels compelled to act her part passively, afraid to step out of character and be herself.

Her full awareness of the duality of her perceptions of their relationship is displayed when she does encounter Carter for the first time in the novel. She tries to define the nature of their marriage, for Maria is fond of facile labels, and as she begins to speak, she is suddenly aware that: "Something real was happening: This was, as it were, her life. If she could keep that in mind she would be able to play it through, do the right thing, whatever that meant" (41). Here she self-consciously adopts a role, knowing that it is destructive to an important aspect of her existence, fully assured of her ability to hide her real emotions. Knowing that prescribed behavior will result in actions and words contrary to her desires, she yet assumes a character and they quickly alienate each other. "Anesthetized," she is unable even to cry at her emotional betrayal of herself (42).

By the time she confronts Carter with her pregnancy, she has so objectified him that she can only deal with herself in the same terms. After she tells him, "it came to her that in the scenario of her life this would be what was called an obligatory scene, and she wondered with distant interest just how long the scene would play" (50). Here, she has completely removed herself from the situation; she seems no longer to have any conception of her own self as she goes through the motions of living her life. Maria, as Carter's wife, is a character with a script, an abstract quality in the realm of "not-I."

That evening, while recalling former friends as merely a set of facts, she thinks back on Carter's reactions to her announcement: "Maria tried very hard to keep thinking of Carter in this light, Carter as a dropper of friends and names and obligations, because if she thought of Carter as he was tonight she would begin to cry again" (52). In this situation, characteristically, her true self begins to emerge and she thrusts off any attempts it might make to impinge on the facade of self she has constructed. She is too afraid to let her feelings come forward, afraid that the process would stir emotions which would complicate the vision of simplicity she has created for order. In her admission to him that she is unsure of the father of her unborn child, Maria makes Carter vulnerable and fears this vulnerability and her own power to create it:

> She wanted to tell him she was sorry, but saying she was sorry did not seem entirely adequate, and in any case what she was sorry about seemed at once too deep and too evanescent for any words she knew, seemed so vastly more complicated than the immediate fact that it was perhaps better left unraveled. (49)

Maria makes her encounters with Carter fail because she wants them to, because any attempt to deal with her immediate situation would threaten the surety of her internalized scenarios. Failure is predictable and safely handled; her repertory for her wife role embraces many easily adopted reactions. Unthinking acting allows her to feel order and meaning, however negative. Such behavior and thinking are obviously self-destructive. They are easy, require no effort for a skilled actress, and provide no obstacles, do not threaten to require her to think, feel, or reveal herself; thus, by passively accepting the role of guilty party, she risks no possibility of exposure and finds a convoluted and false security in knowing she cannot be harmed or rejected while vulnerable. As Kohut observes, narcissists self-impose isolation because of "their inability to love," and they are "motivated by their conviction that they will be treated unempathically, coldly, or with hostility."[11]

Her one touchstone to what she thinks is her inner reality is Kate. But in the year before her treatment, her faith in her child as a salvation is as arbitrary as her list of things she spontaneously decides she will never do (135). Her concept of the child denies the reality of Kate's retardation, and her thoughts about Kate and her own behavior toward her are self-indulgent. Maria believes what she wants and ignores the unpleasant. When Carter mentions the disruptive effect of her excessive visits on Kate's adjustment, Maria obliquely asks, "Adjustment to what?" (42). Similarly, her visits to the institution are attempts at actualizing fantasy and have far more to do with the mother's reassurance of herself than with the child's welfare (71). Significantly, Maria imagines the child most strongly when indulging in self-pity or romantic reverie; her fantasies of home life with Kate include both Goodwin and Costello (70, 113). Kate is a concept to Maria, a selfobject, someone Maria needs to complete herself—even though her affection for her daughter is undoubtedly authentic, if misguided.

The central issue of Maria's unborn child and abortion functions to allow the reader to view her when she is most vulnerable. Her feelings about what she had done are closely associated with the emotions she has for her mother and Kate. She tries to objectify the unborn child and deal with it as an abstract concept, but she cannot, for despite her efforts, she is very much involved in what she does. For the first time, she cannot call up her grandiosity to protect herself; she cannot separate herself from her actions because the abortion is a symbolic killing of her own unborn true self.

Despite her wishes to the contrary, Maria cannot deal with this particular aspect of her life effectively; she is haunted by plumbing, the symbolic representation of her guilt, death, and her concept of the living child, Kate, becomes increasingly unreal. At one critical point in the narrative, the reader is allowed to view Maria absolutely nakedly, and that occasion corresponds to a day symbolic to her, the day her aborted child would have been born. While driving, she pulls to the curb:

> she . . . put her head on the steering wheel and cried as she had not cried since she was a child, cried out loud. She cried because she was humiliated and she cried for her mother and she cried for Kate and she cried because something had just come through to her, there in the sun on the Western street. . . . (140)

She is flooded and overwhelmed by images she has repressed, and one can finally see Maria completely exposed, not only to the reader, but to

herself as well. But again, the experience does not seem to be constructive at this point and it offers her no genuine stability; her self-esteem
plummets and she begins a ritual of self-abuse and degradation that
includes such actions as lead to her pathetic encounters with Larry
Kulik and Johnny Waters (149–53).[12]

The breakdown incident indicates the duality of Maria's reactions and
the complexity of her repression. The invulnerable facade she has constructed allows no such immediacy—these things are the "not-I"—but
these things are obviously central to what the reader recognizes as the
real Maria. Her behavior in the novel, including the thoughts the
reader is allowed to see, is artificial and belongs to the character Maria
is trying to convince herself she is. But clearly, Maria also has another
level of reaction, one which embraces the people and emotions she
works to dissociate herself from. By denying herself empathy for others, she loses her ability to see herself as a subject. Her world is an
aggregate of simple abstractions, and the role she assigns herself is no
more complex or real than the roles she imposes on others. To avoid
pain and vulnerability, she must be reductive in her perception of herself as well as her perceptions of the world around her.

Maria's collapse occurs when she has objectified her life to the extreme. She goes to the desert, wandering about the wasteland of a
town, aware of the emotional complexities and the ugliness of the relationships between Carter, Helene, BZ, Suzannah Wood, and Harrison
Porter. She is no longer capable of reaction. The culmination is, of
course, BZ's death and her institutionalization. But as she leaves for the
desert, her own voice, the one which introduced the novel, begins to
reemerge in the short, intrusive chapters. In these first-person accounts, the reader sees the institutionalized Maria coming to terms
with the role she had adopted throughout the novel; they are accounts
of her realization of what she had done and been. While they do not
signal recovery, they do indicate that she is becoming aware, that she
recognizes that she has plunged as far as she can go and is beginning a
positive reassessment of herself.[13] The stychomythia, or internal debate,
of these distinctly different narrative voices also provides readers an
indication of Didion's own stance to her protagonist. Readers are not
allowed at this point to identify with the disintegrating Maria; rather
they are suddenly elevated above the decay of her personality. In this,
Didion may be indicating her own criticism of Maria's narcissism, forc-

ing readers to recognize that the novel itself is not inherently narcissistic: the alternating voices strongly suggest the infusion of a new sense of subjectivity.

Maria first acknowledges her misguided pattern of objectification when she admits she has been "burdened by the particular" (182), recognizing that she has been avoiding subjective response by escaping it through abstractions. She begins to understand that she is not entirely alone in her perceptions of herself, that others observe both her and the world from positions as objective as hers have been. Her shedding of the latent, artificial romanticism comes with the awareness that she must "play it as it lays," accept life as it comes (199). For the first time, she feels the need to justify what she has done, particularly her participation in BZ's suicide (202), and she recognizes the complexity that Kate represents as a unique individual (205).[14] For the first time, she explores what she thinks might have happened to her (207) and formulates her first rational and viable plan for the future; however slender a hope it might offer, she is beginning to form a sense of order that embraces a truly subjective response to the world, Kate, and herself (209). The last of these interpolations closes the novel and reveals Maria as an inchoate existentialist, a woman unburdened of pretense and romance who can survive knowing the absurdity of the world. She now possesses the capacity for survival because she can say "why not" live (213). These are the reactions of a woman who, beginning to make contact with her true self, can now recognize and exercise individual choice.

Her assertion that, "I try to live in the now and keep my eye on the hummingbird" (8) represents a new understanding of her life and existence in general; she can now say, "I know something Carter never knew, or Helene, or maybe you. I know what 'nothing' means, and keep on playing" (213). But Maria's sense of nothingness is not the same as BZ's nihilism, which drove him to suicide; her sense is one that allows her to continue. She rejects her earlier, destructive belief in external control, in reward and punishment, and she contrasts herself with Carter and Helene, who "still believe in cause-effect" (202). She is willing to accept the present, unembellished by analyses or alterations of the past and unfettered by considerations of the distant future. Her opening lines, "What makes Iago evil? some people ask. I never ask" (1), signal her abandonment of her quixotic search for causes, answers, and motivations; "To look for 'reasons' is beside the point" (1). She is beginning to recreate herself as the woman she is now, not as the daughter-model-lover-wife-actress-mother she was cast as before.

While she knows that "Everything goes. I am working very hard at not thinking about how everything goes" (6), she has also come to realize that *"Carter and Helene still ask questions. I used to ask questions, and I got the answer: nothing"* (209). She is still in treatment and she realizes that she has work yet to do. She must tame her grandiose self and find her true self; to this end, she adopts an existential stance: *"You call it as you see it, and stay in the action"* (209). Her plan is clear, simple, and realistic: *"Now that I have the answer, my plans for the future are these: (1) get Kate, (2) live with Kate alone, (3) do some canning"* (209). Disburdened of guilt, having rejected others' assignment of her role, Maria is beginning to take responsibility for and control of her life for the first time.

Kernberg defines the characteristics of narcissistic personality disorder as follows:

> grandiosity, extreme self-centeredness, and a remarkable absence of interest in and empathy for others in spite of the fact that they are so very eager to obtain admiration and approval from other people. These patients experience a remarkably intense envy of other people who seem to have things they do not have or who simply seem to enjoy their lives. These patients not only lack emotional depth and fail to understand complex emotions in other people, but their own feelings lack differentiation. . . . When abandoned or disappointed by other people they may show what on the surface looks like depression, but which on further examination emerges as anger and resentment, loaded with revengeful wishes, rather than real sadness for the loss of a person whom they appreciated.[15]

Clearly applicable to Maria, this diagnosis also includes another dimension, wherein "the devaluation of objects and object images on the part of patients with pathological narcissism creates a constant emptiness in their social life and reinforces their internal experience of emptiness."[16] This same position is argued by Kohut, who observes that "the patient will describe subtly experienced, yet pervasive feelings of emptiness and depression," while feeling "that he is not fully real, or at least that his emotions are dulled. . . ."[17] Clearly, in diagnostic and therapeutic terms, this is the condition from which Maria suffers and for which she is being treated in the framing narrative.

The essential duality of Maria's selfhood is signaled early in the novel by her feelings about the two movies she has been in. She likes the commercial film because she sees herself in it as another person, objectified, abstract, and well within the realm of the "not-I": "the girl on the screen seemed to have a definite knack for controlling her own destiny" (19). She prefers the sureness of its neat conclusion to the other, which "represented some reality not fully apprehended by the girl Maria played" (18); it is simple, objective, and patently false. The other movie chronicles a day in her own life and exposes *her*, the Maria she tries so disastrously to conceal. "She never thought of it as *Maria*. She thought of it always as that first picture" (20). But the film represents everything Maria tries to avoid yet has passively accepted: "The girl on the screen in that first picture had no knack for anything" (20). Her use of past tenses indicates her purposeful distancing of these contrasting images of herself, and her attitudes toward the films serve as a paradigm for the true self/false self split that has controlled all aspects of her life.

This duality reveals her essential conflict, self-definition, and her relationship to the world. A basic but false sense of superiority provides her with a comfortable distance from others, who seem to her only to offer the possibility of more pain, but she distances herself from herself in the process, losing touch with people, friends, her environment, and finally herself. For these reasons, Maria is "thinking constantly about where her body stopped and the air began, about the exact point in space and time that was the difference between *Maria* and *other*" (169). Only when Maria allows aspects of the true self to reach consciousness can she finally begin to expose herself, be vulnerable, and accept the fact that she cannot reduce her life to a series of abstractions. And in the clinic, stripped of all but self, Maria seems to be beginning the process of rediscovery, one hopes, to reemerge as an existentialist who has control and can build a life around herself, rather than creating a static tableau which simply includes a character she arbitrarily chooses to call "Maria."

NOTES

1. David J. Geherin, "Nothingness and Beyond: Joan Didion's *Play It As It Lays*," *Critique*, 16 (1974), 64–78. Geherin's study is a valuable existential exploration of the novel, concluding that it is ultimately anti-nihilistic; he also notes that "What distinguishes Maria's experience from that of most heroes of existential novels is that hers is uniquely feminine, not that Didion has written a blatantly feminist tract, not that Maria's encounter with nothingness is ultimately qualitatively different from a man's. However, one must understand her experiences as a woman to appreciate fully the nature of her crisis" (68–69).

2. Heinz Kohut, AOS, p. xiv, defines "selfobjects" as "objects which are themselves experienced as part of the self."

3. Lynne Howard Goodhart, "Joan Didion's *Play It As It Lays:* Alienation and Games of Chance," *San Jose Studies,* 3 (1977), observes that because Didion "puts her character first and refrains from judging, interpretation of her point of view is challenging," pointing out the necessity of subjective evaluations of the novel and its protagonist. She notes that the novel is "a finely told tale of horror, the brutal portrait of a woman alienated from herself, from other people, and from the world" (p. 65), and, without making conclusions about the implications of the novel's framing narrative, Goodhart notes that Maria's condition results from the fact that "everything and everyone outside the self is seen as more powerful than the self" (p. 67). Sybil Korff Vincent, "In the Crucible: The Forging of an Identity as Demonstrated in Didion's *Play It As It Lays,*" *Perspectives on Contemporary Literature,* 3 (1977), 58–64, reads the novel as an indictment of "community," which seems to be an overly reductive interpretation of both character and novel.

4. Joan Didion, *Play It As It Lays,* (New York: Pocket Books, 1970), pp. 6, 213; numbers in parentheses in the text refer to this edition.

5. Thomas Mallon, "The Limits of History in the Novels of Joan Didion," *Critique,* 21 (1980), 50, observes that "Ethical coherence, the 'point' of having a code and the ability to live it with consistency, has vanished" for a character such

as Maria. Similarly, H. Jennifer Brady, "Points West, Then and Now: The Fiction of Joan Didion," *Contemporary Literature,* 20, (1979), 465, observes that the novel "ironically supports conservative values by showing their utter absence in the characters' lives."

6. Kohut, AOS, p. 28.

7. C. Barry Chabot, "Joan Didion's *Play It As It Lays* and the Vacuity of the 'Here and Now,'" *Critique,* 21, (1980), 59, suggests that Maria is aware of BZ's actions and that her refusal to join him in suicide "cannot be read as an affirmation: it would simply be a redundancy, for she has already effectively aborted her own life"; Vincent (61) refers to BZ's suicide as his "path of integration," a path Maria refuses "to her credit."

8. Kohut, AOS, p. 119.

9. Sigmund Freud, *Civilization and its Discontents,* trans. and ed. James Strachey (New York: W. W. Norton, 1961), p. 61.

10. Otto F. Kernberg, BCPN, pp. 229–30.

11. Kohut, AOS, p. 12.

12. Kohut, AOS, p. 149, comments that revelations are "accompanied by the discharge of crude, unneutralized exhibitionistic libido" in narcissistic personalities, an accurate description of Maria's promiscuous sexual encounters.

13. Chabot, "Joan Didion's *Play It As It Lays*," p. 60, notes that Maria, "having systematically stripped her life bare, willed her own indifference to the things of this world, this most abstracted of characters, not surprisingly, finds herself before this barest of abstractions," nothingness. But Chabot sees this as a negative process, concluding that, at the close of the novel, "Her final prospects seem bleak indeed: she will not relinquish the comforts of her present estate for the mere chance of achieving something more substantial." Such a reading seems to deny the positive affirmation set out in the framing fiction, the initial assertion that "I try to live in the now and keep my eye on the hummingbird" (8). Geherin, "Nothingness and Beyond," p. 66, more accurately interprets the circular structure of the novel when he observes that Maria's "confinement in the sanitarium is not to be viewed as a solipsistic retreat but as a temporary withdrawal from the world in preparation for a future re-emergence, wounded but wiser, with a wisdom born of pain."

14. Mark Royden Winchell, *Joan Didion* (Boston: Twayne, 1980), refers to the "postexistentialist nihilism" of the novel (p. 137), and asserts that "Maria may actually believe that she is living for Kate: however, the truth—as Didion's narrative forces us to see it—is that Maria continues to live because she does not even share BZ's faith in the meaningfulness of death" (p. 135). This conclusion discounts the circularity inherent in the framing narrative, and by stating that "For Maria there are *no* significant philosophical problems" (p. 136), Winchell does an injustice to a character who is more complex and intelligent than he gives her credit for.

15. Kernberg, BCPN, pp. 228–29.

16. Ibid., p. 237.

17. Kohut, AOS, p. 16.

Index